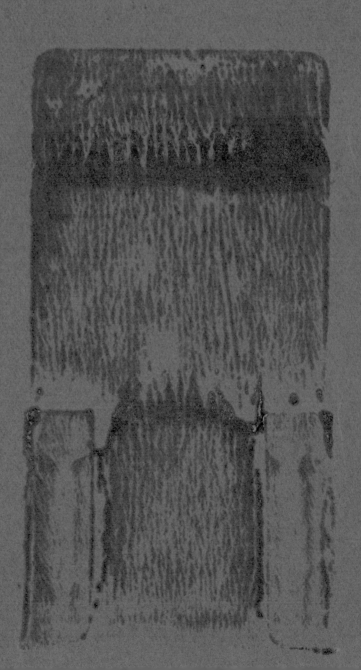

SCIENCE AND JUSTICE

The Massachusetts Witchcraft Trials

EXECUTION OF

A. Hangman   B. Bellman   C. Two

A

D

CHES, A.D. 1655

eants   D. Witchfinder, taking his money

Sanford J. Fox

SCIENCE AND JUSTICE

The Massachusetts Witchcraft Trials

The Johns Hopkins Press, Baltimore

Lovingly dedicated to my wife

FOREWORD

Many years ago Justice Holmes urged that "we must beware of the pitfall of antiquarianism, and must remember that for our purposes our only interest in the past is for the light it throws upon the present." This wise man of law and life went on to say, "I look forward to a time when the part played by history in the explanation of dogma shall be very small, and instead of ingenious research we shall spend our energy on a study of the ends sought to be attained and the reasons for desiring them."[1]

However this may be, Professor Fox demonstrates that sound historical research can point to greatly needed improvement in the practical administration of justice and thus to the main ends of the law. His scholarly treatment of historical evidence is apparent throughout but is particularly well illustrated in the analysis of the defense of insanity (Chapter VIII). There, and notably also in the concluding chapter, the author shows meticulous care to distinguish facts from inferences and inferences from speculation.

Especially thought-provoking is the author's skillful diagnosis of the inadequate law-science relationship during the colonial witch trials. He points out that, while a few writings on law were occasionally consulted, no professional bar was involved in the witchcraft cases, this despite the "operation . . . of a legal system that in many respects showed sophistication and justice . . . in keeping with the best traditions of British due process." He demonstrates that "the administration of the law in the witchcraft

---

[1] O. W. Holmes, "The Path of the Law," Address delivered in 1897, *Harvard Law Review*, 10 (1897):474.

prosecutions was related in some rather complex ways to the world of science and scientists," and then, emphasizing a matter of great relevance to modern law reform, he concludes that "these constitute the framework within which some important contemporary problems may be clarified."

The author skillfully analyzes the religious, psychological, and cultural climate of colonial New England to account for the admixture of scientific and magical explanations of disease, not only by the Salem justices but also by physicians and midwives. In this connection he points out that, despite the anatomical and physiological discoveries in seventeenth-century Europe, there was a general belief that *"maleficium*, the harm produced by witches, was brought about by their manipulation of *natural* forces, so that the presence of naturally caused death was deemed perfectly consistent with the presence of witchcraft." In addition, "the institutional ability to deal with medical judgments openly and on their merits was wholly lacking," even though some of the magistrates were members of the Royal Society. "Their scientific involvement was, in short, irrelevant to their capacity to judge the quality of diagnostic evaluations."

While thus taking ample account of the cultural causes for the uneasy liaison between science and law in the witchcraft trials, Professor Fox concludes that "if justice involves bringing to bear in an informed way all that is relevant to the resolution of conflicts, then it must be said that it was injustice that characterized the use of science in the witchcraft controversy . . . for the reason that relevant and available scientific knowledge was either not used at all or was accepted *in toto* and put to indiscriminate use."

Have we made much progress since the witchcraft trials? The author answers this question in the negative. Despite the fact that we today "think we know more of what science really is and have assigned a learned profession to the caretaking of justice, there is still a discomforting similarity to the kind of injustice that obtained three centuries ago." It is true that patchwork improvements have been made, "yet all these advances leave more than a little to be desired. The ability of those charged with administering the law . . . to deal knowledgeably with scientific issues has not progressed very much beyond the days of the witchcraft trials. With full knowledge of the present and expanding importance of science in the legal process," the author justifiably chides, "we make no requirement that these professionals be anything but illiterates in science when they assume their responsibilities for the liberties, lives, and property of the populace." Bluntly and plainly, he concludes that "the legal profession has the responsibility and the opportunity to serve justice better than this, but it is grossly lacking in the knowledge and training it needs to do so." I have long held a similar view.

There is, however, hope for change. During the past two decades a few law professors have called for greater systematic and continuous liaison between the law and relevant paralegal disciplines; among these men has been Professor Fox, who, several years ago, in a persuasive argument emphasized the need for more effective cooperation between law and biology.[2]

There are, however, several matters to be observed in fruitfully guiding the emerging movement away from disciplinary parochialism toward a more just justice. First, in the law's pursuit of a more realistic justice, the stage must be set for systematic interdisciplinary training of lawyers, both initially and through refresher seminars and clinical participation. Second, adequate interdisciplinary texts must be developed for the new training.

Professor Fox has made a modest but noteworthy beginning toward achievement of the first desideratum. As a law teacher he is realizing in practice the need for interdisciplinary study in his classes on juvenile delinquency at the Boston College Law School; he is trying to have his students view legal goals in the light of the insights and promising potentials of psychiatry, psychology, and social casework.

But a great deal more remains to be done. I have long believed

---

[2] "Delinquency and Biology," *Miami Law Review*, 16 (1961):85–88, and "Legal Aspects of Biogenetic Crime," in *Biological Treatment of Mental Illness*, ed. Max Rinkel (New York: Page and Co., 1966), pp. 967–99.

that there is a need to establish a number of Legal Interdisciplinary Institutes at various universities, under the stimulus of farsighted law faculties. The objectives would be first, the assembling of authoritative materials in fields (among others relevant to the administration of justice) such as family life, delinquency and crime, racial relations, and labor problems; second, the working over of such materials by creative law professors, aided by specialists in various extralegal areas, with the aim of anticipating their probable relevance to major human and societal fields of future legislative and judicial concern; third, the dissemination of reports of such materials to judges, legislative reference bureaus, federal and state policy framers, and, in particular, to law school teachers and libraries.

Apart from its vital value as teaching material in the training of law students, the aim of an Interdisciplinary Institute would be to keep makers and interpreters of the law continuously informed of the progress of thought and experience in those fields of human endeavor with which legislators, judges, and administrators will probably have to deal in the not too distant future. At present, the reading by judges and other lawmakers in the fields of economics, sociology, political science, biology, and psychiatry tends to be rather sporadic and meager. About the only way in which significant research results on issues of business and labor, marriage and divorce, the protection of children, the relation of normal and morbid psychology to questions of criminal responsibility, and many other such problems find their way into the judicial mind is through the occasional exceptional briefs of counsel. But this method has the disadvantage of being drawn upon only as the occasion for litigation arises; it is not *anticipatory* of problems about to arise. Further, since briefs are constructed in the heat of litigation, they are likely to be less thorough, and certainly more partisan, than analyses of objective researches motivated not by particular lawsuits but solely by the search for the facts and their possible implications for future legislation and judicial decision.

As to the education of future lawyers, it needs to be emphasized that something much more fundamental is called for than the occasional tentative experiments in a few law schools. There is a crying need for a series of "West Points" of criminal justice, at which new generations of knowledgeable lawyers would be trained.[3] The proposed educational and training institution would be dedicated to raising the standards and vision of police officials, prosecutors, judges, correctional administrators, and others concerned with criminal justice.

It seems clear that the time has arrived for developing relevantly trained specialist criminal lawyers, or, in more general terms, specialists concerned with problems of law that affect persons more than property, who will dedicate themselves to the public service both in and out of office and whose range of interests will include all stages of the administration of criminal justice and related problems.

I confidently anticipate that Professor Fox will be an effective participant in the attempt to bring about the crying reforms needed in the legal profession. In the meantime, I am certain that the reader trained in law, the historian, the practitioner of various biological and sociological disciplines, and, indeed, the general reader will find his present work both scholarly and lively.

SHELDON GLUECK
Roscoe Pound Professor of Law Emeritus
Harvard University Law School

[3] Sheldon Glueck, "Law and the Stuff of Life," *Harvard Law School Bulletin*, 14 (1963):3–6. Bills to implement the idea are pending in the U.S. Senate and House of Representatives.

PREFACE

Why still another book on witchcraft, in view of the already vast amount of literature on that subject? To the historian for whom studies of the past require no extrinsic justification, the point should be made that the story of the trials is not retold here, nor are the individual tragedies redramatized. Rather, my attempt is to describe the part that science played in the prosecutions, examining first the aspects of science that were inherent in the Anglo-colonial conception of witchcraft and then the actual participation of scientists and awareness of scientific attitudes in the trials. In the light of this examination, it is clear that the witchcraft trials cannot be viewed as entirely, or even largely, the products of superstition and collective insanity. This book undertakes to show, in detail not found in earlier studies, that the investigations and trials were an integral part of the scientific ethos of the time.

In the field of legal history there has been no real attempt to trace the complex relations of the legal order with the scientific community of ideas and persons. It seems impossible to understand this neglect as reflecting a lack of things to describe and analyze. In the past three hundred years, the law could hardly have remained entirely aloof and immune from the ever-widening influence of science, and, in fact, it did not. Nonetheless, very little attention has as yet been directed to the historical interrelationship of law and science. Virtually the only aspects of this relationship that have attracted the interest of historians have been the legal problems engendered by the joint pressures of Enlightenment humanitarianism and the new psychiatry emanating from

France at the turn of the nineteenth century, and even in this area the effort has often been too limited and narrow; we are given, for example, merely descriptions of the villainous rejection by the lawyers of the virtuous doctrines propounded by the doctors. Deepening of our understanding of why law and psychiatry got along as they did still remains a task for the historians.

There are, of course, necessary limits to any historical study, imposed by the focus that is adopted, and dealing with the scientific aspects of the Massachusetts witchcraft cases has entailed making many exclusions. Inquiries such as why the 1690's saw such a proliferation of prosecutions and what effect these cases ultimately had on the law and the community have not been made, not because they lack historical significance but only because they lie beyond the scope of this particular study.

I must also acknowledge that this book has been written with an ulterior purpose: it represents a deliberate effort to shed some light from out of the past on some important current problems in the area of law and science. In that sense it is not "pure" history but seeks to communicate with those whose primary interest is in the proper administration of our system of justice. While much scholarship is now being brought to bear on the problem of the law's use and misuse of science, there is a noticeable lack of application of the wisdom of history, which this book attempts to remedy. My hope is that it will provide food for thought to lawyers and scientists in shouldering the responsibility they must share for designing and operating a jurisprudence that is modern, informed, and just.

My intellectual indebtedness in the preparation of this book has been formidable. The historical sense and sensibility of my wife have been a continuous and enriching resource. To my friend and teacher, Sheldon Glueck, is due more appreciation than can be briefly expressed here for his wisdom, guidance, and generous concern during its preparation. The students who have enthusiastically assisted in the work are, unfortunately, too numerous for individual mention. The secretarial help of Mrs. Mildred Lechiaro was invaluable throughout the course of the research and writing of this book. Stephen Morrison, Librarian of the Boston College Law School, and his staff—in particular Miss Herta Varenais— have provided indispensable, efficient, and gracious assistance in locating and obtaining works with which law librarians are not usually called upon to deal. The staffs of two other libraries, the Medical Library of Harvard University (now the Countway Library) and the Wellcome Library on the History of Medicine, London, have also been extremely helpful in the conduct of research by one initially unfamiliar with their resources.

S. J. F.
Boston College Law School

CONTENTS

Foreword by Sheldon Glueck   ix

Preface   xv

CHAPTER I
A Case Study in Law and Science   1

CHAPTER II
The Roots of Massachusetts Witchcraft   9

CHAPTER III
The Views of Scientists   25

CHAPTER IV
The Law and Nature of Massachusetts Witchcraft   35

CHAPTER V
Maleficium and Cause of Death   45

CHAPTER VI
Witchcraft and Disease   63

CHAPTER VII
Science and the Identification of Witches: 75
                Female Experts

CHAPTER VIII
The Defense of Insanity   91

CHAPTER IX
The Law-Science Relationship Then and Now   109

Index   117

SCIENCE AND JUSTICE

The Massachusetts Witchcraft Trials

I

A CASE STUDY IN LAW AND SCIENCE

✛

The history of science is still a new enough subject for the opening pages in such a work often to be devoted to supplying some reason why it should be studied or written about.[1] Even when this question has been settled, however, there is another level of controversy over whether a writer without professional credentials in a specific field of science has the competence to delve into its history or to comment on its social meaning. Here an affirmative and permissive consensus seems to prevail, so that under the leadership of such outstanding scholars as Arthur Schlesinger, Sr., and Jacques Barzun[2] it is not only those who "do" science who write about it usefully.

Perhaps these matters have been discussed so frequently and fully that the need for any further explanation of what follows in this book is obviated. Yet I do feel that something of the significance of the relationship between law and science must be suggested before the justification for examining a portion of its history can be assumed. This task is neither difficult nor lengthy. Law, as much as any other contemporary social institution, is deeply affected by the rules, discoveries, and ethics of modern

[1] See, e.g., A. Rupert Hall, *The Scientific Revolution, 1500–1800*, 2d ed. (Boston: Beacon Press, 1966), pp. 1–6.
[2] See A. Hunter Dupree, "The History of American Science—a Field Finds Itself," *American Historical Review*, 71 (1966):863–74.

science. The scientific ethos that permeates our culture makes a variety of interrelated demands upon law. First, an outright conflict between what is accepted as truth or reality in science and what is promulgated as truth or fact in law must be avoided. Such a clash would stigmatize the profession of law as unscientific and invite a degree of public disrespect and disrepute that could undermine the whole legal order. Second, relations between legal institutions and personnel and their scientific counterparts need to be, if not intimate, at least superficially cordial. If a significant segment of the scientific community shuns courts, lawyers, and the like with visible disdain, then regardless of the merits of any particular antagonism, the administration of justice becomes negatively valued, even to the point of affecting the self-esteem of the legal community itself. One factor impeding the recruitment of lawyers to the practice of criminal law has undoubtedly been a reluctance to join the ranks of those whose professional practice and theoretical heritage are scorned by leading scientific citizens of the community. Finally, science is a constantly changing body of thoughts and habits, demanding from law a structure capable of evaluating these changes so as to absorb, without undue delay, what has adequate promise of permanence, while at the same time withholding acceptance from the more ephemeral products of science.

With this background, then, one may well feel that what law does about science and scientists is important enough for us to examine a bit of relevant history. The witchcraft trials in colonial Massachusetts have been selected as the historical vehicle for a number of reasons. The leading consideration is that there was a substantial amount of science involved in the trials, in contradiction to the widely held belief that the whole matter was almost entirely an exercise in superstition, with a little psychopathology and back-biting thrown in. Both the preliminary investigations that took place and the witchcraft trials themselves involved important judgments on questions within the domain of the scientific community of the day. Where death or disease was the criminal harm inflicted, heavy reliance was placed on the knowledge and skills of the medical profession in determining whether the offense of witchcraft was involved. Once this question had been settled, the law continued to draw on medical resources in its effort to identify the culprit. The field of forensic psychology is also unavoidably involved: problems are posed familiar enough to any contemporary criminologist but in a context that directs attention to the nature of the underlying issues. Throughout, these prosecutions raise a broad range of questions concerning the ability of the law—in its procedures, concepts, and personnel—to exploit fully the knowledge and experience of the specialists it called on and, more important, to understand and take account of their shortcomings as well. A detailed discussion of this question has been reserved for the last chapter.

Seventeenth-century witchcraft is propitious for this inquiry for the additional reason that in that century the scientific revolution grew and blossomed. More than anything else, this revolution represented a fundamental change in the minds of men, a new orientation that involved pursuing new questions rather than replacing old observations with new ones. No one discovered in this century, for example, that it was *not* the nature of an apple to seek repose on the earth, as Aristotle had suggested as the reason why the apple fell.

More basic than any specific discovery, and near the heart of what was happening in science, was Francis Bacon's attack on scholastic science and creation of a new scientific philosophy that attracted spirited followers, in the persons of the founders of the Royal Society.[3] It was the intellectual inducement to a new outlook and framework for science that was at the core of the scientific revolution. Its visible products were, of course, remarkable. We tend to think that the astoundingly rapid accumulation of knowledge taking place in the mid-twentieth century constitutes a unique advance in man's understanding and control of nature. But on the whole, this century is in the process of perfecting technology, which involves little fundamental change either in

[3] See Margery Purver, *The Royal Society: Concept and Creation* (London: Routledge and Kegan Paul, 1967).

3

knowledge or in orientation toward nature. In contrast, one historian has described the events of the period of the scientific revolution as outshining "everything since the rise of Christianity and reducing the Renaissance and Reformation to the rank of mere episodes, mere internal displacements within the system of medieval Christendom."[4]

The witchcraft cases in Massachusetts are among these leaps into new dimensions in human understanding. When the first witch was hanged in Boston, in 1648, Copernicus' *De revolutionibus* was one hundred years old and man was well into the process of finding new lodgings for himself in the universe after having been evicted from its center. Vesalius' *Fabrica*, which awakened the great interest in anatomy and human biology, was published in the same year, 1543. The destruction of Aristotelian physics accomplished by the work of Galileo was already a quarter of a century old by 1648. It was only twenty years prior to that hanging in Boston that William Harvey effectively demolished all ancient physiology with his demonstration of the circulation of the blood. Well before the famous Salem trials in 1692, Descartes had drawn from the discoveries of his age the theory of mechanically linked causes in human affairs, and his idea found its way even into the court procedures of the Salem cases. From the middle of the century on, societies were being formed in Europe whose members not only set the standards of scientific thought for ages to come but also formed a link between that thought and intellectual development in America. Finally, of course, mention must be made of Newton, whose unique genius served to establish once and for all the new perspectives on the universe and man's place in it. In view of these truly revolutionary intellectual and material advances, we are obliged to ask at the outset how an era of such monumental achievement could tolerate even the accusation and trial, much less the outright execution, of persons as witches.

It must not be thought that this query is misdirected to seventeenth-century Massachusetts. There was in the Colony a lively

[4] Herbert Butterfield, *The Origins of Modern Science*, rev. ed. (New York: Collier Books, 1962), p. 7.

4

interest in scientific goings on. Several persons corresponded regularly with leaders of the Royal Society in London.[5] Contributions to scientific knowledge were made in astronomy,[6] and, as far as medicine is concerned, "the evidence suggests that contemporary European theories were known in Boston throughout the seventeenth century."[7] In their own way the Puritans of New England, no less than the Quakers in Philadelphia, accepted fully the scientific advances that were circulating through their intellectual environment.[8] In a later chapter I shall attempt to reconcile this interest with their simultaneous pursuit of witches.

There are two more factors that support the selection of these particular events as an appropriate historical case study of law-science relations. One is the singular and intense religious quality of the Puritan leadership in the Bay Colony. Few outdid these

[5] See Raymond P. Stearns, "Colonial Fellows of the Royal Society of London, 1661–1788," *William and Mary Quarterly*, 3 (1946):208. The respect entertained in England for the New England scientific setting is attested to by a notation in the Dedication to vol. 40 of the *Transactions of the Royal Society*. It states that Governor Winthrop of Connecticut had often met with men of science when he visited England and had participated in planning the founding of the Royal Society. Dr. Mortimer, Secretary of the Royal Society, writes further in the Dedication that "had not the Civil Wars happily ended as they did, Mr. Boyle & Dr. Wilkins with several other learned men, would have left England, and, out of esteem for the most excellent and valuable Governor, John Winthrop the Younger, would have retired to his newborn Colony, and there have established that Society for Promoting Natural Knowledge, which these gentlemen had formed, as it were in embryo among themselves."

[6] Thomas Brattle, for example, was "a merchant, a mathematician, and an amateur astronomer whose contributions won him the gratitude of Sir Isaac Newton" (Perry Miller, *The New England Mind: From Colony to Province* [Boston: Beacon Press, 1961], p. 196). These latter achievements were comet observations in 1680 which were used in Newton's *Principia* (see Dirk J. Struik, *Yankee Science in the Making* [New York: Collier Books, 1962], p. 49).

[7] O. T. Beal and R. H. Shryock, *Cotton Mather* (Baltimore: Johns Hopkins, 1954), p. 31.

[8] It has been suggested that the most satisfactory explanation for Quaker scientific interest lies in their great concern with man's condition in this world and its progressive improvement through the control of nature. See Brooke Hindle, "The Quaker Background and Science in Colonial Philadelphia," *Isis*, 46 (1955):253. On a somewhat different theological basis, the Puritan ethic was also centrally involved with man in this world. Some aspects of Puritan beliefs served to quicken the interest in scientific works, such as the faith that God had created a universe that was entirely ordered and therefore inviting and hospitable to investigation (see Perry Miller, *The New England Mind: The Seventeenth Century* [Boston: Beacon Press, 1961], pp. 207–35).

settlers in zeal and piety; they have in fact been called the "Left Wing" of Protestantism.[9] Their entire enterprise was devoted to the founding of a godly commonwealth that would provide an example for all the world to see and emulate. No part of the effort, including the system of criminal justice, could be permitted to escape its obligation to contribute to this end, at least that is the way the settlers felt at first. We will observe that later the very success they achieved in establishing a viable, independent, and prosperous society tended to erode their sense of identity as a beacon to mankind and that this loss, in turn, affected their ability to evaluate the scientific issues in the witchcraft cases.

A further argument in favor of the selection of this case study is the unusual autonomy the colonial leaders assumed in the sphere of lawmaking. Fairly early in their new experience the alacrity with which they chose to ignore restrictions on their civil power became manifest. Governor Winthrop relates that the General Court went so far as to declare that "our allegiance binds us not to the laws of England any longer than while we live in England, for the laws of the parliament of England reach no further, nor do the king's writs under the great seal go any further";[10] that was in 1646. More than forty years later it was clear how much this belief had become part of New England thinking. In response to one of the earliest colonial assertions of "the rights of Englishmen," the King's loyal judge, himself a product of the Colony, replied that the colonists "must not think the laws of England follow us to the ends of Earth."[11] Of course, this independence of speech did not indicate a desire to cut themselves off entirely from their legal traditions. It is plain that this would have been an impossible undertaking. The fact that several of the colonial leaders, including Winthrop, had served as justices of the peace in England served to ensure a large measure of continuity, since

[9] See George Rosen, "Left Wing Puritanism and Science," *Bulletin of the History of Medicine*, 15 (1944):375.

[10] Governor John Winthrop, Journal, in *History of New England, 1630–1649*, ed. James Kendall Hosmer, 2 vols. (New York: Barnes and Noble, 1908), 2:301.

[11] Quoted in Miller, *The New England Mind: From Colony to Province*, p. 156.

their experience with English law was a vital and consciously used resource in the construction of a new order. But given the necessity of observing the historical connection between one set of conditions and its neighbors in time, the legal institutions in Massachusetts and the administration of the witchcraft laws do represent a great effort to reflect dominant contemporary ideas and values. One result of this effort was the creation of a sophisticated and mature system of justice that not only carried forward English constitutional development but also anticipated by more than one hundred and fifty years major themes in American constitutional law.[12]

It would thus be a mistake to view the prosecutions as merely one aspect of a cruel, arbitrary, and retributive system of criminal justice. The evenhandedness of the legal system is demonstrated by much historical evidence. During the course of the century, for example, there were many more acquittals for witchcraft than there were convictions.[13] Moreover, the law did not jump in with a

[12] The literature of the legal system of early Massachusetts is large. A comprehensive discussion of the first two decades is found in George L. Haskins, *Law and Authority in Early Massachusetts* (New York: Macmillan, 1960). A recent description of criminal justice in the colony is Edwin Powers, *Crime and Punishment in Early Massachusetts, 1620–1692* (Boston: Beacon Press, 1966). In Appendix C, pp. 551–62, Powers compares the early Massachusetts statutes with civil rights and liberties today and cites the "due process" provision of the Body of Liberties (1641), which reads that "no mans life shall be taken away; no mans honour or good name shall be stayned; no mans person shall be arrested, restrained, banished, dismembered nor any wayes punished; no man shall be deprived of his wife or children; no mans goods or estate shall be taken away from him; nor any wayes indamaged under colour of Law or countenance of Authoritie unles it be by vertue or equity of some expresse law of the Country warranting the same established by a General Court sufficiently published" (Max Farrand, ed., *The Laws and Liberties of Massachusetts* [Cambridge, Mass.: Harvard University Press, 1929], p. 1). There is no question but that this rule of law was faithfully adhered to, even under the most trying circumstances. For example, the death penalty was withheld in the case of carnal knowledge of two girls under the age of ten on the grounds that the law was not sufficiently clear (see Powers, *Crime and Punishment in Early Massachusetts*, pp. 265–66).

[13] See, for example, the acquittal cases of John Godfrey (1669), in George Francis Bow, ed., *Records and Files of the Quarterly Court of Essex County*, 4:153; Mary Parsons, wife of Joseph Parsons (1675), in *Records of the Court of Assistants. Colony of the Massachusetts Bay 1630–1692* (Boston, 1901), 1:33; Hugh Parsons (1680), in *ibid.*, p. 189; James Fuller (1683), in *ibid.*, p. 228; Mary Webster (1683), in *ibid.*, p. 233; Mary Ingham (1676), in Nathaniel B. Shurtleff, ed., *Records of the Colony of New Plymouth in New England*, 12 vols. (Boston: William White, 1856), 5:223–24.

criminal charge each time the cry of "witch" was raised. It was not uncommon, for example, for a slander suit to be instituted by the witch against the "victim" of the purported witchcraft.[14] As to the severity of the law, it should be remembered that only fine and banishment followed a reference to the Church of Boston as "a whoare" and "a strumpet,"[15] and that the frequent resort in criminal punishments to public humiliation—the use of stocks and the wearing of signs—evinces a great concern for humbling the will of the offender as a means to his reformation.[16] There is, in fact, little that represents a community desire for pure retribution. The witchcraft cases in colonial Massachusetts, therefore, provide an opportunity to study the product of self-conscious and progressive lawmaking by a deeply ethical and religious people in an era of unparalleled scientific accomplishment.

[14] The testimony in one such case (1659) is preserved in detail in *Quarterly Court of Essex County*, 2:157–60.

[15] See the case of Francis Hutchinson, in Shurtleff, ed., *Records of the Governor and Company of the Massachusetts Bay in New England (1626–86)*, 5 vols. (Boston: William White, 1854), 1:109.

[16] See Haskins, *Law and Authority*, pp. 204–11.

II

THE ROOTS OF MASSACHUSETTS WITCHCRAFT

✠

One of the major shortcomings of much of the writing on Massachusetts witchcraft is that it concentrates exclusively on the events that arose out of the Salem trials in 1692. While in a strictly numerical sense these trials are the large bulk of the Massachusetts experience, a neglect of the preceding half century of similar events might imply that on matters scientific the Salem cases were basically different from the others. This is not so. In examining facets of the contributions of science and scientific attitudes to the prosecution process, it appears that there were striking similarities among the cases as they arose during the unfolding of the century. Thus we must take as our subject matter the entire range of largely homogeneous cases as they arose, from the earliest days of the settlement through the proceedings in Salem Village in the last decade of the century.

During this period, Puritan society was, of course, continually moving away from the strictly theocratic framework of its founders, and to some degree the aspects of witchcraft focused on here—in particular, the psychopathological concepts involved in the defense of insanity (discussed in Chapter VIII below)—reflect that process of change. But on the whole the developments within the society, despite their importance in other areas, were largely irrelevant to law administration as it affected witches, and

9

the law's use of science remained constant. So, too, the cascading advances in particular areas of scientific knowledge made outside the Puritan community during the 1600's had no observable impact on the prosecutions: this sort of progress directly produced no changes in thought in the society that prosecuted witches that were sufficient to affect the prosecutions. Perhaps the age of science was an age in which attitudes toward science and nature changed, rather than an age of discoveries and inventions.

Even an examination of every witchcraft trial has its dangers, however. Such a broad span of time is still but a moment in the lives of people who were peculiarly conscious both of their past and their future. They valued equally their traditions and their ambitions, and their acts were flavored with a keen sense of their own position in world history. An aspect of this preoccupation—of great interest to us now—is the conception of witchcraft they felt had been passed on to them as an aspect of their political, religious, legal, and scientific heritages. These traditions, from which the Massachusetts cases spring, must be understood at the outset if what followed from them is to be seen in its proper light. Here the major focus of attention is on what meaning events and ideas had for a people at a given time and place in the past. More specifically, the fact that the mid-twentieth-century mind rejects magic and witchcraft as fanciful, superstitious, and perhaps even as a part of a delusional or psychotic outlook is of singular unimportance. It is possible that the set of beliefs that underlay the witch prosecutions may have been part of what has now been called "socially shared psychopathology."[1] But that is not likely, and to make the assertion stand that seventeenth-century Massachusetts was an insane society in this or other respects, a host of brilliant achievements in government, in theology, and in law, as well as a consistent course of ordered and reasoned reaction to the stresses of war, pestilence, and famine, must be explained away. Nothing short of a profound and unreasoning devotion to

[1] Ernest M. Gruenberg, "Socially Shared Psychopathology," in *Explorations in Social Psychiatry*, ed. Alexander H. Leighton, John A. Clausen, and Robert N. Wilson (New York: Basic Books, 1957), pp. 201–29.

the concept of monomania could maintain the belief that the witchcraft trials are simply manifestations of mental illness.

A look backward from Puritan times is therefore essential. In order to arrive at a reasonably clear view of the ideational heritage of witchcraft, it should first be pointed out that belief in witches appears to have been a universal phenomenon. It is, as George Kittredge has noted, "the common heritage of humanity. It is not chargeable to any particular time, or race or form of religion."[2] The discussion of the manner and rationale of scientific participation in the prosecutions which will follow should shed some light on the basis for this universality. But it does seem plain that acceptance of the reality of witches and witchcraft goes back at least as far as there are records to describe it. Henry Charles Lea, the historian of the Inquisition, wrote of sorcery and witchcraft within that context and was working on a detailed history of witchcraft when death deprived the world of his contribution to this field.[3] In his study of the Inquisition, Lea cites the case of the first known prosecution for witchcraft, which occurred in ancient Egypt in about 1300 B.C. Lea's account of the case reveals elements that will appear again millennia later, on the other side of the world. This is his description:

> The proceedings in the case recite, that a certain Penhaiben, a farm superintendent of cattle, when passing by chance the Khen, or hall in the royal palace where the rolls of mystic lore were kept, was seized with a desire to obtain access to their secrets for personal advantage. Procuring the assistance of a worker in stone named Atirma, he penetrated into the sacred recesses of the Khen and secured a book of dangerous formulas belonging to his master, Rameses III. Mastering their use, he soon was able to perform all the feats of the doctors of mysteries. He composed charms which, when carried into the royal palace, corrupted the

[2] George Lyman Kittredge, *Witchcraft in Old and New England* (Cambridge, Mass.: Harvard University Press, 1929), p. 372; Henry Charles Lea, *A History of the Inquisition of the Middle Ages*, 3 vols. (New York: Harper, 1888), 3:386.

[3] Arthur C. Howland edited a three-volume publication of Lea's last work under the title, *Materials towards a History of Witchcraft* (Philadelphia: University of Pennsylvania Press, 1939).

concubines of the pharaoh; he caused hatred between men, fascinated or tormented them, paralyzed their limbs, and in short, as the report of the tribunal states, "He sought and found the real way to execute off the abomination and all the wickedness that the heart conceived, and he performed them, with other great crimes, the horror of every god and goddess. Consequently, he has endured the great punishment, even unto death, which the divine writings say that he merited."[4]

What is noteworthy here is, first, that there is a firm belief that Penhaiben could and did in fact exercise supernatural powers of the sort described. There is no flavor of charlatanism or fraud even remotely implied; he "executed" the abominations. Second, there is no implication of impropriety about the use of these powers *per se*. Presumably, if Rameses III had done precisely what Penhaiben did, there would have been no abomination involved. The book must have been in the Khen for a purpose. To hypothesize further, the "doctors of mysteries" were privileged in the performance of these feats but did not use them for personal advantage. The accused was, in short, a magician without a license. This same prohibition on the *improper* use of magical powers seems to underlie the Exodus edict, "Thou shalt not suffer a witch to live," since the Old Testament is replete with instances of a *proper* alliance with spiritual powers for human purposes, for example, Moses producing water from a rock or Joshua commanding the sun and moon to stand still.[5] This emphasis on the matter of authorized vs. unauthorized sorcery did not end in Biblical days. As we shall see, the Massachusetts witchcraft cases also contain hints that the accused witches were engaging in practices—this time medical—that put them in unlawful competition with the colonial physicians. In view of the extent to which medical procedures of the day relied on astrology, alchemy, and other incursions into fields beyond human biology, the parallel with frank sorcery is apparent.

---

[4] Lea, *Inquisition*, 3:388. See also E. A. Wallis Budge, *Egyptian Magic* (London: Kegan Paul, 1899), p. 3.

[5] Exod. 17:6; Josh. 10:12, 13. The relation between Mosaic and Egyptian magic is discussed in Budge, *Egyptian Magic*, pp. 4–10.

If the belief in witches is the "heritage of humanity," it has been the peculiar heritage of the witches themselves that they be condemned and punished by those who wield secular and temporal power. Lea's collections of statutes and orders directed against them attest vividly to the fact that regardless of the stage of cultural development or the nature of the religious commitment that might be involved, societies have been virtually unanimous in their proscription of illegal magical practices.[6] Much of this opposition was generally based upon notions of good and evil, specifically, upon the alliance alleged to exist between the illicit magician and the forces of evil abroad in the universe, personified in Christianity by the Devil. The lines of battle were clearly drawn:

> As Satan's principal object in his warfare with God was to seduce human souls from their divine allegiance, he was ever ready with whatever temptation seemed most likely to effect his purpose. Some were to be won by physical indulgence . . . ; others by conferring on them powers enabling them apparently to forecast the future, to discover hidden things, to gratify enmity, and to acquire wealth, whether through forbidden arts or by the services of a familiar demon subject to their orders. As the neophyte in receiving baptism renounced the devil, his pomps and his angels, it was necessary for the Christian who desired an aid of Satan to renounce God. Moreover, as Satan when he tempted Christ offered him the kingdom of the earth in return for adoration, there naturally arose the idea that to obtain this aid it was necessary to render allegiance to the princes of hell. Thence came the idea, so fruitful in the development of sorcery, of compacts with Satan by which sorcerers became his slaves, binding themselves to do all the evil they could encompass and to win over as many converts as they could to follow their example. Thus, the sorcerer or witch was an enemy of all the human race as well as of God, the most efficient agent of hell in its empiternal conflict with heaven. His destruction, by any method, was therefore the plainest duty of man.[7]

[6] See Lea, *Materials*, 1:137–43, and *Inquisition*, 3:429–33.
[7] Lea, *Inquisition*, 3:385–86.

In spite of the directness of this injunction, it seems that the actual punishment of witches and sorcerers has had a somewhat checkered history. In the Roman Empire suppression was severe. With the opening of the Christian era vigorous action was taken against them, but this was all but completely abandoned in the period following the disintegration of the Roman Empire. The cycle of enforcement and neglect continued thereafter, evinced in penalties that range from the demand of ninth- and tenth-century continental legislation for mere penance for murder by sorcery to the penalty of death by burning for witches in the late Middle Ages.[8]

A variety of factors must have produced this ebb and flow in the severity of the penalties inflicted upon witches. It seems that the more secure the times—socially, politically, and economically —the less illicit incursions into spiritual mystery evoked official sanctions. But in the presence of widely felt turmoil and upheaval, the wrath of the state appeared in the form of energetic law enforcement. Probably the outstanding precipitating factor in Christian times was the threat posed by heresy. The connection between witchcraft and heresy is pointedly expressed in the above quotation from Lea. On the basis of this nexus one would expect the vigor of anti-heresy actions to be mirrored in the enforcement of the law against witches. Yet the persistent opposition to heresy did not always produce concomitant campaigns against witches; they enjoyed periods of relative peace during early heresy campaigns, probably because the express identification and merger of the concept of witchcraft with the idea of heresy apparently was not made until the Papal Inquisition of the Middle Ages.

While illicit magic had been condemned by the early Church, this prohibition was more in the interest of divesting the populace of pagan beliefs and practices in order to make room for the new Christianity and its ritual than it was an effort to preserve a Christian orthodoxy. The complex process of systematizing belief took centuries, and the refinements of the Schoolmen of the early

[8] *Ibid.*, pp. 392–425.

Middle Ages had to be developed before the opposite of this belief—heresy—could be definitively and systematically confronted. The anti-witchcraft and anti-heresy programs were thus parallel courses followed until the energies of the Church were fully mobilized in the period of the Inquisition, beginning with episcopal inquisitions conducted locally and progressing to the entire domination of the program by the popes and their emissaries. Significantly, this is also the profoundly unsettling period in the development of nation states and the breakup of feudal communities. But it was on the platform of clearing away heresy that the whole campaign of the next centuries was conducted.

Pope Alexander IV, in his bull of 1258, forbade the inquisitors to deal with magicians and required that these persons be left to the regular judges unless there was heresy clearly involved in their practices. This proviso in the bull, however, proved quite adequate as justification for the expansion of inquisitorial jurisdiction to sorcerers and witches. The reasons for this development are complex. Lea's explanation is that

> probably it may be traced to the effort of the theologians to prove that all superstitious practices were heretical in implying a tacit pact with Satan, as declared by the University of Paris. Thus, the innocent devices of the wise-women in culling simples, or in muttering charms, came to be regarded as implying demon-worship. When this conception once came to be firmly implanted in the minds of judges and inquisitors, it was inevitable that with the rack they should extort from their victims confessions in accordance with their expectations. Every new trial would add fresh embellishments to this, until at last there was built up a stupendous mass of facts which demonologists endeavored to reduce to a science for the guidance of tribunals.[9]

To this may be added Lynn Thorndike's suggestion that at these times the witch was the scapegoat for many of the ills of the waning medieval society and was more the victim of psychological and sociological pressures than of religious dogma. With this in

9 *Ibid.,* pp. 492–93.

mind, Thorndike warns that "it is possible to overemphasize the somewhat tenuous connexion between magic and heresy."[10] In the matter of moral responsibility for the prosecutions and actual causation of the executions, Thorndike is certainly correct in drawing into his discussion more than theology and the institutions of the Church. Witches were, after all, cruelly executed long before Christianity came into the world. But it is not witchcraft throughout time that we are here concerned with. In seeking to understand the roots of witchcraft in Massachusetts in the 1600's, it is vital to observe that there *was* a clear and observable "connexion" between magic and heresy on the continent which did not, for reasons to be developed, appear in New England, and the distinction was important in structuring the role of science in the Massachusetts cases.

During the course of almost four and a half centuries, more and more of the practice of the occult arts was assimilated into the conception of heresy. Pacts with Satan, illicit baptisms, unfounded assumptions concerning the Devil's power to act contrary to the will of God, and all manner of other acts came to be deemed a denial of the faith. An influential declaration by the Theology Faculty of the University of Paris in 1398 made virtually all such superstitious observances an error of faith.[11] Paris was the leading center of theological studies of the time, and thus a pattern was established that was widely and respectfully followed. The assimilation became so total that when Innocent VIII, in 1484, issued his bull authorizing the activity of two of the most famous inquisitors, Henry Kramer and James Sprenger (authors of the book for use in such cases, the *Malleus maleficarum*), he announced as his purpose the driving out of all "heretical depravity" and the desire that the "Catholic Faith should especially in this Our day increase and flourish."[12]

---

[10] Lynn Thorndike, "Magic, Witchcraft, Astrology and Alchemy," in *The Cambridge Medieval History* (Cambridge: University Press, 1936), 8:686.

[11] Lea, *Inquisition*, 3:464.

[12] The bull is printed in Montague Summers' translation of the *Malleus maleficarum* (London: John Rodker, 1928), p. xliii.

The significance of this statement is that, from this period on, witchcraft took on a new significance. Lea goes so far as to say that this was a "new witchcraft."[13] The emphasis on heresy considerations introduced a novel and important emphasis on the subjective elements of faith and belief. It was not that inquiry into observable secular harm was then abandoned—far from it. The second paragraph of Innocent's charter to the inquisitors contains a long list of "enormities and horrid offenses" committed by the heretical witches.[14] But as far as the ecclesiastical prosecution of witches was concerned, these abominations had only evidentiary value, and it was not necessary to prove the accused person guilty of such matters. Beliefs and errors of understanding being the central issues in adjudicating heresy, it was a confession that was the evidence most sought after. Thus, the *Malleus maleficarum* makes clear that if an accused is inconsistent in his statements to a judge, this is "sufficient grounds to warrant his exposure to the question and torture."[15] The fact that some punishment is authorized even without a confession is of no more than slight importance, since the availability of rack and screw rarely made it necessary to close a case without a confession.[16] The priests mention that "common justice demands that a witch should not be condemned to death unless she is convicted by her own confession,"[17] but the great emphasis on the abjuring of heresy found in the post-conviction procedures outlined in their

---

[13] Lea, *Inquisition*, 3:493.

[14] Summers, *Malleus maleficarum*.

[15] *Ibid.*, p. 272.

[16] The *Malleus* does call for an individualized use of torture (p. 273):

For some are so soft-hearted and feeble-minded that at the least torture they will confess anything, whether it be true or not. Others are so stubborn that, however much they are tortured, the truth is not to be had from them. There are others who, having been tortured before, are the better able to endure it a second time, since their arms have been accommodated to the stretchings and twistings involved; whereas the effect on others is to make them weaker so that they can the less easily endure torture. Others are bewitched, and make use of the fact in their torture, so that they will die before they will confess anything; for they become as it were, insensible to pain. Therefore there is need for much prudence in the matter of torture, and the greatest attention is to be given to the condition of the person who is to be tortured.

[17] *Ibid.*, pp. 222–23.

handbook makes it certain that saving souls was a much more paramount consideration than procuring "common justice." To this end a penitent confession was an obvious necessity, and all other matters of proof and procedure derived their importance from their relationship to the procuring of it.

To the extent that the views represented in the *Malleus* characterized European witch trials, the above analysis would suggest that the relationship between magic and heresy was, in an absolute sense, a great deal more than tenuous. Once an accused witch was required by inquisitional procedures to respond to inquiries on items of faith, the matter of witchcraft became an incidental aspect of the heretic hunt. From a comparative point of view, however, the great importance of the heresy-witchcraft merger lies in the fact that the heresy factor did *not* play a significant role in the conception of witchcraft that was dominant in seventeenth-century Massachusetts. The central reason for this is that the turning point in the history of witchcraft, highlighted by Lea in his description of the extension of inquisitorial jurisdiction, seems to have had no analogue in English history: in England heresy never became the nub of witchcraft. Thus, the major source from which the Puritans drew their views in this respect was vitally different from the late stages of Continental witchcraft. To the English, and to the New England settlers, the essence of witchcraft was not belief or errors in faith but, as Kittredge puts it, "*maleficium*— the working of harm to the bodies and goods of one's neighbors by means of evil spirits or of strange powers derived from intercourse with such spirits."[18]

This interpretation of Massachusetts witchcraft requires amplification, since as late as the beginning of the fifteenth century witchcraft was a relatively minor problem in England. Pollock and Maitland mention but a handful of insignificant cases,[19] including several prosecutions that terminated in a jury acquittal. These events apparently led Lea to remark that "to the fair and

[18] Kittredge, *Witchcraft in Old and New England*, p. 24.
[19] Sir Frederick Pollock and Frederick William Maitland, *The History of English Law*, 2 vols. (New York: Little, Brown, 1895), 2:550–53.

open character of English law is doubtless to be attributed the comparative exemption of the island from the terror of sorcery."[20] Later, of course, England had a large number of witchcraft prosecutions, convictions, and executions. But of crucial importance to an understanding of both those trials and the Massachusetts experience are the facts first, that England was but little troubled by the problem of heresy and second, that the Papal Inquisition never took strong hold there.

The historians of English law Pollock and Maitland, in speaking of the crime of heresy, describe it as "an offense of which few Englishmen were guilty, and about which therefore our courts seldom spoke."[21] Lea mentions three known instances of heresy prosecutions in England in the early period after the Conquest, and adds, "but practically the orthodoxy of England was unsullied until the rise of Wickliffe."[22] But even the case involving heresy against the Lollards was largely a political problem, and Wycliffe's trial "ended in a scandalous fiasco."[23] Wycliffe himself died in peace, and it was not until more than twenty years after his death that a statute directed against heretics became part of English law.[24] It is, of course, possible that heresy was punished prior to this without a statute, a contingency disputed by Sir James Stephen on the ground that, if there had been some law against heresy earlier, it certainly would have been invoked against Wycliffe and his followers after the Pope and the Archbishop of Canterbury had declared their doctrines heretical and had even excommunicated some of them.[25] It seems that this matter of law enforcement against heretics "is a question that buzzes in a vacuum" by virtue of the paucity of pre-Lollard heresy in England.[26]

Just why England should have been so comparatively little

[20] Lea, *Inquisition*, 3:467.
[21] Pollock and Maitland, *English Law*, 2:543.
[22] Lea, *Inquisition*, 1:114.
[23] Charles William Chadwick Oman, "English History," *Encyclopaedia Britannica*, 11th ed.
[24] This is the famous *De haeretico comburendo*, 2 Henry 4, c. 14 (1400).
[25] Sir James Fitzjames Stephen, A *History of the Criminal Law of England*, 3 vols. (London: Macmillan, 1883), 2:443.
[26] Pollock and Maitland, *English Law*.

bothered with heresy is a fascinating problem, though one which cannot be explored here. But acceptance of the indications that this is so leads to the inference that English witchcraft probably did not trace the evolutionary path seen on the Continent. In the absence of a developing crisis in heresy, such as was experienced in Europe, there was relatively little reason for witchcraft conceptions to have focused on Devil worship and related actions from which the implication of rejection of religious orthodoxy could be drawn. Under these circumstances there is no reason to expect *maleficium* to be assigned a secondary role.

In the rest of Europe this heresy-connected focusing on subjective elements appears to have been brought about largely by the Inquisition, and therefore what experience the English had with the inquisitors is also of central importance. It was apparently quite limited, there being only one recorded instance of the Papal Inquisition operating in England. This related to the campaign against the Templars led by Pope Clement V. On November 22, 1304, Clement set off all the monarchs of Europe to hunt and try the Templars.[27] In the early fall of 1304, Edward II of England had expressed grave misgivings to other kings, even to Clement himself, as to whether there had in fact been any wrongdoing by the highly respected Templars. With the receipt of the bull of November 22, however, Edward initiated the required arrests and investigations. Compliance with royal orders was slow, and it was not until October, 1309, that the two papal inquisitors who had been sent to England to carry on the prosecutions were able to hold their examinations. To the surprise of the examiners, innocence was both stoutly asserted by the accused and warmly supported by most other witnesses. Worse still, the laws of England did not permit torture under ordinary circumstances, and further progress was thus stymied until, in mid-December, the King was induced to order the jailers to permit the clerical examiners to do with the bodies of the Templars what they pleased, "in accordance with ecclesiastical law." Even so, it was not until late May of the following year that confessions were finally obtained

[27] This was the bull *Pastoralis praeminentiae*. See Lea, *Inquisition*, 3:278–79.

from three of the Templars. Three months later, Clement protested to Edward and to all of the bishops of England that the reluctance to use torture in these cases was itself a serious offense against Church law. Thus prompted, in the succeeding year Edward stated again that ecclesiastical law was to govern the procedures used in the investigations by the inquisitors. Only in the last of his decrees on this subject, issued on April 28, 1311, did Edward actually use the word "torture." The ultimate outcome of this reluctant cooperation with the Inquisition was, as might be expected, but few convictions and, as punishment, merely a mild rebuke to the Templars for being defamed for heresy.[28]

From these episodes it appears that witchcraft in England had little association with heresy and consequently cannot be expected to have produced a strong emphasis on the subjective beliefs of the accused persons or on relationships established with Satan. To put the same thing affirmatively, Kittredge's contention that witchcraft presupposes some working of worldly harm seems acceptable in its application to the English experience. The basic heritage of the English *émigrés* to Massachusetts, therefore, was in "the trials of the Elizabethan age [which] did not involve acceptance, either by the people or by the judges . . . of the complicated and systematized doctrine which formed the basis for the inquisitorial proceedings on the continent."[29] The importance of this for our inquiry into the role of science in the colonial cases is that a fundamental issue in which science was frequently involved—the determination of *maleficium*—was a matter central to the whole undertaking and not a last-minute addition to the task of extirpating heterodox belief.

This discussion is not meant to serve as a complete description of the history of witchcraft in England, which is a complex (and fascinating) affair, involving political intrigues, the relatively slow process of Christianization, the influence of Protestant theologians who returned from exile in Europe upon the accession of Elizabeth I, and the persistent tensions between English monarchs

[28] *Ibid.*, pp. 298–301.
[29] Kittredge, *Witchcraft in Old and New England*, p. 24.

and the papacy. All of these factors have been well traced else-where.[30] The point being stressed here is that in spite of all the relationships between English and Continental experience observable in that history, English witchcraft remained an essentially secular offense.

There is no more interesting demonstration of the difference between the English and the Continental tradition than appears from a comparison of two virtually contemporaneous documents. Not only do they appear at about the same time but they also come from the same geographical area, and both issue from the pens of learned clergymen. One is a statement by Dutch and Flemish ministers in New York, written in October, 1692, in response to inquiries concerning the nature of witchcraft put to them by Joseph Dudley of Massachusetts. The other is from Cotton Mather and appears in his *Memorable Providences Relating to Witchcraft and Possessions* of 1689.

The New York clerics declared

> that the formal essence of witchcraft consists in an alliance with the Devil; that is to say, in that men (desert) the realm of God our Creator and Supreme King whom all are bound to obey in everything by reason of our dependence upon him, and whose glory everyone, to the extent of his ability, is bound to maintain against his enemies—and go over to the camp of the Devil in order to fight against God so as to increase and strengthen, as much as they can, the kingdom of the Devil. In return for this defection, the Devil, on his part, promises them his aid to gratify their lusts. Thus man, on one part, throws off the yoke of God bidding farewell to His precepts and promises, in order to belong wholly to the Devil, whom he holds in the place of God.

[30] See, e.g., Wallace Notestein, *A History of Witchcraft in England from 1558 to 1718* (New York: Russell & Russell, for the American Historical Association, 1911); C. L'Estrange Ewen, *Witch Hunting and Witch Trials: The Indictments for Witchcraft from the Records of 1373 Assizes Held for the Home Circuit A.D. 1559–1736* (London: Kegan Paul, 1929), pp. 1–47; Trevor Davies, *Four Centuries of Witch-Beliefs* (London: Methuen, 1947). The last cited work discusses the "rapid spread of continental witch-beliefs in England," but Davies obviously means by this the impetus to enforcement and not the alliance with heresy prosecutions (see his chap. 3).

Mather, on the other hand, defines witchcraft with a distinctly different and more worldly kind of problem in mind: "Witchcraft is the Doing of Strange (and for the most part Ill) Things by the help of evil Spirits, Covenanting with (and usually Representing of) the woful children of men. First, Witches are the Doers of Strange Things. They cannot indeed perform any proper Miracles; those are things to be done only by the Favorites and Embassadors of the LORD. . . . Secondly. They are not only strange things, but Ill Things that Witches are the Doers of."

By the close of the seventeenth century the problem of heresy had largely abated, but, nonetheless, the Continental tradition stands out clearly in the New York clergymen's description of the essence of witchcraft in anti-God, pro-Devil terms. There is, indeed, no mention at all of the problem of worldly harm. To Mather this is the nub of the whole question. Witches are, first and foremost, "Doers," and it is this view that characterizes Massachusetts witchcraft.[31]

English witchcraft cases also focused on the harm produced by witches; it was, in fact, a subject for complaint by George Gifford, writing there, in 1593. He declared that the law was imperfect in not punishing a witch proved to have had dealings with the Devil; proof of murder should not be needed to put her to death.[32] As will appear below, as far as formal legal provisions were concerned, Gifford underestimated the breadth of the proscription. He was quite right, however, regarding the actual administration of the law.

---

[31] The text of the New York clergymen, as well as the questions propounded to them, is found in *Proceedings of the Massachusetts Historical Society*, 2d series 1 (1884):348. Cotton Mather's description is taken from *Translation and Reprints from the Original Sources of European History*, vol. 3, no. 4 (1902):2.

[32] George Gifford, *A Dialogue concerning Witches and Witchcraft* (London: Reprinted by the Percy Society, 1842), p. 95. The same protest can be found in William Perkins, *A Discourse of the Damned Art of Witchcraft* (1608), discussed in Kittredge, *Witchcraft in Old and New England*, 290–93, esp. p. 292.

III

THE VIEWS OF SCIENTISTS

✠

As it is almost impossible for us today to conceive of someone's practicing magic and witchcraft, so we are impelled to believe that it must have been an equally difficult conception to maintain in any age in which scientific fact is given priority over unverified supposition and overt fantasy. How can we explain the fact that in the seventeenth century, the age of the great scientific revolution, which laid the foundations for the science and technology of our own times in virtually every field of knowledge, the belief in witches existed with such vigor that executions took place in New England into the very last decade of the century, or that the English statute against witches was only repealed in 1736? For an explanation it is simple and inviting to rely on the communication gap that then existed (and which has grown larger since) between science and scientists on the one hand and the rest of the population on the other. Witchcraft, in this sense, might be deemed the passion of the unlearned. But the troublesome fact is that it was not merely the non-scientific laity but the most eminent leaders of the scientific community that persisted in the belief.

This is not to say that there was always complete public unanimity on the subject. Dissenting views can be found, and indeed much of what we know of the lore of witchcraft is derived from writers engaged in the debate as active partisans. Not infre-

25

quently, in fact, modern discussion of this subject tends to divide historical characters into heroes and villains, the former, naturally, the contenders for disbelief and the latter the advocates of blind superstition. It is useful to look briefly at two such protagonists of the period because in their views the issues can be seen as they appeared to men of science and learning in those times.

The historians, by acclamation, have declared the outstanding hero to be John Weyer (1515–1588), a physician, who has been variously described as German or Dutch. Gregory Zilboorg has summarized his contributions to the field of psychiatry as follows:

> He was the first physician whose major interest turned toward mental diseases and thereby foreshadowed the formation of psychiatry as a medical specialty. He was the first clinical and the first descriptive psychiatrist to leave to succeeding generations a heritage which was accepted, developed, and perfected into an observational branch of medicine in a process which culminated in the great descriptive system of psychiatry formulated at the end of the nineteenth century. Weyer more than anyone else completed, or at least brought closer to completion, the process of divorcing medical psychology from theology and empirical knowledge of the human mind from the faith in the perfection of the human soul.[1]

Weyer did not hesitate to apply his talents to an attack on the practices of the Inquisition ("it is highly unpleasant to see how people, in order to kill errors, are busy killing human beings"[2]) and to the belief in witches that he found all around him. In a letter to his patron, Duke William of Julich, in 1562, he expressed the essential elements of his position on this subject:

> Of all misfortunes which the various fanatical and corrupt opinions, through Satan's help, have brought in our time to Christendom, not the smallest is that which under the name of witchcraft, is sown as a vicious seed. The people may be divided against themselves through their many disputes about the Scrip-

[1] *A History of Medical Psychology* (New York: W. W. Norton, 1941), p. 228.
[2] Quoted in *ibid.*, p. 209.

tures and church customs, while the old snake stirs the fire; still no such great misfortune results from that as from the thereby inspired opinion that childish old hags whom one calls witches or sorcerers can do any harm to men and animals. Daily experience teaches us what cursed apostasy, what friendship with the wicked one, what hatred and strife, among fellow creatures, what dissention in city and in country, what numerous murders of innocent people through the devil's wretched aid, such belief in the power of witches brings forth. No one can more correctly judge about these things than we physicians whose ears and hearts are being constantly tortured by this superstition.[3]

It is difficult to ascertain the elements of thoroughgoing modern science that Weyer has used to support his position. His attribution of much of the misfortune to "Satan's help," to "the devil's wretched aid," and to the machinations of the "old snake" seems to preclude the assumption that Weyer refused to rely on supernatural interference in human affairs, which the role of pure scientist would seem to imply. Zilboorg, who quite properly designates Weyer as a giant in the evolution of medical psychology, insists that he did not himself believe in evil spirits and that his references to the Devil are nothing more than the use of contemporary jargon to convey ideas about mental illness.[4] This may well be so. The difficulty is that to his contemporaries these references must have seemed to be a concession to prevailing opinion that made his position both illogical and unpersuasive. Dr. Meric Casaubon, for example, noted carefully that Weyer admitted "no small part of what we drive at, when he doth acknowledge *supernatural operations*, by Devils and Spirits."[5] This led Casaubon to suspect Weyer himself of some illicit trafficking with Satan and to suggest "that what he intended was not so much to favor women, as the Devil himself, with whom it is to be feared, that he was too well acquainted."[6] Weyer was

---

[3] Quoted in *ibid.*, pp. 213–14.
[4] *Ibid.*, p. 212.
[5] *A Treatise Proving Spirits, Witches and Supernatural Operations* (London: Pawlet, 1672), p. 35.
[6] *Ibid.*, p. 46.

attempting to inject into the subject of witchcraft both the benefits of his clinical experiences with mentally ill persons and a
heaping dose of common sense, but he lacked a structured philosophy of science into which his observations could be integrated.
More important, he failed even to begin to develop an epistemology that would relegate what was then unexplainable by science
to future scientific activity, as an alternative to accepting present
solutions from the non-scientific framework of theology. For, as
Wallace Notestein has observed, this framework was the real
point at issue: "Given a personal Devil who is constantly intriguing against the kingdom of God (and who would then have
dared deny such a premise?), grant that the Devil has Supernatural powers (and there were Scripture texts to prove it), and
it was but a short step to the belief in witches."[7]

No one illustrates the forcefulness of the argument developed
from these premises better than Joseph Glanvill. He was a Fellow
of the Royal Society and a determined advocate of the values of
the emerging science, yet he stands as the black villain in the
witchcraft controversy, as Weyer is the hero. His writing was
known to the Mathers in Massachusetts, and the Reverend John
Hale of Beverly, writing after the Salem trials, affirmed that
Glanvill "hath strongly proved the being of Witches."[8] Glanvill
noted that the dissensions produced by the Reformation had
promoted a growing theological skepticism, a process of disbelief
that might today be called "creeping atheism." Responsibility
for this state of affairs, he asserted, partly rested with those who
refused to accept orthodox views of witchcraft: "And those that
dare not bluntly say, there is NO GOD, Content themselves (for
a fair step, and Introduction) to deny there are SPIRITS, or

---

[7] *A History of Witchcraft in England*, p. 211.

[8] See Increase Mather's reference to Glanvill in his *Remarkable Providences*
(1684), reprinted in George Lincoln Burr, *Narratives of the Witchcraft Cases
1648–1706* (New York: Barnes & Noble, 1952), p. 33. Cotton Mather's knowledge
of Glanvill is apparent in his Introduction to *Memorable Providences Relating to
Witchcrafts and Possessions* (1689), also reprinted in Burr, *Narratives*, p. 98.
Hale's reliance on Glanvill is indicated in his *A Modest Inquiry into the Nature
of Witchcraft* (1702), reprinted in Burr, *Narratives*, p. 405.

Witches."[9] Furthermore, he noted with authority, there was nothing in the new science that required such a blasphemous denial. Glanvill assigned to the mysteries of religion those areas of knowledge that science had not, and perhaps could not, appropriate to its own methodology and epistemology. It was to him of little consequence that religious doctrine could not explain just how the Devil and the witch go about their malevolent business. After all, he analogized, "we cannot conceive how the Foetus is formed in the Womb, nor as much as how a Plant springs from the Earth we tread on; we know not how our Souls move the body. . . ."[10] Mystery was no impediment to belief. Even that vigorous critic of much of the lore of witchcraft, Dr. John Webster, acknowledged that the Devil can make things invisible "by his spiritual power" and that the witch can accomplish strange deeds "by the strength of her imagination and the motion of her free will. . . ."[11] Webster, too, found murky metaphysics quite acceptable.

Glanvill's arguments were, if anything, more rigorous than those of Weyer. He recognized, for example, that the full force of history was on his side, and he exploited this advantage fully. The burden of proof he therefore assumed for himself was to demonstrate that it might be possible for witches to exist, not that there were, in fact, such persons. All of tradition declared the reality of witches, and, since the protesters asserted that this was absolute sham and untrue, Glanvill keenly undertook to destroy such arguments by proving the possibility of witchcraft: "If I show, how these things may be, and probably notwithstanding their allegations, though I say not down right that they are in the particular way I offer, yet 'tis enough for the design of Defense, though not for that of proof: for when one saith a thing cannot be, and I tell him how it may, though I hit not the

---

[9] *A Blow at Modern Sadducism In Some Philosophical Considerations About Witchcraft* (London: James Collins, 1668). The quotation is taken from the fourth edition, unnumbered page in the Preface immediately preceding p. B2.

[10] *Ibid.*, pp. 13–14.

[11] *The Displaying of Supposed Witchcraft* (1677), p. 252. On the title page Webster is identified as a "Practitioner of Physick."

just manner of it; I yet defeat the Objection against it, and make way for the evidence of the thing de Facto."[12]

As one might expect, the subtlety of Glanvill's distinction was frequently overlooked, for example, by Mr. Hale, in his assertion of Glanvill's proof quoted above. The proof that Glanvill did offer was based on appeals to many agencies of authority. In regard to religion, he declared that a denial of the reality of spirit, as distinct from matter, was a denial of God and of the soul.[13] He appealed to the concept of a Copernican universe where man loses his uniqueness and where creatures similar in spiritual quality to man might reside, beings who might be the agents with whom witches have their supernatural dealings: "And if both the superior and lower Continents of the universe have their inhabitants also, 'tis exceedingly improbable . . . that they are all of the meer sensible nature, but that there are at least some of the Rational, and Intellectual Orders. Which supposed, there is good foundation for the belief of Witches, and Apparitions; though the notion of a Spirit should prove as absurd, and un-philosophical, as I judge the denial of it."[14]

In addition, he suggested that common sense rebels at the thought that all of recorded experience with witches has been but one gigantic conspiracy and deception:

> And I think, those that can believe all Histories are Romances; that all the wiser would have agreed together to juggle mankind into a common belief of ungrounded fables; that the sound senses of multitudes together may deceive them, and Laws are built upon Chymera's; that the gravest and wisest Judges have been Murderers and the sagest persons Fools, or designing Imposters; I say, those that can believe this heap of absurdities, are even more credulous than those whose credulity they repre-hend.[15]

There were, of course, others who entered the lists, and it seems fair to observe that the subject was controversial, at least

[12] *Modern Sadducism*, unnumbered page preceding p. B4.
[13] *Ibid.*, pp. 7–8.
[14] *Ibid.*, pp. 9–10.
[15] *Ibid.*, p. 6.

at a literary level. Reginald Scot, for example, denounced witch-craft beliefs in his *Discovery of Witchcraft* (1584), provoking the equally famous *Demonologie* of James I (1597). But Scot's refutation of witchcraft was deficient in much the same respect as was Weyer's. He granted the existence of evil spirits but failed to deal with the question of why they were not capable of produc-ing the malevolent system of evil known as witchcraft.[16] Another anti-witchcraft work that should be mentioned because it comes from a man with such attractive credentials is Dr. John Webster's *The Displaying of Supposed Witchcraft* (1677). Of Webster, Kittredge remarks that

> he was not exceptionally credulous, and he belonged to that advanced school of English physicians who, in the second half of the seventeenth century, upheld the general theories of Para-celsus and van Helmont in opposition to the outworn follies of the Galenists or regulars. He was a man of great erudition, of vast and varied experience, of uncommon mental gifts, and of pas-sionate devotion to the truth. I admire him, but I must be par-doned if I am unable to see how he can be regarded as a tower of skeptical strength in the great witchcraft controversy. Even his admissions on the subject of the fallen angels are enough to destroy the efficiency of his denial of current notions about witch-craft. Once grant, as Webster does, that our atmosphere is peopled by legions upon legions of evil angels, delighting in sin, eager to work mischief, inimical to God and man, furnished with stores of acquired knowledge, and able to devise wicked thoughts and put them into our minds, and it was idle to deny—in the face of the best philosophic and theological opinion of the ages—that these demonic beings can make actual covenants with witches or furnish them with the means of doing injury to their fellow creatures.[17]

We find, then, that skepticism and attempts to discuss the whole matter of witchcraft in terms of the thought patterns of science were ineffective because they failed to deal directly with the basic structure of good and evil in the universe and to assert

---

[16] See Kittredge, *Witchcraft in Old and New England*, pp. 340–43.
[17] *Ibid.*, pp. 348–49.

unequivocally the inability of evil forces to affect human affairs. Something needs to be said by way of explanation for this ineffectiveness.

The accommodation of the findings and views of scientists to the belief in witchcraft must be viewed as but part of their larger effort to preserve a harmonious relationship between religion and science. A major reorientation in thought was taking place in which priority was beginning to be assigned to knowledge gained from observation and experience rather than from the scholastically applauded channels of revelation and reason. Bacon's exhortations, at the beginning of the seventeenth century, that scientists eschew certain sources of what he considered to be misleading authority and embrace inductive techniques may have provided no precise methodology for actual scientific work; nonetheless, his powerful emphasis on induction furthered greatly the development of new, experimental, and fruitful means of learning the truth about nature. Clearly, an alternative to the truths of revelation was evolving.

There was also much in the world of science that was specifically threatening to traditional religious views, such as the findings and theories of astrophysics and astronomy, which destroyed for all time the anthropocentric view of the universe, a view that had become incorporated into dogma. The response of the scientific community to these and other dangers to religion was to assert that the study of nature, far from being a system competing in any way with the concepts of theology, was properly seen as an effort to advance further the proof of God and His works. Thus, Robert Boyle wrote that "for the sensible representation of God's attributes to be met with in the creatures, occurring almost everywhere to our observation, would very assiduously sollicit us to admire him, did we but rightly discern him in them. . . ."[18] There is probably no more thorough exposition of this view than Cotton Mather's *The Christian Philosopher* (1721), which provides a

---

[18] *Fifth Essay on the Usefulness of Natural Philosophy* (1663), quoted in Harold Fisch, "The Scientist as Priest: A Note on Robert Boyle's Natural Theology," *Isis*, 44 (1954):253.

Norm landing

sophisticated explication of the wonders of scientific findings as a means of demonstrating the genius of divine creation. Mather sees the body of man as "a Machine of a most astonishing Workmanship and Contrivance!"[19] He adds, "Yea, every Writer of Anatomy will offer enough to trample Atheism under foot."[20]

There was some objection made to this blending of science and religion whereby the former's major function was to prove the truth of the latter. Bacon, for example, recommended avoidance of "this unwholesome mixture of things human and divine [from which] there arises not only a fantastic philosophy but also an heretical religion."[21] Hobbes went quite a bit farther and demanded that only the data of natural science be accepted as the foundation of human knowledge, but he acquired few followers in this view. In view of the deep religious feeling of the age, it must have been perfectly plain to men of science that latent conflicts ought to be avoided and that "the way to advance the new learning was to insist upon its limitations."[22] Such a circumscribed role for science was, moreover, more than acceptable to the leadership of New England.

> Puritan receptivity to the new science was encouraged, it seems clear, not half so much by the ocular proofs through which the new methodology was established as by the concomitant attestations of its theological orthodoxy advanced by its proponents. Particularly did the strategic line taken by the defenders of the Royal Society, by Boyle, Bishop Sprat, and Joseph Glanvill, insure Puritan confidence in the respectability of the movement. In order to avoid the accusation of atheism and materialism, in order to distinguish themselves from the Hobbesians, the Academicians put great stress upon their devotion to the spirit of "Scepsis Scientifica" and wrote energetically upon the vanity of Dogmatizing; as long as the conclusions of science could be deliberately advanced as tentative hypotheses, and as long as the scientists themselves were continually assuring laymen that more

[19] *The Christian Philosopher* (London: E. Matthews, 1721), p. 222.
[20] *Ibid.*, p. 223.
[21] Francis Bacon, *Novum organum*, pt. 1, sec. 65.
[22] Perry Miller, *The New England Mind: The Seventeenth Century*, p. 223.

remained to be investigated than had yet been studied, so that any impressions, garnered from our present imperfect knowledge, that seemed for the moment to challenge theological axioms would undoubtedly be corrected by future discoveries, then science contained no threat of heresy.[23]

At the heart of the matter is the fact that men of scientific learning accepted the basic theological framework of witchcraft, which made efforts at disputation by any of them largely futile. They found themselves at pains to demonstrate that their science did not pose any difficulties for religion, emphasizing that they did not know everything and that there were realms of knowledge and experience which were properly the exclusive domain of religion. But what is more important is that the belief in witchcraft followed from an unqualified acceptance of orthodox religious premises concerning good and evil and the potency of spiritual forces, and the rejection of this belief necessarily touched upon atheism. Science and scientists were therefore well advised to take care to avoid rending the fabric of belief in witchcraft. Any fundamental attack of this sort, express or implied, from scientific quarters would have been totally irreconcilable with the central effort to preserve the peace between religion and science. An authoritative condemnation of the belief in witchcraft as unscientific was neither present nor just around the corner.

This much of the discussion has been largely a matter of philosophy. Henceforth it will be concerned with how this philosophy affected the application of scientific knowledge and the use of scientific experts in the actual prosecution of persons accused of witchcraft. I turn now to a brief description of the legal system in which the prosecutions occurred.

[23] *Ibid.*, p. 222.

IV

THE LAW AND NATURE OF
MASSACHUSETTS WITCHCRAFT

✠

At the time of the colonization of New England, witchcraft was a statutory offense under the English law. Just how far back this crime can be directly traced is not clear. Although the *Leges Henrici* (*ca.* 1114) mention homicide by witchcraft as a capital crime, it was not until 1541 that a separate and distinct provision was made by Parliament for punishing witches.[1] In 1604 the final version of this law was enacted, the famous "witch act" of James I that remained on the statute books until 1736.[2] Both this law and its Elizabethan predecessor[3] contained separate provisions to cover the causing of death or bodily injury by witchcraft. They also proscribed the practice of witchcraft even without any resultant observable harm or *maleficium*. These latter provisions were directed at those who "use practice, or exercise invocations or conjurations of evil and wicked spirits to or for any intent or purpose."[4] Under both the 1562 and 1604 legislation these practices were punishable by death. There are, moreover, actual

[1] The first specific legislation, 33 Hen. 8, c. 8 (1541), was repealed by Edw. 6, c. 12 (1547). For a collection of pre-Norman, mostly ecclesiastical, laws, see Ewen, *Witch Hunting and Witch Trials*, pp. 2–4. There is a useful tabulation of the witchcraft acts from 1571 to 1736 in Ewen, p. 25.

[2] 1 Jac. 1, c. 12 (1604), repealed by 9 Geo. 2, c. 5 (1736).

[3] 5 Eliz., c. 16 (1562).

[4] This language is found in both the Elizabethan and Jacobean statutes.

prosecutions under both statutes for witchcraft of this "non-harm-producing" type.[5] In addition, the fact that in the law of James I death was the penalty for a first offense of bewitching a person without causing death is of some importance. Under the earlier statute of Elizabeth this non-fatal witchcraft was a capital crime only in cases of *second* offense. There were also more severe penalties under James for other aspects of witchcraft and sorcery, such as exhumation of corpses.

What these comparisons make clear is that, insofar as the statutory provisions were concerned, witchcraft without *maleficium* was not regarded as a minor offense and that, to some extent, the law in this area was becoming even more harsh under James I in the early years of the seventeenth century. The substance of . the distinction made above between the English and Continental witchcraft cases is, therefore, not that there was no provision in English law for witchcraft of essentially a subjective or victimless nature, but rather that the kinds of prosecutions that were undertaken and their underlying theoretical basis in conceptions of heresy were much more characteristic of Continental experience with the Inquisition than of English. Kittredge's discussion of the English witch trials near the turn of the seventeenth century shows that the almost exclusive concern of law enforcement activity was with *maleficium*, as does Ewen's finding that in only 25 out of 202 convictions in the counties studied did the documents contain no mention of *maleficium*.[6]

In Massachusetts there was no body of written statutes before 1641, when the Body of Liberties was adopted after long discussion and debate.[7] In that compilation was included provision that

---

[5] See Kittredge, *Witchcraft in Old and New England*, pp. 282–86.

[6] See the full discussion of a typical case in Kittredge, *Witchcraft in Old and New England*, pp. 3–22, and his account of the pardons granted by James I to persons convicted of witchcraft, almost all of which did not involve *maleficium*, pp. 314–15. Ewen's list is in *Witch Hunting and Witch Trials*, pp. 102–8. But compare the argument that English witches were part of an illicit European religion in Margaret A. Murray, *The Witch-Cult in Western Europe* (Oxford: Clarendon Press, 1921).

[7] On this subject Governor Winthrop's diary notes: "This session continued three weeks and established 100 laws, which were called the Body of Liberties. They had

"If any man or woman be a witch, (that is hath or consulteth with a familiar spirit) they shall be put to death."[8] (The Laws and Liberties of 1649 reiterated this provision.[9]) The revocation of the charter in 1684 forced reliance on English law, and some of the 1692 Salem trial indictments therefore specifically mention the statute of James I.[10]

The phrasing of this colonial law presents some difficulty. On the face of it, it seems to limit witchcraft prosecutions to cases that do not involve manifest harm. The statute raises the question of whether the Puritans might not, in this respect, be drawing more upon a Calvinistic emphasis on notions of heresy than on the English tradition of requiring evidence of *maleficium*. There is some support for this suggestion in the fact that, while their English brethren left the punishment of heresy almost entirely in the hands of the ecclesiastical authorities, the colonists declared heresy to be a civil offense punishable by banishment, a sanction that fell little short of capital punishment in view of the Indian wars and the problems of survival in a wilderness.[11]

In spite of the restrictive language of the statute, however, the Massachusetts experience, like that in England, makes clear that the offense did encompass, and indeed was almost entirely limited to, the production of bodily harm and death by witchcraft. The first witch trial in Massachusetts, in fact, involved the charge that the accused had severely harmed her victims. Accord-

---

been composed by Mr. Nathaniel Ward, . . . and had been revised and altered by the court, and sent forth into every town to be further considered of, and now again in this court, they were revised, amended, and presented, and so established for three years, by that experience to have them fully amended and established to be perpetual" (Winthrop, Journal, pp. 48–49).

[8] The Body of Liberties is reproduced in William H. Witmore, ed., *The Colonial Laws of Massachusetts. Reprinted from the Edition of 1660, with supplements to 1672. Containing also, the Body of Liberties of 1641* (Boston: Published by the City Council, 1889). The declaration against witches is in Liberty 94, Capitall Laws, p. 55.

[9] See Winfield S. Nevins, *Witchcraft in Salem Village in 1692* (Salem, Mass.: Salem Press, 1916), pp. 29–30.

[10] See *The Laws and Liberties of Massachusetts*, p. 5; reprinted from the 1648 edition in the Henry E. Huntington Library.

[11] See George Lee Haskins, "Ecclesiastical Antecedents of Criminal Punishments in Early Massachusetts," *Proceedings of the Massachusetts Historical Society*, 72 (1957–60):21–35, esp. p. 24.

ing to Governor Winthrop, the witch, one Margaret Jones, "was found to have such a malignant touch as many persons, men, women, and children, whom she stroked or touched with any affection of displeasure, were taken with deafness, or vomiting or other violent pains or sickness."[12] She was hanged at Charlestown in 1648.[13] This was not the first execution of a witch in New England; we know, again on the authority of Winthrop's Journal, that some unnamed person "of Windsor was arraigned and executed at Hartford for a witch."[14] Burr says that this was Alse Young, hanged on May 26, 1647.[15] There are, however, no records at all concerning the facts of this earlier case. It is also clear that the parsimoniously worded Massachusetts statute was invoked as authority for charging death by witchcraft in 1680, for example. The indictment against Mary Hale in that year charged that she "by the abhorred sin and art of witchcraft did kill and bewitch Michael Smith to death."[16] She was found not guilty, however.[17]

It is impossible to examine in detail all the convictions for witchcraft that occurred in Massachusetts or in New England in the seventeenth century in order to determine the precise role of *maleficium*. In some instances, all that is known is that the case occurred. The conviction of the "woman of Windsor" (Alse Young?) is one example; the execution of the wife of Henry Lake of Dorchester[18] is another. The significance of *maleficium* in the New England and Massachusetts experiences must, therefore, be derived from interpolation. Prior to the Salem trials in 1692 and 1693, it seems that there had been five executions for witchcraft in Massachusetts and six in Connecticut. Of the Massachusetts witches, two, Mrs. Lake and Mrs. Kendall of Cambridge, are almost entirely unknown, with Mrs. Kendall only

---

[12] Journal, p. 344.
[13] *Ibid.*
[14] *Ibid.*, p. 323.
[15] Burr, *Narratives*, p. 408, n. 2.
[16] *Records of the Court of Assistants*, 1:188–89.
[17] *Ibid.*, p. 189.
[18] See Burr, *Narratives*, p. 408, n. 4.

briefly mentioned by the Reverend John Hale in his 1704 *Modest Inquiry*. It is significant, however, that Hale gives the charge as bewitching a child to death.[19] A third witch, Ann Hibbins, who was hanged in Boston in 1654, was the upper-class widow of a prosperous merchant and former Assistant of the Colony, as well as the sister of Richard Bellingham, one-time Governor of Massachusetts Bay. Of the charges made against her and of the record of the trial nothing remains. We do know that the jury found her guilty, a verdict which the judge refused to accept—which perhaps is an early example of differential treatment of accused persons based on socioeconomic considerations. Be that as it may, the case came before the General Court, where she was found guilty and sentenced to death.[20]

Of the three remaining Massachusetts cases, that of Margaret Jones has already been mentioned—Winthrop cites her having harmed other persons as the first of the charges against her. The next in chronological order, according to Poole[21] and Kittredge,[22] was that of Mary Parsons; it seems, however, that she was convicted and hanged in 1651 for the murder of her child rather than for any use of the black arts (this, at least, is what the official records state[23]). The last of the pre-Salem witches was Mrs. Glover, who was hanged for afflicting John Goodwin's children with violent fits.[24] Her case was made something of a *cause célèbre* by Cotton Mather's involvement in it, and we shall return to it later.

Thus, of the five Massachusetts cases in which the death penalty was invoked, the information available indicates that

[19] *Ibid.*, p. 409.

[20] This case does not appear in any of the official records. Nevins (*Salem Village*, p. 35) says that there is no trial record. The description in my text is from Thomas Hutchinson, *History of the Colony of Massachusetts Bay* (London: Thomas & John Fleet, 1764), p. 187; and William F. Poole, "Witchcraft in Boston," in *Memorial History of Boston*, ed. Justin Windsor (Boston: Ticknor and Co., 1881), 2:130.

[21] "Witchcraft in Boston," pp. 131–32, n. 20.

[22] *Witchcraft in Old and New England*, p. 367.

[23] *Records of the Governor and Company of the Massachusetts Bay*, 3:229. According to Nevins (*Salem Village*, p. 33, n. 9), Mrs. Parsons was reprieved and not executed.

[24] The case is described by Mather in *Memorable Providences*, pp. 89–131.

maleficium was involved in three (those of Jones, Kendall, and Glover) and was one of the major counts against these accused. In no case does there appear even a hint of a heresy charge, although heresy was itself almost a capital offense under the colonial code.[25] It would be somewhat surprising if the circumstances of the cases of Mrs. Lake or Mrs. Hibbins, now unknown to us, departed radically from this pattern.

The potential role of science in the determination of *maleficium* in the early cases seems, therefore, to have been of central importance. As to the Salem cases that occurred in the last decade of the century, the harm inflicted on the bodies of the tormented girls of Salem Village was the cause of the outbreak of prosecutions. There was, in addition, the charge that livestock had been bewitched;[26] Sarah Good, for example, was accused of bewitching seventeen sheep and hogs to death.[27] The well-known fits of the Salem girls were, moreover, not the only kind of *maleficium* the witches were supposed to have produced on the bodies of their neighbors. One victim complained of an infected foot from which was produced "several gallons of corruption" when lanced, and of sores in his groin "which brought him almost to death's door."[28] In only one of the 1692–1693 cases in which the death penalty was exacted—that of Samuel Wardwell, executed on September 22, 1692—does it appear that a significant part of the indictment involved the covenant with the Devil. It was charged of him that "about twenty years ago with the evill spiritt, the devill, a covenant did make wherein he promised to honor, worship and believe the devill."[29]

[25] *The Laws and Liberties of Massachusetts*, p. 24.

[26] The charge was made against Elizabeth How, who was convicted and executed (see Samuel G. Drake, ed., *The Witchcraft Delusion in New England* [Roxbury, Mass.: Woodward, 1866], 3:109, 111). She was also accused of bewitching a girl to death (see Nevins, *Salem Village*, p. 186).

[27] The victim was Benjamin Abbott; he testified against Martha Carrier, who was also convicted and executed. The testimony is described by Cotton Mather in *Memorable Providences*, p. 242.

[28] See Nevins, *Salem Village*, p. 56.

[29] Quoted in *ibid.*, p. 207. Wardwell was also charged with bewitching Martha Sprague (*ibid.*).

These Salem cases were tried after 1684, when the charter of the Colony was revoked, which placed laws such as the 1641 proscription against witches and its re-enactments in legal limbo. On December 14, 1692, the colonists enacted a new witchcraft statute that followed closely the text of the 1604 Act of James I.[30] The later indictments, such as that against Wardwell, specifically mention violation of the Act of James I. There is, however, no reason to assume that the adoption of the English act signified anything but an attempt on the part of the colonists to assure an independent political status for themselves through this demonstration of loyalty to English law.

A special court of Oyer and Terminar was appointed to deal with the witchcraft complaints emanating from Salem Village. The trials were of persons who had been first granted a preliminary hearing before a magistrate.[31] Earlier cases had all been heard before the regularly constituted courts, in accordance with generally applicable law. The trial of all capital cases took place before the Court of Assistants, composed of the Governor, the Deputy Governor, and the magistrates. In 1636 it was ordered that this court should hold four sessions annually at Boston.[32] In cases arising between these sessions the accused was bound over to appear before the next Great Quarterly Court, as the four sessions were called. In the cases before 1692 a grand jury indictment usually initiated the judicial process.[33] Imprisonment was generally the interim disposition in any event, since the law granting the right to bail did not extend to capital crimes.[34]

Provision was made in the law for carrying a case to the General Court when judge and jury could not agree on the verdict: "And if the Bench and Jurors shall so differ at any time about their verdict that either of them cannot proceed with peace of

---

[30] *Province Laws of Massachusetts* (Boston: Wright and Potter, 1869), 1:90. This statute was disallowed three years later (see Nevins, *Salem Village*, pp. 29–30).

[31] See Powers, *Crime and Punishment in Early Massachusetts*, pp. 469–73.

[32] *Records of the Governor and Company of the Massachusetts Bay*, 1:169.

[33] See, e.g., the indictment of Mrs. Joseph Parsons in *Records of the Court of Assistants*, 1:31.

[34] *The Laws and Liberties of Massachusetts*, p. 28.

conscience, the Case shall be referred to the General Court who shall take the question from both and determine it."[35]

Two witchcraft cases were processed accordingly, with quite different results. Hugh Parsons, husband of the Mary Parsons who had confessed to murdering her child in 1651, was convicted of witchcraft by the jury—a decision the magistrate could not accept. Upon a retrial in the General Court, he was acquitted.[36] As mentioned above, Ann Hibbins was convicted by a jury in the Court of Assistants, the verdict was refused by the judges, and the case was taken to the General Court. There, however, according to Thomas Hutchinson, "the popular clamor prevailed against her, and the miserable old woman was condemned and executed."[37]

One more point needs to be made concerning the efficiency with which the legal system operated. In the great majority of cases, the accusation of witchcraft and of relations with the Devil resulted not in a hanging or even a conviction, but in a dismissal of charges. The records show that before the Salem trials took place there were at least ten such dismissals, as compared with five possible executions at the most.[38] During the Salem prosecutions,

---

[35] *Ibid.*, p. 32.

[36] *Records of the Governor and Company of the Massachusetts Bay*, 3:273.

[37] *History of the Colony.* For a discussion of the general administration of criminal law in Massachusetts during these times, see Powers, *Crime and Punishment in Early Massachusetts*, pp. 424–54.

[38] Unice Cole was indicted for having familiarity with the Devil in 1662 and was found "not legally guilty according to indictment but just ground of vehement suspicion of her having familiarity with the devil" (*Records of the Court of Assistants,* 3:253–54). In 1673 the Court of Assistants dismissed the case against Anna Edmunds because "they saw no ground to fix any charge against her" (*ibid.,* 1:11). In 1651 Mrs. Hugh Parsons was acquitted of witchcraft (Nevins, *Salem Village*, p. 33, n. 9). Her husband, as noted above, was also set free. In 1674 Mrs. Joseph Parsons was found not guilty (*Records of the Court of Assistants,* 1:33). In 1665 John Godfrey was found not legally guilty (*ibid.,* 3:151). Mary Ingham was acquitted by a jury in 1677 (*Records of Plymouth*, 5:223). In 1680 Mary Hale was found not guilty (*Record of the Court of Assistants,* 1:189). A similar verdict was returned in 1683 in favor of Mary Webster (*ibid.,* p. 233). In the same year James Fuller was also acquitted (*ibid.,* p. 228).

Ewen (*Witch Hunting and Witch Trials*, p. 100) says that from 1558 to 1736 fully 78 out of every 100 persons charged with witchcraft in the five counties of the Home Circuit in England were not executed. Earlier (p. 31) he says that "the chance of a witch suffering the death penalty, when arraigned before the regular justice, was small, 81 persons out of every 100 escaping the rope."

twenty died, ten were condemned but not executed, and approximately ninety-six were never convicted.[39] It thus appears that there was much more involved in hanging a witch in Massachusetts than making the accusation. Proof was needed, and we must now turn to the role of science in providing that proof.

[39] The figures in the text are taken from Nevins, *Salem Village*, p. 254; Nevins gives "a partial list of persons accused whether convicted or not." There are 126 names on the list. The following names were omitted: 19 who were executed; Giles Corey, who was pressed to death for failure to plead; 8 who were convicted but released when the prosecutions ceased on September 22, 1693; and two who were convicted and died in prison—a total of 30. Volume 135 of the *Massachusetts Archives*, pp. 1–6, lists 91 names of persons accused of witchcraft from 1656 to 1750, including those executed. No attempt has been made to reconcile the Archives' list with Nevins'. The fact remains, however, that during the entire century, only a small minority of persons accused of witchcraft were convicted or executed.

V

MALEFICIUM AND CAUSE OF DEATH

✠

I t is difficult to say with certainty where a witchcraft case begins—with a garrulous old woman, with an interpersonal relationship of hostility and enmity, perhaps with an unexpected death. It would not be surprising if in many cases a combination of these factors produced the accusation. But whether it confronted the investigators initially or was encountered incidentally as part of the subsequent proof of a witchcraft charge, the issue of whether a deceased met his end by natural means or by witchcraft was a crucial one. In other words, the prosecution was obliged to prove *maleficium* before a conviction could be obtained.

One obvious means of dealing with unexplained death, adopted by the colonists in the early days of their settlement, was to conduct a coroner's inquest. As early as 1630, for example, a jury's inquiry and view of a corpse resulted in a decision that a criminal homicide had been committed.[1] The first codification of the laws, in 1641, showed evidence of support for medical training in anatomy. This policy made possible the carrying out of post-mortem examinations, which might be extremely useful to such inquests. It was implied in an exception made in the law governing disposition of certain corpses: "It is ordered by the Court that no man condemned to dye shall be put to death within four days

[1] *Records of the Governor and Company of the Massachusetts Bay,* 1:77–78.

next after his condemnation, unless the Court see special cause to the contrary, or in case of martial law; nor shall the body of any man so put to death be unburied twelve hours unless it be in case of anatomy."[2]

Six years later, a more specific statement of policy appeared that put the General Court again on record in favor of developing the dissecting and anatomical skills of its medical personnel by permitting them to study cadavers systematically. It is sometimes suggested that enactment of this statute was caused by the need for anatomists created by the return to England of Giles Firman, Jr., who had taught anatomy during his stay in Massachusetts, from 1632 to 1677.[3] In 1677, discussing local medical education in a letter, John Clint wrote that "we never had but one Anatomy in the Country, which Mr. Giles Firman (now in England) did make and read upon very well."[4] Following Firman's departure the law declared: "We conceive it very necessary that such studies as physic, or chirurgery may be at liberty to reade anatomy and to anatomize once in four years some malefactor in case where be such."[5]

These statutes broaden the position taken in England as early as 1540, when Henry VIII's charter to the Guild of Barbers and Surgeons of London gave them the right to four bodies of criminals each year.[6] The Massachusetts colonists also brought with them the English experience with the use of coroners, and in

[2] *The Laws and Liberties of Massachusetts*, pp. 12–13. There is a strikingly similar provision in the Duke of York's laws, in force in Pennsylvania from 1676 to 1682, except that there is no provision "in case of anatomy." See J. B. Linn, ed., *Charter to William Penn, and Laws of the Province of Pennsylvania* (Philadelphia: George, Nead, and McCamant, 1879), p. 24. See also Frederick C. Waite, "The Development of Anatomical Laws in the States of New England," *New England Journal of Medicine*, 233 (1945):716.

[3] See, e.g., Timothy Leary, "The Massachusetts Medicological System," in *Methods and Problems of Medical Education*, 9th ser., vol. 9 (New York: Rockefeller Foundation, 1928), p. 303.

[4] Quoted in *ibid.*, p. 300.

[5] *Records of the Governor and Company of the Massachusetts Bay*, 2:201.

[6] 32 Hen. 8, c. 42 (1540). See William S. Copeman, *Doctors and Disease in Tudor Times* (London: William Dawson & Son, 1960), pp. 27, 40; Waite, "Anatomical Laws," pp. 716, 717.

1641 they enacted a law that "whensoever any person shall come to any very sodain, untimely or unnatural death, some Assistant or the Constable of that town shall forthewith summon a Jurie of twelve discreet men to inquire of the cause and manner of their death, who shall present a true verdict thereof, to some neer Assistant or to the next court (to be holden for that Shire) upon their oath."[7]

It is noteworthy that there is no mention of a physician's carrying out these responsibilities, as contrasted with the practice in colonial Maryland, where it is reported that "a chirurgeon often acted as the foreman of a coroner's jury."[8] There, the use of the expertise of medical persons is often quite clear, as in a Maryland case where the foreman of the coroner's jury, a chirurgeon, declared that the victim had met his end by means of a bullet "which entered the epigastrium near the navel on the right side, obliquely descending and piercing the guts, glancing on the last vertebra of the back, was lodged in the side of the ano."[9] There seems little room for doubt that full advantage was taken of someone's dissecting skill and anatomical knowledge in this case. The role of expertise is even more clear in another Maryland case in which the two physicians assigned to the corpse reported "that after they had cut open the body they found it clear of inward bruises, either upon the diaphragm, or within the ribs"; they added: "The lungs were of a livid bluish colour full of putrid ulcers, the liver not much putrid, although it seemed to be disaffected by reason of its pale wan colour: the purse of the heart was putrid and rotten, by which we gather that this person by course of nature could not have lived long, putrefaction being so near unto that noble part, the heart, even at the door."[10]

To what extent did allegations of death by witchcraft in Massachusetts involve similar examinations? It is important first to

---

[7] *The Laws and Liberties of Massachusetts*, p. 16.

[8] Raphael Semmes, *Crimes and Punishments in Early Maryland* (Baltimore: Johns Hopkins, 1938), p. 236.

[9] Quoted in *ibid.*, pp. 236–37.

[10] *Ibid.*, p. 237. Semmes provides several other examples of professionally conducted post-mortem examinations (see pp. 311–12, 238).

observe the use of medical skills in cause of death investigations generally. The records indicate that the coroner's inquest was used fairly often. As early as September, 1630, a jury reported that it had "vewed" a dead body and returned a verdict that "wee finde that the strookes given by Walter Palmer were occationally the means of the death of Austen Bratcher and soe to be manslaughter."[11]

A search for similar cause of death inquiries in the *Records of the Governor and Company of the Massachusetts Bay* (1678 to 1686), the *Records of the Court of Assistants* (1630 to 1692), the *Records of Plymouth* (1633 to 1691), the *Records of the Suffolk County Court* (1671 to 1680), and the *Records and Files of the Quarterly Court of Essex County* (1636 to 1683) revealed eighty-two such investigations. There were only two reports of murder, the great bulk (thirty-six) being findings of drowning. It is interesting that there were quite a few (twelve) suicides.[12] In only two of these cases, however, does there appear the hand of a medical man. In 1678, a jury report states: "Sir, according to your order, I with the rest of the men have searched the body of one called Edward. I made incision upon the parts of his body which was most suspicious which was upon the temporal muscle; I layed the bones bare: we could not find any fracture in the least, neither was the flesh in any wise corrupt or putrified."[13] The other medical report in the official records concerned the death of Jacob Goodale. In 1676 the jury, with the assistance of Dr. Zerobabel Endicot, made a post-mortem examination which indicated that Goodale had been beaten to death.[14]

---

[11] *Records of the Governor and Company of the Massachusetts Bay,* 1:78.

[12] The murder verdicts are in *ibid.,* 5:41, and in *Records of Plymouth,* 2:132. The drowning verdicts are in the *Quarterly Court of Essex County,* 2:119, 223; 4:98, 211, 212; 5:260, 444; 8:238–39, 442. They are also found in *Records of Plymouth,* 1:88; 2:151, 175; 3:15, 16, 28, 92, 93, 146–47, 158, 208–9; 4:83–84, 169, 170–71; 5:7, 94–95, 121–22, 123, 130–31, 141, 225–26, 262–63, 273; 6:8, 45, 75, 76. The suicide cases are in the *Quarterly Court of Essex County,* 2:421; 3:233; 5:124; 6:397. Also see *Records of Plymouth,* 3:213; 4:13, 83; 5:182, 208, 249–50, 262; 6:142.

[13] *Quarterly Court of Essex County,* 7:14.

[14] See the inquest report quoted in Francis R. Packard, *History of Medicine in the United States* (New York: Hoeber, 1931), 1:57. The trial of Giles Corey for inflicting the beating is in *Quarterly Court of Essex County,* 6:190.

John Winthrop reported two additional instances in which medical skills were used to determine the cause of death. In 1647 a surgeon who was called upon "to search the body" of the deceased found a fractured skull. This examination, however, did not take place until after the murderer had confessed.[15] Winthrop also cites a post-mortem finding of skull fracture in 1639 that led to a murder indictment.[16] Timothy Leary provides accounts of three more cases of post-mortem examination—in 1654, 1667, and 1674.[17]

In most of the cases that are known it appears that a gross view of the corpse was taken by laymen, their report typically concluding, "Wee, the said jury, having diligently serched him." When there were suspicious circumstances, the inquest sometimes resorted to what has been called the "ordeal by touch" or "bier right", an ancient practice based on the belief that when the guilty party touches the body blood will flow from the wounds or the corpse will in some other way indicate the identity of its slayer. Thus we find a Plymouth jury reporting that "further, wee required Anne Batson and seuerall of the family to touch the dead child but nothing thereby did appeer respecting its death."[18] John Winthrop's Journal mentions two other cases in which the touch of the murderer produced a flow of blood in the corpse, and Dow cites indications of this "ordeal by touch" being invoked as late as 1769.[19]

In only one instance does there appear a verdict of witchcraft returned by the jury. This was in New Hampshire in 1679, one year after it had become a royal colony. The setting in the town of Hampton is, however, clearly that of Puritan Massachusetts. According to Page, a jury of inquest viewed the body of a young

[15] John Winthrop, Journal, 2:318.

[16] Quoted in Packard, History of Medicine in the United States, p. 56, n. 14.

[17] "The Massachusetts Medicolegal System," p. 303.

[18] Records of Plymouth, 5:261–62.

[19] Pp. 218–19; George Francis Dow, Every Day Life in the Massachusetts Bay Colony (New York: The Society for the Preservation of New England Antiquities, 1935), pp. 203–4. This practice was not, of course, confined to Massachusetts. See Semmes, Crimes and Punishments in Early Maryland, pp. 126–27, n. 6; Harry B. Weiss and Grace M. Weiss, An Introduction to Crime and Punishment in Colonial New Jersey (Trenton, N.J.: Past Times Press, 1960), p. 47.

child and returned a verdict of "suspicion that the child had been murdered by witchcraft."[20] The jurors cited the appearance of the body to support their opinion, although they did not describe it. In addition, they relied on the odd appearance of the suspected witch and "the testimony that they heard."[21] There is no hint at all of the involvement of medical judgment.

In none of the other sources, however, is there a verdict that even alludes to witchcraft as being involved in the death. In Ewen's study of analogous records in England from 1559 to 1736, witchcraft is similarly absent. He reports: "One would have expected the coroners' rolls and inquisitions to be full of verdicts of death by witchcraft, but the writer has never seen any entry but felo de se, visitation of God, homicide, murder, or misfortune. Possibly, as in some of the gaol calendars, the word murder is used to include death by witchcraft."[22] In the two murder cases I found in the Massachusetts inquest reports, no concealment of witchcraft seems likely. In one, the murderer confessed to having used a knife and in the other, although the verdict did not identify the culprit, it did state that the corpse was "wounded in severall places, whereby, he was murthered."[23]

On the other side of this same coin is the fact that in none of the witchcraft trials does there appear to have been a coroner's inquest of any sort. The case against Rebecca Nurse, for example, included the charge of bewitching to death an eight-year-old child who had "strange and violent fitts for about two days and two nights, and then departed this life by a cruell and violent death."[24] A post-mortem inquiry, similar, perhaps, to the surgeon's search for "flesh in any wise, corrupt or putrified," as was mentioned in the 1678 Essex County report quoted above, might have revealed the cause of death. But none was done.

[20] Elwin L. Page, *Judicial Beginnings in New Hampshire 1640–1700* (Concord, N.H.: New Hampshire Historical Society, 1959), p. 118.

[21] *Ibid.*

[22] Ewen, *Witch Hunting and Witch Trials*, p. 60.

[23] *Records of the Governor and Company of the Massachusetts Bay*, 5:41.

[24] *The Historical Collections of the Topsfield Historical Society*, vol. 13 (Topsfield, Mass.: Published by the Society, 1908), p. 50.

We have, however, an autopsy report from Connecticut, dated March 31, 1662, which, although it did not result in an actual trial, sheds light on the present problem.[25] Elizabeth, the nine-year-old daughter of John Kelley of Hartford, died on March 26, 1662, after an illness of several days. During her sickness, Elizabeth complained several times that Goody Ayres was choking her and causing her other suffering. The same Goody Ayres seems to have been involved earlier with persons who were tried and executed as witches (Mr. and Mrs. Nathaniel Greensmith), but there is no record of any formal prosecution against her. A jury of inquest investigated Elizabeth's death and required Mrs. Ayres to touch the body, as a result of which the corpse "purged a little at the mouth." They also reported that "the backside of both the arms, from the elbow to the top of the shoulders were black and blue, as if they had been bruised or beaten." Five days after the death, on March 31, 1662, a physician named Bryan Rosseter, who had been summoned from Guilford, examined Elizabeth's body and reported as follows:

All these 6 particulars underwritten I judge preternatural: Upon the opening of John Kelley's child at the grave I observed,

1. The whole body, the musculous parts, nerves and joints were all pliable, without any stiffness or contraction, the gullet only excepted. Experience of dead bodies renders such symptoms unusual.

2. From the costal ribs to the bottom of the belly in the whole latitude of the womb, both the scarf skin and the whole skin with the enveloping or covering flesh had a deep blue tincture, when the inward part thereof was fresh, and the bowels under it in true order, without any discoverable peccancy to cause such an effect or symptom.

3. No quantity or appearance of blood was in either venter or cavity as belly or breast, but in the throat only at the very swallow, where was a large quantity as that part could well contain, both

[25] The account of this case is taken from Charles J. Hoadly, "Some Early Post-Mortem Examinations in New England," *Proceedings of the Connecticut State Medical Society*, 69 (1892):207–17.

fresh and fluid, no way congealed or clodded, as it comes from a vein opened, that I stroke it out with my finger as water.

4. There was the appearance of pure fresh blood in the backside of the arm, affecting the skin as blood itself without bruising or congealing.

5. The bladder of gall was all broken and curded, without any tincture in the adjacent parts.

6. The gullet or swallow was contracted, like a hard fish bone, that hardly a pease could be forced through.

BR. ROSSETER.

Rosseter's report is of interest in several respects. For one thing, he opened the body "at the grave," indicating that Elizabeth was first buried and then disinterred for the autopsy. (It is not likely that the body would have remained unburied for five days or that Rosseter would have made his examination at the grave unless it was necessary.) Perhaps, therefore, his findings represent, in part, a failure to recognize as decomposition the changes that took place in the interval between death and the examination, i.e., a lack of experience with corpses after the *rigor mortis* stage.[26] Another point of note is that in only two of the six particulars does Rosseter expressly declare the findings to be to some extent beyond medical experience. The absence of *rigor mortis,* he says, is "unusual," and the discrepant nature of the skin and the underlying tissues and organs mentioned in his second particular is caused by no "discoverable peccancy" or corruption. The other four conditions are presented without any comment on his grounds for judging them to be "preternatural." Even in the first two, it should be observed that nothing expressly concerning witchcraft is reported. Rosseter finds the pliability of the body "unusual," but does not call it unknown or common in the case of witchcraft; he says the peccancy is not "discoverable," not that the symptoms have been induced from outside.

[26] See Theodore Shennan, *Post-Mortems and Morbid Anatomy,* 3d ed. (London: Arnold, 1935), p. 28. Rosseter also seems not to have understood post mortem lividity or gravity-induced settling of the blood in his findings 2 and 4 (see *ibid.,* pp. 23–24).

In short, Rosseter's report is almost entirely an objective description of his observations. He makes no mention of any sign or stigmata of a witch's intervention in the functioning of the body, such as impressions of fingers around the child's throat, etc. He stresses only what is novel or unexplainable to him, e.g., the blood in the back of the arms with no signs of bruising. Yet the central thrust of this medical report to laymen is that the morbid conditions he found were supernaturally induced, even those for which he knew there could be a natural cause. It is difficult to avoid suspecting that Rosseter's medical indictment of Goody Ayres was more the result of his embarking on his task in the belief that witchcraft had killed Elizabeth than it was the result of the autopsy findings themselves. Approximately six weeks after this report, there were court proceedings, apparently a preliminary examination of Goody Ayres on a charge of witchcraft. Undoubtedly, Rosseter's report played a significant role in bringing this action about. Since both Mr. and Mrs. Ayres fled from Connecticut, there is no record of a trial.

We have, then, a history of a not infrequent resort to postmortems in cases of suspicious death; although there were no such investigations in the Massachusetts witchcraft cases, we are given some indication of what an autopsy report might be like where witchcraft was suspected. The attempt to account for the occurrence of any autopsies at all may provide a useful context in which to examine the witchcraft cases. There seems to have been no shortage of medical personnel to conduct these inquiries, in fact, the practice of medicine was a part-time occupation of many persons in the Colony. On the whole, these physicians were trained in a system of apprenticeship, and few had any medical schooling in the universities of Europe.[27] It was not until 1765 that the first American medical school opened in Philadelphia. During the seventeenth century, however, there were a number of doctors

[27] Carl Bridenbaugh, *Cities in the Wilderness*, 2d ed. (New York: Alfred A. Knopf, 1955), p. 447. See also Henry Sigerist, "Boerhaave's Influence upon American Medicine," in *Henry Sigerist on the History of Medicine*, ed. Felix Marti-Ibanez (New York: MD Publications, 1960), p. 202.

who were among the most prominent members of the community. Dr. Samuel Fuller of Plymouth and Dr. John Pratt of Cambridge, for example, were highly respected figures in the Colony.[28] There is, in addition, evidence that medical judgments were relied on strongly in other kinds of legal and semi-legal problems. In 1646 the court in Plymouth decided to allow one Francis Crooker to marry only if he could present a doctor's certificate that he was not an epileptic.[29] In 1651 Thomas Robinson was ordered to consult with physicians and to follow their advice concerning his impotence.[30]

On the other hand, the colonial experience with medicine was not entirely favorable. The regulation of quackery was no easy matter. Fines had to be levied to prevent the sale of medicines of no value.[31] The problem that arose in drawing a line between a permissible medical practice and the quackery that evoked public concern is nowhere more clearly stated than in the order of the General Court of May 3, 1649, regulating the use of novel therapies:

> Forasmuch as the lawe of God, Exod:20:13, allowes no man to touch the life or limme of any person except in a judicyall way, bee it hereby ordered and decreed, that no person or persons whatsoever that are employed about the bodies of men and women and children for preservation of life, or health, as physicians, chirurgians, midwives or others, shall presume to exercise to put forth any act contrary to the known rules of art, nor exercise any force, violence, or cruelty upon or towards the bodies of any, whether young or old, —no, not in the most difficult and desperate cases, —without the advice and consent of such as are skilfull in the same art, if such may be had, or at least of the wisest and gravest then present and consent, upon such punishment as the nature of the fact may deserve; which law is not intended to discourage any from a lawful use of their skill, but rather to encour-

[28] See Packard, *History of Medicine in the United States*, pp. 8–10; John Winthrop, Journal, 2:249.
[29] *Records of Plymouth*, 2:112.
[30] *Quarterly Court of Essex County*, 1:221.
[31] *Records of the Governor and Company of the Massachusetts Bay*, 1:83.

age and direct them in the right use thereof, and to inhibit and restrain the presumptious arrogance of such as through praesidence of their oune skill, or any other sinister respects, dare to bould to attempt to exercise any violence upon or towards the bodies of young or old, to the prejudice or hazard of the life or limme of men, women or children.[32]

Near the turn of the century, perhaps because this problem continued unabated, one university-trained physician in Boston declared the practice of medicine to be "perniciously bad."[33] Nonetheless, there does seem to have been a sufficiently large group of physicians for autopsies to have been undertaken in the witchcraft cases.

Apart from the matter of personnel, another set of factors to be considered are the fields of substantive knowledge involved in autopsy procedures. Foremost among these was anatomy. The scientific revolution had greatly increased knowledge of the human body, and these discoveries, in turn, might be expected to have stimulated medical men to work on cadavers. The new findings in science were manifested earliest in biology and human anatomy, although it is accurate to characterize the great scientific changes of the seventeenth century as primarily in the physical sciences, mostly in terrestrial and celestial physics. As was true in almost all of the divisions of human biology, the main sources of anatomical knowledge were the works of the great Roman physician of the second century, Claudius Galenus. In the centuries that stretched between his life and the dawn of modern times they had, of course, been added to and modified, but the doctrines that survived were clearly Galenic, perhaps even more than the central ideas in physics upon which Galileo worked were essentially Aristotelian.[34] In this sense, the changes in anatomy were more dramatically revolutionary than were those in physics.

Although not so intended at the time, the beginning of the

[32] *Ibid.*, 3:153.
[33] This was Dr. William Douglas. See *Massachusetts Historical Society Collections*, 2d ser., vol. 4 (Boston: John Eliot, 1816), p. 164.
[34] See A. Rupert Hall, *The Scientific Revolution*, pp. 77–92.

end of Galen's hold on men's minds may be dated 1543, the year in which Andreas Vesalius published his *De humani corporis fabrica* in Basel. This was a text based upon extensive practical experience in dissecting and was illustrated with an accuracy and wealth of detail earlier unknown. The *Fabrica* provided the fundamentals of knowledge that were to serve subsequent anatomists and medical men for centuries. However, it was not itself a rejection of Galen; indeed, when Vesalius found discrepancies between his own observations and the descriptions of Galen, he did not hesitate to conclude that Galen might be right.[35] Only infrequently did he state forthrightly that the traditional view was wrong.

Other anatomists followed Vesalius, some making quite significant advances in knowledge,[36] but relatively little of this knowledge had reached English medicine by the beginning of the seventeenth century. The commencement of English involvement in a new biology can probably first be seen when William Harvey announced his discovery of the circulation of the blood in 1628.[37] Largely because of this delay and the American system of apprenticeship training of medical practitioners, the early colonial period has been called almost entirely Galenic.[38]

Despite all the advances made in such areas as anatomy, circulation, respiration, etc., by pioneers such as Vesalius and Harvey, some commentators believe that there was remarkably little change in techniques of medical treatment or in the practice of medicine generally.[39] Even the latest publications in pathology, directly related to post-mortem anatomical findings, barely influenced the incidence or nature of autopsy procedures practiced by medical personnel.[40] The disinterest in anatomy, and perhaps in post-

[35] *Ibid.*, p. 139.

[36] See Charles Singer, *The Evolution of Anatomy* (London: Kegan Paul, 1925), pp. 135–74.

[37] See Kenneth D. Keele, *William Harvey* (London: Nelson, 1965).

[38] Maurice B. Gordon, *Aesculapius Comes to the Colonies* (Ventnor, N.J.: Ventnor, 1949), p. 3.

[39] Richard H. Shryock, *The History of Nursing* (Philadelphia: Saunders, 1959), pp. 134, 146–49.

[40] Seventeenth-century progress in this field is summarized in Esmond R. Long, *A History of Pathology* (New York: Dover, 1965), pp. 47–62.

mortem examinations as a consequence, is probably attributable, at least in part, to the distinction made between the functions of physicians and surgeons, whereby the latter group did almost all of the work we now associate with surgery. They also had a markedly lower social and professional status than the physicians, so that a reluctance on the part of physicians to engage in practice of a menial nature, as dissections and post-mortems may well have been considered, would be quite understandable. It is, in fact, one of the advances attributed to Vesalius that he himself cut up the cadaver in teaching anatomy to his classes, rather than simply lecturing on the parts as they were exposed to the students by an assistant, as was the tradition.

In the colonies the handicap created by the persistence of these traditional roles was aggravated by the fact that the apprenticeship system of educating colonial physicians was not well designed to keep the profession's recruits abreast of new developments in normal or morbid anatomy. Apprenticeship training emphasized the transmission of past knowledge and techniques, not the capacity or opportunity to assimilate novel ideas. Perhaps even if new doctors had been drawn from the English medical schools, this same negative result would have been produced. The fact that these developments in human biology came largely from individual scientists not associated with the established universities tended to insulate formal medical education as well from the changes.[41] To some extent, this was offset by the new means of communication established by the founding of the Royal Society in 1661 and the publication of its transactions. This was not without significance for the colonists. Governor John Winthrop of Connecticut was an original Fellow of the Society, although he was the only New England member elected in the seventeenth century.[42] We may infer, however, that others elected in the second decade of the following century (Cotton Mather, 1713; William Brattle, 1714; John Leverett, 1713; and Elihu Yale, 1717[43]) achieved that honor partly because of an interest in science that went back at

---

[41] Eric Nordenskiold, *The History of Biology* (New York: Tudor, 1928), p. 142.
[42] Stearns, "Colonial Fellows of the Royal Society of London," p. 222.
[43] *Ibid.*, pp. 226, 229, 230, 231.

least as far as the period of the Salem trials. Moreover, there was an active correspondence between eminent scientific members of the Society, such as Robert Boyle and Robert Hooke, and persons in New England.[44] Yet what stimulus might have been derived from the new knowledge was probably hardly felt by the bulk of practitioners. Shryock even suggests that conservative physicians were the chief obstacles to medical progress in the seventeenth century.[45] Thus, although there were probably enough physicians available for an expanded autopsy program that might have encompassed the witchcraft cases, their intellectual distance from dynamic developments in anatomy served to reinforce their traditional lack of interest in the new science.

In addition to anatomy, the physicians naturally drew upon broad theories of medicine and disease in their practice, and this, too, affected the scope of the cause of death investigations. The seventeenth century had inherited the humoral theory. The human body was believed to be made up of combinations of the four fundamental humors—blood, phlegm, yellow bile, and black bile. Health consisted of the proper mixtures and proportions of the humors; disease, even death, resulted from their imbalance or improper distribution. Unquestioning belief in such a theory made it pointless to conduct post-mortem examinations in cases evincing no obvious external traumata, such as would be caused by drowning or by a tree falling on the deceased. Without some understanding of the role of local pathology, doctors could usually hope to discover little of significance from a survey of the internal organs. Yet such examinations were sometimes done, so that we can see that this theory did not completely monopolize medical thought in the colonies or elsewhere. It is important to note that in the sixteenth century there were stirrings of new theories in what might be called chemical physiology, exemplified in the works of Paracelsus (1493–1541), Van Helmont (1578–1644), and the great English anatomist Thomas Willis (1621–1675). At about the same time, an explanation of bodily func-

[44] *Ibid.*, p. 220.
[45] *The History of Nursing*, p. 134.

tion, normal and morbid, was introduced that relied heavily on physical, especially mechanical, principles. This approach was developed in England and Scotland primarily by William Cole (1635–1716) and Archibald Pitcairne (1652–1713). But these ideas were not fully developed, influential, or adequately communicated to the bulk of medical men, at least until the impact of Cartesian and Newtonian mechanics came to be widely felt at the end of the century.[46] As one historian of medicine put it, "The medicine of the early seventeenth century presents no features to distinguish it from that of the preceding century. The practice and theory of medicine was mainly founded upon Hippocrates and Galen, with ever increasing additions from the chemical school."[47] During the course of the seventeenth century, the most significant movement in medical practice away from the dogmas of the ancients was toward a common-sense view that purported to scorn all theory. Perhaps the transitory nature of medicine in this era is best illustrated in the person of the famous English physician Thomas Sydenham (1624–1689), who rejected both the chemical explanations of his time and the humoral hypothesis of antiquity. He insisted that observation and reliance on the healing powers of nature were a safer guide to practice than resort to any abstract theory. Sydenham clearly understood that many diseases were caused by some kind of local pathology rather than by problems associated with the humors. Collaboration with his close friend John Locke, himself an accomplished physician, undoubtedly had an influence on the development of such an empiricism. In a letter Locke puts their view succinctly: "You cannot imagine how far a little observation carefully made by a man not tied up to the four humours (Galen), or sal, sulphur and mercury (Paracelsus), or to acid and alcali (Sylvius and Willis) which has of late prevailed, will carry a man in the curing of diseases though very stubborn and dangerous; and that with

[46] See Joseph F. Payne, "History of Medicine," in *Encyclopaedia Britannica*, 11th ed.

[47] *Ibid.*, p. 49; Shryock, "The History of Quantification in Medical Science," *Isis*, 52 (1961):220–26.

very little and common things, and almost no medicine at all."[48]

Thus, although significant work in pathology and morbid anatomy did not begin before the eighteenth century,[49] and progress in anatomy generally was out of the intellectual orbit of most colonial physicians, it may well have been an inquiring and developing empiricism that explains the limited number of autopsies that were in fact done in Massachusetts.[50] However, this interest in scientific investigation was not carried over into the matter of witchcraft. The administration of the law seems to have continued as though humoral theory were still unquestioned gospel. Still, the scientific community was not entirely unaware that some of the old medical dogmas were giving way and that its position on the power of witches could not remain completely static. It did face up to the necessity of reconciling its support of belief in witchcraft with the existing and expanding knowledge of the natural causes of death and disease. Its solution was to assert that the *maleficium,* the harm produced by witches, was brought about by their manipulation of *natural* forces, so that the presence of naturally caused death was deemed perfectly consistent with the presence of witchcraft. An expert scientific witness in one famous seventeenth-century English witchcraft case, Sir

[48] Quoted in *ibid.,* p. 50. See also David A. Givner, "Scientific Preconceptions in Locke's *Philosophy of Language," Journal of the History of Ideas,* 23 (1962):34; Patrick Romanell, "Some Medico-Philosophical Excerpts from the Mellon Collection of Locke's Papers," *ibid.,* 25 (1964):107. A close analysis of Sydenham's writing suggests both the presence of medical theory and something less than the thoroughgoing empiricism he believed he had adopted (see Kenneth Dewhurst, *Dr. Thomas Sydenham* [1624–1689]: *His Life and Original Writings* [London: Wellcome Library, 1966], pp. 60–67).

[49] Morgani's pioneering work, *The Seat and Causes of Diseases Investigated by Anatomy,* was published in 1700 and was translated into English in 1769. The first systematic treatise on morbid anatomy appeared in 1795, by Mathew Baille (see Payne, "History of Medicine," p. 52). Anatomical instruction from corpses was given for the first time in America in 1750 by Dr. Peter Middleton and Dr. John Bard in New York City. It was not too long before the public dramatically stated its opposition (see Jules C. Ladenheim, "The Doctors' Mob of 1788," *Journal of the History of Medicine,* 5 [1950]:23).

[50] See Sigerist, "Boerhaave's Influence upon American Medicine," p. 208. It is still true, however, that humoral theory was slow in dying out. As late as 1679, for example, Dr. John Barton of Massachusetts reported treating "an aching humor" by bloodletting (*Quarterly Court of Essex County,* 7:303).

Thomas Browne, summed up this position in his testimony relating to the fits suffered by certain of the witch's victims:

> And his opinion was, That the devil in such cases did work upon the bodies of men and women, upon a natural foundation, (that is) to stir up, and excite such humours super-abounding in their bodies to a great excess, whereby he did in an extraordinary manner afflict them with such distempers as their bodies were most subject to, as particularly appeared in these children; for he conceived that these swooning fits were natural, and nothing else but [what] they call the mother, but only heightened to a great excess by the subtility of the devil, co-operating with the malice of these which we term witches, at whose instance he doth these villanies.[51]

Browne spoke in terms of humoral doctrine, but the important point is that, no matter what *natural* causes of death an autopsy might reveal, the witch could still be held guilty for having brought about those causes. According to Cotton Mather, this English trial was "much considered" by the Massachusetts jurists.[52]

Such a view was affirmed by a man who attacked much in the traditions of witchcraft, Dr. John Webster. He declared that "what effects soever Devils or those called Witches do bring to pass in humane bodies are wrought by natural means, and proceed from natural causes."[53] To the inquiring mind, all of this leaves open the question of how natural causes can be thus supernaturally induced, a problem that did not escape the attention of Webster's contemporaries. After quoting at length the eminent physiologist Van Helmont as authority to show that the Devil did work by natural causes, Webster addressed the puzzle of the natural-supernatural nexus by asserting that the Devil can make things invisible "by his spiritual power" and that the witch "by the strength of her imagination and the motion of her free

---

[51] A Trial of Witches at the Assizes held at Bury St. Edmonds for the County of Suffolk: 17 Charles 2, A.D. 1665, in *Howell's State Trials*, 6:698.

[52] *Wonders of the Invisible World*, quoted in Kittredge, *Witchcraft in Old and New England*, p. 581, n. 16.

[53] *The Displaying of Supposed Witchcraft*, p. 247.

will . . . doth convey or inject these strange things into the bodies of those she would hurt or torment."[54] Joseph Glanvill, F.R.S., in defending the belief in the power of witches, grasped at essentially the same kind of explanation. He admitted that he did not know just *how* spirits did what they did. But, after all, "we cannot conceive how the Foetus is form'd in the womb, nor as much as how a Plant springs from the Earth we tread on; we know not how our Souls move the Body."[55] As a practical matter, Dr. Rosseter's report in Connecticut indicates that this difficult question need not be confronted. The autopsy surgeon need only describe the conditions he finds and then rely on the generally accepted belief that a witch could have produced them.

This constellation of ideas constitutes a perfect justification for neglecting post-mortem examinations where witchcraft was alleged or suspected. There was no post-mortem finding that could either confirm or deny the existence of the unknown forces suggested by Glanvill that were not within human understanding. In summary, it seems, that in spite of their distance in geography and in training from the locus of scientific progress in biology, the fetters of ancient doctrine did not prevent colonial medical men from engaging in some post-mortem examinations. When it came to witchcraft, however, this emancipation was quite irrelevant because the demonological theories propounded by them made evidence of witchly intervention wholly indistinguishable from their other findings.

[54] *Ibid.*, p. 252.
[55] *Modern Sadducism.*

VI

WITCHCRAFT AND DISEASE

✠

It will be recalled that the offense of witchcraft extended to *maleficium* short of death as it did to witchly homicide. The harm of this sort that a witch might inflict took a variety of forms. One victim testified, for example, that he felt "as if living creatures did run about every part of my body ready to tear me to pieces."[1] Another related that he had pains in his side and sores in his groin.[2] The victims of Margaret Jones, hanged in 1648, "were taken with deafness or vomitting or other violent pains or sickness."[3] And, of course, the physical suffering complained of by the girls in Salem Village is probably the best known instance of non-fatal *maleficium*. Even where death did result, there are cases where a pre-mortem investigation was made of the illness.

In the previous chapter the discussion largely centered around the absence of medical participation in the investigation of witchcraft. In the instances now being considered, where the victim still lived, the positive impact of medical science can be observed. Medical help was almost invariably sought to relieve the suffering, as it would be in any case of sickness. In the preliminary phase of

[1] This was the testimony of William Bradbury against Mary Perkins Bradbury, who was convicted in 1692 but not executed (Nevins, *Salem Village*, p. 212).

[2] Benjamin Abbott, testifying against Martha Carrier, executed in 1692 (*ibid.*, pp. 185–86).

[3] John Winthrop, Journal, 2:345.

the Salem incidents, for example, the Reverend John Hale reports that not only Doctor Griggs, but several other physicians as well, were consulted concerning the afflictions.[4] In an earlier case of suspected witchcraft, according to Cotton Mather, "skilful physicians were consulted for their help, and particularly, our worthy and prudent friend, Dr. Thomas Oakes."[5]

This was the common pattern. The colonists seem to have adhered quite closely to the injunction of Insitor and Sprenger in their *Malleus maleficarum* that the first test for the presence of witchcraft in these cases was the verdict of the physicians.[6]

The "verdict" that was forthcoming from the forensic scientists of the day was, however, not a simple one. Michael Dalton, an English writer of legal texts whose authority the settlers respected enough to have sent to England for two copies of his *Country Justice* as early as 1647,[7] dealt with the matter of the offense of witchcraft arising out of sickness of one sort or another: "Now to shew you farther, some signs to know, whether the sick party be bewitched. 1. When the healthful Body shall be suddenly taken, without probable reason, or natural cause appearing."[8] The first sign involves the diagnostic skill of the physician. Dalton appears to be saying that witchcraft is likely to be afoot when the illness lies beyond medical understanding—when a differential diagnosis rules out a natural cause. But immediately following his enumeration of signs, Dalton appends an important caveat, derived from Richard Bernard's *Guide to Grand Jury Men*: "But withal observe, with Mr. Bernard, cap. 2. that divers strange diseases may happen only from Natural causes, where he sheweth eight such several diseases; therefore, unless the Compact with the Devil be proved or evinced by evident marks or tokens . . . , it is not to be supposed that the Devil is the agent."[9]

Here is a skeptical view of the significance of "strange"

---

[4] *A Modest Inquiry*, p. 413.
[5] *Memorable Providences*, p. 101.
[6] Summers, *Malleus maleficarum*, p. 87.
[7] *Records of the Governor and Company of the Massachusetts Bay*, 2:212.
[8] Michael Dalton, *County Justice*, 4th ed. (London: John More, 1630), p. 274.
[9] *Ibid.*

diseases: they well may have hidden natural causes uninfluenced by witchcraft. In this warning Dalton reflected an opinion also held by some scientists, even by those who, like Dr. Meric Casaubon, were firm believers in witches. Dr. Casaubon's caution in this regard is especially significant because it is directed partly at what was then a poorly understood area of mental disorder ("melancholy") where ignorance—and hence a diagnosis of witchcraft—was highly likely:

> And indeed, that the denying of Witches, to them that content themselves in the search of truth with a superficial view, is a very plausible cause; it cannot be denied. For if anything in the world, (as we know all things in the world are) be liable to fraud, and imposture, and innocent mistake, through weakness and simplicity; this subject of Witches and Spirits is. . . . How ordinary is it to mistake natural melancholy (not to speak of other diseases) for a Devil? And how much, too frequently is both the disease increased, or made incurable; and the mistake confirmed, by many ignorant Ministers, who take every wild notion, or phansie, for a suggestion of the Devil? Whereas, in such a case it should be the care of wise friends, to apply themselves to the Physician of the body, and not to entertain the other, (I speak of natural melancholy) who probably may do more hurt, than good; but as the learned Naturalist doth allow and advise? Excellent is the advise and counsel in this kind, of the Author of the book de morbo Sacro attributed to Hippocrates, which I could wish all men were bound to read, before they take upon them to visit sick folks, that are troubled with melancholy disease.[10]

To what extent did medical men in Massachusetts observe these caveats advocated both by lawyer Dalton and physician Casaubon? The doctors did seem to have attempted to effect cures in the cases they attended, and it would be somewhat astonishing if they had not. Widow Carr, whose ailments helped to convict Mary Bradbury in 1692, was treated by Dr. Crosby.[11] Dr. Prescott attended the afflicted side, foot, and groin of Benjamin Abbott,

[10] *A Treatise Proving Spirits*, pp. 29–30.
[11] See n. 1 above.

whose testimony was instrumental in hanging Martha Carrier in 1692.[12] Dr. Fuller joined Dr. Crosby in treating Mrs. William Brown in 1669. The Browns testified against Susanna Martin in 1692 concerning this earlier bewitchment.[13]

In most cases we do not know the diagnosis upon which treatment was based, the nature of the treatment itself, or the course of the illness. But where this information does appear, it seems to be rationally related to both medical theory and the presenting symptoms. Thus, Dr. Prescott lanced Benjamin Abbott's sore, "from which several gallons of corruption did run out."[14] The Reverend Samuel Willard (1640–1707) described his experience with Elizabeth Knapp of Groton, who was apparently an hallucinating epileptic: "On the Sabboth the Physitian came, who judged a maine part of her distemper to be naturall, arising from the foulnesse of her stomacke, & corruptnesse of her blood, occasioning fumes in her braine, & strange fansyes; whereupon (in order to further tryall & administration) shee was removed home & the succeeding weeks shee tooke physicke & was not in such violence handled in her fits as before; but enjoyed an intermission & gave some hopes of recovery."[15]

This is full-blown humoral theory, and is a competent diagnosis for the times. But eight days later young Elizabeth "was again with violence . . . roaring, & yelling extreamly . . ."[16] Medical assistance was summoned once more: "The Physitian being then agen with her consented that the distemper was Diabolicall, [and] refused to administer . . ."[17] Elizabeth continued in this condition for several days, after which she regained some control and told

[12] See n. 2 above.

[13] See Drake, *The Witchcraft Delusion in New England*, 3:99.

[14] See n. 2 above.

[15] Willard's account, an enclosure to a letter to Increase Mather, is reproduced in S. A. Green, *Groton in the Witchcraft Times* (Cambridge, Mass.: J. Wilson & Son, 1883).The quote here is from p. 10. This Elizabeth Knapp is often confused with the woman of the same name who was executed as a witch in Connecticut in 1653 (see Drake, *Annals of Witchcraft* [Boston: W. E. Woodward, 1869], pp. 76–77).

[16] *Ibid.*, p. 11.

[17] *Ibid.*

Reverend Willard that she was bewitched. For reasons that Willard's note does not make clear, the accused woman was "by 2 evident and cleere mistakes . . . cleered."[18]

It is important to note that this pattern of attempting natural treatment and then, upon failure to arrest or reverse the condition, making diagnosis of diabolical intervention does not seem to be a uniform one. Concerning the afflicted girls in Mr. Parris' house at Salem, Reverend Hale reported several doctors in consultation but only one "gave his opinion, that they were under an Evil Hand."[19] Of this one, Dr. Greggs (or Gregg), it has been said that "he had expressed the same opinion of many of his patients when he could not understand their disease."[20] This was also true of Dr. Crosby, who told his patient he was "behaged"[21] and who, with Dr. Fuller, said that Mrs. Brown's fits were supernatural.[22] However, there is no indication that Dr. Prescott said that his patient, Benjamin Abbott, was bewitched, although Abbott was at times near death.[23] In Topsfield Joseph Ballard's wife was unsuccessfully treated by the local physician, but it was not until Ann Putnam arrived there from Salem Village that witchcraft was mentioned.[24] The doctor who was called in to treat the Putnams' child seems to have made no such diagnosis, even though "all he did give it could do it no good," and it died.[25] In some cases it is difficult even to know with certainty whether any treatment at all was attempted prior to the medical declaration of witchcraft. This question arises, for example, in connection with

[18] See Burr, *Narratives*, p. 23, n. 1.

[19] Quoted in *ibid.*, p. 413.

[20] Samuel P. Fowler, *An Account of the Life, Character, etc., of the Rev. Samuel Parris* (Salem, Mass.: Ives and Pease, 1857), p. 6. Fowler goes on to suggest that "it is highly probable that the opinion of these physicians went far to form the belief of not only Parris, but also of his ministerial friends, in the existence of witchcraft in the village. Mr. Parris appears to have been much astonished, when the physicians informed him, that his daughter and niece were, no doubt, under an evil hand" (*ibid.*).

[21] Quoted in Nevins, *Salem Village*, p. 212.

[22] Quoted in Drake, *The Witchcraft Delusion in New England*, 3:100.

[23] See n. 2 above.

[24] Nevins, *Salem Village*, p. 195.

[25] Deposition of John Putnam and Hannah Putnam v. Rebecca Nurse, *Historical Collections of the Topsfield Historical Society*, 13:50–51.

Cotton Mather's narration of the case against Mary Glover, who was executed in 1688. Mather states, concerning the illness of the victims, that one of the physicians "found himself so affronted by the Distempers of the children that he concluded nothing but an hellish Witchcraft could be the Original of these Maladies."[26]

There are a variety of factors that might account for the differing reactions of doctors to the baffling medical problems that confronted them in these cases. One that cannot be ignored is the variation in skill, experience and sophistication among the physicians involved. Kocher's evaluation of this problem in England may be equally applicable to the New England scene. There is, he suggests, a state of mind concomitant to sophisticated knowledge that is something in the nature of a belief that medical secrets still locked in mystery will some day yield to the accumulation of experience and experiment. The stronger this expectation of earthly progress, the more reluctant the practitioner will be to affirm that he faces supernatural forces in treating his patient.[27] On the other hand, those medical men with little awareness of medicine as an integral part of a culture's evolution will be more inclined to accept a fairly static state of knowledge and will resort more willingly to the notion of witchcraft.

However, this is only a partial explanation. The diversity of medical judgments is probably more directly related to the contemporaneous theology of medicine than to the professional sophistication of individual practitioners. Even among the most skilled there was likely to be a division of opinion that might well manifest itself in the witchcraft issue. The traditions of medicine affirmed that all human maladies, disease included, were traceable to God. It is true that in England, and probably in America too, there was a small number of atheistic, radical physicians who practiced within a completely materialistic framework.[28] But for

---

[26] *Memorable Providences*, p. 101. For similar ambiguities in reports of experience in England, see, e.g., Kittredge, *Witchcraft in Old and New England*, p. 302.

[27] Paul H. Kocher, *Science and Religion in Elizabethan England* (San Marino, Calif.: The Huntington Library, 1953), p. 142.

[28] *Ibid.*, p. 263. Weyer is somewhat affiliated with this group by virtue of his belief that "those illnesses the origin of which is attributable to witches come

the most part within the medical profession there were varying degrees of acceptance of the traditional view of divine causation. One position, taken by the less pious members of the group, was to acknowledge perfunctorily God as the ultimate cause but then to virtually ignore Him in an all-consuming concern for the natural forces that were deemed the proper business of medicine. Spiritual matters, if they played a part in a medical case at all, were entirely the domain of the clergy.[29] In this view is the seed of the modern attitude that distinguishes, with a high degree of mutual exclusiveness, the material and spiritual sides of man. In the seventeenth century such a position was likely to produce intense efforts at cure on the part of the physician and then, if the therapy failed, his passive acquiescence in witchcraft proceedings without any formal declaration by him that *maleficium* was present.

Considering the high incidence of sickness among the settlers, sometimes on an epidemic scale, and the relatively small number of witchcraft cases that arose, it seems fair to infer that most of the medical men in the colony kept their religious beliefs at a distance from their professional judgments, which thereby precluded their making a diagnosis of witchcraft when treatment failed. It is equally plain that a minority were involved in a mixture of piety and practice. Dr. Oakes, Dr. Fuller, and Dr. Greggs did not hesitate to use witchcraft as a diagnosis. Kittredge relates that in England even a man reputed "the greatest physician of his time" was first baffled by a patient's fits and then "ascribed the fits to witchcraft, remarking that he himself 'had some experience of the malice of some witches.' "[30] These men evince not a lack of

---

from natural causes" (quoted in Zilboorg, *A History of Medical Psychology*, p. 214). But, as has been discussed in Chapter III, Weyer's readers could quite properly take this as merely a description of his own experience, since he makes all the concessions concerning Satan and God that are necessary to support contrary assertions from the experience of others that witches can and do cause illness. His position is further undermined by the belief that the Devil works through natural means and that, therefore, a finding of natural causes does not preclude the possibility of evil interference.

[29] Kocher, *Elizabethan England*, pp. 264–65.
[30] *Witchcraft in Old and New England*.

medical skill—there are still a good many illnesses which might
be described as "fits" that elude scientific mastery—so much as a
belief that God's role in human affairs is not limited to the Creation, but that His intervention can be seen all through the course
of life. God was seen as the cause of particular cases. In one's
professional activity, therefore, one always had to be on the look-
out for signs of supernatural forces.[31]

Perhaps the best representative of this latter group is Cotton
Mather, whose emphasis on religion was accompanied by an extraordinary erudition in scientific affairs; he has, in fact, been
called by one scholar the first significant figure in American medicine.[32] His willingness to draw a firm line on one side of which
lies the impact of spirits is revealed in his description of John
Goodwin's child, who was afflicted by witch Glover with "strange
Fits, beyond those that attend an Epilepsy, or a Catalepsy, or those
that they call the Diseases of Astonishment."[33] Mather had, of
course, no doubts about the existence and power of witches and
could in no way accept the implication of atheism that a denial
of them would have entailed. Yet he devoured scientific literature[34]
and as a consequence sought a rational way of resisting the materialism that the scientific progress he observed seemed more and
more to imply. This he accomplished by postulating a *"Nismath
Chaim"* (breath of life) as a vital principle that functioned somewhere between the immortal soul and the physical body.[35] The
consequence of this was an imperative to go beyond mere physical
factors, for "most certainly, the Physician that can find out Remedies . . . that shall have a more immediate Efficacy to brighten,
and strengthen, and Comfort, the *Nismath Chaim*, will be the most
successful Physician in the World."[36] It is but a small step from

---

[31] See Kocher, *Elizabethan England*, pp. 263–64. The printed records reveal only
one instance in which a physician is alleged to have diagnosed witchcraft and yet
no prosecution took place (see *Quarterly Court of Essex County*, 4:207).

[32] O. T. Beal, "Cotton Mather, the First Significant Figure in American Medicine," *Bulletin of the History of Medicine*, 26 (1952):103.

[33] Cotton Mather, *Memorable Providences*, p. 101.

[34] See Miller, *The New England Mind: From Colony to Province*, p. 345.

[35] See Beal and Shryock, *Cotton Mather*, pp. 67–68.

[36] Quoted from Mather's *The Angel of Bethesda*, in *ibid.*, p. 69.

the *Nismath* and its effects on health to acceptance of an active role of evil spirits in health and illness. A firm belief in such a God-centered vitalism needed only the addition of the common belief in witches to propel the frustrated physician into a diagnosis of witchcraft.

It is important to note that this insistence that spirit effects material events was not limited to clerical efforts to preserve the concept of the omnipotence of God. There was impressive scientific authority to support an attending physician who refused to limit his conception of the human body to its physical dimensions. William Harvey, for example, had demonstrated a materialistic and mechanical circulation of the blood in 1628. But in 1651 he wrote:

> The blood considered absolutely and by itself, without the veins, in so far as it is an elementary fluid, and composed of several parts . . . possesses but few, and these not very obvious virtues. Contained within the veins, however, inasmuch as it is an integral part of the body, and is animated, regenerative, and the immediate instrument and principal seat of the soul, inasmuch, moreover, as it seems to partake of the nature of another more divine body, and is transfused by divine animal heat, it obtains remarkable and most excellent powers, and is analogous to the essence of the stars.[37]

Nor should the fact be overlooked that Newton, too, was often thought to be resorting to a non-material force (gravity) in his explanation of heavenly motions. While it may be true that he was, in fact, content to describe and analyze phenomena mathematically without accounting for the causes of what he described, the *Principia* nonetheless produced a rash of accusations of mysticism from the Cartesians, who insisted that a force could not operate at a distance and that all explanations must include a description

[37] *Anatomical Exercises on The Generation of Animals; to which are added Essays on Parturition; On the Membranes, and Fluids of the Uterus; and on Conception* (1651), in *The Works of William Harvey*, ed. Robert Willis (London: The Sydenham Society, 1847), p. 510. For a discussion of Harvey's metaphysics and vitalism generally, see T. C. Allbut, *Science and Medieval Thought* (London: Clay, 1901).

of the strictly mechanical linkages at work.[38] The attribution to Newton of abandonment of Cartesian mechanics and embracing of the idea that force can operate at a distance was "the strongest obstacle to the acceptance of Newtonianism." Great scientists like Huygens and Leibniz attempted, but in vain, to restore vitality to the view that motion can take place only by matter pushing on matter.[39] The effect of this somewhat controversial idea of gravity on the relationship of science to theology, and hence on the matter of diagnosis, is well illustrated by John Locke's reaction to the issue:

> I admit that I said (*Essay on Human Understanding*, Book II, ch. VIII, par. 11) that body acts by impulse and not otherwise. This also was my view when I wrote it and even now I cannot conceive its action in any other way. But since then I have been convinced by the judicious Mr. Newton's incomparable book that there is too much presumption in wishing to limit the power of God by our limited conceptions. The gravitation of matter toward matter in ways inconceivable to me is not only a demonstration that God, when it seems to Him good, can put into bodies powers and modes of acting which are beyond what can be derived from our idea of body or explained by what we know of matter; but it is furthermore an incontestable instance that He has really done so. I shall therefore take care to correct this passage in the new edition of my book.[40]

[38] See the excellent discussion of this aspect of Newton's work and resulting misconceptions of it in Hall, *The Scientific Revolution*, pp. 246–76, especially the quotation from a letter by Newton (pp. 273–74) that is an explicit denial of any resort to occult forces: "It is inconceivable that inanimate brute matter should, without the mediation of something else, which is not material, operate upon and affect other matter without mutual contact. . . . That gravity should be innate, inherent, and essential to matter, so that one body may act upon another at a distance through a vacuum, without the mediation of anything else, by and through which their action and force may be conveyed from one to another, is to me so great an absurdity that I believe no man who has in philosophical matters a competent faculty of thinking, can ever fall into it."

[39] See Alexandre Koyré, *Newtonian Studies* (Cambridge, Mass.: Harvard University Press, 1965), pp. 115–38.

[40] Quoted in *ibid.*, p. 155.

It must have appeared to many others, at it did to Locke, that, far from tending to exclude or limit the role of God, the new science often served to affirm and reiterate it. Assertions from Huygens, Leibniz, and others that only matter can influence matter came too late for anyone to revise or reject the concept of witchcraft.[41] This skeptical view, of course, came to prevail but only as science narrowed its focus so as to exclude spiritual factors, not because scientific findings forced its acceptance. A strictly mechanistic conception of the human body, one that could have constituted a source of scientific opposition to findings of *maleficium* in the trials, was known as early in the century as 1628, when Harvey demonstrated the circulation of the blood. In some limited areas—theories of respiration, for example—this view was in fact adopted and produced a wealth of new insight.[42] But mechanism as a substitute for religious vitalism had to await the eighteenth century, a time when even Cotton Mather could call for the expulsion of metaphysics from medicine and could suggest "by the Laws of Matter and Motion to find out the Cause and Cure of Disease."[43] Until then "inaccurate diagnosis and complete misunderstanding of the cause of the diseases and accidents of the victims," as Ewen puts it,[44] was not a fair description of the role of medical men in the witch prosecutions. For the most part they were passive in the matters of accusation and trial, and when they did affirm the presence of witchcraft, they were reflecting not

[41] Probably the most vigorous debate on the gravity question is in H. G. Alexander, *The Leibniz-Clarke Correspondence* (New York: Barnes and Noble, 1964).

[42] See Leonard G. Wilson, "The Transformation of Ancient Concepts of Respiration in the Seventeenth Century," *Isis*, 51 (1960):161, 172:

The entire structure of Galenic physiology had been dismantled and its debris removed. Following the discovery of the circulation of the blood by Harvey, it had been shown in succession: that the lung tissue is composed of membranes surrounding minute air spores (Malpighi), that the blood circulates through these membranes in capillary vessels (Malpighi), that the essential requirement in respiration is a constant supply of fresh air (Hooke), that the change in colour of the blood during its passage through the lungs is due to its contact with the air (Lowen), that some portion of the air is removed in respiration (Mazow) and that this is the same portion of the air as is consumed by fire (Mazow).

[43] Quoted in Beal, "Cotton Mather," p. 112.

[44] *Witch Hunting and Witch Trials*, p. 113.

only the traditions of their general culture but also the relevant attitudes of the giants of their own scientific community.

In addition, it should be pointed out that it is not at all clear that doctrines of mechanism could not be made to serve the processes of prosecution. In 1692, for example, we find Thomas Brattle discussing the procedure for determining guilt that involves the accused touching the victim. If relief of the victim's suffering is forthcoming, the guilt of the accused is indicated:

> The Salem Justices, at least some of them, do assert that the cure of the afflicted persons is a natural effect of this touch; and they are so well instructed in the Cartesian philosophy, and in the doctrine of *effluvia*, that they undertake to give a demonstration how this does cure the afflicted persons; and the account they give of it is this; that by this touch, the venomous and malignant particles, that were ejected from the eye, do by this means, return to the body whence they came, and, so leave the afflicted persons pure and whole.[45]

The judges in Salem, like several of the doctors at the bedside, found scientific theory a valuable and relevant tool.

---

[45] Letter of Thomas Brattle, Fellow of the Royal Society, quoted in Burr, *Narratives*, p. 171.

VII

SCIENCE AND THE IDENTIFICATION
OF WITCHES: FEMALE EXPERTS

✠

The witchcraft cases presented many issues in which law relied upon science to aid in the discovery of witches. Scientific support for the belief that witches could cause sickness and death still left unsolved the identity of the witch in any given case. To any system of law, the identity of the accused is a vital question; to the settlers of Massachusetts, whose highly developed conceptions of due process of law permeated their legal order, this matter was a most essential element of the proceedings.[1] The priority accorded this view of justice was well expressed in part of a 1692 essay which responded to the protest that, if the law contained too many safeguards, no one would be convicted: "This is a dangerous Principle, and contrary to the mind of God, who hath appointed that there shall be good and clear proof against the Criminal; else he is not Providentially delivered into the hands of Justice,

---

[1] Willingness to let guilty persons free of the full punishment of the law because of a defect in the legal system can be aptly illustrated in the area of adultery. In 1631 it was declared to be a capital offense (*Records of the Governor and Company of the Massachusetts Bay*, 1:92). Six years later three persons were convicted and under ordinary circumstances would have been promptly executed (*ibid.*, p. 202). But a question was raised as to whether the law had been adequately publicized, and the opinion of the elders was sought. Then, as Governor Winthrop relates the story, "it was thought safest, that these three persons should be whipped and banished; and the law was confirmed and published" (Journal, 1:262–63).

to be taken off from the earth. Nor hath God exempted this case of Witchcraft from the General Rule. Besides, reason tells us, that the more horrid the Crime is, the more Cautious we ought to be in making any guilty of it."[2]

There were, of course, a variety of ways by which the identity of the witch in question could be established. One way was to see whether the touch of the suspected witch on the victim produced a remission in the sufferer, a method described in Thomas Brattle's famous letter of 1692. The confession of the witch was another proof, although it is in this connection that the question of mental disorder arose, discussed in the next chapter. In the Salem trials it was obvious to many that the accused were confessing merely in order to escape punishment, since repentant witches were spared the gallows.[3] The use of confessions to convict witches also involves the question of torture, and there is some evidence that it was used illegally in Massachusetts.[4]

Perhaps the most controversial method of proving the guilt of the accused involved the use of what was called "spectral evi-

[2] The essay is entitled *Some Miscellany Observations on our Present Debates respecting Witchcrafts*. The authorship is in doubt but is traditionally assigned to the Reverend Samuel Willard of the Old South Church (see Perry Miller, *The New England Mind: From Colony to Province*, pp. 204–6). The quotation is taken from p. 205.

[3] This disposition of confessed witches greatly undermined, almost destroyed, the theological base on which the whole society rested (see *ibid.*, pp. 200–4, 207–8).

[4] Torture was authorized by law, but only in certain cases after conviction: "It is ordered, decreed, and by this Court declared; that no man shall be forced by torture to confesse any crime against himselfe or any other, unles it be in some Capital case, where he is first fully convicted by clear and sufficient evidence to be guilty. After which, if the Case be of that nature that it is very apparent there be other Conspirators or Confederates with him; then he may be tortured, yet not with such tortures as be barbarous and inhumane" (*The Laws and Liberties of Massachusetts*, p. 50).

One complaint about torture in the witchcraft cases appears in a letter from John Proctor to certain ministers concerning his son: "My son William Proctor, when he was examin'd, because he would not confess that he was Guilty, when he was Innocent, they tyed him Neck and Heels till the Blood gushed out of his Nose, and would have kept him so 24 Hours, if one more Merciful than the rest, had not taken pity on him, and caused him to be unbound. These actions are very like the Popish Cruelties." Robert Calif printed the letter in his *More Wonders of the Invisible World* (1700); it is reprinted in Burr, *Narratives*, p. 363; see also *ibid.*, p. 363, n. 2.

dence." This was based upon the common belief that demons could take the form of a person and, as his specter, either inflict harm on the body of another person or simply appear and converse on some evil subject. In such a case, at the trial the victim would testify that the accused came to him on a certain occasion and acted in a witchly way; the defense of the accused that he was miles away or knew nothing of the incident would be quite beside the point because at the time in question it was his specter, not his person, that bore witness to his being a witch. The question of whether the testimony of the victim to this effect was admissible and, if so, what weight it should be given was troublesome in the Salem trials. The issue that proved of major importance in the trials was that of whether an innocent person could be represented by a specter. Under the influence of Judge Stoughton, in 1692 the court at Salem ruled that this was not possible.[5]

There was still another means of identifying the witch, namely, by the signs of guilt that could be discovered in an expert search of the accused's body. Any modern law enforcement official would find his task greatly simplified if he could have suspected persons examined for the presence of certain physical signs that would generally be accepted as strong evidence of guilt. The witchcraft investigations enjoyed just such an advantage, and they exploited it fully. The search for the so-called Devil's marks was sanctioned by all authorities. Michael Dalton, whose *Country Justice* was a cornerstone of precedent, described the signs as

> some big or little Teat upon their body, and in some secret place, where he (the Devil) sucketh them. And besides their sucking, the Devil leaveth other marks upon their body, sometimes like a blew spot or red spot, like a flea-biting; sometimes the flesh sunk in and hollow, (all which for a time may be covered, yea taken

---

[5] For a collection and discussion of English cases in which spectral evidence was admitted, both before and after the Salem trials, see Kittredge, *Witchcraft in Old and New England*, pp. 363–65. Perry Miller places much of the responsibility for the devastating use of spectral evidence on leading members of the Puritan clergy, who, although they came out in support of the proposition that the innocent could be represented, refrained from making an effective protest (see *The New England Mind: From Colony to Province*, pp. 193–95, n. 2, 198–200).

away, but will come again to their old form.) And these the Devils marks be insensible, and being pricked will not bleed, and be often in their secretest parts, and therefore require diligent and careful search.[6]

The employment of this investigative technique was not without its critics, however. Thomas Brattle, for example, included among his objections to the Salem trials the reliance on these witch's marks. Speaking of this process of proof, he says: "They are searched by a Jury; and as to some of them, the Jury brought in, that [on] such or such a place there was a preternatural excrescence. And I wonder what person there is, whether man or woman, of whom it cannot be said but that, in some part of their body or other, there is a preternatural excrescence. The term is a very general and inclusive term."[7] There is also the remarkable Connecticut document protesting witchcraft prosecutions that requests "that ye unusuall excresencies found upon their bodies ought not to be allowed as evidence against them without ye approbation of some able physitians."[8] One of the two signers of this document was a physician "of great ability."[9]

The reply that was made to objections of this sort relied heavily on the authority of the scientists and their ability to make an accurate differential diagnosis. Thus Cotton Mather responded: "I add, why should not witches marks be searched for? The properties, the qualities of those marks are described by divers weighty writers. I never saw any of those marks, but it is doubtless not impossible for a surgeon, when he sees them, to say what are magical."[10] Perhaps one of the "divers, weighty writers" to whom

---

[6] P. 273.

[7] Letter of October 8, 1692, in Burr, *Narratives*, p. 175.

[8] Quoted in John M. Taylor, *The Witchcraft Delusion in Colonial Connecticut* (New York: Grafton Press, 1908), p. 74.

[9] See *Genealogical and Family History of the State of Connecticut*, 1 (1911):45.

[10] Quoted in Rossell Hope Robbins, *The Encyclopedia of Witchcraft and Demonology* (New York: Crown Publications, 1959), p. 136. See also the statement of a physician to Henry IV of France, which equates skepticism on this point with professional incompetence: "Writers who say that it is difficult to distinguish devil's marks from natural blemishes, from a carbuncle, or from impetigo clearly show that they are not good doctors" (*ibid.*).

Mather was referring was Mathew Hopkins, the famous witch-finder in England. In his well-known book, *The Discovery of Witches*, Hopkins constructed a dialogue concerned with this problem which identified more accurately than had Mather or the Connecticut petitioners the scientific experts whose authority and skills were involved. Hopkins sets about answering a number of questions, among them "Quereie 5. Many poore people are condemned for having a Pap, or Teat about them, whereas many People (especially antient People) are, and have been a long time, troubled with naturall excressencies as Hemerodes, Piles, Child-bearing, &c." To this question Hopkins replies that the existence of witch's marks is supported by "many ancient skilfull matrons and midwives present when the women are tryed," who attest that "such token cannot in their judgments proceed from any of the above mentioned Causes."[11]

That it was, in fact, "matrons and midwives" who did the searching of the female accused, rather than surgeons, is borne out by the cases reported in both Massachusetts and the other colonies. Mather was probably referring to what may have been a common practice of assigning the formal responsibility for certain examinations to a medically trained male, while the actual search was done by women. In New Hampshire, for example, a magistrate (who was also a physician) issued to a constable one of the earliest search warrants to be found, authorizing the search of a house for a "child or an embryo of which a woman was said to be delivered. A bit irregularly, but with an eye to decency and expertness . . . , the warrant was addressed to two midwives and three other women, as well as to the constable."[12] In Massachusetts the first signature that appears on the report of the search conducted on the accused witch, Rebecca Nurse, in 1692 was "J. Barton Chyrugen," although it is clear from the papers in the case that he took no active part.[13] The names of nine women follow

---

[11] Hopkins' text is in Montague Summers, *The Discovery of Witches. A Study of Master Mathew Hopkins Commonly Call'd Witch Finder Generall* (London: Cayne Press, 1928). The question and answer quoted appear on p. 52.

[12] Quoted in Page, *Judicial Beginnings in New Hampshire*, p. 105.

[13] Quoted in *The Historical Collections of the Topsfield Historical Society*, 13:53.

Barton's. They had been ordered by the sheriff to examine six accused women. Their report was as follows: "The first three, namely: Bishop, Nurse; Proctor by diligent search have discovered a preternatural excrescence of flesh between ye pudendum and Anus much like to tetts and not vsuall in women and much vnlike to ye other three that hath been search by us and that they were in all three women neer ye same place."[14] All six were executed as witches.[15] Below is the petition for a second examination that Rebecca Nurse submitted to the court in Salem. It is provided not only because it illustrates the point just made concerning the exclusive role of women experts regarding female accused but also because it presents dramatically the conflicts engendered by reliance on these experts and their knowledge.

The humble petission of Rebeccah Nurse of Salem Village. Humbly Sheweth

That whereas sum women did search your Petissioner at Salem, and I did then conceive for sum Supernaturall Mark, and then one of the sd. women which is knoun to be, the Moaste Antiente skilfull, prudent person of them all as to any such conceive: Did express herself to be: of a Contrary opinion from the Rest, and Did then Declare that she saw nothing in or about yoer Honor's poare pettissioner But what might Arise from a Naturall cause: and I then rendered the said persons a sufficient knoun reason as to myself of the moueing cause thereof which was by Exceeding weaknesses: decending partly from an ouerture of Nature and difficult Exigences that hath Befallen me in the times of my travells And therefore your pettissioner: Humbly prayes that your Honour's would be pleased to admit of some other women to Enquire into this Great: concern; those that are Moast Grand wise and skillfull; namely: Mrs.: Higgenson senr: Ms. Durkstone: Ms: Woodberry two of them being Midwives: Ms. Parter:

---

[14] Quoted in *ibid.*, pp. 52–53.

[15] According to Hutchinson, there is one additional case of an execution even when no witch's marks were found, that of Ann Hibbins in 1655 (*History of the Colony*, p. 187). Hutchinson notes also that the judges refused to accept the verdict of guilt brought in by the jury and the case was appealed to the General Court, "where the popular clamour prevailed against her and the miserable old woman was condemned and executed" (*ibid.*).

together with such others, as may be choasen on that Account: before I am Brought to my triall: All which I hoape your Honour's will Take into your prudent consideration; and find it requisite soe to doe: for my life lyes now in your Hands, under God: And Being Conscious of my owne Innocency. I humbly begg that I may have liberty to manifest it to the wourld partly by the Meanes abouesaid: And your Poare pettissioner shall Evermore pray as in duty bound Sc.

REBECCA NURSE:
hir Marke †[16]

Another examination was made a few hours later, not only of Nurse but of Bishop and Proctor as well. It was, however, done by the same persons as the first one. This time on the person of Rebecca Nurse the examiners found that "instead of that Excresence within mentioned it appears only as dry skin without sense . . . and that the piece of flish . . . formerly seen is gone and only dry skin nearer to ye anus in another place."[17] The jury refused to convict her, and it was only after it was forced to reconsider its position by the judges that it returned a verdict of guilty. Then Rebecca Nurse was hanged.[18]

These incidents reveal that expert testimony could change radically within a span of only a few hours, and that the searching women sometimes differed among themselves concerning what they observed. Nevertheless, from the outset, such evidence seems to have been considered important in the witchcraft cases. In the very first trial, that of Margaret Jones of Charlestown in 1648, Winthrop noted that "she had (upon search) an apparent teat in her secret parts as fresh as if it had been newly sucked, and after it had been scanned, upon a forced search that was withered, and another began on the opposite side."[19] This procedure was used early and widely. In the search of a Connecticut witch the women found "on her secret parts Just within ye lips of ye same growing within sid[,] sumewhat as broad[,] and reach without ye lips

[16] *The Historical Collections of the Topsfield Historical Society*, 13:55–56.
[17] *Ibid.*, pp. 56–57.
[18] Calif, *More Wonders of the Invisible World*, pp. 258–59.
[19] John Winthrop, Journal, 2:344.

of ye same about an Inch and half long lik in shape to a dogs eare[,] which wee apprehend to be unusuall to women."[20] In Virginia, it is reported, juries of women were impaneled in 1675 and 1679 to search " 'according to the 118th chapter of Dalton' for the Devil's marks."[21] As late as 1705 a Virginia jury of women reported the accused was "not like them nor noe Other woman that they knew of, having two things like tetts on her private parts of a Black Coller, being Blacker that the Rest of her Body."[22] In Maryland there was an unusual case of a woman who, after she had been called a witch by others, petitioned the court for what was, in effect, an injunction against the defamation. In the petition she asked for an examination by able women to show that she was in fact not a witch.[23]

There were cases, as has been indicated, in which the accused was executed as a witch in spite of the finding of searchers that she had no witch's marks. Their absence was no obvious sign of innocence, although there is some indication of a belief that a person could not be a witch if he had no physical signs. What may have been a common view in this matter was expressed by Thomas Cooper, who had been appointed to guard one Mary Parsons, accused of witchcraft. There seems to have been a question as to whether she or her husband had murdered their child. She told Cooper that she could prove her husband was the witch in question. To this, the guard replied, "Methinks, if he were a witch, there would be some apparent sign or mark of it upon his body, for they say witches have teats upon some part or other of their body; but so far as I hear there is not any such apparent thing upon his body."[24]

[20] Quoted in Taylor, *The Witchcraft Delusion in Colonial Connecticut*, p. 43.

[21] Burr, *Narratives*, p. 436.

[22] *Ibid.*, p. 442. In this same case, however, one group of women who were summoned to perform the search refused to do so (*ibid.*, p. 440).

[23] Francis N. Parke, *Witchcraft in Maryland* (Baltimore: n.p., 1937), pp. 44–47.

[24] Quoted in Poole, "Witchcraft in Boston," p. 140. The marks found on men were mostly of the kind that "being pricked will not bleed," as Dalton puts it. The phenomenon of supernumerary breasts (polymastia) may also have been involved. This condition is twice as frequent in men as in women (Max Thorek, *Plastic Surgery of the Breast and Abdominal Wall* [Springfield, Ill.: Charles C Thomas, 1942], pp. 94–101).

The witchcraft cases were not the only instances in which law administrators called upon the female experts. There are many instances, for example, where the possible offense of fornication was involved, in which the midwives were ordered to make a search to find if a woman was or had been pregnant.[25] Even in civil actions, where there was a question as to whether a female plaintiff in an assault and battery case had suffered injuries, or as to what kind they were, it was a female independent expert who made the search and reported to the court.[26] In some cases, although the sexual identity of the searching expert is not mentioned, the inference is quite strong that it was a midwife rather than any male, for example, "Robert Wyor & John Farland beeing indited for ravishing two yong girles, the fact confessed by the girles, & both upon search found to have bin defloured."[27] There is also, however, some evidence that law enforcement officials did not always consider themselves bound to refrain from engaging in searches on some occasions. There is the deposition of the Constable of Salisbury in the *Massachusetts Archives*, in the case of Eunice Cole. He said that "being about to strip Eunice Cole to be whipt . . . looking upon her breast under one of her breasts (I think her left breast) I saw a blue thing." He then asked that the court send some women to take a look for themselves.[28]

The female experts in the witchcraft cases, in seeking to distinguish the natural from the unnatural, to identify what was usual or unusual in women, were involved in somewhat the same difficulties as were encountered by the physicians faced with explaining difficult cases of death or disease. It was a specialized problem of differential diagnosis. In regard to the witch's marks, there was here also a residual category of "witchcraft" that piety demanded they respect. Their task was more limited, however, in

[25] See the cases in *Quarterly Court of Essex County*, 4:91 (1669); 5:291 (1674); 8:145 (1681); and in "Records of the Suffolk County Court 1671–1680," in *Publications of the Colonial Society of Massachusetts*, 29:91, 185. See also Semmes, *Crimes and Punishments in Early Maryland*, p. 192.

[26] *Quarterly Court of Essex County*, 2:443–46.

[27] *Records of the Court of Assistants*, 2:121.

[28] Massachusetts Archives, Massachusetts State Library, State House, Boston, Mass., Vol. 135, p. x3.

the sense that the whole of their judgment turned on familiarity with anatomy, particularly that of the female genitalia and, to some extent, with the field that is now known as gynecology. It was theoretically possible for them, as for the physicians, to declare that, although they had never seen a growth, a structure, or an organ that appeared as it did in a particular accused woman, still there was probably a natural explanation for it—one that, as yet, they had not encountered. Such a position would certainly have made convictions more difficult in some cases and might well have saved some lives.

The explanation of why this was not done must rest, in part, on their reluctance to reject witchcraft and thereby to appear to be atheists. But, as was true with the doctors, such a clinging to orthodoxy is only part of the picture. It should be realized, moreover, that such an affirmation would not have amounted to the wholesale rejection of traditional belief that would have been involved in a physician's declaration that sickness and death could not be, and in any given case was not, caused by the power of spirits. It would have been quite possible to believe wholeheartedly in spiritual interferences in human affairs, even to believe that a certain person was a witch and had produced the *maleficium* alleged, while at the same time believing that one part of the case against the individual was not proved. The judgment of the midwives, in other words, was a more circumscribed piece of expertise. The conflict of opinion in the case of Rebecca Nurse and the others indicates that a finding of "non-witch" could be made with little fear of betraying any sympathy with the forces of evil. Yet there must have been some reluctance of this sort involved.

In looking for an explanation, one must first appreciate the precarious position of the female medical practitioner and the midwife (the two were virtually the same during these times). Margaret Jones, hanged in Boston in 1648, is a case in point. She seems to have been a medical practitioner who encountered the censure of her male colleagues. Fiske describes her as having "had some sensible ideas about medicine. She disapproved of wholesale bleeding and violent emetics, and used to work cures by means of herb tonics and other simple prescriptions."[29] But the sufferings of some of those she treated seem to have continued, and their complaints might well have easily ripened into the accusation of witchcraft.

There was a tradition of associating female quackery with witchcraft that can be seen in the preamble to Henry VIII's statute regulating medical practice:

> For asmuch as the science and cunning of physick and surgery, is daily within this realm, exercised by a great multitude of ignorant persons, of whom the greater part have no manner of insight in the same, nor any other kind of learning, that common artificers as smiths, weavers and women, boldly and accustomably take upon them great cures and things of great difficulty in which they partly use sorcery and witchcraft; partly apply such medicines unto the disease as to be noxious and nothing meet therefore to the high displeasure of God great infamy to the faculties and the grievous hurt damage and destruction of many of the King's liege people most specially of them that cannot discern the uncunning from the cunning.[30]

Even disregarding the peculiar role of women in medical practice, the fact must also be considered that there was a strong relationship between diagnostic procedures and resort to occult knowledge. Astrology, for example, was a means of forecasting the course of an illness that roused the ire of the clergy for its implicit determinism; the esoteric nature of the pharmacopoeia presented another link with dark knowledge.[31] In short, medical judgment itself sometimes contained a mysterious element that made distinguishing between it and conjuration a difficult matter. All of these suspicious circumstances were apparently put together into a sinister pattern at least as early as 1441, when the Duchess of Gloucester was accused of witchcraft, an accusation which was, in

---

[29] John Fiske, *New France and New England* (Boston: Houghton Mifflin, 1902), p. 145.

[30] 3 Hen. 8, c. 11, 1511–12.

[31] Kocher, *Elizabethan England*, pp. 201–24.

part, "owing to her 'uncanny' knowledge of medicine and astrology."[32]

There was still another danger of impiety in seeking non-witchly interpretations of the searchers' observations. The Puritans would no doubt have seconded Nicholas Remy's argument that "to make nature the standard and measure of all things, to believe only what was credible, in effect tied the hands and circumscribed the power of God."[33] Some room had to be left for incredible and, more important, supernatural events.

In view of the colonial problem of controlling quackery and the risk of accusations of witchcraft taken by medical practitioners, it is quite understandable that the midwives might hesitate to question any part of orthodox belief and practice and tend to resolve all questionable cases against the accused. Something also needs to be said about the quality of the expertise that was exercised in the searches. Our assumption that physicians might have disavowed the notion of the spiritual causation of disease and death was partly based on the premise that the growth of knowledge in the medical field was accelerating and that they were generally aware of the exploding boundaries of scientific insight. In both these respects, the position of the midwife is quite dissimilar to that of the physician.

As to the substantive knowledge of the female sexual anatomy that was involved, it is difficult to assess exactly whether, considered in the abstract, it was sufficient to permit recognition of the "marks" as natural phenomena. While it is true that advances in female anatomy were made as the study of anatomy as a whole progressed, this field presented some real difficulties. For example, a widely used anatomical text by the Italian Mondino (1270[?]–1326) was based on the female anatomy of animals,[34] and the

[32] Lea, *Inquisition*, 3:467–68; and Copeman, *Doctors and Disease in Tudor Times*, p. 136. These problems were not peculiar to Massachusetts. See Walter R. Steiner, "A Contribution to the History of Medicine in the Province of Maryland, 1636–1671," *Bulletin of the Johns Hopkins Hospital*, 13 (1902):194.

[33] Quoted in John L. Teall, "Witchcraft and Calvinism in England," *Journal of the History of Ideas*, 23 (1962):35.

[34] Arturo Castiglioni, *A History of Medicine* (New York: Alfred A. Knopf, 1941), p. 344.

most popular basic source book for midwives, Roslin's *Rosengarten* (imitated in English by Thomas Raynalde in 1540 under the title *The Byrthe of Mankynde*), appeared in 1513, before the corrections stimulated by Vesalius had been made.[35] Raynalde's version was still being issued, largely unchanged, as late as 1676.[36] Vesalius himself provided no assistance on this score. His textual descriptions of female sex organs are sketchy, and the drawings that appeared in the *Fabrica* are counted as among the most inaccurate in an otherwise outstanding set of illustrations.[37] But it would be quite wrong to say that this field was neglected entirely. As early as the middle of the fifteenth century Ferrari had described the female ovary,[38] and work on the internal organs by

[35] For a description of an earlier but unprinted treatise, see J. H. Aveling, "Account of the Earliest English Work on Midwifery and the Diseases of Women," *Obstetrical Journal of Great Britain and Ireland*, 2 (1875):73. The 1545 and subsequent editions of *The Byrthe of Mankynde* included several anatomical plates from Vesalius' *Fabrica* (see J. W. Ballantyne, *The "Byrthe of Mankynde": Its Author, Editions and Contents* [London: Sherratt and Hughes, 1909], pp. 343–48); see also L. Clendening, *Source Book of Medical History* [New York: Hoeber, 1942], pp. 170–79).

[36] There were fourteen editions altogether (see Ballantyne, *The "Byrthe of Mankynde,"* pp. 324–25).

[37] J. B. de C. M. Saunders and Charles D. O'Malley, eds., in the *Illustrations from the Works of Andreas Vesalius* (New York: World, 1950), p. 170, comment:

> This extraordinary figure of the female genitalia has been the subject of much comment. Some have called it "monstrous" and others have implied that a Freudian quirk in the author had resulted in its assuming a resemblance to the male organ. However, if one is familiar with the circumstances under which Vesalius obtained the specimen, it is not difficult to interpret. It was obtained from the body of a woman who had been the mistress of a certain monk. Vesalius and his pupils, hearing of her death, snatched the body from the tomb, but, unfortunately, the monk together with the parents of the girl complained of the outrage to the city magistrates so that the anatomist and his students were compelled to dismember and free the body from all skin as rapidly as possible to prevent its being recognized. Since they had stolen the body expressly to examine the female organs, the best they could do was to encircle the external genitalia with a knife, split the symphysis and excise the vagina and uterus in one piece after severance of the urethra. Later, the uterine cavity was exposed by sectioning the body longitudinally and turning up the anterior half. We imagine that the uterine tubes were lost in the hurried method of preparation.

A somewhat different story is told in Henry Morley, "Andreas Vesalius," in *Toward Modern Science*, ed. Robert M. Palter (New York: Noonday Press, 1961), 2:76–77.

[38] Castiglioni, *A History of Medicine*, p. 368.

leading anatomists such as Fallopius (1523–1562)[39] and Graaf (1641–1673) continued.[40] Truly outstanding figures in medical history also participated in the research, including Ambroise Paré, the great surgeon (1510[?]–1590), who conducted a small school for midwives in Paris,[41] and John Weyer, who not only pioneered in psychological medicine but also invented a speculum for examination of the vagina and described retention of menstrual flow and occlusion of the neck of the uterus.[42]

The concern of the searching midwives, however, was with pathology of the external organs, and historical judgment is rendered most difficult here. Around the turn of the seventeenth century some descriptions of the external organs were made, for example, by Adriaan van den Spieghel (1578–1625),[43] and Fallopius had included mention of the clitoris in his work.[44] Moreover, in 1579 there had been a fairly complete enumeration of the relevant anatomy by Cabial, surgeon to the King of France.[45] There was also a treatise (1595) on gynecological rarities by Van Granfenberg (1530–1598).[46] Whether these and other contributions[47] brought the things observed by the searching women into the realm of what was understood as natural is impossible to know. All we can say is that the probability of seeing a natural phenomenon rather than a witch's mark would have been increased if extant knowledge had been applied to the searching process. We know, for example, that when a really first-rate medical mind participated in a search for witches' marks the result was exculpatory. During the prosecution of the Lancashire witches in 1634 to 1635 four suspected women were ordered searched by ten midwives,

[39] Nordenskiold, *The History of Biology*, p. 104.
[40] *Ibid.*, pp. 171–73.
[41] Kate C. H. Mead, *A History of Women in Medicine* (Haddam, Conn.: Haddam, 1938), p. 393.
[42] Zilboorg, *A History of Medical Psychology*, p. 208.
[43] James V. Ricci, *The Genealogy of Gynaecology* (New York: Blakeston, 1943), p. 343.
[44] André Pecker, *Hygiène et maladies de la femme au cours des siècles* (Paris: Decasta, 1961), p. 17.
[45] *Ibid.*
[46] Ricci, *The Genealogy of Gynaecology*, p. 327.
[47] See *ibid.*, pp. 285–333.

six surgeons, and no less a figure than William Harvey, then physician to Charles I. Of the four women examined by this panel, three were cleared completely. On the fourth it was reported there were "two things which may be called teats." But these were not accepted as incriminating evidence: "The first in shape like a teat of a bitch but in our judgement nothing but the skin as it will be drawn out after the application of leeches. The second is like the nipple or teat of a woman's breast but of the same colour with the rest of the skin, without any hollowness or issue of any blood or juice to come from thence."[48]

There were a host of reasons why nothing resembling the judgment of a William Harvey was applied to the Massachusetts cases. An understanding of the role of the midwives may be advanced by reference to the gap that generally existed between new knowledge in medicine and its acceptance and implementation in common practice. In the case of female practitioners, the gap was further widened by virtue of their exclusion from any formal medical education in the English universities,[49] by their lack of any significant amount of non-medical education (only one of the eight examining women in Rebecca Nurse's case could write her own name; the others each made "hir Marke"), and by their general non-participation in the intellectual life of the community at large.[50] They thus tended to be insulated from printed works and from any feeling for the dynamic growth of knowledge during the period of the great scientific advances. It is not at all surprising that there is not the smallest sign that any of the women whom the law called upon hesitated to assign to the realm of witch-

---

[48] The report is quoted from Keele, *William Harvey*, p. 71. For discussion of the probability of Harvey's disbelief in witches, see Notestein, *A History of Witchcraft in England*, pp. 160–63.

[49] Some English women were educated at Italian medical schools, however (see Mead, *A History of Women in Medicine*, p. 401).

[50] This is well illustrated by an entry in John Winthrop's Journal concerning a Mrs. Hopkins "who was fallen into a sad infirmity, the loss of her understanding and reason which had been growing upon her diverse years, by occasion of her giving herself wholly to reading and writing, and had written many books. . . . For if she had attended her household affairs, and such things as belong to women, and not gone out of her way and calling to meddle in such things as are proper for men, whose minds are stronger, etc., she had kept her wits" (2:225).

craft things they observed which were beyond their experience. It may be suggested further that this commitment to a wholly static state of knowledge was supported by the unhospitable attitude of a male-dominated medical profession, which was not likely to react favorably to attitudes that seemed contrary to its own. It is true that direct professional competition between men and women in the area of obstetrics and gynecology was yet to come. It was only during the course of the seventeenth century that these matters began to enter the list of subjects taught men in their medical preparation,[51] and formal lectures on obstetrics did not take place in America until they were instituted by the famous Dr. William Shippen, Jr., in 1765.[52] Nonetheless, it would be a mistake to explain the role of the midwife in the trials strictly on the basis of a lack of any direct male participation in her particular medical activity during the times in question, since there was a fair amount of "general practice" by women, which did put them directly in contact with men. The male attitude was probably more a function of their reaction to women in medicine generally than of any question as to where the formal lines of professional competence fell between the two sexes. At any rate, the women tended to keep "in line" and were among the last members of the seventeenth-century medical community to voice any opinions that were new to their profession.

[51] Castiglioni, *A History of Medicine*, p. 569.
[52] Packard, *History of Medicine in the United States*, 1:53. See also Herbert Thomas, *Chapters in American Obstetrics* (Springfield, Ill.: Charles C Thomas, 1932).

VIII

THE DEFENSE OF INSANITY

✠

One of the most widely held views concerning the witchcraft trials is that virtually all of the persons who were prosecuted as witches were mentally ill. Regardless of how accurate this belief may be in so far as the Continental cases are concerned, it cannot be applied to the Massachusetts experience merely because of a presumed analogy to the European trials.

The first factor supporting the distinction between the two is the firm establishment of the defense of insanity in the common law of England before the American colonization was undertaken.[1] This defense would operate to prevent mentally ill persons from being convicted of *any* offense. Mental illness is, of course, a concept that has to be considered in its historical context. In Massachusetts, for example, a specific statute that was enacted in 1641 was phrased to reflect the two major considerations that were relevant to all the Puritan experience, religion and reason, made it clear that mental abnormality, along with other extenuating conditions, was not to be passed over in assessing criminal liability in the Bay Colony. It read: "Children, Idiots, Distracted persons, and

---

[1] See Sheldon Glueck, *Mental Disorder and the Criminal Law* (Boston: Little, Brown, 1925), p. 125. The defense also seems to have been known to the heresy prosecutions, at least in the early stages of the Inquisition. See the case of the heretic Eon de l'Etoile, whose insanity saved him from punishment, described in Lea, *Inquisition*, 1:66.

all that are strangers or new comers to our plantation, shall have such allowances and dispensations in any Case whether Criminal or other as religion and reason require."[2]

There is, furthermore, ample evidence that this statute was no mere pious reference, to be ignored in practice. Its application can be seen in several instances. In one case a stranger to the Colony, accused of stealing silver from a box that was found floating in the harbor, was acquitted on the grounds that "it was not usuall" to give up anything so found in his country.[3] Nor was the policy of dispensation for strangers limited to minor offenses of this sort. In one case that must have kindled many emotions, the kind of unfamiliarity that was implied in the term "stranger" stands out. An Indian who had committed forcible rape upon an English girl was held not liable for the usual death penalty. The trial court noted that "although in an ordinary consideration hee deserued death, yett considering hee was but an Indian, and therefore in an incapasity to know the horiblenes of the wickednes of this abominable act, with other cercomstances considered, hee was centanced by the Court to be seurly Whipt att the post and sent out of the country."[4] This was certainly a broad reading of the spirit of the law.

The insanity defense of the 1641 statute was also part of the active jurisprudence of the Colony. There was, for example, the fornication prosecution in which the accused woman was discharged, "the court judging by her carriages and testimonies concerning her that shee was a distempered crazy woman."[5] So too with a Mrs. Wilson, who was charged with frequently absenting herself from the public ordinances. She was dismissed from the court after it had been informed that she was "distempered in her head."[6]

In seeking to determine the role of the defense of insanity in the witchcraft cases, however, very few things can be said with certainty. There is only one instance in which a person charged

---

[2] The Body of Liberties, No. 52 in *The Colonial Laws of Massachusetts*, p. 45.
[3] *Publications of the Colonial Society of Massachusetts*, 30:1156.
[4] *Records of Plymouth*, 6:98.
[5] *Publications of the Colonial Society of Massachusetts*, 29:436.
[6] *Quarterly Court of Essex County*, 4:88.

with witchcraft seems to have been discharged or acquitted on this ground, that of Elizabeth Johnson of Andover, granddaughter of Reverend Dane of that village. She was convicted in 1692 but was reprieved because she was "simplish." Her grandfather described Elizabeth, who had confessed to being a witch, as "but simplish at best."[7]

As to those who were executed as witches, the question of whether the defense might have been useful to them had it been in some way presented in their behalf involves more than the usual difficulties of such historically precarious speculation. The unfortunate fact is that we have no record at all of executions before 1692 on which to make a judgment. There are only a few fragmentary data. Regarding Margaret Jones, Governor Winthrop remarks that at her trial she "was very intemperate, lying notoriously, and railing upon the jury and witnesses, etc., and in the like distemper she died."[8] This description seems to show little more than extreme anger, which, under the circumstances, seems quite appropriate and not the behavior of a deranged person. There is nothing in the case of Ann Hibbins to suggest mental abnormality save the statement of a later writer that she was not "well settled in her mind."[9] As to Mrs. Lake and Mrs. Kendal, there is virtually no information at all except Reverend Hale's statement that both denied their guilt to the end.[10]

This leaves the fifth remaining pre-Salem execution which we know of, that of Mary Glover, to be accounted for. Here the material is more than fragmentary. In 1688 she was charged with using witchcraft on the children of John Goodwin so that they suffered greatly from fits. Cotton Mather provides us with the narrative. She confessed in open court to these deeds of witchcraft. "However," Mather continues,

> to make all clear, The Court appointed five or six Physicians one evening to examine her very strictly, whether she were not craz'd

[7] Quoted in Claude Moore Fuess, "Witches at Andover," *Proceedings of the Massachusetts Historical Society*, 70 (1953):14.
[8] Journal, 2:344.
[9] Poole, "Witchcraft in Boston," p. 139.
[10] *A Modest Inquiry*, pp. 408–9.

in her Intellectuals, and had not procured to herself by Folly and Madness the Reputation of a Witch. Diverse hours did they spend with her; and in all that while no Discourse came from her, but what was pertinent and agreeable; particularly when they asked her, What she thought would become of her soul? she reply'd "You ask me a very solemn Question, and I cannot well tell what to say to it." She own'd herself a Roman Catholick; and could recite her Pater Noster in Latin very readily; but there was one Clause or two alwaies too hard for her, whereof she said, "She could not repeat it, if she might have all the world." In the upshot, the Doctors returned her Compos Mentis; and Sentence of Death was pass'd upon her.[11]

In some respects Mrs. Glover was examined even more thoroughly than are criminal defendants today. The gathering for consultation of five or six doctors and their examination for "divers" hours compares quite favorably with the personnel and time now generally expended on the investigation of the criminal capacity of an accused person. But what is important here is the question of how well Mrs. Glover fared in the context of seventeenth-century Massachusetts law and psychology. This discussion should shed some light on the intriguing matter of why the insanity defense was not raised more often in the witchcraft cases.

The important thing to note in the Glover case is that it was in order to assess the state of her "Intellectuals" that the court called in the physicians. They, in turn, found her reasoning ability to be functioning well and, therefore, could claim for her no exemption from the processes of the criminal law. Her replies were "pertinent and agreeable," and her response to the specific question concerning her soul was completely consistent with an intact cognitive functioning. The focus of the examination was on her reason, a concern that appears in other criminal cases as well. In one instance a witness testified to an incident in which he was eating at the same table with the defendant, "and he did eat after all other had done and also licked the crumbs left on another's

[11] *Memorable Providences*, pp. 104–5.

94

plate—20 persons looking on at this and his other foolish tricks; I never could perceive he was at all ashamed, all of which makes it clear to me he hath not the use of his reason as other men."[12]

It is not at all surprising that reason here appears as the central and governing mental faculty. The preoccupation in Massachusetts with reasoning powers seems to illustrate what Gregory Zilboorg has called "the old tendency to consider all mental diseases as diseases of intellect or reason."[13] Of great importance was the fact that much of the then most recent work in human biology served to confirm and support a conception of insanity that was rooted in the malfunctioning of the intellect. Viewing modern "psychiatry proper" as being concerned primarily with emotional disorders, Zilboorg suggests that, looking back in time,

> one may safely conclude that the trend toward the purely scientific which had developed in the medical world of the seventeenth century had comparatively little effect in the domain of psychiatry proper. Idiocy, cretinism, apoplexy, certain aspects of epilepsy, certain consequences of obvious brain injuries, and certain paralyses —a number of conditions which were due to actual brain defects, congenital or acquired—attracted the attention of the medical man. Passing over some of his flights of theoretical imagination, we should credit him with the successful advancement of our knowledge of what we learned in later centuries to recognize as organic diseases or defects of the central nervous system, which are accompanied with more or less gross mental disturbances—disturbances characterized mostly by deviations from normal intellectual functioning. . . . These allegedly purely intellectual disturbances were viewed as results of anatomical or physiological abnormalities. Even those diseases in which the symptoms were primarily emotional such as melancholy (known later as depression) and mania were viewed as conditions produced by organic causes. . . . The severe psychological conditions such as hysterical, convulsive states, or hyster-epilepsies as they were later called for a short period, the

[12] Testimony of John Trumble in the case of John Jackson, *Quarterly Court of Essex County*, 6:27.

[13] *A History of Medical Psychology*, p. 268; see also I. E. Drapkin, "Remarks on Ancient Psychopathology," *Isis*, 46 (1956):223.

ecstacies, the hallucinatory, persecutory states—in short, the vast majority of severe neuroses, so-called borderline conditions, and psychoses—were disregarded by those who felt themselves fully wedded to physics, chemistry and physiology.[14]

The colonists provided much evidence that they too were "fully wedded" to the physical sciences in their conception of mental illness. Cotton Mather discussed the physical basis of insanity in terms strikingly similar to the twentieth-century thesis of the biochemists and physiologists: "A great Philosopher observes and affirms, that the Clearness of our Fancy depends on the regular Structure of the Brain; by which it is fitted for the receiving and compounding of all Impressions with the more Regularity. In Fools the Brain is deformed. The Deformity is not easily noted in other people: But, no doubt, a smaller Difference than can be imagined may alter the Symmetry of the Brain, and so the Perspicuity of the Fancy."[15]

The therapy that was provided for mentally disordered persons was rational in that it followed this organic orientation of the etiology of their disease. On board the *Hannah & Elizabeth* on his way from Dartmouth to New England Dr. John Barton treated a Mrs. Killegroue for the "Maladie of Histericall vapors" with what was then fairly standard therapy, "suppository, a compound Clyster with Hisyricall Carmanitiue seeds and a stomachicall Emplaister."[16] Joane Brownstist's hysterical fits Barton treated with "Spiritt of Castar & oile of Amber seurall times."[17] In Salem Dr. Zerobabel Endicott's prescription for a distracted woman provides another example of the application of the pharmacopoeia to the problems of mental illness: "Tak milk of a Nurse that giues suck to a male child & also take a hee Cat & Cut of one

---

[14] *A History of Medical Psychology*, pp. 268–69. See also the discussion of the central role of reason in the conception of insanity in George Rosen, "Social Attitudes to Irrationality and Madness in Seventeenth and Eighteenth Century Europe," *Journal of the History of Medicine*, 18 (1936):220.

[15] *The Christian Philosopher*, pp. 234–35. A modern example is given in Sanford J. Fox, "Delinquency and Biology," *Miami Law Review*, 16 (1961):85–88.

[16] Quoted in Gordon, *Aesculapius Comes to the Colonies*, p. 6.

[17] *Ibid.*, p. 7.

of his ears or a piece of it & Lett it blede into the milk & then Lett the sick woman Drink it. Doe this three Times."[18]

Of course, this resort to drug therapy to put the humors back in balance often went hand in hand with prayer therapy. The amalgam is well illustrated by a letter of William Pynchon to Edward Hopkins in 1664, in which Pynchon declares, "Yet I must tell you that that hot subtell vapor which hath taken possession of her brain is hard to be removed though it may be much helped through Gods blessing uppon the event." He went on to recommend sweet milk and saffron so that "her body will be brought to a sweating temper which I conceive will be a good help to nature."[19]

It thus appears quite clear that intellectual functioning and the right use of reason were firmly established cornerstones of seventeenth-century conceptions of insanity both in and out of New England,[20] and it would be surprising indeed if a non-organic or functional view of mental illness—one that emphasized emotional pathology—had achieved any foothold at all in Puritan thinking. It must be recalled that "mind" was equated with "soul" and that nothing could be admitted as true that implied the possibility of sickness and, therefore, mortality, of the soul. The brain itself could become afflicted; a soul (and a mind) could be wicked, but not sick. Two hundred years later this same view was expressed by Pliny Earle, M.D., one of the leading American psychiatrists of the time:

> Were the arguments for the hypothesis that in insanity the mind itself is diseased tenfold more numerous than they are, and more weighty, I could not accept them. My ideas of the human mind are such that I cannot hold for a moment that it can be diseased, as we understand disease. That implies death as its final consequency, but Mind is eternal. In its organization, it was created for

[18] Quoted in Dow, *Every Day Life in the Massachusetts Bay Colony*, pp. 183–84.
[19] Quoted in *Proceedings of the Massachusetts Historical Society*, 48 (1914):56.
[20] Insanity included, of course, the concept of lunacy. See, for example, testimony in 1676 concerning a man "outrageously mad and distracted" but only during "one parte of the moone" (*Quarterly Court of Essex County*, 6:228–29).

immortality, consequently, it is superior to the bodily structure, and beyond the scope of the wear and tear and disorganization and final destruction of the mortal part of our being.[21]

Seen in the context of the deeply religious position of the Massachusetts leadership, this mind-soul equation greatly reinforced the view that insanity was an entirely organic problem. This in turn, as Zilboorg has pointed out, perpetuated that notion that defects of reason are the essence of the symptomatology. Thus Mrs. Glover and several others were tested in their "Intellectuals."

Although only a heretic could openly suggest that the mind-soul could become defective, in its entirety or in its parts, yet it must have been clear to all that forms of insanity did exist and that there were unfortunate fellow humans whose reason was grossly impaired and whose behavior was grossly deranged. The reaction of the colonists to such people sheds some light on the problem at hand. If they harbored a harsh and punitive attitude towards those whom they recognized as being mentally ill, this might help to explain why mental illness was so infrequently used as a legal defense in the witchcraft cases. In other words, the consequence of ignoring a perceived mental illness would be imposition of the death penalty, and such a result would be acceptable if it were felt that the mentally ill ought to be punished anyway.

This thesis does not seem to be supportable, however, in spite of the general belief today that cruelty and abuse were the characteristic response to mental illness in colonial Massachusetts.[22] In the first place, the colonists shared with their English brethren what was for the times the quite progressive idea that care of the mentally ill was a public responsibility. In 1676 it was enacted that

> whereas there are distracted persons in some tounes, that are vnruly, whereby not only the families wherein they are, but others suffer much damage by them, it is ordered by this Court and the

[21] Quoted in Norman Dain, *Concepts of Insanity in the United States 1789–1865* (New Brunswick, N.J.: Rutgers University Press, 1964), pp. 64–65.

[22] See, for example, Albert Deutsch, *The Mentally Ill in America* (New York: Columbia University Press, 1949), pp. 25–39.

authoritie thereof, that the selectmen in all tounes where such persons are are hereby impowred & injoyned to take care of all such persons, that they doe not dmnify others; and also to take care & order the management of their estates in the times of their distemperature, so as may be for the good of themselues & families depending on them, and the charge to be paid out of the estates of all such persons where it may be had, otheruise at the publick charge of the toune such persons belong unto.[23]

Where insane persons were cared for at home, public funds bore the expense. There were, for example, orders for the payments of five pounds per year to parents for care of a distracted child[24] and of fifty shillings per year for care of a "distempered" child.[25] Even before the 1676 statute mentioned above, public guardians were imposed to look after the welfare of persons unable to care for themselves, as in the case of a Widow Willix; being in no capacity to "order and improve her estate by reason of a strange kind of distracted and distempered condition" from which she had been suffering for a long time, three men were appointed to take care of her estate, her comfortable subsistence, and to see that the building of her house was finished according to a contract entered into by her.[26]

This is not to say that the colonial attitude towards the mentally ill was always one of enlightened benevolence. In some instances, the particularly outrageous behavior of disturbed persons met with whipping and fines, as with two women who went naked to church in 1663.[27] Here, however, the inference that the women may be mentally disturbed may not have been shared by the colonists. There is also probably a good deal of truth to observations that the lot of the insane was not a happy one. "The insane poor languished in jails and almshouses, wandered aimlessly around the countryside, or were auctioned off to work for those who

[23] *Records of the Governor and Company of the Massachusetts Bay*, 5:80–81.
[24] *Ibid.*, 3:232.
[25] *Ibid.*, p. 363.
[26] *Quarterly Court of Essex County*, 3:149. See also the similar case of Widow Jackson in *ibid.*, p. 176.
[27] *Ibid.*, p. 64.

would support them at a minimal cost to the country. The well-to-do and middle class patients wasted away at home, chained in unheated attics, ill-fed and ill-clothed, and occasionally attended by doctors whose remedies included bleeding, purging and emetics."[28]

Even so, this picture does not seem to be one of a cruelty to the mentally ill approaching the intentional, into which can be fitted the explanation posited above—that the defense of insanity was not used in witchcraft cases because insanity was felt to be punishable. What may be enlightening, however, is the question of the absence of the defense from capital cases generally. It is a curious fact that even apart from the witchcraft cases there is not one criminal case involving the death penalty in which the defense of insanity is even alluded to. Of course, this omission may reflect the obvious and uniform sanity of capital offenders in Massachusetts. Yet there is at least one case where the assumed uniformity fails, that of Dorothy Talbie. She was convicted of murdering her daughter, Difficult Talbie, on December 4, 1638,[29] and was hanged two days later. Winthrop's account of this case includes a strong hint that the child's name derived from a serious illness of some sort. But what is more important is that his journal entry amounts to a virtual acknowledgment that Dorothy was mentally ill:

Dorothy Talbye was hanged at Boston for murdering her own daughter, a child of three years old. She had been a member of the church of Salem, and of good esteem for godliness, etc.; but, falling at difference with her husband, through melancholy or spiritual delusions, she sometimes attempted to kill him, and her children, and herself, by refusing meat, saying it was so revealed to her, etc. After much patience, and divers admonitions not prevailing, the church cast her out. Whereupon she grew worse; so as the magistrate caused her to be whipped. Whereupon she was reformed for a time, and carried herself more dutifully to her

[28] Norman Dain and Richard Carlson, "Social Class and Psychological Medicine," *Bulletin of the History of Medicine*, 33 (1959):445.

[29] *Records of the Governor and Company of the Massachusetts Bay*, 1:246.

husband, etc.; but soon after she was so possessed with Satan, that he persuaded her (by his delusions, which she listened to as revelations from God) to break the neck of her own child, that she might free it from future misery. This she confessed upon her apprehension; yet, at her arraignment, she stood mute a good space, till the governor told her she should be pressed to death, and then she confessed the indictment. When she was to receive judgment, she would not uncover her face, nor stand up, but as she was forced, nor give any testimony of her repentance, either then or at her execution. The cloth, which should have covered her face, she plucked off and put between the rope and her neck. She desired to have been beheaded, giving this reason, that it was less painful and less shameful. After a swing or two, she catched at the ladder.[30]

Perhaps a similar case is that of Mary Parsons, who was acquitted of witchcraft but was convicted of murdering her child in 1651.[31] Of her, Samuel Drake remarks that she was permanently insane.[32] Probably one reason for the absence of the insanity defense is the fact that there was no defense counsel involved in these cases. Without some such assistance an accused person would perhaps not plead insanity on his own. Yet the Glover case is one instance where the judges looked into this matter entirely on their own, so it must be acknowledged that there was at least some means by which the question could be raised in the prosecution process without the intervention of partisan lawyers.

Another possible explanation for the absence of the defense is the very limited use the colonists made of capital punishment. Of the seven common-law felonies for which death was the penalty under English law—homicide, rape, burglary, arson, robbery, larceny, and mayhem—the Massachusetts law recognized only the first two.[33] There was no vague category of "felony," as there was in England, for which the death penalty would be inflicted. Whenever the word "felony" was used in Massachusetts,

---

[30] Journal, pp. 282–83.
[31] Records of the Governor and Company of the Massachusetts Bay, 3:229.
[32] Drake, The Witchcraft Delusion in New England, p. 66.
[33] The Laws and Liberties of Massachusetts, p. 6.

it seems to have been an imprecise term meaning nothing more than "serious."[34] Restriction in the use of the death penalty can also be seen in statutes, unknown in English law, that authorized it only upon the third commission of the same offense.[35] And, of course, the numerous English capital crimes of purely statutory origin, such as "congregations and confederacies holden by Masons,"[36] were completely absent from Massachusetts law. One cannot but conclude that one of the major innovations of Massachusetts lawmaking was a greatly reduced use of capital punishment.[37]

It may not be amiss to speculate that concomitant with this limited definition of capital crimes was the attitude that, when an offense that had been denounced as capital was committed, the full rigor of the law should be felt. Account had been taken of the necessity for allowing for human failings, such as provisions for reformation of offenders, in the definition of what was capital and what was not, and the process largely resulted in a narrowing of the former category. After this legislative decision there was very little room left for considering the individual circumstances of the murderer or the witch, even when they were as striking as were the delusions of Dorothy Talbie. While there is no evidence that this view was verbalized, the assumption that it did prevail may make more intelligible the approach the colonists took to capital offenders generally.

Regarding witchcraft specifically, however, we must keep in mind that, whatever tendency there was for the courts to be alert for signs of insanity, its recognition depended upon the use or misuse of intellect and reason by those accused. It thus becomes highly important to observe that there was nothing irrational,

[34] For example, in 1671 Alice Thomas was convicted of "felonious theft" but was sentenced only to make treble restitution and to public humiliation (*Publications of the Colonial Society of Massachusetts*, 29:82–83).

[35] "Burglary and Robbery," in *The Laws and Liberties of Massachusetts*, pp. 4–5.

[36] Dalton, *Country Justice*, p. 276.

[37] I am grateful to Mr. Geoffry Paul Hellman for making available to me his 1965 Honors Thesis from Harvard College, in which he thoughtfully develops and documents this matter of restricting the death penalty.

nothing evincing defective reason, in the practice of witchcraft *per se*. We may tend today to think that anyone who seriously confesses to the perpetration of such deeds needs to have his head examined, but in the view of the seventeenth century he needed only to be punished, for the same reasons that a murderer was punished. A witch's confession and the testimony of victims and witnesses were all entirely reasonable to the uncraz'd intellectuals of the society. Virtually everyone fully believed that such things as were described could easily take place. Not only was witchcraft consistent with the functioning of normal intelligence and reason, it was, in a very significant sense, anticipated, awaited, and almost welcomed by the keenest minds of Puritan Massachusetts. It was seen as rational within a broad social context, rather than involving only the mental ability of individuals.

Appreciation of this last point depends upon knowledge of the particular form and nature of the Puritan religious beliefs on which the Colony was founded and the course of their evolution during most of the seventeenth century. Perry Miller has traced these beliefs in a brilliant study to which no summarizing can do full justice, but at the heart of the matter was the doctrine of the contract or federal covenant which the Puritan community had with God. Appreciation of this covenantal relationship is central to approaching any aspect of the history of colonial Massachusetts, and it is of major importance in understanding why insanity was barely mentioned in the witchcraft experience, especially in the events of 1692 and 1693. The covenant related to society as a single entity and was quite distinct from the individual's relations with his deity. It had, according to Miller, three distinct features:

> It has to do with conduct here and now, with visible success or tangible failure. Secondly, since a society cannot be rewarded in heaven for its obedience . . . and cannot be punished in hell . . . it must perforce contract with the Almighty for external ends. Its obedience, in short, means prosperity, its disobedience means war, epidemic or ruin. . . . In the third place, a community is not joined to God by so irrevocable a contract as will endure no matter how depraved it becomes. . . . If a society, no matter how many

saints may still be in it, sinks so deep into corruption that its abominations call for destruction, then the national covenant is ended.[38]

In such a view, the adversities suffered in New England could not be accidents or merely the logical concomitants of wilderness living. They were the consequences of breaches of the covenant, "exquisitely proportioned to the amount of depravity" in the community. Spiritual impurity bred hardship. Repentance, fasting, days of humiliation, etc., purged the sin and restored prosperity and peace. In the context of this ideological structure, the hanging of Margaret Jones in 1648 can be seen as the Puritan's performance of the secular side of the covenant—the suppression of vice. This cleaving to the path of godliness through law enforcement by a society enjoying a special relationship to its God presumably was as efficacious in keeping the community "covenanted" as was other related activity, such as keeping the community free from heretical opinion or maintaining proper intercongregational relationships. It was, in short, one aspect of a true society of God and a part of the example New England was setting for the rest of the world. Certainly there was no laxity in the judicial part of the demonstration, for, as Governor Bradford of Plymouth Plantation observed, "the churches look narrowly to their members and the magistrates over all, more strictly than in other places."[39]

In addition, there was another possible significance to criminal acts, including witchcraft. On the one hand, the sure administration of the criminal law was, as has been suggested, a covenantal obligation and was part of the light that was to shine "round the world from the city on a hill." On the other hand, the social harm produced by criminal conduct might have been felt as a wrathful communication from God visited upon the community as a consequence of its sinfulness. As such, it would call forth the ritual of prayer and rectification of the evil appropriate to purging the

[38] Miller, *The New England Mind: From Colony to Province*, p. 22.

[39] William Bradford, *Of Plymouth Plantation 1620–1647*, ed. Samuel Eliot Morison (Boston: Houghton Mifflin, 1912), p. 316.

underlying sin and therefore providing assurance of a continuation of the covenantal status. This interpretation, however, seems to overemphasize the degree to which crime was generally experienced as a community disaster on the scale of a drought or an Indian war. Winthrop's journal, for example, contains numerous references to murders, rapes, and other serious offenses with no indication that these events did or should evoke a collective repentance. The records of the General Court contain no orders for fasting or days of humiliation upon discovery of criminal harm. There was, at least in these early years, a strictly observed difference between sin and the afflictions that were its wages. The problem of individual crime was experienced on too small a scale to project the inference to the Puritan mind that there was serious underlying and causative sinfulness.

Later in the history of the Colony, says Miller, "the conception of the relation of society to the divine was unwittingly (and unintentionally) transformed into a thesis which positively reversed primitive doctrine."[40] The sinfulness of the society was no longer seen as a condition to be eradicated upon a vivid demonstration that it existed; rather, sin and corruption were themselves deemed visitations of the wrath of God. A pervasive and chronic state of spiritual impurity that could not be expiated replaced the sense of sin that had been experienced only at times and that even then could be removed through demonstrations of renewed adherence to covenant obligations. The "mental anguish" of the second and third generations in Massachusetts concerning their spiritual decline could no longer be measured by the external and objective phenomena of epidemic, war, famine, etc. These events were no longer the yardsticks for measuring culpability, and the expiating procedures became empty ritual and, in fact, devices for further reinforcing the pervasive sense of sin.

Miller attributes this change to the impact of a particular type of sermon, which he calls the "jeremiad" because its central theme was that the populace was being systematically taken to task for

---

[40] Miller, *The New England Mind: From Colony to Province*, p. 28.

its sins, a theme whose text frequently came from Jeremiah in the book of Isaiah.[41] In the course of collective assimilation of jeremiad thinking during the century, criminal acts acquire increased potential for signifying the perversity of the community, all the more so as the offenses take on the appearance of an epidemic directed at society at large. For this reason, it is of central importance to note Miller's statement that "an appearance of witchcraft among the afflictions of New England was from the beginning as much to be anticipated as Indian raids; by 1692 several instances had been encountered, and a more organized assault was altogether predictable."[42]

In view of Miller's thesis about the great significance of the jeremiad in the approximately thirty years from 1660 to 1692, the discovery of witches in the 1690's was more than predictable— but not at the beginning. It was, like the notion of the revocation of their charter, a shining confirmation of all that the Puritans had been led to believe for two generations concerning their abiding sinfulness and the dire calamities that would befall them as a consequence of that state. As more and more witches were discovered through the Salem investigations, the whole fiendish enterprise by the Devil and his workers must have become all the more understandable. Far from taking on the appearance of irrationality, the confessions of witch after witch would seem highly constructive and rational events in the life of the society. The presence of witches was clearly a calamity on the scale of epidemic or war. In this context how could anyone claim that the confessions sprang from madness? It followed logically from the collective fall from grace which the colonists had come to believe in. Significantly enough, the one person who did make such an assertion of madness, Thomas Brattle,[43] interpreted the Salem experience wholly outside of the traditional covenantal context, decrying the great stain on New England's reputation, not the

[41] *Ibid.*, pp. 27–39.
[42] *Ibid.*, p. 192.
[43] See Thomas Brattle's letter dated October 8, 1692, in Burr, *Narratives*, p. 173.

jeopardizing of her covenantal status.[44] Thus it seems that if the defense of insanity had a relatively small role in the witchcraft cases, it was not because of cruelty to mentally ill defendants. In the context of psychology and of New England covenantal history, the witchcraft that was charged and acknowledged was highly rational and far removed from the seventeenth-century concept of insanity.

[44] Miller, *The New England Mind: From Colony to Province*, pp. 196–97. The warning about impossible confessions was also made in England by Dr. John Webster, writing to several Justices of the Peace (see Kittredge, *Witchcraft in Old and New England*, p. 348). Webster's book was known to the Mathers (*ibid.*, p. 349), although the trustworthiness of the confession seems to have played no role in Increase Mather's *Cases of Conscience*, which Miller credits with putting a stop to the Salem trials (*The New England Mind: From Colony to Province*, pp. 198–200).

IX

THE LAW-SCIENCE RELATIONSHIP
THEN AND NOW

✠

Since this book's central concern is with law and science, it is fitting that it close with some mention of the problems lawyers now face, although it should be obvious from the previous chapters that there was no involvement of any sort of professional bar in the Massachusetts witchcraft cases. What we have observed instead is the influence of writers such as Michael Dalton, the administrative hand of men like John Winthrop, who had had some judicial experience, and the operation of a legal system that in many respects showed sophistication and justice. These latter virtues appeared often in the administration of the law and in its substantive content, both of which were in keeping with the best traditions of British due process and were in some details, such as the recording of the law in writing and the restricted use of capital punishment, well in advance of legal progress in the mother country. What this system of colonial justice might have been like if there had been a class of professional lawyers in New England can only be a matter of speculation. Given the low regard in which the English bar was held at the time, their presence might have been more of an impediment to the attainment of justice than anything else. But what is clear beyond speculation is that the administration of the law in the witchcraft prosecutions was related in some rather complex ways to the world of science and scientists, and these constitute the framework within which some important contemporary problems may be clarified.

The theme that runs through an examination of these cases is that the law was keeping very much in step with the scientific thought of the day. What emerges as the really difficult historical task is to identify any way in which law enforcement against witches actually conflicted with science. The neglect of post-mortem examinations certainly involved no disagreement between law and science, for, as the Rosseter report from Connecticut reveals, the demonological theory made the findings of a necropsy either irrelevant or confirmatory of a witch's involvement. There were no observations a doctor could record that would rule out the suspect's capability. This suggests, incidentally, that it is not our scientific sophistication that prevents us from taking witchcraft seriously now. We could term Elizabeth Kelley's terminal illness bronchial pneumonia or diphtheria, but the question of its spiritual causation would remain open. Science still remains the provider of only penultimate answers if we concede the potency of supernatural forces, as one may assume most persons who are orthodox in their religious beliefs would. It can be suggested that the principles of religion that were at the heart of the neglect of science in the death cases, far from being a demonstration of seventeenth-century fanaticism, were hardly more than an acknowledgment of the omnipotence of God that continues to be recognized today. The view that the universe of things is not merely a matter of insensible physical particles is commonly found among men of science, past and present. In one form or another, the scientist's rejection of a thoroughgoing materialism lent much support to the view that witches could cause the elements of nature to combine in fatal proportions.

So too there was no conflict when physicians were consulted during the course of a victim's illness. For the most part, it appears that purely medical procedures were followed, and, in a few cases, the inefficacy of these ministrations gave rise to suggestions of witchcraft. There was no infidelity to science even in these latter cases, for there was no doctrine or ethic that demanded limitation

110

of the physician's role to an assessment of known symptoms, and widely held beliefs in some form of spiritualism supported a medical opinion that supernatural elements were at work.

But to say that the witchcraft trials had no anti-scientific elements tells much less than the whole story. The law-science amalgam in these cases reveals a great over-reliance on and uncritical use of science. An outstanding example is the matter of differential diagnosis. The validity or basis of a physician's pronouncement that his patient was a victim of witchcraft is nowhere questioned. Such judgments were readily accepted and given weight; there was none of the reluctance or hesitation inherent in Lawyer Dalton's *medical* observations. There was no inquiry into the problem of why, in some incurable and baffling physical illnesses, witchcraft appeared, and in others it did not. Why some physicians quickly reached the conclusion that a witch was involved in their patients' suffering, while other practitioners never ventured such an opinion, seemed to be a matter of no concern to anyone. The pervasive belief within the scientific community in spiritual control or influence over bodily functions, whether called an *élan* or a *Nishmath Chaim,* never appears openly as the premise for finding disease or death to have been supernaturally induced.

What tended to preclude a critical analysis of medical judgments was the universality and strength of the belief that people could and did behave as witches, causing the kind of harm that the expert opinions merely confirmed. But there is also the crucial question of who was to put forth the criticism, and where. The institutional ability to deal with medical judgments openly and on their merits was wholly lacking. It is true that several of the magistrates were personally involved in the world of science—through their membership in the Royal Society or otherwise—but the details of medical practice, both theoretical and practical, were not within their area of interest. Their scientific involvement was, in short, irrelevant to their capacity to judge the quality of diagnostic evaluations. Perhaps some of the witches who were themselves medical practitioners, such as Margaret Jones, had some sort of intellectual tools to voice a critique, but they were obviously not in a position to do so effectively. Furthermore, there was no requirement that the physician who was instrumental in launching a prosecution, as Dr. Griggs in Salem Village may have been in 1692, should testify at the actual trial. None of the validity testing that inheres in open judicial inquiry reached what may well have been the instigating factor of a case. The assumption that the victim was indeed suffering from witchly harm, with which the trial started, persisted throughout the proceedings, and no attempt was made to verify it by confronting and scrutinizing the underlying diagnostic judgment. There was thus neither the personnel nor the procedures for recognizing the limits of scientific expertise or for subjecting individual expert opinions to any sort of test.

Virtually everything said here about the uncritical acceptance of physicians' reports applies to the use of midwives as well. Their involvement in these cases ranks as the outstanding example of justice being blind when its eyes needed to be wide open. No doubt some evaluation of the women's reports could have been made, since standards of medical practice were evolving in the Colony by which their opinions might have been judged. It had been known for some time that substandard medical work was being carried on. There is even evidence of the prosecution of quacks, and, as has been suggested, some of the witchcraft cases may have been directed as much at controlling illegal medical practice as at *maleficium*. Yet no limitation seems to have been imposed on the use of the judgments of the searching women in the witchcraft cases. It may be recalled that in Connecticut a demand for "approbation" of physicians in these cases *was* made. It is not unlikely that in Massachusetts, too, some practitioners privately cautioned against relying strongly on the opinion of the women. If there were such reservations, however, little attention seems to have been paid to them. To some extent the use of a group of women rather than a single midwife did constitute an invitation to dissent, as well as an opportunity to obtain an opinion whose validity was vouched for by the unanimity of the panel or by the process of argument among its members when a consensus

112

could not be reached. But for the most part this validity factor remained of only potential value to the judicial process, since there was no institutional way of bringing before the court the facts or opinions disputed among the women or of resolving issues raised by the accused's objection to the women's report. The judges seemed to consider that both they and the jury were incapable of dealing with these disagreements and that all that could be done, as the Nurse case illustrates, was to have the women take another look. But then, as before, the report was received by administrators of the law who were in no position to evaluate it.

In the areas where the law's use of scientific judgments should be characterized as an "under-use," the same problems appear. When the victim of an alleged witchcraft was dead, the theory of the Devil's working through natural causes was perhaps, as has been suggested, itself sufficient to make irrelevant post-mortem investigations. But this theory did not preclude medical ministrations while the victim lived, and it is likely that, if a cure could have been effected by the physician's manipulation of the right physical factors, a charge of witchcraft would have been extremely difficult, if not impossible, to maintain. Similarly, if autopsy in any case had revealed an obvious and familiar natural cause of death, it is unlikely that prosecution would have continued, in spite of demonological theory. There was, in other words, room to use scientific skills in far vaster areas than those in which they were in fact employed. But the local scientific community was not in a position to take the initiative in making a post-mortem examination; and no impetus to do this came from the legal system itself, in spite of the statutory framework that would have supported a broadened program of autopsies. Here was an instance in which the law might have demanded more from the scientists than they knew themselves capable of. In the absence of an awareness of the potential use of science on the part of those responsible for the legal system, the "apathy" of the scientists prevailed.

In the area of mental abnormality there was also statutory authority to do more than was actually done; dispensation for

113

"distracted" persons was considered in only one witchcraft case. But even routine mental examinations in all cases probably would not have changed the outcome of a single trial, although this kind of guess can be made only most diffidently. All that can be said with assurance is that the law did not seek to apply what local skills there were in the field of psychodiagnosis in any case but that of Mary Glover. Perhaps it is important that of all the persons executed as witches in Massachusetts, Mrs. Glover was the only one who openly confessed her misdeeds. All of the pre-Salem offenders and all of those executed in that last series of prosecutions went to the gallows protesting their innocence to the end. The only sign of mental abnormality in the confession of a witch appeared in her case. There were, of course, other confessions—those of the Salem accused who realized that confession and repentance would allow witchcraft to go entirely unpunished. But this kind of absolution ritual was so deeply embedded in Puritan thought, even though the confessions were obviously meretricious, that there was no possibility of considering them to be a sign of insanity. If those who acknowledged their sin returned to a state of grace, so those who denied it were wicked and damned. It was almost entirely a question of one's status before divine judgment. The over-riding nature of this question tended to crowd out of consideration the matter of mental abnormality. There was, in short, such great cultural relativity involved in the use of physicians to diagnose the mental status of accused witches that the over-all result was a virtual neglect of the entire problem.

A serious question must now be raised concerning the justice of Massachusetts law administration in the cases. If justice involves bringing to bear in an informed way all that is relevant to the resolution of conflicts, then it must be said that it was injustice that characterized the use of science in the witchcraft controversy. To say this is not to point the finger of blame at those who were responsible for running the legal system or those who contributed their skills to the judicial process. There are a wealth of good reasons why a different pattern of law-science relations should not be expected. But, nonetheless, unjust it was, for the reason that relevant and available scientific knowledge was either not used at all or was accepted *in toto* and put to indiscriminate use.

Now that we think we know more of what science really is and have assigned a learned profession to the caretaking of justice, there is still a discomforting similarity to the kind of injustice that obtained three centuries ago. We do not try witches any more, although the exact reason why is not as obvious as one might expect. But more to the point is the question of what the administration of justice now does to bring in all the extralegal material that bears on the attainment of just results. One might advert initially to the process of judicial notice, whereby judges may take as proved anything that has become a recognized and accepted scientific fact. Obvious progress has also been achieved by allowing each side in a court case to call its own scientific expert and to crossexamine openly the scientists brought in by the other side. We know also that thinking about the problem of mental illness and legal responsibility is a great deal more sophisticated today. In some states a mental examination has become a routine matter in certain serious cases, and it would be highly unusual for a homicide trial to conclude without the testimony in court of a medical expert concerning his autopsy findings.

Yet all these advances leave more than a little to be desired. The ability of those charged with administering the law—lawyers and judges for the most part—to deal knowledgeably with scientific issues has not progressed very much beyond the days of the witchcraft trials. With full knowledge of the present and expanding importance of science in the legal process, we make no requirement that these professionals be anything but illiterates in science when they assume their responsibilities for the liberties, lives, and property of the populace. A student can come to law school with an undergraduate education that has no science in it at all, and law schools make no pretense at making up the deficit while he is in their charge. The brutal fact that even the best trained and most experienced scientists can differ among themselves on a precise question raised in court, thereby making the accuracy and sophistication of the judge's clarifying explanations to the jury crucial, has not prevented our elevating to the bench lawyers whose experience with science ended with a high-school biology course. The development of the adversary system and of the rule requiring a jury to limit its decision to the evidence openly presented to it provide the opportunity for skilled lawyers to bring forward and explain appropriate material from the world of science. But this reliance on the intellectual ability of an individual practitioner to teach himself a body of knowledge that is fast becoming more and more esoteric and specialized is surely a far from satisfactory means of dealing with the problem. The kind of critical evaluation of scientific material that this approach produces can be little more than minimal. The legal profession has the responsibility and the opportunity to serve justice better than this, but it is grossly lacking in the knowledge and training it needs to do so.

INDEX

Acquittals: examples of, 7, n. 13, 38; proportion of, 42–43

Alexander IV, Pope: on magicians, 15

Anatomy: criminal's body studied, 45–46; of female organs, 86–88; Galenic basis of, 55–56; as impetus for autopsies, 55–58; influence on English medicine, 56; legal authority to study, 45–46; and pathology, 56, 58; and Scientific Revolution, 55–56; taught by Giles Firman, 46; training in, 45

Astrology: in medical diagnosis, 85–86

Atheism: and disbelief in witches, 28–29

Autopsies: Connecticut report by Bryan Rossiter, 51–53, 110; demonological theory in Rossiter report, 110; Maryland cases, 47; Massachusetts cases, 48–49; modern use of, 113, 115. *See also* Medical theory; Physicians

Bacon, Francis: and new science, 32; on scholastic science, 3; and on science and religion, 33

Bible: Exodus proscribes witches, 12; magic in Joshua, 12

Bier right (ordeal by touch), 49

Bishop, Goody, 80

Boyle, Robert. *See* Religion

Brattle, Thomas: astronomer, 5, n. 6; on Cartesian philosophy in trials, 74; member of Royal Society, 57; non-covenantal basis of criticism by, 106–7; opposes search for Devil's marks, 78

Browne, Sir Thomas: known in Massachusetts, 61; on witches' use of natural forces, 60–61. *See also* Medical theory

Cartesianism. *See* Descartes, René

Confession: of Elizabeth Johnson, 93; and execution of witches, 114; by heretics, 17; by Mary Parsons, 42; number of, in Massachusetts, 106; untrustworthiness of, 107, n. 44; viewed as rational, 103; witches' use of, to escape punishment, 76

Connecticut: witch's marks found in autopsy, 51–53, 110

Covenant, Puritan: and defense of insanity, 103–7; effect of crime on, 104–5; and Thomas Brattle, 106–7. *See also* Insanity

Dalton, Michael: describes witch's marks, 77–78; influences trials, 109; on medical proof of witchcraft, 64–65; on medicine, 111

Descartes, René: attack on Newton by Cartesians, 71–72; influence on medical theory, 59; influence in trials, 74, 76; mechanism of, and trials, 4

Devil: as source of witchcraft, 13; superstition as pact with, 15; Wardwell's covenant with, 40

Devil's marks. *See* Witch's marks

Dudley, Joseph, 22

117

Due process of law: example of, 75, n. 1; in witchcraft trials, 75–76

Edward II, King: and prosecution of Templars, 20–21
England. *See* English law
English law: criticized by George Gifford, 23; death penalty in, 102; early witchcraft cases, 18–19; felony, 101; heresy prosecutions, 18, 19–20, 21–22; insanity defense, 91; Massachusetts departure from, 6; punishment of heretics, 19; requirement of *maleficium* in, 18, 35–36; witchcraft acts, 35, 36
Executions for witchcraft: Alse Young (1647), 38; Ann Hibbins (1654), 39, 42, 80, n. 15; confession necessary for, 17; frequency of, 42–43; insanity defense in capital cases, 100; Margaret Jones (1648), 38; Mary Glover (1680), 39; Mr. and Mrs. Greensmith, 51; Mrs. Henry Lake, 38; Mrs. Kendall, 38; restricted in Massachusetts, 102; Samuel Wardwell (1692), 40; mentioned, 40

Galen (Claudius Galenus): contribution to human biology, 55–56; influence on colonial medicine, 56
Glanvill, Joseph: influence in Massachusetts, 28; proves possibility of witchcraft, 28, 29–30; reference to Copernican universe, 30; on witch's manipulation of natural forces, 62
Gloucester, Duchess of: charged with witchcraft (1441), 85–86
Glover, Mary: bewitches John Goodwin's children, 39; confesses, 93; declared sane, 94; harm produced by, 70; mental examination of, 93–94; mentioned, 40, 114

Griggs [Greggs, Gregg], Dr. (Massachusetts physician): diagnoses witchcraft, 67; medical theology of, 68, 69–70; not required to testify, 112; treats victims, 64

Harvey, William: discovers circulation, 56; and mechanism, 73; physiology of, 4; searches for witch's marks, 88–89; and vitalism, 71
Heresy: in bull of Pope Innocent VIII, 16; in England, 18, 19–20, 21, 37; and Inquisition, 17, 20–21; light punishment for, 14; and Lollards, 19; in Massachusetts law, 37; and Massachusetts witchcraft, 40; merges with witchcraft, 14–23 *passim*; prosecutions, 19–20; and prosecutions of witches, 14–15; related to witchcraft in *Malleus maleficarum*, 18
Hobbes, Thomas: epistemology of, 33
Hopkins, Mathew: and witch's marks, 78–79

Innocent VIII, Pope: bull of 1484, 17; and Inquisition, 16, 20
Inquests: of Elizabeth Kelley, 51–53; first Massachusetts case (1630), 45; empirical medicine in, 60; kinds of verdicts, 48; Massachusetts statute, 46–47; and murder verdicts, 50; natural death and witchcraft, 60–62; New Hampshire witchcraft verdict, 49–50; new science in, 56–57; report by Governor Winthrop, 49; sources of Massachusetts data, 48; supernaturally induced injuries, 52–53; theoretical basis for witchcraft verdicts, 62; witchcraft verdicts in England, 50
Inquisition: encompasses witchcraft,

5; in England, 20–21; in history of witchcraft, 17; Pope Clement V and, 20

Insanity: Ann Hibbins, 93; attitude toward, 98–100; in capital cases, 101–2; and confessions, 103; Cotton Mather's view of, 96; Dorothy Talbie [Talbye], 100–1; in English law, 91; examinations for, 113–14; examples of, 92; and human biology, 95–96; Margaret Jones, 93; Mary Glover, 93–94; Massachusetts law, 91–92; Mrs. Kendal, 93; Mrs. Lake, 93; as plea to avoid execution, 92–93; and role of lawyers, 101; role of reason, 94–98; routine examinations for, 115; theological views on, 97–98; treatment for, 96–97; in witchcraft, 102–7

Interdisciplinary Institute, ix–x

Jeremiad: as anticipation of witchcraft, 105–6

Jones, Margaret: accused, 84–85; charged with *maleficium*, 38; covenant obligations, 114; injury of victims, 63; medical criticism by, 111–12; as medical practitioner, 84–85; sanity of, 93; witch's mark, 81

Justice: in witchcraft cases, 114–15

Kittredge, George Lyman: historian of witchcraft, 11; on John Webster, 31; on *maleficium* in English witchcraft, 18; mentioned, 21, 36, 39

Lawyers: interdisciplinary education of, ix, x–xi; low status in England, 109; scientific training of, 115–16; and witchcraft cases, 109

Lea, Henry Charles (historian of the

Inquisition and witchcraft), 11; on Inquisition, 15, 17; mentioned, 13, 14

Locke, John: influenced by Newton, 72; medical theory of, 59–60

Lollards: and heresy, 19

Magic, illicit: Bible prohibits, 12; in Massachusetts cases, 12; punished by early Church, 14

Maleficium: affirmed by midwives, 84; bewitching of animals, 40 and n. 26; bodily pain, 40, 63; deafness and vomiting, 63; defined, 18; in England, 35–36; infection of foot, 40; in Massachusetts law, 37; medical treatment of, 64, 65–68; and natural forces, 29, 60–62; theory rejected, 73

Malleus maleficarum: authors, 16; on individualization of torture, 17, n. 16; on role of physicians, 64; on witchcraft, 18. See also Confession; Heresy; Innocent VIII; Inquisition

Maryland: autopsies in, 47; inquests in, 47; witch's marks in, 82

Massachusetts Charter: revoked, 37; witchcraft law after revocation, 41

Massachusetts law: constitutional law 7; courts, 41; on felony, 101–2; grand jury in, 41; protects strangers, 91–92; spectral evidence in, 76–77; on witchcraft, 36–37. See also Due process

Mather, Cotton: knew Glanvill's work, 28, n. 8; on Glover case, 39; on insanity, 96; on medical theology, 70–71; member of Royal Society, 57; rejects vitalism, 73; on science as evidence of God, 32–33; scientific status of, 70; on witch's marks, 78

Medical theology: Cotton Mather on,

Medical theology—*cont'd.*
70–71; diverse views on, 68–69; importance of, 68; perfunctorily acknowledged, 69; supported by Harvey and Newton, 71–72; views of physicians, 69–70

Medical theory: chemical physiology, 58, 59; empiricism, 59–60; European, in Boston, 5; Galenic orientation, 59; humoral, in inquests, 58; influence on magistrates, 111; mechanism, 58–59; treatment of witchcraft victims, 66–67

Medical training: apprenticeship, 53–57; first American medical school, 53; Giles Firman's anatomy, 46; Galenic outlook, 56

Medicine. *See* Medical theory; Medical training; Midwives; Physicians

Midwives: affirm *maleficium*, 84; area of expertise, 84; aware of new knowledge, 86; compete with physicians, 84, 90; criticized, 112; diagnoses of, 84; on female anatomy, 83–84; female quackery and witchcraft, 85; in intellectual life, 89; judgment sought, 83; Remy's caveat on diagnosis, 86; searches of Rebecca Nurse, 80–81

Murder, charge of: against Dorothy Talbie, 101–2; against Mary Parsons, 39; inquest verdicts, 50; and witchcraft in England, 50

New Hampshire: search for embryo in, 79; witchcraft verdict in, 49–50

Newton, Isaac: attacked by Cartesians, 71–72; impact on religion, 73; influence on Locke, 72; rejects materialism, 71–72 and n. 38; contribution of, 4

Nismath Chaim: in Cotton Mather's medical theology, 70; example of vitalism, 70–71; mentioned, 111

Ordeal by touch, 49

Pharmacopoeia: occult nature of, 85

Physicians: compete with midwives, 90; Dalton urges participation of, 64–65; declaration of witchcraft without treatment, 67–68; diagnose witchcraft, 66–67; diagnostic alternatives, 110–11; diagnostic skill compared with midwives, 89; distinguished from surgeons, 57; examine Mary Glover, 93–94; importance of skill, 68; inaccurate diagnoses, 73–74; issue search warrant to women, 79; *Malleus maleficarum* on, 64; and Margaret Jones, 84–85; Maryland inquests, 47; Massachusetts inquests, 48; and medical progress, 58; midwives compete with, 84, 90; quackery, 54–55, 112; relativity of diagnostic views, 114; reliance on judgment of, 54, 111; Remy's caveat on diagnosis, 86; summoned to relieve victims, 63–64, 65–68; treatment in Topsfield, 67; use of occult knowledge, 85; vitalism of, 71; and witch's marks, 78 and n. 10, 79. *See also* Anatomy; Autopsies; Medical theory; Medical training

Religion: and preservation of orthodoxy, 14; of Puritans, 5–6; scientific support for, 32–33

Retrials: of Ann Hibbins, 39; in disputed verdicts, 41–42; of Hugh Parsons, 42

Rossiter, Dr. Bryan: autopsy report of, 51–53, 62; demonological theory of, 110

Royal Society of London: and Joseph Glanvill, 28; Massachusetts correspondents, 5; Massachusetts members, 57–58; move to Connecticut, 5, n. 5; philosophy of, 3

Science: conflict among experts, 115–16; conflict with religion, 32–34; evidence of God, 32–33; and materialism, 73, 110; Newtonian science and religion, 73; Puritan acceptance of, 33–34; significance to law, 1–2; as threat to religion, 32; use of experts, 115
Scot, Reginald: refutes witchcraft theory, 31

Thorndike, Lynn: on causes of prosecutions, 15–16
Torture: *Malleus maleficarum* on, 17; in Massachusetts, 76
Trials, witchcraft: Court of Assistants, 41; disagreement on verdict, 41–42; indictment, 41; influence of Cartesian philosophy on, 74, 76; judge pressures for conviction, 81; opposition to, 26–28, 65; preliminary hearing, 41; pre-Salem cases, 9–10; role of science in, 2–3; significance of, 2–3; special court in 1692, 41; as superstition and insanity, xiii; testimony of Sir Thomas Browne, 60–61. *See also* Due process of law; English law; Massachusetts law

Vesalius, Andreas: *De fabrica*, 56; and Galenic anatomy, 55–56; influence on anatomy, 53–54; teaching technique of, 57
Vitalism: Harvey's description of blood, 71; and Newton, 71–72; Nismath Chaim, 70–71; witchcraft diagnosis, 110–11.

Weyer, John: contributions to psychiatry, 26; criticized, 27–28; opposition to witchcraft, 26–28; work in gynecology, 88
Witchcraft, history of: in Egypt, 11–12; and Inquisition, 17; punishments for, 13, 14. *See also* English law; Heresy
Witchcraft theory: as alliance with the Devil, 13; basis for belief in, 28; Cotton Mather on, 22, 23; Glanvill's proof of, 28–30; as insanity, 10; New York ministers on, 22; scientists' belief in, 25–26
Witch's marks (Devil's marks): absence of, 82; Ann Hibbins, 80, n. 15; Connecticut case, 81–82; criticized by Thomas Brattle, 78; described by Michael Dalton, 77–78; distinguished from natural growths, 83; formal responsibility for search, 79; identifiable by physician, 78 and n. 10; Maryland cases, 82; on men, 82, n. 24; physician's supervision of search for, 78; reports of searches for, 80, 83; Virginia cases, 82; William Harvey on, 88–89

Designed by Arlene J. Sheer

*Composed in Intertype Garamond (text) and Monotype Garamont (display)
by Monotype Composition Company, Inc.*

Printed offset on 60-lb. P & S R by Universal Lithographers, Inc.

Bound in Columbia Fictionette by L. H. Jenkins, Inc.

Too Good to Be True

Too Good to Be True

The Rise and Fall of Bernie Madoff

Erin Arvedlund

PORTFOLIO

PORTFOLIO
Published by the Penguin Group
Penguin Group (USA) Inc., 375 Hudson Street, New York, New York 10014, U.S.A.
Penguin Group (Canada), 90 Eglinton Avenue East, Suite 700, Toronto, Ontario, Canada M4P 2Y3
(a division of Pearson Penguin Canada Inc.)
Penguin Books Ltd, 80 Strand, London WC2R 0RL, England
Penguin Ireland, 25 St Stephen's Green, Dublin 2, Ireland (a division of Penguin Books Ltd)
Penguin Books Australia Ltd, 250 Camberwell Road, Camberwell, Victoria 3124, Australia
(a division of Pearson Australia Group Pty Ltd)
Penguin Books India Pvt Ltd, 11 Community Centre, Panchsheel Park, New Delhi – 110 017, India
Penguin Group (NZ), 67 Apollo Drive, Rosedale, North Shore 0632, New Zealand
(a division of Pearson New Zealand Ltd)
Penguin Books (South Africa) (Pty) Ltd, 24 Sturdee Avenue, Rosebank,
Johannesburg 2196, South Africa

Penguin Books Ltd, Registered Offices: 80 Strand, London WC2R 0RL, England

First published in 2009 by Portfolio, a member of Penguin Group (USA) Inc.

1 3 5 7 9 10 8 6 4 2

Copyright © Erin Arvedlund, 2009
All rights reserved

LIBRARY OF CONGRESS CATALOGING-IN-PUBLICATION DATA
Arvedlund, Erin.
Too good to be true : the rise and fall of Bernie Madoff / Erin Arvedlund.
p.   cm.
Includes index.
ISBN 978-1-59184-287-3
1. Madoff, Bernard L.   2. Swindlers and swindling—United States—Biography.   3. Ponzi
schemes—United States.   4. Commercial crimes—United States.   I. Title.
HV6692.M33A78 2009
364.16'3092—dc22
[B]   2009026093

Printed in the United States of America

To Patrick,

My Life Is Yours

Too Good to Be True

Introduction

O n the morning of March 12, 2009, Bernard Lawrence Madoff stood inside courtroom 24-B on the twenty-fourth floor of the Daniel P. Moynihan U.S. Courthouse in downtown Manhattan. Outside, a strong, wintry spring wind blew, but inside the air was stuffy and hot with tension. The seventy-year-old Madoff sat just past the wooden barrier that separated the public seating gallery. He did not look at anyone, just stared straight ahead, as everyone in the room and on the closed-circuit television watched his every move. Always impeccably dressed, Madoff wore a bespoke business suit in his trademark charcoal gray, paired with a lighter gray silk tie. He was flanked by four attorneys, two on either side of him. His longtime lawyer, Ira Sorkin, was seated on his immediate right, and another attorney, Daniel Horwitz, sat to his left. In front of Madoff and his lawyers were another table and chairs, full of federal prosecutors, but Madoff could see only the backs of their heads.

Just a few months before, Madoff had commanded the respect and admiration of Wall Street, of his wealthy friends and his charities, of his thousands of investors and believers. But on this day, he commanded nothing and no one, except his own voice. On this morning, at ten a.m. exactly, Madoff faced up to 150 years in prison on eleven criminal counts.

Madoff rested his fingers on the top of the table in front of him and occasionally took a sip of water from a glass. As U.S. District Judge Dennis Chin entered, everyone in the room stood, including Madoff, the phalanx of attorneys, dozens of reporters, and a court sketch artist. There was also a mob of angry Madoff investors, calling themselves "victims" and "casualties," who had come to seek vengeance on the man who had done them wrong.

"You wish to plead guilty to all eleven counts?" Judge Chin looked up matter-of-factly and spoke somewhat kindly to Madoff.

Nodding his head of wavy, pewter-colored hair, Madoff listened and answered calmly throughout Judge Chin's many questions and clarifications that followed: "You understand you are giving up the right to a trial? If there were a trial, you could see and hear witnesses, offer evidence on your behalf," and so forth. Judge Chin wanted to make sure this was what Madoff had chosen: to plead guilty, and thus not to cooperate with the government's investigation or to indict anyone else in his crime, the $65 billion Ponzi scheme that was proving to be America's largest financial fraud ever. No, Madoff didn't want a public trial; he didn't want to have to point the finger at anyone else. Given the scope of the charges against him, it was a stubborn move.

To each question, Madoff answered, "Yes, I do." Madoff was waiving his right to due process in a court of law. He was going to plead guilty and would alone admit to everything he was charged with, including securities fraud, mail fraud, wire fraud, money laundering, making false statements, and perjury.

And that was exactly how he wanted it.

Madoff's blue eyes looked weary and his expression resigned. No longer was he sporting that insane-looking smirk, the smile—of what? the unburdened?—that had incensed everyone who had seen him walking around freely while he was out on bail in the days after his December 11, 2008, confession and arrest. Now, three months later, the smirk had vanished. He began wringing his hands. One of the prosecutors in front of him, Acting U.S. Attorney Lev Dassin, stood up to address the court. "The charges reflect an extraordinary array of crimes committed by Bernard Madoff for over twenty years," Dassin said. "While the alleged crimes are not novel, the size and scope of Mr. Madoff's fraud are unprecedented." Assistant U.S. Attorney Marc Litt, the chief prosecutor in the case, then stood up and told the judge that Madoff could face up to 150 years in prison under federal sentencing guidelines.

Finally, it was Madoff's turn to speak. The room stilled.

"Mr. Madoff, tell me what you did," Judge Chin said.

Madoff had prepared a statement, which he read out loud from stapled paper pages. He took full blame. He wasn't going to cooperate with the prosecutors, wasn't going to help them out and bargain for leniency or a lesser sentence. He wasn't about to indict his family or anyone else for helping in this fraud—a fraud so large, encompassing more than four thousand client accounts, that even the Nobel Peace Prize winner and Holocaust survivor Elie Wiesel, whose charity had lost millions, had been driven to calling Madoff "a thief and a scoundrel" in public.

Madoff wanted everyone to believe that the crime was his and his alone—even though investigators suspected that his wife, his sons, his brother, and other relatives and top lieutenants helped carry it out.

Madoff's voice was a strange blend of Queens-accented Noo Yawk and a soft but firm monotone: "Your honor, for many years up until my arrest on December 11, 2008, I operated a Ponzi scheme. . . . I am actually grateful for this first opportunity to publicly speak about my crimes, for which I am so deeply sorry and ashamed. . . . I am painfully aware I have deeply hurt many, many people.

"When I began my Ponzi scheme, I believed it would end shortly and I would be able to extricate myself and my clients from the scheme. I am here today to accept responsibility for my crimes by pleading guilty and, with this plea allocution, explain the means by which I carried out and concealed my fraud. . . . I always knew this day would come. I never invested the money. I deposited it into a Chase Manhattan bank."

Madoff's statement took only about ten minutes, and while he spoke he did not turn to or eye the packed crowd in the gallery. When he finished, he sat down, and the courtroom broke out into a series of murmurs. Madoff would not have to spell out any details of his crime, nor would he implicate anyone else. There was just his guilty plea and no further explanation.

The tension crescendoed, for now it was time for three victims to make short statements. The first, George Nierenberg, took the podium and glared over at Madoff.

"I don't know if you've had a chance to turn around and look at the victims!" Nierenberg snapped.

Madoff then glanced over his shoulder, but Judge Chin admonished Nierenberg to return to the argument at hand. For what reason, if any, should the judge not accept Madoff's guilty plea, and not send him to jail?

A filmmaker whose family had lost everything, Nierenberg wanted to know why there was no conspiracy charge by the government—surely there were other people who had helped Madoff in his decades-long fraud who should be held accountable too. "He didn't commit this alone. I'm not suggesting that you reject the plea, but that there is another count to consider," Nierenberg said. Madoff had just said that the fraud had started in the early 1990s, but even the prosecutors disputed that claim, saying they thought it had started much earlier.

The second victim to address the court, Ronnie Sue Ambrosino, pointed out that the full extent of Madoff's crimes might never be uncovered if he was not forced to provide more information. Madoff's two sons, Mark and Andrew, and his brother, Peter, worked at the same firm too but had not been charged in the Ponzi scheme.

"Judge, I believe you have the opportunity today to find out where the money is and who else is involved in this crime," Ambrosino said. "And if this plea is accepted without those two pieces of information, I object to it being taken."

After the victims had made their statements, Judge Chin nodded and thanked them for speaking. Then he ordered Bernard Madoff remanded to prison. He would be sentenced three months later, in June 2009.

Applause broke out in the courtroom. The thief would not be going back to his million-dollar penthouse apartment on the Upper East Side of Manhattan, where he had been under house arrest for the previous three months.

Outside the courthouse, at 500 Pearl Street, near the intersection of Pearl and Cardinal Hayes Place, the people who had invested with Madoff felt eerily unsatisfied. Some got a small thrill from seeing and hearing the metal handcuffs click around Madoff's wrists as Judge Chin ordered Madoff to prison for the first time since his confession to the FBI.

"He wasn't speaking the truth. It was a disgrace to the court," said Brian Felsen, a twenty-three-year-old Minnesotan whose grandfather had invested with Madoff in the 1980s. "I'm happy my grandfather didn't live to see this. His life's work was stolen. He would have been horrified." Felsen's family had come to Madoff through Minneapolis-based money manager Michael Engler, a pillar of the local Jewish community who'd also been duped by Madoff. "To see Madoff in the flesh . . ." Felsen said. "It opened the wound."

Other victims couldn't have cared less that Madoff had pleaded guilty and would probably go to jail for life—the time he served would not repay the lives he hurt. Adriane Biondo of Los Angeles asked out loud on the sidewalk, among a crowd of reporters and Madoff victims, "Where's the money, Bernie?"

Where *was* the money? It was a question that everyone across the nation—and the world—had been asking ever since news of the scam had broken. Was it in London, where two of Madoff's longtime fund-raisers had set up an office? Was it in Switzerland, where Madoff had successfully courted Swiss banks like Safra Bank and Edgar de Picciotto's UBP? Was it in Asia, even, where Madoff had traveled in a desperate last bid to raise money before the scam unfolded?

Just three months earlier, Bernard L. Madoff had been relatively unknown outside of the close-knit circles of Wall Street. Now Madoff was a household name, a verb meaning "to rip off," as in, "I was Madoffed." His name was now equated with a crime bigger than Enron, bigger than WorldCom, bigger even than those of Charles Ponzi himself, the man whose name would grace the type of scheme that Madoff had taken to a whole new level. Madoff's crime spanned the world and involved tens of billions of dollars, all of which had seemingly vanished overnight.

Among financial traders on the Street and within the halls of the Securities and Exchange Commission (SEC), the government agency that regulates financial institutions, Madoff had been a prominent figure for decades. "Bernie," to those who knew him well, and his brother, Peter, had made names for themselves in the 1970s and 1980s by starting a then-revolutionary electronic trading business. Their system, which allowed them to buy and sell stocks in seconds—instead of hours or even days—helped promote a onetime backwater exchange known as the NASDAQ. Today it is one of the largest trading venues in the world. Aside from a few close associates, few of Madoff's Wall Street contemporaries ever suspected that he was at the same time pulling off one of the greatest cons in history.

Madoff had also made a name for himself in Washington, D.C., and specifically on Capitol Hill, as a generous donor to both Republican and Democratic election campaigns and as an aggressive lobbyist for stock market restructuring. Wall Street regulators knew Madoff because, as an expert on market structure and trading, he sat on committees and volunteered as an adviser to the SEC. At elite beach clubs in Palm Beach and Los Angeles, ski resorts in Switzerland, and aristocratic dinner parties in London, Madoff was highly sought after, but only a few actually knew him. "Bernie," as he was also known to his investors, would manage your money and promised a guaranteed 10 percent, even 12 percent or higher, annual return—as long as you didn't ask any questions.

Until his arrest in December 2008, however, Madoff was relatively unknown outside the financial world. It wasn't until he admitted to his massive $65 billion fraud scheme over the course of—potentially—several decades that Main Street began to take notice.

Overnight, America came to know Bernard Madoff as a man living a life of luxury and deception—not just for months or years, but possibly for his entire adult life—paid for with other people's money. It quickly became apparent that much of the vanished money had never existed except on paper. The numbers represented profits that Madoff told investors he had made for them, when in fact he had spent the money they had given him and not invested it at all. The exact amount of actual money lost may never be known. What we do know is that, for decades, Madoff looked his investors in the eye with a smile, shook their hands, and never showed any indication—let alone remorse—that he was robbing them blind. He fooled his closest friends and family, as well as hundreds of university endowments, charities, and pension funds; he stole people's hard-earned savings, their futures, and their dreams by faking investment returns under the cover of a legitimate Wall Street firm. And when he was caught, there was little recourse for his victims because, by then, the money had disappeared. Such is the nature of the pyramid scheme.

Madoff's crime, painstakingly carried out over many years, was audacious but based on a simple premise: he paid earlier investors with later investors' money. This type of scam was made famous in America at the turn of the twentieth century by Charles Ponzi. Although he was not the first to engage in the practice, Madoff expanded the scam across decades and on a multibillion-dollar scale. The effects of Madoff's lies rippled across the globe, and when he was exposed, investors around the world wondered how he could have managed such a vast fraud for so long without regulators catching on, despite numerous red flags and warnings.

This is one of the many revelations that infuriated Madoff's victims. How did regulatory agencies such as the SEC or FINRA (the Financial Industry Regulatory Authority), which are charged with monitoring financial institutions, fail to notice that one man was operating the largest Ponzi scheme in history? The SEC has said it found no evidence of foul play at Madoff's firm, but there were plenty of warning signs that something was amiss.

In the spring of 2001, I first heard about Bernard Madoff while working for *Barron's* magazine. Several of my contacts mentioned his name to me and told me he was a hotshot in the hedge fund world, churning out consistent 15 percent annual returns on investments despite fluctuations of the market. Like legendary hedge fund managers George Soros and Julian Robertson, Madoff supposedly ran a $6 billion hedge fund, but unlike Soros or Robertson, Madoff's performance numbers never seemed to show up in any of the usual databases or magazines. Strangely, Madoff asked his investors not to tell anyone he was managing their money; investors were intensely loyal to Bernie and were willing to keep their money with him for years. But others I spoke to were wary of Madoff and said his investment strategy did not make sense; even experts in his so-called strategy couldn't duplicate his returns. After no luck getting an interview, I phoned his office one more time to say the story was running anyway. Suddenly, he was made available. Over a scratchy international phone line, Madoff told me he was in Switzerland; I asked Madoff how he was able to accomplish his amazing returns. "I can't go into it in great detail. It's a proprietary strategy." Madoff further dismissed skeptics who tried to reverse-engineer his secret formula, saying they "didn't do a good job. If he did, those numbers would not be unusual." He sounded untroubled, affable, and didn't tell me much of anything.

In May of that year, my article on Madoff ran in *Barron's*. It quickly became watercooler fodder in Wall Street circles as it questioned how Madoff could be making such great returns using a strategy that other investment professionals could not replicate. Unfortunately, despite the buzz generated by my article, the SEC, Madoff's investors, and others connected to the scam turned a blind eye. Madoff continued to recruit unsuspecting clients around the world.

I was not alone in my suspicion of Madoff. A week before my article ran, Michael Ocrant, a reporter at the industry publication *MAR Hedge*, published a similar story asking the same questions. His article received the same response: immediate buzz but otherwise a surprisingly lackluster reaction by those who could have intervened. Harry Markopolos, a financial analyst who had been introduced to Madoff's firm in 1999 and was familiar with the strategy Madoff said he used—known as the "split-strike conversion"—realized that Madoff was running a fraud and made it his mission to expose him for the thief he was. Unfortunately, despite Markopolos's years of attempts to out Madoff—including warning the SEC on multiple occasions—Madoff continued to fly under the radar.

Madoff's story is not just that of a financial mastermind and criminal. It is a complex, ever-changing, and expanding tale of a fraud of unprecedented proportions. How did Madoff defraud so many of his clients? How did human nature and his investors' willingness to delude themselves play a role? In a sense, the fraud was a vast, unwitting conspiracy among Madoff, his colleagues, family, friends, and investors. The conspiracy perpetuated a fantasy. Madoff promised returns that were too good to be true, and everyone else conspired to believe his unbelievable promises. Madoff was a master illusionist.

There are many frustrating questions looming over *l'affaire* Madoff. Why would one of Wall Street's icons create a web of so much deception and rob so many people of what would amount to billions of dollars of their money? Why did Madoff's investors put all their financial eggs into one basket, including what they'd intended to bequeath to children and grandchildren? Why did so few people heed the warning signs that were evident all around Madoff? What motivated Madoff? Was one month of losses enough for him to start faking returns? What was the turning point, the moral line of demarcation between just some lax business practices and a much larger betrayal? Was Madoff a good person covering up a bad decision, or was he a lifelong sociopath? Who helped him perpetuate the fraud: his family, the feeder funds who enabled him, or people inside the regulatory agencies? Are there other

Madoffs in the hedge fund world, and if so how can they be found out and stopped? Perhaps one positive to come out of this breathtaking crime is that secretive hedge funds will be dragged out into the light for public scrutiny, and there will be fewer shadows where crooks like Bernie Madoff can hide.

—Erin E. Arvedlund
June 2009
erinarvedlund@yahoo.com

Chapter One

At just after eight o'clock on the morning of Thursday, December 11, 2008, FBI agent Theodore Cacioppi and another agent presented themselves to the doorman at 133 East Sixty-fourth Street in Manhattan. Outside on that gray morning, the twelve-story prewar apartment building on New York's tony Upper East Side didn't stand out as special, but inside the space reeked of money. Just past the outside awning and entrance is the lobby, replete with leather chairs and live orchids, understated and sumptuous. The wealthy tenants don't want or need to advertise their affluence, but their prosperity and lives of luxury are obvious. In the past, the building, between Lexington and Park avenues just three blocks east of Central Park, had housed its share of famous tenants, including heirs to the writer Henry James. The residence was profiled in an issue of *The New Yorker* in 1927, the year of its construction. Today the famous occupants, several of whom are billionaires, range from Wall Street tycoons to Matt Lauer, the crooked-smiling anchor of the *Today Show*.

The older couple that Agent Cacioppi and Agent B. J. Kang were about to meet had lived in the building since 1984, when the wife smartly purchased the palatial spread in the midst of a New York real estate bust. Today the agents took the elevator to the penthouse apartment, 12A, the couple's $8 million, ten-thousand-square-foot home.

Agents Cacioppi and Kang didn't have to wait long at the door. They had been expected. The FBI had been summoned to the apartment after the New York branch received puzzling phone calls the evening before. The two sons of the man who lived in apartment 12A had contacted federal officials to turn their father in. They had asked their lawyer to contact Wall Street regulators, who then called New York's Southern District prosecutors, who then alerted the FBI. The sons had made emotional statements, claiming that their father, Bernard Lawrence Madoff, a pillar of Wall Street, was a fraud.

It sounded like a joke. Cacioppi didn't know exactly what to believe. The suspect's sons claimed their father had defrauded his investors and family members out of $50 billion, possibly more. If that was true, the man who lived in this splendid apartment was the biggest con artist in history. But as the agents emerged from the elevator, it was hard to imagine this penthouse was the home of a thief and a swindler.

Bernard Madoff answered the door wearing pajamas, slippers, and a pale blue bathrobe. He let the agents in.

"Do you know why we're here?" Cacioppi asked Madoff. "We are here to find out if there is an innocent explanation" for the strange summons the agency received. They spoke to the older man somewhat quietly now since they were all standing inside the apartment.

Madoff paused, then said, "There is no innocent explanation."

Madoff went on to say that everything his two sons, Andrew and Mark, had told law enforcement was true. His investment advisory business, a hedge fund he had supposedly been running from an office one floor below his brokerage firm in an upscale midtown building, was a fraud. The brokerage business, Bernard L. Madoff Investment Securities, which he, his brother, and his extended family had built up since 1960, was legitimate, but the hedge fund was "a lie" and "a giant Ponzi scheme."

Madoff claimed he was broke. His clients were penniless too. There was no money left of the estimated $50 billion in assets Madoff had been overseeing for more than four thousand client accounts.

Cacioppi wasn't anticipating this. It was going to be one hell of a busy day. He hadn't expected a full confession or to have to arrest Madoff on the spot. Usually these kinds of high-end criminals stonewall as long as possible.

But Madoff had just spilled his guts. He had admitted to stealing billions of dollars from and lying to his family, friends, colleagues, clients, and Wall Street regulators for nearly a quarter of a century. The agents had no choice.

"You're under arrest," Agent Cacioppi said before he read Madoff his rights. Agents Cacioppi and Kang brought Madoff downstairs and their team drove the onetime Wall Street legend to the Southern District prosecutor's office downtown. Agent Cacioppi left in a separate car. He needed to speak to Madoff's two sons to swear out a complaint against their father. In the complaint, Andrew and Mark Madoff were listed anonymously, saying only that Madoff had confessed the night before to "senior employee 1 and senior employee 2."

Madoff had his reasons for confessing. He very likely had seen this day coming, and once his sons turned him in for securities fraud, he would be arrested by the Feds. He might escape state prison, or the dreaded Rikers Island, New York City's infamous jail. He would be eligible for bail and potentially house arrest. If he did go to prison, Madoff could end up in a federal facility, which might be more comfortable than a state one. His lawyer, Ira Sorkin, had advised it. Sorkin was worth all the money Madoff paid him over the years. He had gotten Madoff out of scrapes as far back as 1992. They were old friends.

Later that afternoon, after the stock market's four o'clock close—and the end of a daylong plummet on the Dow Jones—Michelle Caruso-Cabrera, a pretty brunette news anchor on CNBC business television, asked Wall Street to "stop what you're doing for one second. . . . Bernard Madoff has been arrested." The legendary pillar of Wall Street had crumbled.

Bernard Madoff was born at the dawn of World War II, on April 29, 1938, the second child of Ralph and Sylvia Muntner Madoff. He grew up near the Atlantic Ocean in New York City, in the town of Laurelton, Queens. Throughout his adult life he would have homes near the sea. Over the years, the mansions he and his wife, Ruth, bought became bigger and more expensive, but apart from the Manhattan penthouse, all of them were a stone's throw from the water.

Eventually, Bernard and Ruth would spend their summers at an oceanfront retreat in Montauk, at the far eastern tip of Long Island. They wintered in a $9.4 million Palm Beach, Florida, house that had once been owned by the Pulitzer family. Palms, banyan trees, and bougainvillea surrounded the estate, and an asymmetric stone swimming pool occupied the backyard. Sometimes the Madoffs, who rarely spent time apart, would spend weeks at a villa in Cap d'Antibes in the south of France. But this opulent lifestyle came decades, and hundreds of millions of dollars, after Bernie's early years in Laurelton.

———

Though Madoff became synonymous with abundant wealth, he came from a relatively humble background. When he was growing up, in the 1940s, Laurelton was a town of twenty-five thousand people, many of them immigrants looking to move up and out of the area. Laurelton resembled other middle-class American towns, except that its residents spoke either Yiddish or English with a thick accent. Today Laurelton is still a neighborhood of immigrants, but it is the languages, patois, and accents of the West Indies, Haiti, or elsewhere in the Caribbean that fill the air.

Bernie Madoff's paternal grandparents, Solomon David and Rose Madoff, emigrated to the United States in 1907. Solomon Madoff, who went by the name David after his move to America, was born in 1882 in the town of Pshedbersh, located on the shifting boundary between Russia and the Austro-Hungarian Empire (today it is part of the Czech Republic). Rose was born in Sopooschna, Russia. David and Rose married and fled tsarist Russia in search of a better life together. They arrived in New York via Hamburg, Germany, on May 11, 1907, aboard the steamship *Graf Waldersee*. In his U.S. naturalization petition, David listed his wife, Rose, and his three children, Abraham, Zookan, and Broocha, all born in Pennsylvania. Mr. Julius Segal and Mr. Louis Shiffman were the witnesses who signed the Madoffs' 1913 petition for naturalization, submitted in U.S. District Court for the Middle District of Pennsylvania in Scranton.

"It is my intention to become a citizen of the United States and to renounce absolutely and forever all allegiance and fidelity to any foreign prince, potentate, state or sovereignty, and particularly to Nicholas II Emperor of all the Russias," David Madoff attested in his petition. According to 1920 U.S. census records from Pennsylvania, Madoff's grandparents listed their birthplace as Russia and their mother tongue as Hebrew. David's occupation was listed as "laborer" and Rose was not employed outside of the home.

David and Rose resided for several more years in Lackawanna County, Pennsylvania. They had a fourth child, a daughter they named Rae, moved to New York City, and were living in the Bronx by the time the 1930 census was taken. They once again listed Russia as their birthplace, but then crossed that out and wrote, "Warsaw." The borders back in Europe continued to shift.

David, who was now forty-eight years old, wrote that he worked as a tailor in wholesale clothing. Their second son, Zookan, who would become Bernie Madoff's father, was now nineteen years old and known as Ralph. He was an assistant manager in the wholesale jewelry business.

During the Great Depression, Ralph Madoff married Sylvia Muntner, and together they had three children: Sondra, Bernard, and Peter. Sylvia's parents came from equally humble beginnings. Her parents had been born in Austria and Romania and also emigrated to the United States; her father, Harry, was the proprietor of a bathhouse, according to the 1930 Manhattan census. Ralph and Sylvia settled in Laurelton, Queens, in the 1950s.

Despite its proximity to bustling Manhattan, Laurelton is a rather isolated place. During Bernie's early years, it did not have its own subway stop, so there was no easy access to the lifeblood and transport network of New York City's five boroughs; its only rail connection was a station on the Long Island Rail Road's Atlantic Avenue branch. Today most of Laurelton is crisscrossed by highways that are lined with strip malls, giving it a semi-industrial feel.

But when Bernie Madoff and Ruth Alpern, the woman who would become his wife, were growing up in Laurelton, it was much more pastoral. Nearby Far Rockaway Beach provided a perfect venue for relaxation. The sand dunes stretched so far back that one classmate of Madoff's, Carol Marston, recalled riding horses on land that would be paved over for runways at Idlewild Airport, later renamed the John F. Kennedy International Airport.

Jay Portnoy, a childhood friend of Madoff's, had rich memories of their grade school years at Public School 156. In an interview with the *Saratogian*, the local newspaper of Saratoga Springs, New York, where Portnoy now lives, he recalled how Bernie and his best friend, Elliot, created a social club called the Ravens. They even had sweaters with the Raven emblem. "This club was the status organization for my age group," Portnoy said. "There was a counter-popular club. . . . This club was called the Maccabees. I was one of its earlier members." Both clubs met in the Laurelton Jewish Center, across the street from PS 156. The Maccabees club was comprised mostly of Jews; the Ravens were pretty much split between Jews and non-Jews.

In the fall of 1951, Portnoy was invited to join the Ravens. He was surprised by the invitation but he eagerly accepted. "The Ravens had a reverse quota system," he explained. "Since they were housed in a Jewish synagogue, the Ravens always had one more Jew than non-Jew. This way they could justify their presence as a Jewish organization. If a popular Gentile was wanted as a member, they had to search for a less popular Jew to invite." Only decades later did Portnoy realize that this was probably the reason he was drafted. He was being used by Bernie Madoff and Bernie's best friend.

In the 1950s, the area had only one high school, Far Rockaway High School, and students from a few surrounding towns, including Laurelton, commuted daily by bus or train to attend classes. The beachside town of Far Rockaway had an aura of life without crime or concerns. Think *Happy Days* meets *Beach Blanket Bingo*. Life in Far Rockaway was lovely and clean but exceedingly strict. Children could play on the sandy boardwalk, but they enjoyed summer days and nights under watchful eyes. If kids even sat on the boardwalk railing, a local beat cop would tap their knees with a nightstick and roust them off. Bungalow houses dotted the side streets from Beach Twenty-fifth to Beach Forty-sixth streets.

Nora Koeppel, a student at Far Rockaway High School during the same years as Bernard Madoff, recalled the area and her morning commute by bus to the school, which was located just a few blocks from the beach. "In those years, even at the age of twelve, you could catch a bus on Rockaway Beach Boulevard, which would take you to Central Avenue in Far Rockaway. . . . [After school] you could go to the movies at the Strand or Columbia Theater or to the bowling alley, which was above the stores. Of course the day also consisted of going to the Pickwick luncheonette for a snack. The Rockaways were always safe and fun. Rockaway Playland, Fabers Fascination, the boardwalk, the pool at the Park Inn Hotel on Beach 115th Street were places we all frequented."

As a teenager Bernie was slender and sometimes wore glasses. He began his years at Far Rockaway High School in 1952. At the time, it was considered one of the best high schools in New York City. Its notable alumni include three Nobel Prize winners—Baruch S. Blumberg, Richard Feynman, and Burton Richter—as well as the financier Carl Icahn and psychologist and advice columnist Dr. Joyce Brothers.

At Far Rockaway, Bernie joined the swim team, the Mermen, his sophomore year. Since most of the meets were held right after school, his friends sometimes stayed after class to watch him compete. Bernie usually swam as part of the medley relay, doing either the butterfly or the breaststroke. Portnoy said he recently found a 1954 issue of the Far Rockaway newsletter, *The Chat*. "It mentioned that the Mermen finished their season with a 4–4 record, but also noted that Bernie's medley team had won their last two contests," Portnoy said. Bernie learned discipline from his swim coach, who then hired him as a lifeguard at the Silver Point Beach Club in Atlantic Beach, Long Island.

Harry Colomby was a favorite teacher among students at Far Rockaway. Colomby, who eventually left teaching for Hollywood, noted that there were other far more illustrious graduates of Far Rockaway. Colomby said that all he remembered of Madoff was that "the kid was on the swim team."

Some of Madoff's high school contemporaries paint him as a Zelig-like figure, a chameleon. "Bernie was around when we were in school. But nobody seemed to know him," said Sanford "Sandy" Elstein, who graduated in 1955. "I wasn't the most popular guy. I was in the band, had a lot of friends who were with the 'in' group, so to speak. But nobody remembers this guy."

The people who do remember Madoff remember him as a bright guy who didn't work too hard. Fletcher Eberle, cocaptain of the swim team, who'd applied for the lifeguard job that Madoff got, told the *New York Daily News*, "The Bernie I knew was a good-natured, happy-go-lucky guy, always smiling and kidding, who swam the butterfly very well and never got overly serious. . . . If you had said to me that Bernie was going to be chairman of the NASDAQ and make all this money, I never would have believed it possible."

Jay Portnoy and Madoff were in the same music and English classes. "We rode on the train together and sometimes sat together," Portnoy said. "There was a group of nine or ten of us who would do things. I wasn't his best friend by any means. He was a bit above average, but he wasn't an honor student. When it came to studies, at least at that time, he wasn't going to his full potential." Portnoy recalled a particular English class in which each student was scheduled to give an oral book report. Prior to their presentation, Madoff took a quick look at Portnoy's book and pronounced it "boring . . . hardly any pictures." Bernie was one of the first to give his report. Even though he had apparently not read any book, he wasn't visibly concerned. He smoothly announced his title as *Hunting and Fishing*, by an author no one had ever heard of, Peter Gunn.

Classmates snickered but quickly suppressed their laughter, because, according to Portnoy, "no one really wanted to see Bernie fry." Madoff smoothly went through his book report, explaining that he didn't have the book in hand because he had returned it already to the public library. "Perhaps the teacher saw through it. . . . She was less than a decade older and pretty sharp. But nobody could really get mad at Bernie. He had a put-upon Charlie Brown persona that carried him through."

But Bernie's hijinks didn't end in the classroom. He volunteered as a locker room guard as part of his student service assignment. The 1956 Far Rockaway High School yearbook lists only two school activities next to Bernie's name: varsity swimming and "locker guard." The yearbook photo shows Bernie dressed neatly in a patterned jacket and sideways-striped tie, presenting an uneven smile.

"He would tell his buddies how dumb most of [the guards] were and how they liked to play 'punch for punch'—hitting each other in the fists until one gave up," Portnoy recalled. "Bernie himself often showed bruised knuckles. When asked about it, he ventured that he could not let the idiots think he was chicken." Bernie and Elliot rushed for a fraternity near the end of their sophomore year in high school. "They thought the hazing was stupid, but felt that they wanted to prove themselves," Portnoy explained.

Another one of Bernie's favorite hobbies was cruising—a favorite 1950s pastime meaning driving around looking at girls, *American Graffiti*–style. At that time, New York State allowed seventeen-year-olds to apply for junior driver's licenses as long as they didn't venture into New York City. Bernie, Elliot, and two neighbors got their junior driver's licenses near the beginning of senior year. Each took turns driving to school. They would take the back streets of Laurelton and Rosedale to reach Nassau County, drive down Peninsula Boulevard to the New York City line, and then take back streets to school. "We would park about two blocks from school so as to make sure none of the teachers would see us," Portnoy said.

During the fall of 1955 and into the winter of 1956, Portnoy and

Madoff's group of friends formed an amateur football team called the Long Island Spartans. Bernie's father was the coach. Bernie often played quarterback and defensive end. They played on the grass apron between the Belt Parkway and its parallel service road, Conduit Boulevard, near the Aqueduct Racetrack. While they chalked the outer boundaries of the playing field, there were no yard lines. Portnoy, who was small and had terrible vision, was the linesman.

But the best diversion turned out to be girls. At graduation time, fellow 1956 graduate Judi Asch was pleased that Bernard Madoff signed her Dolphin yearbook and wrote on the page with his picture: "I really think that every school should have you. But I'm too selfish to give you up. Lots of luck & happiness to the greatest. Bernie."

Madoff clearly liked Asch, but he had already set his sights on someone else: his future wife, Ruth Alpern, from the class of 1958. A few months before he graduated, in June 1956, Bernie started seeing Ruth. Portnoy and other old friends described her as "a very pretty petite blond with green almond eyes. Elliot thought she was an airhead, but she was no more so than most fifteen-year-old girls. Perhaps Elliot was a bit envious of being displaced by Ruth in Bernie's attentions."

Following high school, Bernie went to the University of Alabama but left after just one year. Stan Hollander was a year ahead of him at Alabama and a member of Sigma Alpha Mu, or Sammy House, when Madoff pledged that fraternity. Bernie was "shy, vanilla, very quiet—and by vanilla I mean no flavor, no excitement. Why he came to Alabama, I don't know. Our house was very popular, more eastern pledges than southern." Among the Jewish fraternity houses on campus, such as Alpha Epsilon Pi, Kappa Nu, and Zeta Beta Tau, "Sammy, of all the frats, was the best one of the group. He got into the pledge class, even though he didn't really know anybody, and then he left a year later." Stan Hollander said he was surprised that Madoff, who was basically a social wallflower at the fraternity, would work so hard to get in and then leave. "I couldn't understand it. He spent a whole year trying to get in, pledging, swinging in, and then, *boom*, he left." Bernie returned to New York.

Back in New York, Bernie enrolled at Hofstra College. Jay Portnoy remembered an incident while he was a student there that he believes in retrospect hinted at what was to come.

It was in early 1958, and Bernie was giving Portnoy a ride to a card game. There was snow on the streets and parked cars on either side of a narrow driving lane. As Portnoy recalled, Madoff was driving about forty miles an hour. Because of the conditions, Portnoy said, "I would have driven much slower, perhaps twenty miles an hour. And I said, 'Bernie, why are you going so fast? You could nick one of the parked cars.' He replied that the vehicle had the same width at forty miles an hour as at a lesser speed, and so he wasn't increasing the risk of crashing." Madoff was right about the width of the car, but in Portnoy's opinion, he was discounting the fact that at the higher speed there was a better chance he would crash and the resulting damage would be greater.

Bernie's youthful misdeeds and lapses in judgments didn't necessarily portend a life of crime. Lots of high school kids drive recklessly and fudge their way through book reports and go on to become good citizens. But Portnoy's take on Madoff many years later was that "he showed pride of appearance, willingness to deceive, [and] no fear of the eventual consequences when there was a good chance of success."

Bernie Madoff graduated from Hofstra with a degree in political science in October 1960. Earlier that year, in March, he had passed the Series 7 licensing test that would allow him to work in securities, and the month after he graduated he founded his Wall Street firm. Madoff nurtured a misperception that he had actually graduated from law school after college, but in fact Bernie left the law to his younger brother, Peter.

Peter joined his brother's firm in 1970, after earning his undergraduate degree from Queens College and his law degree from Fordham Law School. "When Bernie was working next door to me, I remember Peter would come in and do stuff while he was still in college," recalled Michael Murphy, who worked at Martin J. Joel brokerage, another small firm with offices next door to Bernard L. Madoff Investment Securities.

Madoff himself helped foster the myth that he had a law degree. He even alluded to attending law school on his company's Web site in 2008, which stated that he founded the firm "in 1960, soon after leaving law school." Michael Allison, chairman of International Business Research, a due diligence firm specializing in hedge funds, confirmed that Madoff took some classes but never graduated from law school. It was a small but significant lie, and also a red flag. "One of the flags of

[his] fraud is that investors assumed some law school training or that he was a lawyer," Allison said.

Bernie Madoff and his future wife, Ruth, grew up in the same neighborhood and commuted to the same high school, but she had a more outgoing and studious reputation than he did.

Like Madoff, Ruth grew up in a family of recent immigrants who had arrived in America at the dawn of the twentieth century. Ruth's paternal grandmother, Beile Alpern, hailed from a town called Jedwadne, which was then part of tsarist-era Russia but is now located in Poland. Beile arrived in New York in 1905 at the age of thirty on a steamship called the *Manchester*. On the journey she carried Ruth's father, Israel, also known as Sol, in her arms, as he was just a year old. Beile spoke Yiddish, and the ship's manifest indicates that she was bound for East Liverpool, Ohio, her passage already paid by her husband and father. But instead, the Alpern family ended up regrouping in New York.

Sol Alpern grew up in New York and eventually married Sara, with whom he had two daughters, Joan and Ruth. On the Far Rockaway High School reunion Web site, Joan Alpern recalled moving to Laurelton in 1950, when she was in the eighth grade. Sol Alpern founded his own accounting firm in midtown Manhattan with his partner, Sherman Heller, and they did business as Alpern & Heller from the respectable address of 10 East Fortieth Street, not far from Grand Central train station.

In high school, Ruth worked on the school newspaper and was a member of Phi Delta Gamma, a Laurelton-area sorority, according to sorority sister Marion Sher. The sorority was a social club that included Laurelton students from other high schools, most of whom were Jewish. Ruthie, as she was known by friends, was sociable and preppy. During her senior year, she earned the designation Josie College, a flattering nickname implying that this bright girl would go on to be successful. After graduation, Ruth enrolled at Queens College and graduated with a degree in psychology.

Bernie Madoff and Ruth Alpern were married the Saturday night after Thanksgiving in 1959. It was a traditional Jewish wedding at the

Laurelton Jewish Center. Bernie and Ruth started out as many young couples do—with very little. Their first home was a modest one-bedroom apartment in Bayside, Queens.

Far Rockaway graduates of the Madoffs' generation still get together for reunions—but not at the high school anymore. Today the place where they grew up could not be more different than it was in the 1950s. Far Rockaway is now mostly impoverished, and the high school is no longer a paradise where kids come and go safely and innocently, or flit between classes and the local candy store. Upon entering the high school building, a masterful William H. Gompert architectural design that was one of hundreds of high schools New York City constructed in the 1920s, visitors encounter a sign posted on the right-hand wall: THERE IS A NO-WEAPONS POLICY AT THIS SCHOOL. New York Police Department officers patrol the hallways and carry guns.

Most of the high school reunions these days take place somewhere far away. In November 2008, Bernie Madoff accompanied Ruth to her fiftieth reunion at a swanky hotel in Fort Lee, New Jersey. According to Karen Lutzker, a schoolmate of Ruth's, the Madoffs were treated like rock stars. A few months later, however, the hundreds of photographs posted on the class reunion Web site would include only one of Ruth Madoff, and that one a side view of her talking to someone else. You couldn't see her face.

At the reunion, just a month before Bernie's arrest, everything about the couple shined like gold. Ruth reflected on her and her husband's success in the Far Rockaway memorial booklet. "I graduated from Queens College in 1961," she wrote. "[Bernie and I] worked together in the investment business he founded. We have 2 sons, 5 grandchildren. After spending some years in the family business, I went back to school to study nutrition and received a masters from NYU. During that time I co-authored *Great Chefs*, only available on eBay these days. I travel and hang out with my grandchildren. I'm on the board of Queens College, and the Gift of Life Bone Marrow Foundation."

By 1959, Sol Alpern had enough money to help his young newlywed daughter and son-in-law. Bernie had some money saved from his stint as a lifeguard and also from a summer job installing sprinklers, but he needed more, so he took a $50,000 loan from his in-laws to start Bernard L. Madoff Investment Securities in November 1960.

"The only time I was in debt was when I borrowed $50,000 from my wife's parents to start my own firm, and I paid that back," Madoff would later boast to Credit Suisse and other investors. At the time, $50,000 was a lot of money, so it was no small feat for a struggling college graduate to pay it back. A decade later, his brother Peter would join the firm.

Stan Hollander, Bernie's fraternity brother at the University of Alabama, heard over the years that Bernie and Peter had started an electronic brokerage and trading firm. Hollander himself worked on Wall Street for two different firms, Gruntal & Co. and Ladenburg Thalmann, in corporate finance. He recognized that the two Madoff brothers were on to something, by taking advantage of the speed offered by computers to make money. "Prior to electronic trading, people who wanted to buy and sell stock had to go down to a human broker on the trading floor, who would charge, say, a one-dollar bid and a three-dollar ask, or selling price. That was an enormous spread, enough for brokers to make a lot of money," Hollander explained. Madoff capitalized on that two-dollar spread, or difference, and offered to execute trades faster and more cheaply than other brokers. Eventually, he also capitalized on the use of computers to set up a completely automated trading desk—*sans* human beings—which put him way ahead of his time.

Hollander claims he has a nose for frauds and prides himself on avoiding them. He had been introduced to Jordan Belfort, who went on to start the bucket shop Stratton Oakmont, the inspiration for the movie *Boiler Room*, and Barry Minkow, who also acquired a white-collar criminal record. But unlike those two, Hollander admits, he did not suspect anything dubious about Madoff.

As early as the 1970s, the Madoffs were starting their ascent to royalty status in New York social circles. At the time, Hollander was friends with the Wilpons, future owners of the New York Mets. "According to them," Hollander said, "the Madoffs could do no wrong." Other mutual friends in Hollander's circle said they were making 2 percent a month investing with Madoff.

Around the time that Bernie was starting up his business on Wall Street, his mother, Sylvia, was running a brokerage firm named Gibraltar

Securities. The broker-dealer firm was registered in Sylvia's name and listed at her and Ralph's home address until the SEC forced her to shut it down, in 1963.

Technically, a broker is an agent who executes orders on behalf of clients, whereas a dealer acts as a principal and trades for his or her own account. Because most act as both brokers and principals, the term "broker-dealer" is commonly used to describe these firms. Not only was it strange to be running a brokerage firm out of their house, but the Madoffs had no background on Wall Street. What's more, in an era when most women didn't work outside the home, it was especially unusual for a woman to work in the securities trading business. Some suspected it was a front for her husband.

Sylvia Madoff closed her business after the SEC ran a sweep of "bucket shops," as these small operations were known. The agency announced in a statement issued in August 1963 that it was "instituting proceedings . . . to determine whether" forty-eight broker-dealers, including "Sylvia R. Madoff [doing business as] Gibraltar Securities," had "failed to file reports of their financial condition . . . and if so, whether their registrations should be revoked."

An SEC litigation release a month later announced hearings in the case of Sylvia Madoff and many of the other firms. But in January of the following year, the SEC abruptly dismissed all the administrative proceedings against a number of the firms, including Sylvia's. "The firms conceded the violation," the litigation release noted, "but requested withdrawal of their registrations; and in this connection they represented that they are no longer engaged in the securities business and do not owe any cash or securities to customers. The Commission concluded that the public interest would be served by permitting withdrawal, and discontinued its proceedings."

Apparently, the SEC had struck a deal: if these little storefront operations and their suspect operators agreed to get out of the business—and stay out—the SEC would let them off with a warning.

So Sylvia Madoff wound down her career in the investment business, just as her son Bernie was building his.

It appears that as early as the 1960s Bernie Madoff was building two businesses. The one he registered with the SEC, the broker-dealer firm

Bernard L. Madoff Investment Securities, was the one that executed stock trades. But Madoff had another business that was growing in its shadow. Thanks in part to the bragging of his father-in-law, Sol Alpern, Madoff quickly developed a reputation as a savvy investor. Alpern told everyone how successful his son-in-law was, and soon people were giving him money to invest for them.

Bernie Madoff's early investment clients were friends and relatives in the New York Jewish community. For many years, Ruth's parents vacationed in the Catskills, a favorite spot for many Jewish families of that era. For them, the Catskills represented the American dream and was a reward for all their hard work in the hot city. It was a place to get away and enjoy leisure time in a natural setting, far away from the asphalt jungle they called home. Not only did the Catskills foster a sense of physical refuge, but the socializing there also allowed these first- and second-generation immigrants to feel like they were really fitting in, assimilating into America at the same time they were building bonds within their own community. There were more than five hundred retreats, including children's camps, hotels, and other summer getaway spots, similar to the one immortalized in the Hollywood film *Dirty Dancing*. Wives and children trekked to the mountains sometimes for the whole summer while husbands took the train up on weekends and worked during the week.

The Alperns stayed at the Sunny Oaks Hotel, in Woodridge, New York. Sunny Oaks was a collection of wooden bungalows where many families would return year after year. Guests became like family to one another. The hotel was owned by the Arenson family, and over the years the Alperns and the Arensons became close friends. According to Cynthia Arenson, who inherited the property from her parents (it closed in 1999), Sunny Oaks naturally became "fertile ground" for Madoff. Eventually, even Cynthia came to invest with Madoff's firm, as had her parents, who had been referred by their good friends the Alperns. Cynthia's father was a retired attorney, and many of his friends were retired teachers. The Arenson family was hardworking but not wealthy, and they provide a perfect example of Madoff investors who were not high-fliers but average Joes and Janes just trying to hold on to and increase their nest eggs.

Sol Alpern told anyone who would listen that his son-in-law had a firm on Wall Street and that "he was doing very well," Arenson told

Bloomberg News. "Wouldn't you encourage your friends to invest with him? Sometimes they got 18 percent, sometimes they got 19 percent" annually in returns. Many of Madoff's early investors were retired, and their accounts, which ranged from $5,000 to $50,000, were puny by Wall Street standards.

Madoff's name was synonymous with "bank," according to David Arenson, Cynthia's stepson, who wrote about his family's involvement with Madoff on his blog. Most of the Arenson family had Madoff accounts, and over the years so did many others who stayed at Sunny Oaks. Investors with Madoff "radiated out through the guest population, through our distant relatives and the distant relatives of guests. I can think of a dozen people I know" who had invested at least $5 million all together, David recalled. "Madoff had wormed his way into the system to such an extent that everyone felt comfortable with him."

But Sunny Oaks was only the first of many vacation spots on the emerging recruiting circuit for Madoff investors. Later they would come from country clubs in Palm Beach, near Boston, and in the Hamptons, from churches and synagogues in Florida and New York, Minnesota and Los Angeles. Each of these were places that fostered an atmosphere of trust, which helped soothe prospective investors.

Meanwhile, the Alpern & Heller accounting firm was thriving, and as new clients came in Sol would tell them what a great investment manager Bernie was. Soon Sol and Sherman were having trouble keeping up with all of the work coming their way. To help handle their growing business, they hired two young accountants named Frank Avellino and Michael Bienes. The two young men were roughly the same age as Madoff, who also sometimes helped out around his father-in-law's office.

Eventually, nearly everyone in the accounting firm started referring clients to Madoff. Frank Avellino began recruiting clients in 1962, according to the SEC. Bienes started fund-raising for Madoff in 1968.

Starting in the 1960s, and continuing over thirty years, Alpern, Bienes, and Avellino would refer, or raise directly, nearly half a billion dollars' worth of business. That money was promptly filtered to Madoff, Avellino and Bienes instructing their customers to open a brokerage account with Bernard L. Madoff Investment Securities. The accounting firm raised money for Madoff by promising investors fixed returns of between 13.5 percent and 20 percent a year on their money. The accountants would then give their investors' money to Madoff, who usually paid them at an even higher rate. They paid themselves by keeping what was left after giving investors the agreed-upon return. They were acting as money managers, as investment advisers, although they were not licensed to do so.

The name on the door of the accounting firm would change over the decades, but the investment operation inside never did. All told, over a period of thirty years, continuing until 1992, when the SEC stepped in to stop the practice, the accounting firm had raised $441 million from roughly thirty-two hundred people. In exchange, the investors got promissory notes and usually their returns sent to them quarterly in the form of a dividend check. Many were retirees living off the quarterly checks.

This was to be the template for all of Madoff's future fund-raising: friends and family were guaranteed a certain return on their money annually, and, pleased and grateful, they were converted into an instant sales force. Who better to refer new clients than current satisfied clients? They came with indubitable references and glowing reports about the young Bernie Madoff. Sometimes the people who referred clients to Madoff took a commission. Sometimes it was disclosed; other times, it wasn't. What people didn't know wouldn't hurt them.

It's unclear if Sherman Heller knew that the rest of his accounting firm was so eagerly raising money for Madoff. Heller died on December 8, 1967, leaving behind his accounting practice, a wife, and three children. In an obituary, Sol Alpern wrote that "members of the firm of Alpern and Heller record with sorrow the passing of an esteemed colleague and friend and extend heartfelt sympathy to the bereaved family."

After Heller died, Sol took his old partner's name off the firm. He made the two young men his new partners, and the firm became known as Alpern, Avellino and Bienes. Sol Alpern retired at the end of 1974, and by the 1980s the accounting firm Alpern & Heller had fully changed hands and become Avellino and Bienes, according to court records filed by the SEC.

In 1981, the successor firm, Avellino and Bienes, was sued for a shoddy audit, unrelated to their work for Madoff. Avellino and Bienes

was a certified public accounting firm in New York City and was hired
by M. Frenville Co. as an independent auditor and accountant. As
part of its duties, Avellino and Bienes prepared certified financial statements of the company for fiscal years 1978 and 1979. In July 1980,
creditors of Frenville filed an involuntary petition for bankruptcy
against the company under Chapter 7 of the Bankruptcy Reform Act of
1978. In January 1981, creditors also filed involuntary petitions under
Chapter 7 against two principals of the company, Rudolph Frenville,
Sr., and Rudolph Frenville, Jr.

More important, the company's lenders argued that Avellino and
Bienes had signed off on financial statements that did not reflect the
company's true failing health. The banks Chase Manhattan, Fidelity,
Fidelity International, and Girard International filed suit in the Supreme
Court of New York on November 16, 1981, against the firm, alleging
that Avellino and Bienes "negligently and recklessly prepared the Frenville financial statements, that the statements were false, and that because of their reliance on the statements, the banks had collectively
suffered losses in excess of five million dollars."

In a 2009 documentary about the Madoff scandal on PBS's *Frontline*,
Bienes admitted he never asked questions about how Madoff generated
his returns but insisted that Sol Alpern had reassured him that the securities industry was so highly regulated he didn't need to worry.

"Sol, his father-in-law, had been doing it," Bienes recalled. "One
of the first things Alpern said to me when I went to work for him
was: 'Listen, you got money, you can invest it with my son-in-law,
Bernie. You'll get 20 percent.' Well, I didn't have any money, and I
wasn't even thinking 20 percent—I didn't even know. But then, a few
short years later, my wife had saved up $5,000, and she says, 'I want to
open an account with Bernie.' And he let her do it. And she started with
$5,000."

With Madoff's guarantee of 20 percent or more, they pocketed a few
percentage points, and by the 1980s the two accountants were pulling
down $10 million a year just for passing on money to Madoff. The two
men never questioned how he was making his returns.

"I was gonna walk in and say, 'Bernie, let me see your books'? He'd
show me the door," Bienes said. "He was my income. He was my life.

How could I do such a thing? First of all, Sol once said, 'He is in the most heavily regulated industry in America.' And I knew that the SEC investigates brokerage houses, and I knew that NASDAQ did. So who am I? Who am I to say, 'Bernie, show me your books'? And if he did, what would I know? What would I see? How could I judge? How could I figure it out? I had no way."

Chapter Two

B ernie Madoff didn't need to be a crook. This was one of the things that most stunned Wall Street when the truth came to light. The fraud was huge, by far the largest financial scam in history. He had stolen billions of dollars from thousands of investors, and he had managed to keep it going for probably three or four decades. The crime was spectacular in many, many ways, but nothing about it was more shocking than the fact that Bernie Madoff was the man who did it.

In the world of stockbrokers, Bernard Madoff was a real, legitimate big-league player. He and his brother had built from scratch one of the most successful broker-dealer firms in New York. The Madoffs helped create what is known as the "third market," or the trading of stocks outside of the primary New York Stock Exchange and American Stock Exchange, by making trades faster and cheaper for other brokers and investors. Their firm executed trades on millions of shares every day, receiving a commission on every one of them. In addition, the firm had a highly successful—and profitable—operation making trades for its own accounts.

Bernie Madoff was a very astute businessman. He had started out as a tiny operator in a tiny part of the market for public companies that didn't qualify for trading on either of the established stock exchanges. But, by recognizing before many others the possibilities for computerized trading and by bold marketing, he was able to build Bernard L. Madoff Investment Securities into one of the largest stock traders on Wall Street. He wasn't a big-name retail broker like Merrill Lynch or Charles Schwab, and in fact very few people on Main Street, outside the world of investments, had ever heard of him. But those in the business, those who needed fast, inexpensive stock trading, knew just where to go. Bernie Madoff was the man.

He grew to be rich and powerful and highly respected in many circles. He didn't need to resort to crime to be successful. So why did he do it? Looking back, we can compare him to a World Series–winning baseball slugger taking steroids—he didn't need to do it, but it helped.

Every business has a first big client who gives them credibility in the marketplace. For Madoff, this client was Carl Shapiro. When Shapiro first came to Madoff in the 1960s, Madoff was a young stock trader with almost no reputation on Wall Street. Shapiro had made a fortune in the garment industry as the founder of Kay Windsor, a women's dress design and manufacturing company. Kay Windsor's shares had been listed for public trading by 1961, and Shapiro had made even more money. He came to Madoff via the same route as many other Madoff clients: through a friend. Shapiro had money to put into the stock market and reportedly wanted to do some arbitrage trading, which required the ability to move in and out of positions quickly. Madoff offered Shapiro a tempting proposition: he would clear Shapiro's trades in just three days, which at the time was an unheard-of turnaround time on Wall Street. Shapiro gave Madoff $100,000 to start an account.

In the 1960s and into the early 1970s, everything on Wall Street was done manually, in person or over the telephone, and recorded on paper. At most brokerage firms back then it could take weeks to execute a simple stock trade. And only the little brokerage firms even bothered to do any trading in stocks for tiny companies, listed on what were called "pink sheets." (Pink sheets got their name because the list of the companies and the brokers who traded them were printed on pink paper.) Brokers who traded these pink sheets, or over-the-counter (OTC) stocks, like Madoff did, would call around to three or four different firms to get a quote and find a buyer or seller for their clients' stock. Afterward, they would hand a completed trade ticket to a young, often teenaged, "runner," who would then take the ticket to the back office for the necessary paperwork and mailing of stock certificates. Credit Suisse CEO Oswald Grübel, who started as a trader in 1970, recalled in an interview with Bloomberg that, for orders taken over the phone, "every word you said on the telephone was a contract—you had to deliver on that. You learned very quickly that you have to be careful when you open your mouth, when you make promises, when you do business, because you have to deliver."

The whole process could take days—or even weeks—and the system was ripe for fraud. For instance, it was impossible to tell if customers who called up and "sold" their shares for cash actually owned the stock (it was akin to a homeowner claiming he or she had a house to sell, and then delivering an empty lot). As late as 1969, the National Association of Securities Dealers (NASD) had to pass a rule "penalizing members for failing to deliver securities sold for clients within five business days." NASD president Richard Walbert warned broker-dealer members not to sell shares from the initial public offerings of newly listed companies for their customers unless they actually had the securities in their possession. Wall Street trading shared many characteristics with the Wild West.

It's hard to comprehend now, in the age of twenty-four-hour global exchanges, but back then Wall Street closed every Wednesday, just to deal with the onslaught of paperwork that would pile up throughout the week. "You kept track of your trading positions on a long piece of paper," recalls E. E. "Buzzy" Geduld, co-founder of Herzog Heine Geduld, a competing brokerage firm. Geduld also served on industry committees with Bernie Madoff over the years.

A postal strike in 1970 made matters even worse. In 1971, the SEC put yet more pressure on brokers by passing a new rule that required them to provide immediate notice "by telegram" to their clients if they were unable to keep records up-to-date. "Good firms were going out of business because they couldn't handle the order flow, and people did everything by hand. They couldn't handle the paperwork," said Michael Murphy, who started his career as an over-the-counter trader. His pink sheet brokerage firm, Martin J. Joel, had offices next door to Madoff's, and the business was later absorbed by Bernard L. Madoff Investment Securities.

With this archaic system in place, trading just couldn't be done more quickly. Carl Shapiro couldn't find a broker to trade as quickly as he wanted—until he met Bernie Madoff, who embraced then-fledgling technology and promised Carl Shapiro that he could make the trades and deliver securities in just three days.

Once Shapiro became a client of Madoff's, word of the hustling young broker's quick turnaround time spread. Others in Shapiro's social circle began lining up to trade with Madoff, and new clients begat new clients. After all, they figured, if Shapiro was so rich, he must know something about making money—and about who to trust with their fortunes.

Bernard L. Madoff Investment Securities was instrumental to the establishment of today's computerized, electronic stock market operations. Initially, BLMIS was a purely manual and telephone brokerage business. It quoted bid and ask prices via the National Quotation Bureau's pink sheets and executed transactions on behalf of clients. But very rapidly, the firm embraced technology to disseminate its quotes, and it started focusing on electronic trading.

In 1971, NASDAQ, a computerized communications web that would come to compete against the New York Stock Exchange and the American Stock Exchange, was established. It started quoting bid and ask prices, as well as total daily volume, for the tiny over-the-counter public companies that weren't listed on either exchange. NASDAQ, which stands for National Association of Securities Dealers Automated Quotation system, wasn't a single physical facility, as an exchange is, but a nationwide electronic network of broker-dealers. And broker-dealers could use the network not only to show prices of pink sheet stocks, but also to trade them. Madoff incorporated NASDAQ trades into his business early on.

Then, another boon came Madoff's way: the National Market System (NMS), which was mandated by the Securities Acts Amendments of 1975 to stir up competition in U.S. equity markets. "The SEC was told by Congress to bring more transparency to the marketplace," said Peter Chapman, a longtime correspondent for *Traders Magazine*. No one knew what prices were for over-the-counter stocks; the pink sheets were quoted only once a day. The NMS, on the other hand, quoted prices from several sources in real time, making it easier to trade more efficiently.

Contrary to popular wisdom on Wall Street, and among his many investors, Madoff did not invent the NASDAQ. He did take advantage of it, though. When it was formed, Madoff was a small broker hustling for business, and his was one of the original five broker-dealer firms that joined the NASDAQ system in the early 1970s. It was only later that he became active within the organization, largely because it helped his business and gave him face time with regulators.

Chapman interviewed Gordon Macklin, the creator of the NAS-DAQ, before Macklin died in 2007. "Madoff made it sound like he was Al Gore inventing the Internet, like he invented NASDAQ," Chapman said. But, according to Macklin, Madoff was not on any of the early NASDAQ committees in the 1960s. "Bernie was around, but in the 1960s he was just a young guy trying to make it in a world of big firms," Macklin explained. "He wasn't a major player. Certainly NAS-DAQ was a big help for him. He and his brother were technologically savvy, so certainly that aligned his interests with those" of the SEC and regulators trying to induce competition.

When Madoff did get involved, Peter DaPuzzo, who headed the over-the-counter trading for Shearson at the time, sat on NASDAQ trading committees with him. DaPuzzo recalled that "just creating a real-time market on computer screens for OTC stocks was a very big deal." Not only that, but NASDAQ created a window into real-time prices, which forced broker-dealers like Madoff and Shearson to compete with one another. "It legitimized the OTC market, made NASDAQ into a real market, and ultimately NASDAQ trading volumes became even bigger" than the NYSE and AMEX by the 1980s.

Madoff ultimately joined the NASD National Market System Design Committee in 1979, and headed the design committee again from 1981 to 1983. Madoff took an active role in the discussions that led to the creation of the Intermarket Trading System. Subsequently, the Intermarket Trading System (ITS) exploded onto Wall Street. It was an order-routing system linking all the country's backwater regional stock exchanges with the NYSE and AMEX. "The Madoffs survived in the horrible times during the 1970s because they adopted the technology a lot sooner than everybody else," said Michael Murphy, who rose from his roots at the small over-the-counter brokerage firm Martin J. Joel to head Wachovia Securities' institutional client business.

This was the major leap. The ITS was the network Madoff needed to bring his revolutionizing touch to the trading of stocks and other securities. It also made him look good to regulators, since he was encouraging competition in the market. And the policy of becoming "helpful, so to speak, followed him throughout his career," Chapman added. "Some people on the Street are expected to do that. The way it works is that if you're a prominent industry person, at a big firm or a small one, you get involved. He became much more involved than anyone."

Madoff's work on market structure consisted of helping to devise a set of rules that would dictate how brokers and exchanges were to work together. Aside from his promotion and use of NASDAQ, noted Chapman, "what made Madoff popular with regulators was the desire of the SEC to introduce competition to New York Stock Exchange–listed stocks. The SEC didn't like the monopoly. It wanted to blow the doors off and bring about better markets, more liquid markets, and benefit American consumers with better prices" for stocks.

Bernie and Peter Madoff quickly adopted the SEC's agenda as their own. After Congress passed its mandate in 1975 to crack the exchanges' monopoly, the SEC had to come up with a way to make that a reality, and the Madoffs embraced setting that agenda, taking on the task for themselves. They decided to trade, to make markets, in stocks that up until then had only been traded on the centuries-old New York Stock Exchange and the American Stock Exchange. The NYSE, or Big Board as it is also known, had an arcane rule, Rule 390, which stipulated that if you were a member of the exchange—like, for example, Goldman Sachs— you could not make markets in listed shares—say, IBM—anywhere off the floor of the NYSE during the hours that the market was open.

So the only broker-dealers who could make a market in IBM, or any other NYSE-listed stock, off the exchange floor were those who were *not* members of the exchange. This rule presented a stumbling block in the SEC's quest to get rid of the NYSE's monopoly on exchange-listed public companies. But Madoff helped circumvent that rule by telling the SEC he would show them the way to create a so-called third market for NYSE- and AMEX-listed shares. "The SEC loved him for that," Chapman said. "His and the SEC's interests suddenly aligned."

Madoff had always been somewhat of an outsider, but now he was capitalizing on that outsider status. Madoff was not a member of the NYSE and so the rule did not apply to him. "Bernie was a competitor to the exchanges—no doubt about it," said a compliance officer at a competing specialist firm. "Initially he and his operation were not perceived as a threat—only in hindsight. But Madoff probably was the death knell to old exchanges like the AMEX."

Eventually, Madoff also became a regional specialist through his involvement with the Cincinnati Stock Exchange, a regional exchange that could also compete with the NYSE, so Madoff was helping the SEC in two different ways: first, by trading listed stocks "off board" as a market maker, and, second, by trading heavily through competing regional exchanges.

In the late 1980s, *Forbes* ran a glowing story about Madoff in which it described a *Star Wars*–like atmosphere at Madoff's midtown offices. "Unlike in most trading rooms, where negotiations are still done largely by telephone, the phones hardly ring," the article said. "When they do, it is for orders of over 3,000 shares, which are negotiated. Anything under 3,000 shares, that is to say 95 percent of the orders, is handled by their computers. An order comes in from computers at Charles Schwab & Co. to buy 3,000 shares of IBM, for instance. Madoff's computer software system, designed by his younger brother, Peter, 43, director of trading, automatically sells the stock at the best 'ask' price in the markets and sends a confirmation back to Schwab untouched by human decision or hands. Time elapsed: 4 seconds."

The computer executions lowered Madoff's costs, but that wasn't the only advantage. Peter Madoff had also built the computer programs to show his traders various ways of hedging, or offsetting the risk, in their trading positions as well as the costs if they decided not to hedge. All that information can be had on a handheld BlackBerry today, but at the time Madoff's system was far more advanced than anything even the specialists on the trading floors had.

On the ten-year anniversary of NASDAQ, in 1981, the *New York Times* asked NASDAQ president Gordon Macklin what made the system different from the exchanges. "There are a number of differences," he said. "But the central one is our system of competing market makers, rather than a single specialist, as the exchanges have. The average NASDAQ company has eight dealers making markets in its security."

The NASDAQ, in which Madoff specialized, was a breeding ground for small growth outfits—like Carl Shapiro's Kay Windsor—that might one day make it big. When they did make it big, those companies might move their trading symbol and list on the more prestigious AMEX or NYSE. But by 1981, more than three thousand companies had their share prices quoted in NASDAQ, more than the combined total—about twenty-five hundred companies—listed on the New York and American stock exchanges.

Madoff's vision of electronic trading crystallized just as trading in

NASDAQ issues was exploding. He and Peter decided that the computer age and Wall Street would finally meet on the customer end as well. They invested heavily to make good on this vision, and soon they were making the SEC's agenda of competitive markets a reality. By the mid-1990s, the regional exchanges, plus the third-market dealers like Madoff, had lured away from the NYSE and AMEX almost 10 percent of all trading in shares listed on those exchanges.

By 1986, the magazine *Financial World* listed Bernie Madoff as one of the top one hundred best paid on Wall Street, estimating he had earned $6 million that year. Aside from being very rich, he was a man ahead of his time. Before most people on Wall Street had really grasped the power and speed of electronic stock trading, Madoff had automated his trades using computers. At least a decade before the Internet made electronic commerce possible—before eBay, Amazon, online dating, Google, and Facebook—Madoff was creating an electronic commerce network for stocks. Frank Christensen, a friend of his, remembers Madoff discussing his plans for the big technology purchase of IBM computers that would help his firm trade faster than other market makers on Wall Street.

What made Bernie Madoff so revolutionary? Before he helped to create the third market, people who wanted to buy and sell stocks that were listed on either the AMEX or the NYSE had no other choice but to trade through the exchanges' antiquated auction systems. They had to call a person, a broker on the exchange trading floor, who, under exchange rules, was obligated to post a "bid," or buying price, and an "offer," or selling price. Once the floor trader had quoted his customer a bid and an offer, an auction took place. What Madoff developed was completely different from the auction market. He wasn't a member of either the AMEX or the NYSE—nor did he want to be. He wanted to help create a "dealer market," a marketplace outside the confines of the old physical buildings—outside the AMEX on Trinity Place and the NYSE on Wall and Broad streets, both in lower Manhattan. Madoff existed in a place where all the dealers, all the buyers and sellers could meet in the ether, in the computerized NASDAQ network, rather than in person. In this new system, traders weren't always regulated the same way. "We all knew Bernie, because he was running a third market," said Dale Carlson, a former Pacific Stock Exchange executive. Essentially,

Madoff had built his own alternative exchange, with the SEC's blessing. "He was running an exchange without being an exchange," Carlson added.

Madoff wanted to build up his trading volume, and he was able to do that by attracting orders away from the AMEX and NYSE. To that end, his next bold play was to pay customers to attract their orders. That was revolutionary too—paying customers for their business? Madoff gave clients a small but perfectly legal rebate of one cent a share. This was so-called payment for order flow, a sort of financial thank-you to the client for sending the transaction to Madoff instead of to another firm. Madoff aimed to make money on every trade he executed—buying shares at one price, selling them at a higher price, and pocketing the difference. The more trades he executed, the more money he made. So, it was good business for him to increase his trading volumes, even if he had to pay customers to come to him. Payment for orders was the second idea of Madoff's that would become standard operating procedure decades later on Wall Street.

By the 1990s, the NASDAQ was completely electronic, and regulators could barely keep up with the changes. Trading became so heavy and out of control that a scandal involving NASDAQ price manipulation erupted in the mid-'90s. The animal that the SEC had pushed to compete with the old exchanges was taking advantage of its customers. Congress issued a report examining how the system could be cleaned up, and roughly thirty firms settled with both the Justice Department and class action investors. (Madoff wasn't named or implicated in any of the government or civil suits.) NASDAQ, founded as the anti-exchange, had itself become corrupt.

Meanwhile, the traders over at the NYSE were furious at the competition. Richard Grasso, who was president and then chairman and CEO of the NYSE from 1988 to 2003, would call big customers of the NYSE and ask them, "'Why are you trading off board?' There was a lot of pressure" from him, Chapman recalled. By dint of his persuasion and his sometimes thorny personality, Grasso was able to keep much of the volume on the NYSE.

Still, the Madoffs ingratiated themselves whenever and however they could. They would make themselves available to journalists. At first Bernie and Peter were the public faces of the firm, but by 1999 and 2000 their roles on the broker-dealer side and the trading desk were slowly being handed over to Bernie's sons, Mark and Andrew. Both sons were taking more prominent roles, and they too were eager to help journalists and regulators and appear at conferences. "They weren't one of the giants, so everything they did was good for their business, like having a public face, and a forum," Chapman recalled. And because they were so willing to talk, they were able to help "set the market structure agenda. It is a very complicated subject, and all the politicians needed people like him to explain it clearly."

Madoff's relationship with the SEC had grown quite cozy during the 1970s and early 1980s, when the agency was grappling with how to implement more competitive markets, as one former SEC lawyer who worked there attested.

"I was in the market regulation division at the SEC," said this lawyer, who'd started working there in 1979 as the agency was still grappling with implementing regulatory changes. "The SEC was struggling with how to create a National Market System, and the NYSE still had a monopoly on trading," the attorney recalled, referring to the challenge posed by Congress's 1975 legislation mandating that the agency foster the development of a national market system to trade stocks. NASDAQ was a fledgling, and AMEX was the backwater. Companies who listed on either graduated to the NYSE "as soon as they could get out."

So Madoff offered to help. "He came in to the staff [at the SEC] and said, 'I can show you how to do it,'" said the lawyer. "I heard Madoff spoken about at the SEC in hushed tones as a wonderful guy. Everybody knew he was coming in to feather his own nest, but he was going to bring more competition, to invigorate NASDAQ market makers, to break down the restrictions. He was a master at cultivating the SEC staff so that he was a beneficiary."

To the SEC, Madoff was "a great American. He was amazing at cultivating the staff on a day-to-day basis. And to his credit, on the market-making side he was an honest dealer. He helped create a legal trading environment" for stocks. "It was that sort of working relationship over the years—that's why the SEC staff thought he was so wonderful." In truth, "Bernie was very shrewd at matching his agenda with the SEC's," the former agency lawyer added.

Madoff extended his spirit of volunteerism elsewhere. At the influential Securities Industry Association, Bernard Madoff sat on the trading committee and was the go-to person for questions on market structure. "He was a statesman, a peacemaker who really understood this stuff like nobody did," said a former SIA employee. After the terrorist attacks on September 11, 2001, the SIA's offices at 120 Broadway in lower Manhattan were a disaster. The air reeked of burning metal and debris. Madoff offered the SIA some space in his midtown Manhattan offices. "We all figured it was just typical of Bernie to offer."

Over at the NYSE, Richard Grasso, naturally, was increasingly furious that Madoff was stealing business. Grasso had risen to be chairman and chief executive of the New York Stock Exchange after being hired by the exchange as a floor clerk in 1968. The exchange was his life. Grasso felt that Madoff had the regulators eating out of his hand—and to some extent, he was right. Napoleonic and forceful, Grasso argued that trading in NYSE-listed stocks off the exchange floor "would happen over his dead body," according to the SIA employee.

"Grasso once came to speak at the SIA. He shook everybody's hand and called everyone by name. He was a real smooth guy." Then Grasso reached his last handshake of the group: Bernie Madoff. Like two mafia dons, Madoff and Grasso stood up, faced each other, said nothing, then hugged as they smiled. They knew everybody was watching them.

On the broker-dealer side of the firm, the Madoffs were making a killing. Their most significant weapon in the battle against the traditional way of trading stocks was a large computer sitting in the middle of Chicago. It was from there that Madoff revolutionized stock trading.

Madoff believed in computers and realized that the business needed to move past its old-fashioned ways. The Madoffs' automated system would accept any order, check out prices in the marketplace, and turn the order around in just a few seconds. That was pretty advanced, considering their major-exchange rivals had ninety seconds to send an order down to the exchange floor into the trading pit crowd. A customer might get a better price on the NYSE, but they would get an order filled faster with

Madoff. "It was the difference between going to 7-Eleven and paying more for convenience," said Peter Chapman, "or going a mile down the road to the supermarket, where the price might be cheaper."

In a 1993 story in *Wall Street & Technology*, Roger Hendrick, vice president of marketing at the Midwest Stock Exchange, said flat out that the chief threat to the old way of doing things was "the emergence of the Cincinnati Stock Exchange." The Cincinnati Stock Exchange, originally founded in 1885 in Cincinnati, had been pretty much defunct by the time Madoff came along. Under the leadership of Bernie Madoff, it closed its physical trading floor and became an all-electronic stock market in 1980. The Cincinnati Stock Exchange wasn't a place—it was a box, a computer.

Madoff essentially took the old jalopy and turned it into a starship. Cincinnati still had an old license allowing it to be an exchange, and that was what Madoff wanted. With the Cincinnati license, he constructed a supercomputer through which he could route trades completely electronically, without a single human being intervening. "He's carved out his own business niche," said Dave Mainzer, a spokesperson at the Midwest Stock Exchange, which lost order flow to Madoff as a result of his black box.

The Cincinnati system was completely automated, without a trading floor or specialists. By using the Cincinnati system, Madoff finally became a member of a stock exchange—albeit a computerized one. This gave him access to the Intermarket Trading System, which he had helped develop several years prior. In 1995, the Madoffs and the other Cincinnati members voted to move the black box to Chicago. By that time, the Chicago Board Options Exchange had struck a membership deal with the Cincinnati exchange, and Madoff's bet on the little jalopy had paid off.

In the finance world, the ITS was the precursor to the Internet. It was an early electronic network linking all U.S. stock exchanges, including the five regional stock exchanges—Midwest, Cincinnati, Boston, Philadelphia, and Pacific—to the New York, American, and NASDAQ exchanges. It allowed orders to be routed from one exchange to another exchange, to whoever was offering a better price.

At first, the system was limited to so-called 19(3)c stocks, comprising securities issued after April 1979. Under this restriction, Madoff would not have been able to trade blue-chip companies that went public prior to 1979—such as IBM, AT&T, Eastman Kodak, or General Motors. (Eventually that ban was lifted.)

Competitors argued that another reason Madoff joined the Cincinnati exchange was because the trading rules were more lenient. Bernie and his brother, Peter, never stated that this was the case, but they believed in the concept enough to invest a large amount of their own money—roughly $250,000—to update the Cincinnati exchange. Needless to say, floor brokers, whose jobs the computer would eliminate, did not welcome Madoff's improvements to the system.

Still, Madoff managed to convince forty-eight Wall Street firms to become members, link up to the Cincinnati Stock Exchange black box via terminals in their offices, and start trading. Volume totaled sixty to seventy million shares daily by 1985—a respectable amount of traffic. Madoff even publicly acknowledged that the investment community would resist the concept of totally automated trading. "The politics of trading off the exchange floor has been hard to overcome," he said in 1986. "The very concept of a floor is to keep the business in one place. Allow trading off the floor, and that business is threatened." In 1987, NASDAQ Workstation software was introduced that allowed almost any personal computer to serve as a trading terminal.

The heart of Madoff's technological success was inside his own firm—the Madoff Integrated Support System (MISS), an automated trading system designed by TCAM Systems Group, a New York systems integrator. The system, conceived in 1983 and customized to meet Madoff's business requirements, was completed in 1988. Madoff trading rivals like Knight Trading and D. E. Shaw later asked TCAM to build similar systems for them.

Meanwhile, the computerization of stock trading in America and the rest of the world was outstripping the ability of regulators to keep up. Junius Peake, a onetime professor of finance at the University of Northern Colorado's Monfort College of Business, noted that "the quantum leaps made in technology have made decentralized trading, away from a physical exchange floor, not only possible but far preferable. You could even be at home and see all bids and offers—from anywhere in the world—on your computer screen, but regulatory barriers imposed on the trading systems by the SEC and the self-regulators have prevented this from happening," he told *Wall Street & Technology*.

Even by 1993, nearly two decades after Congress's 1975 call for a national market system, a true, full link between all exchanges still did not exist. But it was getting closer. Still, the patchwork of rules and regulations guaranteed a degree of chaos, and that meant that a professional intermediary remained involved in the trading process. "The present systems cost investors billions of dollars a year, which could be readily saved by moving to automated decentralized trading systems," added Peake, who also worked on Wall Street for four decades and had been governor and vice chairman of the NASD.

Armed with the technology to trade faster, cheaper, and longer, Madoff next went after order flow—by paying for orders to come his way. Madoff paid other brokers and customers one cent per share to allow him to execute their retail market orders—a highly controversial practice. Madoff wasn't the first to pay for order flow, but he did popularize it openly. Basically legal kickbacks, Madoff's payments for order flow rapidly brought him business.

In the 1980s, prices for stocks were still quoted in fractions of a dollar, often in eighths, or 12.5 cents. If a stock was trading at thirty dollars a share, for instance, a trader might see a bid price of 29 7/8 and an offer price of 30 1/8 quoted on a computer screen. Madoff guaranteed a quote for two thousand shares, meaning his firm would buy or sell up to two thousand shares of the most popular companies at the best quoted price in a matter of seconds. As an added bonus, the clients were receiving the small but perfectly legal rebate of one cent a share.

Here's how the system worked: A client would send Madoff a sell order on, say, two thousand shares of a stock at the market price. Madoff would pay the client a $20 rebate for the order on top of the $29.875 bid price. If Madoff got an order from another brokerage to buy two thousand shares at market, he would sell them the stock for $30.125. Madoff would, in exchange, receive the spread of 25 cents a share, or $500 on the two orders, minus the $20 rebate on each, for a total of $460, overall 0.77 percent on $60,000. A round-trip transaction like that hundreds of time every day adds up to a very lucrative business.

"Madoff started going out to all the small, regional brokerage houses, like Piper Jaffray in Minneapolis or Bateman Eichler in Los Angeles," recalled Alex Jacobson, who worked for the Chicago Board Options Exchange. Madoff would tell them, "'Send me your order flow, and I'll guarantee you the best market.' Plus, he was paying them," Jacobson recalled.

Toronto-based Dominion Securities, in particular, "loved it," said Doug Steiner, an employee there at the time. "We charged our own clients a commission on the trades, we were guaranteed the best price fills, and Bernie took the risk—which was that he could quickly rebuy what he sold and resell what he bought, and do it at a profit. And his operation was totally automated," he told *The Globe and Mail*. Steiner was so inspired that in 1993 he founded his own online trading business in Toronto called Versus Technologies, which ran E-Trade Canada until it was bought by E-Trade in 2000. Steiner kept in touch with Madoff in the '90s and urged anyone in the industry who would listen to study Madoff's electronic trading and how it had enhanced market liquidity for everyone.

Big customers like Fidelity, Schwab, and others also redirected "a significant share of the trading volume, creating what was known as 'the third market'" for listed stocks, wrote Greg N. Gregoriou and François-Serge Lhabitant in a paper examining the Madoff scandal. Edward Mathias was on the NASD committee Madoff chaired in 1990 when the subject of payment for order flow came up for discussion. The NASD was NASDAQ's so-called self-regulatory organization, its in-house watchdog, and that same year, Madoff became chairman of NASDAQ. Thus, on the issue of payment for order flow, he was acting as both judge and jury. Mathias explained, "He got on the committee and took control of the task force" charged with deciding whether payment for order flow would remain legal—if it did, that would help Madoff tremendously, and if it didn't, that would kill off the trading volume business he had built by paying a rebate of one cent on every share traded.

Mathias, who at the time was working at T. Rowe Price, the mutual fund company based in Baltimore, remembers that the subject "was a big deal at the time—to get a penny a share back. Somehow he was able to persuade people who were against payment for orders. It wasn't a clear-cut issue. Traditional brokers didn't like it, and for a lot of firms it was a necessary evil." In the end, Madoff won out, recalled Mathias, now a managing director at the Carlyle Group in Washington, D.C. Payment for order flow became, and still is, legal. Madoff's various weapons to win orders worked. By 1989, Bernard L. Madoff Investment Securities was a market maker handling more than 5 percent of the trading volume in NYSE-listed stocks—without even being a member of the NYSE. By 1990, Madoff was trading 275 NYSE stocks, 100 NASDAQ issues, and 300 convertible bonds and preferred stock

By 1993, he had raised his maximum buy or sell order for clients to five thousand shares on S&P 500 stocks, and he offered the same execution for convertible bonds, preferred shares, warrants, and share purchase rights. In the late 1990s and into 2000, Madoff's business grew significantly, and he operated such a sophisticated brokerage trading that many of his employees went on to work at big hedge funds or become portfolio managers.

One Madoff trader left to work at Renaissance Investment Management, a Russia-specific hedge fund, in its London office. Another trader left for Thomas Weisel, a so-called buy-side firm in San Francisco. Sharon Fay, another former employee, became chief investment officer for value equities at AllianceBernstein, while yet another Madoff employee joined Clinton Group, a New York hedge fund founded by George Hall. According to New York headhunter Ben Ross, Madoff's broker-dealer firm was "a pool for real talent," and those who left often went on to take high-profile jobs. With Madoff's success came scrutiny and criticism. Madoff began to be demonized by his rivals in public. In 1993, the *Wall Street Journal* wrote a story revealing that Madoff and other members of the Cincinnati exchange were using the computer box for something called "preferencing." Bernie Madoff originated the idea of preferencing, by routing customers' trades through Cincinnati, but he conceded: "There are a lot of people who don't like what we are doing."

Other firms such as Shearson Lehman and Pershing & Co. (then a division of Donaldson, Lufkin & Jenrette) also engaged in preferencing, which was a hidden way for Wall Street firms to make money by trading against their small, or retail, customers. For example, when a John or Jane Investor type bought or sold a NYSE-listed stock through Shearson, the order was sent to Shearson's computer first. Then Shearson held on to the order briefly—long enough to decide whether it could fulfill the order out of its own inventory for a profit.

If Shearson could fill the trade out of inventory and make a profit on the trade, then Shearson would take the order and trade with itself on the Madoff-controlled Cincinnati Stock Exchange, where Shearson was a member dealer. If the computer decided that Shearson didn't have any inventory that would make the trade a profitable one, the customer's order was sent to the NYSE or some other exchange. Cincinnati Stock Exchange chairman Frederick Moss argued Wall Street firms that preferenced trades for the retail customer—often referred to on Wall Street as "dumb money"—still got the customer the best price even though the firm was making money on the trade.

With controversy about preferencing came more questions about payment for order flow, which would dog Madoff for years. The central question about the practice was: is the customer getting the best price or, as critics argued, is Madoff just trading a buy and sell order quickly and paying clients off to send the order his way? The big exchanges, the AMEX and the NYSE, would argue for years afterward that the customer was being cheated out of getting a better, fairer price.

Madoff revolutionized trading on Wall Street, in part by embracing the regulators' agenda. And in the process he had grabbed business away from the old-time trading floors, made millions of dollars in profits, and made many enemies.

Chapter Three

All the time that Bernie Madoff was making a public name for himself revolutionizing trading on Wall Street, he was also building his largely secret "advisory" business. This business would later be known as a "hedge fund," even though technically it was nothing of the sort.

The advisory operation was there all along. It started out in the 1960s, not long after Madoff hung up his shingle as a registered broker-dealer. At first, the advisory business was informal. Madoff's family, friends, and other key clients would open brokerage accounts with him and then let him decide how to trade for them.

As a broker-dealer, Bernie Madoff attracted clients because he did a good job for them. He executed trades quickly and efficiently, and his clients got fair prices and good service. They trusted him, so they recommended their friends to him to trade. On the investment side, the business was boosted the same way. Madoff promised, and delivered, amazingly good returns to his investors. They were happy, they trusted him, and they were eager to recommend him to their friends.

It wasn't just the infectious enthusiasm of happy clients and investors, however, that kept either of Madoff's businesses growing. There was also the money that he paid to people to bring him business. As a broker-dealer, Madoff paid other broker-dealers a commission, or rebate, to send orders his way so that he could execute them and make money on the trades. So too on the advisory side, he paid commissions to people for finding new investors and delivering them to his door. The commissions were based on how much money they brought in.

Many of the early investors who gave Madoff the first round of money, raised between 1962 and 1992, were referred to him by his father-in-law, Sol Alpern. Alpern, who had lent the young Madoff $50,000 to get the broker-dealer business going, also helped to get the advisory operation off the ground. Alpern was always singing Madoff's praises as an investor, and soon two of his young accountant employees, Frank Avellino and Michael Bienes, also set up a side business of their own, bringing investors to Bernie Madoff. Among other fundraisers who became staggeringly rich by bringing money to Madoff were his old friend Maurice "Sonny" Cohn, who set up a firm called Cohmad Securities, which was located right in Madoff's office; Walter Noel of Fairfield Greenwich Group; Austrian banker Sonja Kohn; and Ezra Merkin, who ran a fund of hedge funds, Ariel, Ascot, and Gabriel. Eventually the Madoff feeder network would be so broad and so deep that investors and portfolio managers would find themselves unwittingly caught up in it.

Pati Gerber's family typified the early Madoff investors. Her family ties to Madoff went back forty years. Her father, Abraham Hershson, was the founder and chairman of Hygiene Industries, a manufacturer of shower curtains, plastic table covers, and bath accessories. His accountant, Alpern & Heller, referred Hershson to Bernard L. Madoff Investment Securities. It's possible Madoff acted as the quick-turnaround broker when Hygiene's pink sheet shares traded. Like the Madoffs and the Alperns, Abraham Hershson came from humble Eastern European origins. He was born in Krasnik, Poland, in 1900, and came to the United States when he was nineteen. He founded Hygiene Industries in 1933, which was eventually sold to Nabisco.

Hershson's fortune from selling his company went not just to Madoff, but to philanthropic activities, including the establishment of a community center in Tel Aviv in 1945 and the creation of a fund to help Polish émigrés in Israel. He supported Brookdale Hospital Medical Center in Brooklyn, the Hillcrest Jewish Center in Queens, United Jewish Appeal, and many other charities. His story was not unlike those of many others who invested in Madoff from the early years: they would start with a small amount and invest millions of dollars over the decades. By 2008, Hershson's extended family's entire investment with Madoff had grown to nearly $20 million—at least on paper.

"My father was investing with him from the beginning," Pati Gerber said in an interview with the *Chicago Tribune*. Hershson started trading through Madoff on the (legitimate) brokerage side but soon started putting some savings aside with Madoff's advisory firm. Madoff acted as a sort of informal bank or money market fund for his clients. They could take money out anytime, usually with very little advance notice, and if Hershson or his family had spare cash, they would give it to Madoff to invest. Hershson got a quarterly dividend from this savings-like account, and ultimately set up similar accounts for his daughter and his grandchildren.

Pati Gerber also encountered Madoff several times over the years at social events and, in recent years, at The Breakers, a Palm Beach hotel and beachfront resort. Madoff even cosponsored Gerber when she decided to become a member of the more exclusive Palm Beach Country Club. After all, if her father couldn't trust his accountant and his accountant couldn't trust his son-in-law, Gerber said, "Who do you trust?"

In the 1970s, Michael Engler, a small-business owner in Minneapolis who also founded a brokerage firm for small, newly public companies, became another rabidly loyal investor with Madoff. He referred countless friends, neighbors, and members of his Minnesota country club. Engler had served as a fighter pilot during World War II, and many of his referrals were fellow veterans. Engler was so highly regarded and so well thought of in his suburban community that many people unquestioningly trusted his advice. After all, they decided, if Madoff was good enough for Engler, he was good enough for them. "These were people who had survived the Holocaust together, or their parents had," said the son of one Madoff investor who had been referred through Engler. "They had served in the military, they came back alive, and they trusted one another with their lives."

It was this high level of trust that led smart and savvy people—especially in the Jewish community—to invest with Madoff over the ensuing years without asking serious questions. And they were not driven by greed, as many commentators on the scandal have since implied, but rather by the desire to invest in their futures with someone they felt they could trust.

"Part of the Jewish mentality is prudence, especially financial prudence, conservatism, not taking risks," said one Madoff investor whose family made a fortune in East Coast fitness franchises. "Madoff was the opposite of risk—he was anti-risk. He would tell prospective investors flat out: 'I'm not hitting the ball out of the park every year. Not me, I'm not a hotshot. If you invest with me, you'll get consistent, less-than-

average returns every year—but you'll get them every year.' He played
to that sense of conservatism, that he was not a get-rich-quick scam."
The trust in Madoff was so great that many men even told their wives
to never sell their Madoff holdings after they died. Wanting to honor
their husbands' dying wishes, many of these widows kept their money
with Madoff's advisory business up until he was exposed in 2008.

Madoff had other close friends who helped with fund-raising. And,
like Avellino and Bienes, they were soon receiving sizable commissions
for their efforts. Two of Madoff's most important fund-raisers were
Maurice Cohn and Alvin Delaire, Jr.

In his early career, Cohn, who was known as Sonny, worked as a
so-called two-dollar broker for the American Stock Exchange and the
New York Stock Exchange. Two-dollar brokers were broker's brokers,
firms that handled orders that larger firms were too busy to take care
of. Sonny Cohn cofounded the two-dollar brokerage firm Cohn, Delaire
& Kaufman in the 1960s. Most of their clients were at the time recognized names on Wall Street, such as the investment bank White Weld
(later taken over by Credit Suisse).

In 1963, Cohn partnered with Alvin Delaire, Sr., and founded
Cohn & Delaire, which traded on the NYSE. After Delaire's death, in
1968, his son, Alvin Delaire, Jr., took over his father's partnership.
Sometime before 1971, the firm also began operating on the American
Stock Exchange. In 1978, the firm became Cohn, Delaire & Kaufman,
with Joseph L. Kaufman, an AMEX member since the fifties, steward-
ing the operation. "Kaufman was a classy guy," said the compliance
officer at one of the NYSE's last remaining specialist firms. "I doubt
Kaufman had any idea what his other partners got up to after they left
the trading floor."

By 1985, Cohn and Delaire had left the AMEX trading floor and
were raising money for Madoff. Cohn partnered with Madoff in forming
Cohmad. Because of its name—a combination of Cohn and Madoff,
Cohmad sounded like a separate firm, but in reality it functioned as a
feeder to collect funds for Madoff and as a sort of payroll account for
the friends and family of the two men. Cohmad officially listed its address in the Lipstick Building in midtown Manhattan, operating out of
Madoff's broker-dealer offices on the eighteenth and nineteenth floors.
It also had a Boston office that was managed, starting in 1989, by Robert

M. Jaffe, the son-in-law of Carl Shapiro, Madoff's first big investor. Alvin Delaire, Jr., appears to have evolved into a point man for Madoff's investment operation. Some Madoff investors contended that he was their main contact for account information, withdrawals from the fund, and other administrative questions. Delaire worked for Madoff and was paid by him directly but held himself out as a registered representative at a separate and independent brokerage firm, Cohmad, according to at least one lawsuit filed against Delaire. Delaire "was merely a salesman" and a "shill" for Madoff's scheme, "and not in any way even a quasi-independent source for the validity" of Madoff's operation or investment strategy, alleged Dr. Martin Schulman of Manhasset, New York, who filed the suit in April 2009.

Madoff got to know Cohn and Delaire because the three men were part of a chummy group of Long Islanders, all in the securities business, who commuted together into downtown Manhattan. Together, the Long Islanders chartered a Cessna seaplane that brought them to a dock on the East River near Wall Street. This may seem like an outlandish extravagance—especially just for a morning commute—but it was one of the fastest and easiest ways to get to Manhattan from Manhasset Bay, Long Island.

In the 1970s, Frank Christensen and Ed Beauchamp were the first to charter the plane to work, but over the years the flight club grew. Frank Christensen was the head of a rapidly growing NYSE firm and eventually became an elder statesman of the trading floor by helping to negotiate a deal that would modernize the exchange through the use of technology and electronic trading. A few more people started flying—including Madoff himself, Sonny Cohn, Roger Hoffman, Walter Hirshon, and Kevin Reilly of Quick & Reilly, and Richard "Dick" Spring. Peter Madoff, who had joined his brother's firm shortly after finishing law school in 1970, also took the plane to work sometimes.

Some of the men were already legends on Wall Street, especially Hirshon, who had started his Wall Street career in 1927 as an independent broker at the New York Stock Exchange. With the exception of some years in Army Air Corps intelligence during World War II, he was with Hirshon & Company until 1957, then cofounded Hirshon, Roth & Company, where he worked until his retirement, in 1982. Hirshon was so wealthy that once, after he'd tripped and fallen off the seaplane's little dock into the East River, he told a surprised young insurance adjuster, "Son, my *shoes* cost $500."

The flying club socialized off the plane too. Madoff showed Christensen around his office in downtown Manhattan. Alvin J. Delaire, Jr., and his wife, Carole, went skiing in Zermatt, Switzerland, with Bernie and Peter. Christensen once sold Sonny Cohn his used moped.

The men also sometimes did business together. Madoff would occasionally call Christensen's firm to buy or sell stock traded on the NYSE, since Madoff was not a member of the exchange and couldn't trade there himself. "This was before computers," Christensen said. "Madoff would be making a market in IBM, so he would call down to my office or to the floor and put in an order for shares."

Christensen recalled that Madoff was even-tempered and rarely got angry. One day in the mid-1970s, Madoff called Frank's firm and an assistant happened to pick up the phone. Madoff gave her five market-on-close orders, or shares that are purchased at whatever price the market closes at for that day. "But she couldn't make out the symbol—she wrote it down wrong. And these were big orders, for five thousand, six thousand shares," Christensen said. The next day the assistant was despondent over her mistake, but Madoff made good on the trades anyway, even though he didn't get the closing price. He even joked about it. "He told her, 'I want you to buy MHP. That stands for Madoff . . . has . . . a prick!'" Everyone laughed, smoothing over the mistake.

On another occasion, Madoff rang Christensen's office in a panic. This time Frank answered. "What's up?" he asked.

"I need the airplane to pick me up at Twenty-third Street!" Madoff growled. "My captain sank my brand-new Rybovich, Frank!" Madoff had two boats in Montauk—an older one and this new Rybovich.

The flight club's regular pilot picked up Madoff at the Twenty-third Street pier and flew Madoff out to Montauk, at the tip of Long Island. The captain of Madoff's brand-new boat, a Rybovich sportfisher, hadn't noticed when the bilge pump backed up—and the boat sank.

"I'm gonna kill that guy! I'm gonna kill my boat captain!" Madoff screamed most of the way out, according to the plane's pilot.

But he didn't kill the captain. By the time Madoff got to the marina, the boat's captain was slouching on the dock looking miserable. Madoff met the captain and put his arm around the man, joking, "You sunk the wrong boat!"

In the 1980s, Bernard L. Madoff Investment Securities moved to the high-profile Lipstick Building at 885 Third Avenue between Fifty-third and Fifty-fourth streets in midtown Manhattan. Even when he was out of the office, Bernie made sure he was always in touch by telephone, especially now that the brokerage business was growing. Even when he was out of town, he called the office every morning at seven thirty to check in with one of his sons.

Michael Murphy, who had started out at Martin J. Joel, a little over-the-counter brokerage next to Madoff's old offices in downtown Manhattan, went on to have a big career on Wall Street. Ultimately, Murphy ended up on the so-called institutional side of the business working for Wachovia Securities, acting on behalf of the firm's large pension fund and corporate pension plan clients.

Murphy would often stop by and have lunch at Madoff's offices in midtown. "They were smart—they always seemed to be a step ahead, and they rarely got in trouble" with regulators, he said about the Madoff brothers. "They were very buttoned up as well. I never saw the Madoffs without a tie on, and their suits were better than anyone else's I knew." In the 1970s and 1980s, their wives were always with the Madoff men at conferences. "And this was before women went to conferences!" Murphy added. "It didn't seem like Bernard was fooling around. They seemed above all that—smart, educated, admired, respected."

Shearson's then–head trader, Peter DaPuzzo, and his wife, Mary Jane, also socialized with both Madoff couples at industry functions like Security Traders Association of New York dinners and annual industry conferences in Boca Raton, Florida. Of the two couples, "Peter and Marion were more outgoing, more gregarious, sitting by the pool with other people or having cocktails," said Mary Jane DaPuzzo. "I always joked that Peter would be the one to get himself in trouble, not Bernie." Ruth and Bernie, on the other hand, "were quiet, unassuming people, dignified and reserved, definitely more unavailable." Ruth wasn't the type to drip with diamonds or heavy jewelry, instead sporting expensive but subtle taste.

Murphy said he had no idea that Madoff managed money, even

when Murphy was a high roller at Wachovia. Since Murphy was working on the institutional side of Wachovia's business, Madoff could have
easily pitched Murphy as a natural client of his advisory business, which
he operated on the seventeenth floor of the Lipstick Building, just downstairs from his broker-dealer firm. But Madoff never did. "They didn't
advertise it. I was very surprised," Murphy said, when Madoff confessed to running a phony billion-dollar hedge fund.

DaPuzzo said he too was "shocked" to find out Madoff was managing money after Madoff's arrest. Even many of those closest to Madoff
in the brokerage industry had no idea he had been building up a billion-
dollar advisory business. Frank Christensen said he didn't hear about it
until November 2008, when he visited a mutual friend in New York
and inquired about Madoff. "He's more of a money manager now," said
the friend. "He's pretty much out of the market maker business." Christensen was stunned. All these years, he said, he had never known Madoff managed money on the side.

Bernie Madoff wasn't registered as an investment adviser, so his investment advisory business was always illegal. But was there a time when
it *wasn't* an outright fraud? Probably not.

It's a good bet that the fraudulent advisory business was actually
Madoff's very expensive way of borrowing money from the public.
That was how he raised capital to trade in his legal broker-dealer business. Madoff didn't want the scrutiny of borrowing from a bank, so
instead he "borrowed" capital from friends and family.

In the early years, both sides of Madoff's business were profitable:
the illegal advisory business would bring in money, then Madoff would
take that money and make big profits on his legal brokerage side. Then
he would pay back the 20 percent rates he promised.

At that time, Wall Street trading was still very profitable. Wall Street
had long traded stocks in increments of one-eighth of a dollar, or 12.5
cents. As part of a broader market restructuring in 2001, the industry
converted prices to decimals—which contracted those fat profit margins to tenths of one cent, down from 12.5 cents. This sharply reduced
the amount of money Madoff and other broker-dealers made on trades.
For example, instead of offering to buy General Motors at $1.00 a

share, then turn around and sell at $1.125 or even $1.250 a share as they had in the past, Madoff and other brokers now had to offer to sell at penny increments, $1.01 or $1.02. So the spread between bid and ask prices contracted down to almost nothing. Profits evaporated for traders across Wall Street, and the Madoffs' trading business would have been particularly hard hit because of its policy of paying other brokers a penny a share just for the opportunity to handle their trades.

Despite this, Madoff didn't have any trouble raising and making money throughout the 1970s and 1980s. Madoff was one of the few broker-dealers who stayed open for business during the crash of 1987, and he got a letter from the SEC thanking him for that.

Although Madoff was taking investors' money and using it all along to fund his legitimate and illegitimate businesses, it is very likely he didn't see this as a rip-off. In his mind, he was paying his "advisory" clients a 20 percent rate of return, and how he did it was not their affair. He was trading heavily and making profits. He was giving some of the profits back to the investors and also keeping a certain amount for himself.

It's possible the Ponzi scheme part of the fraud started way before the crash of 1987, as some have speculated. That's because nobody, no trader, no matter how good he is, wins every month or even every quarter. The fact that Madoff promised and appeared to deliver consistently high returns from the very beginning was a tip-off that some people noticed and that many others should have. So, when the profits weren't enough to cover the payouts, Madoff would even things out. Sometimes he might take the money from the broker-dealer side, or sometimes he might use incoming money to subsidize the payments to investors. According to the testimony of whistle-blower Harry Markopolos, who tried to turn Madoff in to the SEC on numerous occasions, Madoff even told some investors that he would "subsidize" losing months with gains from other winning months.

Further, there was the fact that some of the payouts that Madoff was promising in the early years were impossibly high. Stanley Chais, a money manager based in Los Angeles who also invested with Madoff's advisory business, and Carl Shapiro, for example, were asking for and receiving cumulative returns as high as 900 percent starting in the mid-1980s. According to SEC fraud charges leveled in June 2009, Chais would order up gains and losses at will, and Madoff would produce them on Chais's statements. The agency alleged that both men knew the results were simply made-up.

A last straw that may have tipped the "investment" operation over to being a total Ponzi scheme was the fact that the SEC closed down two of Madoff's big fund-raisers, Frank Avellino and Michael Bienes, in 1992.

The two accountants, who had become involved with Madoff while working for his father-in-law, Sol Alpern, in the early 1960s, were investigated by the SEC for an illegal "notes" scam through their money management operation, which they had not registered. The commission found that the two accountants were issuing promissory notes to their investors that guaranteed as much as 20 percent returns each year. The SEC, fearing this was a scam, or even a Ponzi scheme, ordered the two men to shut down their operation and return all of their investors' money.

All the while, Avellino and Bienes had been funneling money to Madoff and receiving commissions for their services. But, oddly enough, the SEC did not implicate Madoff at all in the scandal. Instead, former clients of Avellino and Bienes were able to set up new accounts with Madoff directly, and many of them did.

Ultimately, a lot of the Avellino and Bienes money stayed with Madoff through these new client accounts, but the pair had brought in nearly a half billion dollars, and for a while it appeared that Madoff might have to give it all back to investors. Coming up with this amount likely almost killed him. Around this time, Madoff lowered the returns he was promising to 10–15 percent a year. Still, the broker-dealer side was making money by trading in the market, so Madoff could hope to make the returns he needed.

By 2005, however, decimalization and other regulatory changes had cooled off the trading business to the point that Madoff's legal side just wasn't producing the profits he needed to pay back even 10–15 percent a year. But Madoff still had thousands of investors to whom he had promised good returns, and he was having trouble raising new money. He even tried to borrow money from banks in Europe at this point—signaling that the Ponzi was starting to unravel in a big way. (Frank Casey, the North American president for UK-based Fortune Asset Management, helped long-ignored Madoff whistle-blower Harry Markopolos closely track Madoff's cash balances and feeder funds. In June 2005, Markopolos and Casey determined that Madoff's Ponzi was unraveling and that Madoff had approached banks such as Paribas to borrow money since he was in need of additional funds to keep the scheme going. The banks turned Madoff down).

Once he started using significant amounts of incoming dollars to fund payouts to prior investors, there was no turning back. He hadn't invested the money, so it wasn't making any gains. This meant that he needed more new "investors" whose money he couldn't invest either, because he needed it to pay off the earlier clients who were expecting a return on their "investment."

Finally, in 2008, he couldn't make it work anymore. The crash of 2008 brought a slew of investors to Madoff's door asking for upward of $7 billion back. He just didn't have it. At this point, he made the choice to confess to his sons and turn himself in. It would have been only a matter of time before he was revealed anyway, but he wanted to go on his own terms.

For many years, Madoff's successful broker-dealer business offered the perfect cover for his phony hedge fund. To observers in the various markets where he operated, the flow of trades from Madoff's legitimate activities was indistinguishable from those that came—or didn't come—from the investment side.

One of the people who watched Madoff's trading activity in the market was Alex Jacobson. Then the head of investor education for the Chicago Board Options Exchange, Jacobson knew a lot about Bernard L. Madoff Investment Securities because it was his job to know. Jacobson was paid to travel all over the country, call on dozens of different brokerage firms, and try to educate them on options trades. He also tried to sell them on making their options trades in Chicago instead of elsewhere. "It was hard for us in Chicago to compete with other options exchanges in New York for business—they were friendlier with the customers, went to their kids' bar mitzvahs, and carpooled together. My job was to kiss the ass of every customer in New York and get them to trade on the CBOE."

Options are sometimes called "poor man's stock." A call option on General Electric gives you the right to buy GE at some predetermined price in the future. GE trades at $60 a share, but an options investor pays just a fraction of the price—say, $3 per GE call option—for the right to buy GE at $65 a year from now. A put option on GE would give you the right to sell the stock down the road, again at a predetermined price. Options are not unlike lottery tickets or bets on horses at the track, which pay out amounts that depend on the odds for both winners and losers.

Madoff and the Cincinnati exchange, which he had revamped and used to make himself a regional specialist, were interchangeable. BLMIS made markets in the top one hundred most liquid stocks—such as General Electric, General Motors, DuPont, Procter & Gamble—and because of that, Madoff generally carried an inventory that closely correlated to the Standard & Poor's 100 index or 500 index, the more widely followed benchmark. Madoff's business, "as we understood it, was that he bought all this order flow, paid a penny a share, but still earned a small profit, and by the end of the trading day, Madoff had some sense of what sort of portfolio they would be taking home," Jacobson said. If BLMIS had an inventory, say, of $100 million in stocks that was close to or exactly matched the S&P 100 index, the firm would buy S&P index options as a kind of insurance policy, just in case the stocks in Madoff's inventory started trading up or down with big swings in price.

While BLMIS's offices were still downtown on Wall and Broad streets in the heart of the financial district, Jacobson began calling on the Madoff firm regularly. His aim was to convince the Madoffs, like other clients, to trade their options through Chicago rather than another options exchange. However, the Madoff offices "were not a friendly place," Jacobson recalled. "Unlike other firms, I couldn't walk in and get introduced and wander around. We sat there waiting to get thrown out."

Nevertheless, Jacobson did win some of the Madoff options business, and by the late 1980s BLMIS was regularly trading S&P index options through the Chicago options exchange. "Late in the afternoon, they'd adjust their collar, which was their hedge on their inventory," he recalled. BLMIS would buy this collar, which involved simultaneously buying put options and selling call options on the S&P index, trying to lock in gains or minimize losses on the portfolio. "As we understood it, the collar wasn't a moneymaker or loser," Jacobson recalled, just a sort of insurance policy to protect against big price swings in Madoff's firm inventory.

This regular afternoon trade for the broker-dealer eventually would go on to become Madoff's cover for his investment strategy. Years later, in sales marketing literature for various feeder funds into Madoff's phony advisory business, many of the pitches described such a strategy as a collar, or split-strike conversion, on the most liquid S&P 100 stocks.

Strangely enough, in the early 1990s, Jacobson said, he heard from traders in the Chicago pit. "All of a sudden, Madoff's collar trade just stopped."

At this point, it appears that Madoff stopped executing this strategy on the broker-dealer side of his business. And it's doubtful he was ever doing this collar or split-strike strategy for his advisory business clients anyhow: the billions of dollars' worth of options required for this trade would have shown up in the markets. Instead, Madoff was nowhere to be seen on the trading floor. His "strategy" was just a marketing story that he would tell to lure in new money.

Jacobson didn't think anything of it until years later. He was in Florida at an options conference, and some of the wealthy clients were gloating about being in a Madoff hedge fund. Jacobson explained, "They kept telling me, 'Isn't it great, all the money I'm making?' They said they were making returns of high teens to low 20 percent" every year, even when the stock market was flat or down for the year. "It made no sense."

The eighteenth and nineteenth floors of the oval-shaped Lipstick Building, where the real trading took place, provided the perfect backdrop for meetings Madoff held with potential investors in his side operation. In his conference room on nineteen, Madoff met with potential investors who would watch the busy activity on the trading floor and gain confidence that Madoff's advisory business must also be legitimate. How else could he keep churning out the steady positive returns?

Moreover, Madoff's brokerage firm was known on the Street as customer-friendly. Big mutual fund firms and professional trading outfits like Bear Stearns and Lehman Brothers were customers of Madoff's. In fact, because Madoff's brokerage business gave big clients like

Lehman Brothers and Charles Schwab such fast and easy trades, some customers even thought they were getting too good of a deal. Fidelity and other big Madoff clients "would get executions that seemed impossible—they were so good as to be unbelievable," said one person who did business with Fidelity Investments at that time.

Doug Steiner, of Dominion Securities in Toronto, visited Madoff's office for the first time in 1986. A devotee of computers, Steiner was immediately impressed by the trading room. "The screens were the first nineteen-inch IBM 3290 flat glass plasma models I'd ever seen," he recalled to the *Globe and Mail* after Madoff's arrest. "The orange hue they cast on the traders' faces was the only bright color in the room. The machines could display up to four windows of market information at once. I was drooling: This was the business I wanted to emulate."

At the time, Steiner knew Madoff ran some money on the side, but he was not interested in this side of the business. "What we wanted was immediate execution of buy and sell orders for the most popular NASDAQ stocks," he said. "Although there were online services that quoted stock prices, you still generally had to phone a broker to do the trade for you. It was a pain in the ass. The market prices could shift quickly, and brokers could make you pay an unfavorable price if they felt like it."

To Steiner and other clients who experienced him in his element, Madoff even looked like the archetypal Wall Street broker. He dressed in French-cuffed shirts and suspenders and raced between phone calls, employees vying for face time. Once, Steiner remembered, a phone call came in from "his yacht captain trying to nail down a trip." Ed Mathias of the Carlyle Group remembers that when Madoff was pushing NASDAQ's trading committee to give the go-ahead on his practice of payment for order flow, "we always met in his offices. They were quite sterile, with all the computers lined up" in the trading room floor. In appearance, Madoff was notably "fastidious." Geduld recalls Madoff "always looked like a million bucks, custom suits, custom everything."

Bernie's own office was not lavish, especially when compared to those of other investment tycoons of the 1980s, the Gordon Gekko "greed is good" era. Bernie hadn't lost his Queens accent and "wasn't an ostentatious person," said one former employee. "Yes, he would buy a nice car, but almost all the traders could enjoy a nice car. For someone who owned a trading operation and was making $20 million a year, he had a very different lifestyle."

Despite his understated nature, Bernie did have his quirks. For one thing, he was obsessed with the appearance of his offices, both in New York and London. He would scuttle around to the windows at the Lipstick Building and make sure the blinds were all drawn at the same level. Madoff also didn't allow employees to write with anything but black ink pens. He hated paper and banned it from the desks of all employees. His avuncular reputation didn't always square with his personal demeanor, which was sometimes strange. "Bernie acted aloof sometimes when you were alone with him, like in the elevator. He was just one of those people, you could walk next to him for twenty blocks, and he was perfectly fine being silent," said one former employee who worked in the automated trading department.

Employees at Madoff's London office, Madoff Securities International, recalled similar oddities about Madoff's personality. Despite the fact that Madoff's U.S. offices were headquartered in the elliptical-shaped Lipstick Building, Madoff was obsessed with right angles and insisted on things being arranged in straight lines. In an interview with *The Mail on Sunday*, one London employee recalled how an entire wall was rebuilt to accommodate this obsession. The wall on which the video-conferencing system had been arranged was shaped in a semicircle, but Madoff could not stand it. "'I can't have that in my office,'" the employee recalled Madoff saying. "'I can't live with it. It has to be square.'"

According to Julia Fenwick, a manager at the London office, whenever Madoff would come to visit, employees rushed around to make sure everything was arranged as he liked it. They would match up computer screens so that they were at an even height with one another and make sure that each picture frame hung perfectly straight. If a desk or a door had been scratched, it was colored in with a marker so that Madoff wouldn't notice. "Things like that would drive him nuts," Fenwick told *The Mail on Sunday*.

Peter Madoff, on the other hand, was known as a screamer. "Bernie was a softie, very easy to deal with, laid-back and even-tempered," recalled Peter DaPuzzo, who was a contemporary of the Madoff brothers and head of the Shearson over-the-counter trading desk for many years.

Peter was considered a "fast talker" and "one of the toughest with whom to do business, a very tough trader."

One former employee recalled a time when Peter Madoff "started screaming at us one day about not using the blue pens" that Bernie hated. "I had just gone to the supply closet to get a pad of paper, and he was in the midst of throwing out hundreds of uni-ball Micro blue pens. Peter insisted. He said, 'Throw them all out!' " The employee still has some of the blue pens today.

Despite his occasional outbursts, Peter, bespectacled and graying with close-cut hair, had a reputation as being "warm" and "very open" among those who served on panels or regulatory committees with him. But among his workers, Peter was considered "a ballbuster. Anytime I asked a question, he gave me a lawyer's response," said the former brokerage and trading employee. "If I needed anything, or any help, I never went to Peter or Shana. I always went to Mark. He gave a shit about me professionally. If it could wait, I went to Mark." Shana Madoff, Peter's daughter, a tall, lithe brunette, also had a reputation as being "difficult" in her role as a lawyer in charge of some trading compliance for the firm.

The people raising money for Madoff seemed to know Wall Street. Some of them had actually worked as brokers in the securities industry before coming to work for Madoff. For example, several Cohmad executives, including Jaffe, Marcia Cohn (Sonny Cohn's daughter), and Jonathan Greenberg, had worked in the early 1980s at Cowen and Company, a small, regional New York broker-dealer that subsequently expanded to major U.S. cities, before joining Madoff.

Many of Cohmad's fund-raisers who had not worked at Cowen had acquired experience elsewhere, usually from having worked as stockbrokers or analysts at other firms. For instance, Richard "Dick" Spring was also on the Cohmad payroll. Spring joined Cohmad in January 1986. He had worked at David J. Green & Co., a New York–based investment firm that had grown to manage more than $1 billion in assets and was listed in 1996 as the 357th largest money manager of tax-exempt assets by *Pensions & Investments* magazine.

Some of those who raised money for Madoff's illegal asset management operation were paid commissions through Cohmad, according to the dollars they brought in. Cohmad was just the toll-taker, the bank where money came in and then was passed on to the quasi–hedge fund Madoff was running. The money to pay these commissions came from Madoff himself.

In July 2001, for example, the Madoff firm made a monthly payment to Cohmad of almost $1.3 million, and for several years after that the monthly amounts regularly exceeded $750,000. Six people listed on Cohmad's payroll earned more than $12 million combined between 2003 and 2008. But by 2008, Madoff's payments had slid, to slightly more than $200,000 most months. Perhaps Madoff was running out of money, or perhaps investors were withdrawing because the stock market had collapsed. The S&P 500, the benchmark index used by investors to gauge how the stock market is doing, had slid almost 50 percent in one year alone. The stock market hadn't seen such a bad year since the Great Depression.

Spring, who had brought in client assets totaling more than $500 million as of January 2007, was one of the highest-paid fund-raisers at Cohmad. He received at least $4.8 million from Cohmad between 2003 and 2007, according to company payment records. Spring's attorney, Kenneth Lipman, of Boca Raton, Florida, later told the *Wall Street Journal* that Spring was merely a million-dollar victim who had no knowledge of the fraud. But for years Spring received payments from Cohmad in exchange for bringing investors, and possibly investment ideas, to Madoff. Jaffe was paid roughly $100 million in commissions over a decade.

Ponzi schemes require more money coming in than is going out— and once investors withdraw more than they deposited, the account is a liability for the Ponzi scheme. Cohmad's payment records reflect such a pattern, according to the SEC charges. Madoff stopped making payments on Cohmad accounts where the investor had withdrawn more than their original investment, and all the brokers working for Cohmad, which was essentially an in-house marketing operation for Madoff, accepted this arrangement year after year.

Indeed, the compensation setup gave Cohmad and the Cohns every incentive to discourage investors from withdrawing funds. Madoff's fees to Cohmad brokers declined over time from 1 percent of funds brought in by Cohmad to 0.25 percent. The percentage was calculated based on the cumulative amount of funds that Cohmad representatives had brought into Madoff—not on Madoff assets under management for those accounts.

Cohmad received no credit for any purported gains or profits earned on those funds. Moreover, if any portion of the original "cost basis" of funds was withdrawn by clients, Cohmad no longer received commissions on those client assets. Cohmad maintained a database tracking the net capital for each client brought in by Cohmad representatives. But the returns that Madoff provided to those investors were not included in the database. For example, if a client placed $10,000 with BLMIS and it grew to $100,000 through supposed management by Bernie, and then the client withdrew $15,000, Cohmad no longer received any payments on the funds, despite the $85,000 that remained in the customer accounts. In short, Bernie Madoff didn't treat his clients' gains as if they were real.

Cohmad also steered Madoff investors to use the accounting firm Marder Sosnik, later renamed Sosnik, Bell & Co. Burt Ross, the former mayor of Fort Lee, New Jersey, was referred to Sosnik Bell by Cohmad fund-raiser Robert Jaffe, with the explanation that Sosnik Bell could handle tax accounting for complex trades. Eventually, Sosnik Bell would come to provide accounting services to hundreds of Madoff's clients.

In 1993 Scott Sosnik and Larry Bell acquired the accounting practice of Melvin Marder. Marder, a lawyer and accountant who lived in Scarsdale, New York, retired to Florida and sold the practice that Sosnik and Bell took over. It was through Marder that the two accountants met Madoff for the first time.

In 1996, Scott Sosnik and his family invested millions of dollars with Madoff as well. Marder said he couldn't remember how he met Madoff or much about the deal with the younger accountants. "I gave them my paperwork, and that was it," he told a local paper. Lawyers for Sosnik and Bell said the two men met Madoff about a dozen times but were not personal friends. Nevertheless, Marder's firm name appears more than two hundred times on the 162-page list of Madoff victims that was made public. Sosnik and Bell's firm name appears roughly seven hundred times.

Robert M. Jaffe, who ran Cohmad's Boston office, was another key fund-raiser for Madoff. Jaffe had a reputation for being a bit of a dandy.

He had married well; his wife, Ellen Shapiro, was one of Boston's wealthiest heiresses and the daughter of Carl J. Shapiro. Shapiro and his wife were fixtures on the Boston charity circuit and were considered among the most generous donors in the entire state of Massachusetts.

Jaffe seemed an odd match for Ellen Shapiro because they came from two completely different worlds. He grew up in a then-working-class Newton, Massachusetts, and was a self-described clotheshorse. To put himself through school, he worked at men's clothing stores like Louis Boston, whose flagship store offered top quality men's clothing from Italy and boasted four floors and forty thousand square feet of space. He cultivated a fine—and expensive—taste for clothes, with a penchant for labels such as high-end Kiton suits. He was once quoted as saying, "The clothing I wear is more—dare I say this—cutting-edge. Once you've had filet mignon, you don't want to go back."

According to federal records, Jaffe began his Wall Street career in May 1969 with a job at the old-line brokerage E. F. Hutton & Co., where he worked until 1980, before joining Cowen and Company's Boston branch. It was while he was at Cowen that Jaffe was investigated for money laundering for the Boston mob. The Angiulo family, Boston's criminal syndicate, opened nine accounts with Cowen. In 1982 the Angiulos purchased $270,000 worth of cashier's checks from the Bank of Boston payable to Cowen and Company. In 1983, the five Angiulo brothers were indicted.

Jaffe initially denied that he had accepted any money from the Angiulos. But later, when the SEC examined brokerage accounts held by the Angiulos, it discovered that Jaffe had actually brought the accounts to Cowen when he moved over from E. F. Hutton five years earlier. He insisted in news reports at the time that the commissions Cowen earned from the Angiulos' accounts were "peanuts." Lawrence S. Leibowitz, Cowen's then–general counsel, said that Jaffe inherited the Angiulo accounts from a colleague at E. F. Hutton and brought them with him when he transferred. S. Paul Crabtree, regional vice president for E. F. Hutton in Boston, told *Business Week* magazine that "members of the Angiulo family did have accounts here in the past." The accounts became inactive when Jaffe left Hutton.

Jaffe was cleared of any wrongdoing, but the odor of the mob trailed him for years. At best, he was guilty of stunning naïveté in not checking on the identity and background of his own customers. Those were the same characteristics he would demonstrate in *l'affaire* Madoff many years later—a willingness to look the other way and not question the source or destination of funds.

Jaffe started raising money for Cohmad in the same sorts of places where Madoff's original network of investors sprang from. One was an elite Jewish country club in Weston, Massachusetts, called Pine Brook. A *Boston Globe* reporter described him as "a fellow who didn't spend a lot of time kind of pushing papers at a desk. . . . Rather, he golfed and did the charity circuit and charity balls, that sort of thing."

And why shouldn't he? After all, Jaffe was the son-in-law of Carl Shapiro, an elderly multimillionaire and noted philanthropist, a mainstay of Palm Beach's socialite and charitable circles. Shapiro along with his wife, daughter, and son-in-law were long-standing members of the Palm Beach Country Club, which had been founded by affluent Jews wintering in Palm Beach who were barred from joining the Waspy country clubs like the Everglades or the Bath & Tennis Club.

Shapiro and Jaffe even backed Madoff's membership application when he joined the Palm Beach Country Club in 1996, which wasn't a surprise. At that point, Shapiro would have been worth hundreds of millions of dollars. It was Madoff who had launched Shapiro from the ranks of the wealthy to the ultrawealthy—and everyone in Palm Beach knew it. Jaffe made easy sales for Madoff in elite circles everywhere "for a small commission, a common practice" in the hedge fund industry, he would say later. It is common practice to be paid for raising money for legitimate hedge funds—but it *wasn't* common practice to hide that fact from investors. Jaffe didn't tell investors he was being paid to put their money with Madoff—even though, for example, everyone who belonged to the Palm Beach Country Club had heard of Madoff, and by 2008 roughly one-third of the Palm Beach club's members had given Madoff money. For his fund-raising, Jaffe was paid roughly $100 million in commissions by Madoff through Cohmad over nearly a decade, according to SEC fraud charges brought against Jaffe and other Cohmad executives.

Carl Shapiro was so rich that by the 1990s his full-time job was donating money. One of Shapiro's favorite causes was Brandeis University, an American college with a traditionally Jewish student body. In 2008, the Shapiros donated $14 million to Brandeis to build a new admissions center that would bear their name. This came fifteen years after they had funded construction of the original Carl and Ruth Shapiro Admissions Center. "It is impossible to overstate the importance of the Shapiro family's dedication to Brandeis University," Brandeis president Jehuda Reinharz said at the time of the donation. "For more than a half century, Brandeis students and faculty have been the beneficiaries of their enduring commitment to this university." Beginning with a gift of ten dollars in 1950, the Shapiro family has over the years made gifts totaling more than $80 million to Brandeis alone.

But the Shapiros avoided the spotlight. They did not seek thanks or publicity. Mostly, they just wanted to do good with the enormous piles of money they had made, largely thanks to Madoff. In 2008, the Brandeis school newspaper, *The Hoot*, published a profile of Carl and Ruth Shapiro because, although their names were chiseled into buildings all over campus, few students at the college actually knew who they were.

Aside from Bernie's personal quirks, there were other unusual aspects about the Madoff firm—in particular, that so many family members worked there.

It was, and still is, common in finance for a son or daughter to follow in their father's footsteps and join the industry or, sometimes, even the same firm. New York Stock Exchange or American Stock Exchange seats were often passed down within families for generations. For example, the sons of former AIG CEO Maurice "Hank" Greenberg joined AIG, though one ultimately left to join Marsh & McLennan, a competing insurance firm. At BLMIS, family members, including Bernie's brother's daughter, Shana, and his two sons, Mark and Andrew, controlled all the key positions. Even on Wall Street, this sort of extended nepotism within a firm was very unusual.

Peter Madoff was a senior managing director, head of trading, and chief compliance officer for both the investment advisory and the broker-dealer businesses. Bernie's nephew Charles, the son of his sister Sondra, joined the firm in 1978 and served as the director of administration. Bernie's older son, Mark, joined in 1986 and was director of listed trading. His younger son, Andrew, joined in 1988 and was director of NASDAQ trading. Peter's daughter, Shana, joined the firm in 1995 and served as the in-house legal counsel and rules compliance attorney for the market-making arm on the broker-dealer side.

Ruth was a constant presence. She had worked with Bernie since the beginning, when he borrowed office space from her father, and decades later she still kept an office near her husband's on the Lipstick Building's nineteenth floor. Ruth and Bernie often arrived at the office together before trading started. Usually, they would arrive in the morning, generally stopping at the newspaper and sundries shop down in the lobby to pick up a yogurt for breakfast or a snack, and then take the elevator upstairs.

Ruth had a penchant for secrecy. One investor, who came to visit Madoff's offices and seated himself in the office next to Ruth's for the day, recalled that "every time Ruth got up to go out of her office, even just to visit the bathroom, she would lock the door of her office."

Sonny Cohn, Madoff's partner at Cohmad, was a close friend, almost like a family member. His daughter, Marcia, also worked in the offices shared by the two firms as Cohmad's chief compliance officer. "Nobody at the firm really understood what she did," said Mark Kashar, who trained and worked at Madoff's firm in the 1990s. She sat at the end of one of the rows of desks in the eighteenth-floor trading room, and every now and then she would process a trade through Madoff's trading desk, their trading symbol, COHMAD, popping up on everyone's screen.

Every two traders had an assistant, and Kashar was paired up with another trader named A. J. Delaire. A.J.'s father was Cohn's former partner Alvin Delaire, Jr., who worked on the mysterious and off-limits seventeenth floor, but again, "no one knew what he did. We all knew he was down there, and sometimes he'd come up to see his son A.J." The younger Delaire ultimately left to work at the New York Stock Exchange.

Cohmad as an entity billed the Madoff firm monthly for rent, the electric bill, market data and exchange fees, a phone lease, long-distance calls, and other expenses. But most important, Cohmad acted as the Madoff family bank, where cash was available for anyone raising money for Madoff. Cohmad also handled Ruth's personal account. Cohmad didn't have any other major source of income beyond wrangling investors to put more money into Madoff's advisory business. Those payments represented roughly 85 percent of Cohmad's total income from 2000 to 2008.

According to Massachusetts secretary of state William Galvin, who filed a complaint against Madoff after his arrest, Madoff used

Cohmad to pay out at least $67 million between 2000 through 2008 to his fund-raisers—among them, Sonny Cohn. Monthly payments were made for "professional services," "brokerage services," and "fees for account supervision." Secretary Galvin's complaint alleges that Cohmad also distributed monthly dividends to its equity owners. The owners included Bernard Madoff, who controlled approximately 15 percent of the firm, and Peter Madoff, who held a 9 percent stake. Cohmad's registration with the Financial Industry Regulatory Authority indicates that Maurice "Sonny" Cohn was the largest stakeholder in Cohmad, owning between 25 and 50 percent of the firm. Marcia Cohn, Milton Cohn, Robert Jaffe, and an employee named Rosalie Buccellato also had stakes in Cohmad.

Although 85 percent of Cohmad's income came from BLMIS for the assets it brought in, employees there never said up front who was managing the money. Sometimes, Cohmad described Madoff's strategy as if Cohmad brokers were managing the money. "Cohmad displayed a mixed reaction to its relationship with Madoff's firm," said Lars Toomre, of Toomre Capital Markets, who has maintained an ongoing analysis of the Cohmad–Madoff web of relationships. "It both downplayed its asset management business and, at times, described the activities of Madoff Investments as if they were its own."

In a November 21, 1991, letter to a prospective investor in Lexington, Massachusetts, Cohmad's then-president Maurice Cohn wrote: "Our primary business is not managing client accounts. We do manage accounts for family and friends using a simplistic, and most important, a very conservative strategy in a disciplined manner, always 'insuring' the accounts against major loss by using put options."

Another letter from Cohn to an investor, dated July 17, 1992, explained Cohmad's goals: "Our 'mission' is to protect your investment (and mine!). To accomplish this, we maintain our discipline and stick with the same strategy, by buying a portfolio of 'blue chip' equities, selling call (index) options on your portfolio, and buying put (index) options to protect your portfolio against violent bear markets. Once again, we are not economists or security analysts. We are risk managers and our associates are very good at what they know best—namely, trading."

The preponderance of Madoff friends and family members in the office might have seemed normal in any other business. But, on Wall Street, the maintenance of systems and financial controls to safeguard

investors' money from fraud is supremely important. Family ties tend
to weaken those controls. So the proliferation of family and friends,
along with the intertwined relationship with Cohmad, should have been
questioned by investors.

One former employee described his experience working closely with
Madoff's sons. "They were my direct managers, and they had made a
lot of money as traders. But they also had all their personal savings in
the advisory business," he said, adding that he felt sorry for them in the
wake of the scandal. "Now they're bankrupt." This employee graduated
from college in 1996 and soon began working for the Madoffs on the
market-making side of the broker-dealer business. His job was to make
a market—set a price at which they would buy or sell a stock—for any
of Madoff's customers who did a brisk business in listed shares. Listed
shares are any shares trading on the New York Stock Exchange or the
American Stock Exchange. Others at the firm traded the newly popular
NASDAQ stocks such as Intel and Microsoft. This was during the technology boom and many of the newly public start-ups preferred to trade
on NASDAQ.

"We did mostly 'agency' trades," he explained, in which he acted as
an agent, or "pass-through," for the customer. A mutual fund firm or a
retail brokerage such as Schwab might "send us an order for ten thousand shares, and I either [bought or sold]. On each share, I earned a
penny or a half-penny commission."

This employee, like many other traders at Madoff's firm, was eventually allowed to trade for his own proprietary, or "prop," account.
Through this account, he began to learn about taking risk, and the job
was more intellectually stimulating than just buying and selling stocks
on behalf of customers all day.

"I was a risk taker—maybe I was just more of a curious person,
wanting to learn—so I ended up making more prop trades, sometimes
worth a few hundred thousand or a million dollars." Madoff's firm
fronted this young man the capital to make these trades—provided he
turned a profit. "So I was both a market maker and a prop trader."

In the mid- to late 1990s, Madoff's trading firm still looked and sounded
much like any other on Wall Street: a cadre of about thirty or forty
young people sat on the nineteenth floor of the Lipstick Building in the

trading section, an open area with rows of desks. Traders sat next to each other, but each person was "really doing their own thing," recalled Mark Kashar. Not everything was automated yet. "People still yelled and screamed, called trades in over the phone—it was like *Animal House*. You really had to think on your feet," he said, although he acknowledged that this activity began to wane as more was done over the computer. Madoff was doing "really well, probably trading 10 percent of all NYSE volume."

Kashar trained for a year at Madoff's firm, which, like many traditional Wall Street firms, ran a yearlong trainee induction program. The broker-dealer brought in well-recognized industry experts to school their trainees, such as market technician Steven Nison. Nison popularized something known as "candlestick charting," a technique originally developed by Japanese rice traders in the 1600s. Stock traders latched on to candlestick charts to predict turning points in the stock market. Candlestick charts marshal the same basic data used in traditional Western bar charts—a security's opening price, high and low for the trading session, and closing price—but represent data using a combination of thick and thin shadow bars.

"After a year or so, they gave you your own book, your own P&L, and they let you loose," said Kashar. He traded mostly listed stocks such as AOL, IBM, and other "big-name stocks, essentially anything that was really liquid. I had to automatically execute orders from Merrill or Bear Stearns or Lehman, meaning I would take the other side of the order and decide if I had to cover my position. It was stressful, but it was a great training ground."

One striking difference between BLMIS and other firms was that traders there had no limit to the amount of capital they could wager. This was a stunning risk, especially considering that Madoff did not have a credit line at a bank. Other aspects of the trading business were unusual too. Madoff did not use other "prime" brokers but instead cleared all his own trades and kept custody of the securities at his own firm. Unlike some trading desks, he couldn't borrow from the bank that owned the firm, so he had to find a different source of capital. That source would be his roster of "investors" on the illegitimate advisory side of the business.

In 1998 Kashar wanted to relocate closer to his home in Texas, so he moved to a new job at a securities trading firm in Dallas. For him it was like swapping a Ferrari for a Datsun. "At my new trading firm, my limits for trading were really tight on the amount of capital," or money given him to gamble for his personal P&L account. "To start out, every trader was allowed to have $1 to $2 million on the 'long' side," or betting on stocks rising, and an equal amount on the "short side," or betting on stock prices falling, he recalled. "At Madoff, it was never really expressed what my limits were. I could have as much as I wanted. Nobody questioned how much capital I had at stake unless I was doing something stupid."

Kashar left in June 1998, when the stock market was rollicking. The Asian currency crisis had started sweeping the globe, from one market to the next, faster now that they were connected electronically. He left wondering how it was that Madoff had such an uncanny sense for when to buy when the stock market was cratering. "Once, in 1997, the Dow was down something around 500 points. The next day the market opened even lower, down 200. And Bernie was running around the firm telling everybody to buy . . . and he was right! He knew whenever there was something going on. And invariably he was right."

Throughout the 1990s, Mark and Andrew Madoff ran the trading floor of the broker-dealer side of Madoff's operation. Andrew took over the NASDAQ desk around 1995. "They were a very hardworking family. Andrew didn't take a vacation for about four years after he started," according to one trader who worked with them. Occasionally, employees would try and race Andrew or Mark, or even Bernard or Peter, into the office. But invariably, one of the Madoff clan would already be in by six forty-five or, at the latest, seven a.m. every day.

Madoff and Ruth often traveled to Cap d'Antibes, France, where they had an apartment, or to their house in Palm Beach. But Bernie was never out of touch with the firm. "He would call in every morning to talk about the P&L," or profit and loss statement, or about where the firm stood in terms of its own trading account, said a former trader. "He wanted to know which of us was making or losing money. They never told me how to trade, they left me alone. But they kept track of what you were doing."

The Madoff philosophy with regard to customers was clear, this trader explained: "Don't fuck the client, don't make them look bad. If you were a market maker and you had an order, you were supposed to be conservative on how it was priced, and don't screw over the client." Madoff made it his job to ensure all of his employees were following this policy.

Once, in 2002, the S&P index was reorganizing which companies would be included in the index, deleting and adding names—a process known as "rebalancing." Index mutual funds that are pegged to the holdings in the S&P, Wilshire, or other indexes, have to buy and sell shares if new companies are added and old companies deleted. "I cleaned house that day," recalled the trader. "My buddy and I on the trading floor did really well."

By that evening, Mark Madoff was the only person around the office, but Bernie called in and found out the two traders had made a killing. Later he came into the office and walked up quietly behind the young man. "'Hey, Robo-Trader!'" he joked. "Sometimes Mark or Andrew would yell out when they saw a bad trade, 'Who's fucking up this stock?' But they never told me how to trade, they always left us alone to do our thing."

In 1996, Madoff hired Neil Yelsey to run what was known as a statistical arbitrage business within Madoff Securities, the broker-dealer. Prior to joining Madoff's firm, Yelsey had worked for Salomon Brothers (now part of Citigroup), where he had various roles, including stock research analyst for telecommunications in the mid-1980s, when that industry was deregulating, and proprietary trader in the 1990s. Yelsey had graduated from Swarthmore College in 1980 with a degree in engineering and was widely regarded as an enormous brain.

Madoff wanted what Yelsey had already helped create at Salomon Brothers. Within Yelsey's unit there, Salomon traded directly with customers at low cost to both sides. While that sounds like something anyone could do today, in the pre-Internet days of the early 1990s it was considered revolutionary. Customers even used Salomon-provided software to see the exact commission rates they paid to trade four hundred or so stocks in the quantitative group's inventory. "A customer might scan the commission charges for each of, say, 100 stocks in a program package and choose to eliminate a few with high commissions," reported the *Wall Street Journal* in a glowing profile of the Salomon trading desk. "The benefit for customers: lower commission rates than conventional trading and no fuss, since the trades don't show up in the public markets," the article noted.

A hire like Yelsey was a coup for Madoff. Salomon's high-tech trading arm, the Quantitative Trading Group, already did what Madoff desired to do—use computers to execute off-the-exchange trades for big customers such as mutual fund portfolio managers at commission rates lower than his competitors.' Yelsey's quantitative-trading unit was "exchanging" long lists of stocks from Salomon's inventory directly with customers at previously agreed-upon prices. "We would like to drive the cost of trading down as much as possible," said Yelsey, who at the time was just thirty-five years old. His boss, Jonathan Sandelman, added that the group held down both Salomon's risks and customers' costs.

Madoff had Yelsey design a similar trading system from scratch, just as he had at Salomon Brothers. He did that, and by the late 1990s Yelsey was using the automated trading program to oversee a portfolio of "something between $500 million and $750 million," according to a former Madoff proprietary trader. The Madoffs re-created Yelsey's strategy, pairing two competing stocks together and betting that one price would fall as the other rose, or vice versa. They made these bets based on the trading history and the relationship of the two prices over a long time. The strategy was called "statistical arbitrage," and the Madoffs took it to a whole new level. "They did it on a massive scale, and instead of just trading pairs, the computer systems [that Yelsey created] would trade three thousand stocks at a time. For instance, all the oil service stocks versus all the oil and gas drilling companies," explained the former employee. "The Madoffs took [Yelsey's] concept and applied it to their market-making business," trading thousands of stocks at once.

The returns from the strategy were fantastic, reaching about 20 percent a year. The strategy was so successful that the trades basically ran themselves. This made the human role in trading almost obsolete. "They got rid of a lot of the traders," said the former employee, who, fortunately, wasn't affected by the new system since he worked as a proprietary trader there.

But by the late 1990s, Madoff's cutting-edge technology was no longer so novel. The SEC, under Chairman Arthur Levitt, was pushing all of Wall Street to embrace electronic trading and help retail investors receive better prices for their portfolios. Madoff was now just one of many firms and literally dozens of "alternative trading networks" offering split-second electronic order execution. The seismic shift came in 2001, when U.S. markets completed the switch to stock pricing in pennies, rather than in fractions of a dollar. The spreads between quoted bid and ask prices, which had once been twenty-five cents or more, shrank to one cent or even less.

As more and more people began adopting the electronic trading model, this same system, which had made Madoff famous, ended up cannibalizing his own business. The efficiency of computers and the switch to decimal prices decimated the big profits from his and everyone else's market-making operations.

Decimals "killed everyone" among the market-making firms on Wall Street, recalled one former AMEX executive. When "the markets were still trading in eighths," Kashar recalled of his years at Madoff, "and if you had good order flow, you could buy on the bid and sell the offer and make money all day long. That was all before decimals."

Decimalization also made it less economical for Madoff to pay for orders to come the firm's way. "They paid one cent a share to bring their order flow to Madoff, but once decimals came around, their profit margins shrank from one-eighth," or 12.5 cents, to a penny. And they were paying a penny for every share. "So suddenly they weren't making as much and the market-making business didn't make any sense," said Kashar.

Moreover, Yelsey's successful trading beast, his automated system, begat imitators, and over time Madoff's returns from that started to drop down to about 2 percent or 3 percent—way down from the 20 percent a year when the program was first implemented.

All during the 1980s and 1990s, more and more money was pouring in to Madoff's illegitimate advisory operation. Although the broker-dealer and advisory businesses remained completely separate from one another, Madoff continued to use the success of his legitimate firm to dupe his victims and the SEC. He would wave papers from the legitimate broker-dealer business in front of them to deceive them into thinking he was making real trades.

What he didn't tell them was that none of the activity at the broker-dealer operation on the eighteenth and nineteenth floors had anything to do with his advisory business on the seventeenth. Madoff wasn't doing any trading for the phony hedge fund downstairs. He was simply taking investors' money, depositing the money into his Chase Bank in Manhattan—account number 140081703—and sending it back out to earlier investors. "By placing before SEC investigators reams of information showing legitimate trading activity through the market-making division, the SEC did not delve deeper into Madoff's investment advisory business," claimed one Madoff investor in a lawsuit against JPMorgan Chase.

Although the advisory business was growing, it was illegal, so Madoff did not like to talk about it. He never took any outsiders to the seventeenth floor. Even when the SEC started showing some interest in 2006, Madoff didn't make it easy for his clients to learn much of anything about how he managed the money. While most mutual funds, and even some hedge funds, provide timely electronic access to their investment accounts for their clients, Madoff never did so—despite his having revolutionized electronic trading over previous decades.

Paper tickets for trades supposedly made on their behalf were mailed to investors, but often they had no time stamps, so the exact transaction was unclear. Officially, this offered protection from others who might try to replicate it or trade against Bernie's secret moneymaking formula, but what it really did was allow Madoff to manufacture trade tickets that confirmed his steady, terrific annual returns on investments that had never actually been made.

Madoff also lied about how many people worked at the seventeenth-floor advisory operation and about how much money he was overseeing. In January 2008 regulatory filings with the SEC, which were signed by his brother, Peter Madoff, Bernie Madoff said he only employed fewer than five employees in investment advisory functions, including research, and yet they were managing $17 billion of assets. How was it possible that such a large sum of money was managed by such a small group of people?

While Madoff claimed more than $17 billion of positions, his 13F form, a regular disclosure the firm filed with the SEC, usually mentioned only smatterings of positions in small (non–S&P 100) equities. Madoff's explanation for this discrepancy was that his strategy was mostly in cash at the end of each quarter in order to avoid making information about the securities he was trading public. Again, this explanation beggared belief. If Madoff had been doing that, there would have been massive movements on money markets.

Another way Madoff hid the scope of his advisory operation from regulators was by lying about the number of clients he had. The SEC required that financial advisers register with the agency if they had more than fifteen clients. Madoff, however, encouraged clients to invest through so-called feeder funds that would channel their money to the firm indirectly. So, even though Madoff was managing money for thousands of individual clients, he counted these feeders as only one investor. Under this guise, he was able to operate below the radar and avoid random SEC audits. That worked until 2006, when the SEC changed its rules and required advisers to count each final investor as a client for registration purposes rather than counting one fund as a single client. Even so, Madoff still did not register immediately.

That year, the SEC spent several weeks at Madoff's broker-dealer operation. Between May and August of 2006, the SEC pored over BLMIS's trades and account statements trying to insure that he was not, in fact, engaged in the illegal practice known as "front-running." Front-running occurs when a broker receives an order from a customer but buys or sells for his or her own account before executing the trade for the customer. As a result, the broker's trade may move the price of the stock up or down before the customer gets in to buy or sell, and the broker has, in effect, cheated the client out of the best price. Front-running is still illegal today.

The SEC's investigation also focused a bit on his advisory business. In particular the agency examiners criticized Madoff for not registering as an investment adviser. He claimed he had only nine clients on that side of his business and it didn't meet the threshold of fifteen. It was only after the SEC probed further that he admitted he had more than fifteen final clients and therefore was finally forced to register in the fall of 2006.

Although the SEC never charged the Madoff firm with front-running, many traders suspected that he was doing just that. There was persistent chatter on Wall Street that Madoff was on to something special that gave him an edge, and many thought he was using his knowledge from trading with big customers on the eighteenth and nineteenth floors to trade ahead of those clients.

Traders recall this as one reason why Madoff's broker-dealer business didn't have a lot of clients in the hedge fund community, which was becoming a growing force on Wall Street. By 2006, some estimates showed that hedge funds controlled $1.3 trillion in assets and accounted for one-third or even half of all NYSE daily trading—a staggering amount.

"A lot of hedge funds wouldn't send us trades" as a result of the front-running rumors, said a former trader at Madoff's broker-dealer. "Everyone thought the hedge fund business downstairs was front-running, so most other hedge funds avoided us. But [front-running] would have been basically fucking the retail customers we were dealing with, so we wouldn't have done that."

Even more strange was that Madoff's hedge fund on the seventeenth floor rarely, if ever, sent trades through its own trading desk on the eighteenth or nineteenth floors.

"We never got any hedge fund business, or if we did, it was very little. But as a trader I gave much better executions to customers than they got anywhere else," said the former trader. "I'd have to drive the stock up twenty cents or thirty cents in price to buy five thousand shares for my client. I was giving a lot more liquidity than existed [in the marketplace]. I just assumed that the seventeenth-floor hedge fund didn't send us trades on the eighteenth or nineteenth floor because the Madoffs thought it was a conflict of interest. I thought maybe Bernie was concerned about how it might look to regulators. They were particularly sensitive about the regulatory nature of their business."

Most of the employees at Madoff's broker-dealer operation knew that Bernie was also running a separate business overseeing money or a portfolio down on the seventeenth floor. But few of them had ever seen the operation or knew details about it.

In September 1998, however, one of Madoff's key employees finally did emerge from the hedge fund on the seventeenth floor. His name was Frank DiPascali.

"I'd seen him at the Montauk summer weekend, the company party," said the former trader. Madoff would put up his entire staff for two nights out in Montauk, Long Island, where Bernie and Ruth had a home and kept their boats. That particular year the party was a lobster bake held at the Montauk Yacht Club. "I'd say hello to Frank, but he didn't really fit," the trader recalled.

"The market makers would not socialize with the people from the seventeenth floor," said Doug Kass, who runs the Seabreeze Partners hedge fund in Palm Beach, Florida, and interviewed several of Madoff's former employees for jobs. Many of those who worked on the seventeenth floor were foreign-born computer programmers of East Indian or Orthodox Jewish backgrounds. By hiring nonnative English speakers on the seventeenth floor, Kass added, "it shows that he encouraged an absence of socialization" between the people operating the real business on the eighteenth and nineteenth floors and the fraudulent hedge fund.

In September 1998, the stock market started sliding on news that a major hedge fund, Long-Term Capital Management, was collapsing. The hedge fund had made highly leveraged bets with money borrowed from all over Wall Street. Founder and fund manager John Meriwether and his Nobel Prize–winning partners were borrowing a hundred dollars for every dollar in the fund, to the tune of $120 billion. "The market was going bonkers. Bernie and Peter had a meeting with all the traders, and Bernie said, 'We're well capitalized. We can play big if we need to,'" he recalled.

Later that day, the stock market began to plummet. Suddenly Frank DiPascali appeared on the eighteenth floor—something he rarely did. DiPascali and Madoff started sending huge orders to buy stocks to market makers on their own trading floor—orders as big as five hundred thousand shares in names like Pfizer and GE. "Every time they did a trade I would see it pop up on my computer screen," he recalled. But this time, the mnemonic, or call sign, representing Madoff's firm, the letters MADF, didn't show up.

Every trader had their own special letters assigned to their proprietary trading account, like a pilot has a call sign. "This was one I hadn't ever seen. But I knew it wasn't external."

The incident raised more questions than it answered. What was this mysterious internal trading account and why was Madoff encouraging people to buy in the midst of so much panic?

Kass posits that money was flowing back and forth between the fraudulent hedge fund and the trading desk. Like many other observers, Kass thinks that the Ponzi scheme began in earnest when Madoff "incurred big losses in the late 1980s" and then tried to make up for them by borrowing money from his advisory clients. On that day in 1998, Kass said, "it sounds like the Madoffs took client money from the seventeenth floor and used it on the prop desk," perhaps because they were losing money in the market. Eventually the fraud grew so big that it became, as Kass would put it, a "financial holocaust."

Chapter Four

In the early 1990s, Frank Christensen dropped in on his old pal Bernard Madoff at his Manhattan office. He figured they would chat about the markets and reminisce about the days when they used to take the float plane to Wall Street together from Long Island. Madoff had since moved his offices to midtown Manhattan. Madoff's operation had expanded—all over the globe it seemed—but Bernard, his brother, and their children were all working on a few floors of the Lipstick Building on Third Avenue.

"I stopped by the office one day, and I sat with him for a few minutes," recalled Christensen, who'd happened to be in midtown after checking in on his NYSE trading operation. Afterward, on an impulse, he'd called Madoff's office.

Something about Bernie was different, Christensen noticed, but he couldn't put his finger on it. "He had changed—dramatically. He had definitely aged from the last time I had seen him," which was in the 1980s. "He wasn't his usual affable self—he was a changed man. Even though we chatted only briefly, I could tell."

Madoff's mood was heavy. He seemed to have a lot on his mind.

Christensen left Madoff's offices that day wondering what had caused his old friend to change so markedly. After that brief meeting, aside from a few short phone calls, Christensen never encountered Madoff again.

Madoff's mood may have been somber because the phony money management operation he had created as a side business had become a hungry beast. By the mid-1990s, it was overshadowing his legitimate and successful broker-dealer business. He had also recently received a scare from the SEC, which had shut down two of Madoff's main fundraisers, Frank Avellino and Michael Bienes, in 1992. Although the two had been forced to pay fines totaling roughly $700,000 for selling illegal notes to investors and then giving the money to Madoff, Madoff himself was somehow miraculously spared. It seemed the SEC was so relieved that all the money Avellino and Bienes had taken from their clients was still in their accounts with Madoff that the agency didn't implicate him for wrongdoing. Madoff claimed to the SEC that he had no idea the money had been raised illegally and publicly shrugged the whole thing off.

Nonetheless, it had caused him a big problem. In the span of thirty years, from 1962 to 1992, Avellino and Bienes had raised more than $440 million in exchange for "notes" returning 15–20 percent annually—a scheme that, like Madoff's entire billion-dollar fraud, was simply too good to be true. After the shutdown, Madoff had to offer all the money back to investors. Luckily for him, he had been able to keep most of it, so he didn't have to come up with nearly a half billion dollars in cash, but it had been a frightening possibility. In the end, he simply opened up new brokerage accounts with his firm for the unsuspecting investors. The clients, for the most part, were happy with the returns and didn't understand or probe the details of why their "advisers" had been shut down.

During the early 1990s, even though Madoff's illegal hedge fund operation was growing exponentially, it was still largely a secret. Even Madoff's longtime secretary, Eleanor Squillari, thought there was only one business, the market-making business. She didn't know the advisory business even existed. "It wasn't until 1993 that I became fully aware that there was a second business, in which Bernie invested money as a favor to a limited number of individuals," she told Vanity Fair in 2009. After Avellino and Bienes's clients switched their accounts to Madoff, they "contacted us in droves," Squillari said. "They didn't call asking to open accounts; they called expecting accounts to be opened for them. Most of them were elderly retirees, many of them widows. They had been accustomed to living off the double-digit dividends they'd been promised by Avellino and Bienes. Now they put their money in Bernie's hands."

With Madoff at the center, the money-raising apparatus would continue to rely on songbirds like Avellino and Bienes. But starting in 1993, a new generation of money-raisers—many of them amateurs, some of them professionals in the hedge fund community—began scouring the world to attract new clients to what Madoff was now describing as an elite "hedge fund." Technically, it was nothing of the sort—but for Madoff's believers, simply having access, a way to hand over to him their money, was the key. "Madoff was not a hedge fund," insists Richard Baker, former Louisiana congressman and now head of Managed Funds Association, Washington, D.C., a lobby group for the hedge fund industry. Madoff didn't offer investors a typical limited partnership like most hedge funds do, nor did he offer quarterly letters or annual conference calls.

But what form Madoff took didn't seem to matter to most of his investors. The fact that he called his scam a hedge fund only made the industry and regulators' nonexistent oversight look bad.

The hedge fund industry was growing, and demand for hedge funds meant that even more people would be interested in a secretive investment pool that had an exclusive air. Madoff's phony hedge fund—which for some time now wasn't investing in the markets but just paying old investors with new investors' money—found an audience easily. The hedge fund was under the radar, it made for good cocktail conversation, and the 1990s bull market was now in full swing.

After the 1992 SEC scare, Madoff needed big money to keep the pyramid going. And he found it. Chief among the big money scouts was Fairfield Greenwich Group. By the mid-1990s, Fairfield founders Walter Noel and his partner, Jeffrey Tucker, in Greenwich, Connecticut, were helping vacuum up cash for Madoff via their feeder fund, Fairfield Sentry, to the tune of hundreds of millions of dollars a year.

Noel managed to build the perfect global hedge fund marketing machine in-house by marrying off four of his five daughters to promising young men whom he then hired. His son-in-law, Yanko Della Schiava, was based in Lugano, Switzerland, and sold Fairfield Greenwich funds in southern Europe. Another son-in-law, Andrés Piedrahita, was by 1997 the biggest equity holder in Fairfield Greenwich and eagerly peddled the funds to Europeans and Latin Americans out of bases in London and Madrid. A third son-in-law, Philip Toub, marketed the funds in Brazil and the Middle East. By 2008, Fairfield Greenwich was pulling in annual fees of $135 million—just for raising money for Madoff.

Sandra Manzke and Bob Schulman of Tremont Capital Management in Rye, New York, also acted as another important feeder, packaging Madoff's low volatility and consistent return stream in the wrapping of retail funds sold across America.

In Europe, Arpad "Arkie" Busson was luring in new investors from the ski slopes of Switzerland to the tune of $230 million, and Sonja Kohn at Bank Medici in Vienna, Austria, was scouting around the newly free former Soviet countries and central and eastern Europe for what became $3 billion worth of investors' money. She even traveled as far as Moscow to appeal to Russian oligarchs' new wealth.

FIM Advisers LLP, whose Kingate Europe and Kingate Global funds oversaw about $3.5 billion, was run by two Italians, with Manzke on the board. FIM marketed the Madoff funds to wealthy Italian families, and in exchange Kingate collected a 5 percent entrance fee into the funds and a management fee of 1.5 percent of assets.

Run by a French aristocrat, Access International Advisors was another feeder into Madoff that charged a 5 percent fee up front, a 0.8 percent management fee, and a 16 percent performance fee on its Luxalpha SICAV–American Selection fund. Access investors paid 2.15 percent of assets in fees. Access was one of many funds that were willfully blind to Madoff's red flags. "He can't be a fraud," Access's founder René-Thierry Magon de la Villehuchet quipped once of Madoff. "I've got all my money with him."

Spain's largest bank, Banco Santander, invested with Madoff through its Optimal Strategic U.S. Equity fund. Santander later admitted its private clients and institutional clients had invested upward of $3 billion (2.33 billion Euros) and offered to repay private banking clients close to half of their losses—on the condition they not sue the bank and keep doing business with Santander. It was the first bank to make such an offer.

Back in New York, J. Ezra Merkin capitalized on his father's reputation and family name in the Jewish community to raise hundreds of millions of dollars for his funds of hedge funds Gabriel, Ariel, and Ascot. Really, Merkin was simply handing $2.4 billion in client money over to Madoff. "Fairfield at least was up front about the fact that they were just salespeople, running a fund of funds picking managers," said a private equity investor with Brookstone Partners who often competed with Madoff for investors. "Merkin failed to disclose the fact that he was no longer pulling the trigger, but simply handing the money over to Madoff." Referred to Merkin by a family member, actor Kevin Bacon and his wife, actress Kyra Sedgwick, invested in his fund of funds and lost everything to Madoff.

In Los Angeles, Stanley Chais and Gerald Breslauer brought in other Hollywood types, such as screenwriter Eric Roth, whose film credits include *The Curious Case of Benjamin Button*, and the charitable foundations of movie and entertainment moguls Steven Spielberg, Jeffrey Katzenberg, and David Geffen (the three men control DreamWorks Animation studio, which created *Shrek* and other films). "Stanley Chais was a beneficiary of this Ponzi scheme for at least 30 years," the Madoff victims' trustee alleged in a lawsuit filed against Chais.

Even Elie Wiesel, a Holocaust survivor and Nobel Prize winner, was swept up in the Madoff marketing machine. Through Ezra Merkin's father, Hermann, the Elie Wiesel Foundation for Humanity was introduced to Madoff and eventually lost more than $15 million in the scheme. Wiesel and his wife also sustained $7 million in personal losses. The senior Mr. Merkin had known Madoff for decades and connected Wiesel with Madoff. Thus Wiesel felt he had checked out Madoff indirectly through experts he trusted. "We thought he was God," Wiesel told a conference in February 2009. "We trusted everything in his hands."

All of these money scouts helped direct a river of cash into Madoff's operation. And they were paid commissions based on how much they brought in.

In the fifteen years between 1993 and 2008, the marketing of hedge funds was becoming a very lucrative industry unto itself. So Madoff's fund-raising efforts weren't unusual. Marketers for bona fide hedge fund managers—who really bought and sold investments for their advisory clients—were also out raising money right alongside Madoff. However, Madoff wasn't raising money through the usual channels.

"There's a whole industry of these third-party marketers who pitch hedge funds. That is all they do," said Tom Lauria, a onetime Wall Street equities analyst who conducts independent hedge fund research and attended many of the marketing events by prime brokers for hedge funds. "Say a marketer for hedge funds raises $1 million for a new fund. The marketer normally would get 1 percent of those assets as a commission and, going forward, 25 percent of any performance the fund returns" the next year. Madoff, however, was never at these events or "capital introduction" parties. He was raising money from family and friends by word of mouth, and usually from investors who didn't have a background in finance. With this system in place, it was less likely people would start asking questions.

Madoff seemed to be everywhere—taking capital away from real hedge funds, private equity funds, and other alternative investments. A private equity investor was incensed to find out he was competing with Madoff out in the fund-raising arena, especially given that no one seemed to know a thing about Madoff's secret hedge fund. "I was sitting down with Banco Santander one day to raise money for a private equity fund, and all the man across from me would say was, 'Why should we invest with you when we can get 10 percent a year?' That's when I realized I was competing against Madoff. He was all over the world."

Everyone connected to Madoff's fund-raising operation was getting such good kickbacks for bringing assets to him that it wasn't in their interests to worry about any warning signs surrounding him. "They had serious disincentives to vet out and do the due diligence," added Doug Kass, who was approached to invest with Madoff. Kass, who runs his own hedge fund in Palm Beach, noted that the depth of conflicts for all the marketers is impossible to overlook. "Everyone was on the tit."

Meanwhile, Cohmad continued bringing money in. Sonny Cohn and Alvin Delaire were working on Madoff's seventeenth-floor offices in the Lipstick Building and bringing investors in through their own operation. Cohn's daughter, Marcia, was sitting on the Madoff trading desk. Even Madoff's personal secretary, Annette Bongiorno, was recruiting residents—for a fee, of course—from her neighborhood of Howard Beach, Queens.

Robert Jaffe and Sonny Cohn would work the golf courses in Palm Beach and Long Island, respectively, and recruit investors right off the green. Their unsuspecting golf buddies had no idea Jaffe and Cohn were being paid hundreds of thousands of dollars a year in commissions to bring them to Madoff.

"I was introduced to Madoff by a man named Sonny Cohn. He got me in with Madoff," said one investor from Great Neck, New York. "When Madoff first went into business, he and Sonny Cohn were friends. Sonny helped him to get accounts to start his company." The individual said he had no idea Cohn "was getting commissions on all the people he steered to Madoff. He never told people like me he was earning commissions. It should be against the law."

Years after his last visit to Madoff in the early 1990s, Frank Christensen had long since sold his successful NYSE specialist trading firm for a mint and retired. In late 2008, as the market was crashing, he visited the New York Stock Exchange. The scene was reminiscent of Black Monday during the 1987 crash—except worse. Now trading volumes equaled billions of shares a day. Visions of another Great Depression loomed.

Christensen made the rounds, chatting with the boys on Button-wood South, the southern end of the exchange floor where John Thain, the still fairly new head of the exchange, was still nervous to walk without a buddy as an escort. At one point in his conversations, Madoff's name came up. This didn't surprise Christensen, considering that in his Wall Street heyday Madoff had not only been his friend but also a fierce competitor. Madoff had literally created a third market to compete with the NYSE and the AMEX to trade stocks they had once listed exclusively.

"He's not in market-making as much as he is managing money now, Frank," one exchange official said breezily. After his initial surprise wore off, Christensen figured that it made sense. After all, Madoff's pioneering move into electronic stock trading wasn't so futuristic anymore. Computers had infiltrated all kinds of industries. There were not only online retail stores, but university libraries that hosted their collections on the Internet and countless service businesses from takeout food to pornography.

Bernard L. Madoff Investment Securities, by now one of the Street's most prominent stock trading firms, was being overtaken in the market-making business. Instinet, Knight Capital Group, and a host of other superfast electronic communication networks (ECNs) had made sweeping advances to the model that Madoff had invented.

So now Madoff was running money—big money, apparently—through another arm of his business. Talk was that Madoff oversaw a hedge fund portfolio with assets on the order of $15 billion. This was not so strange in and of itself. After all, some of the most successful hedge funds were run by former traders. Millennium, for example, was founded by Israel "Izzy" Englander, a former AMEX trader. What was strange was Madoff's structure—or lack thereof. It was customary for hedge funds to charge a 2 percent fee on assets and a 20 percent fee on profits, but Madoff only charged commissions. Just by passing up on the 2 percent management fee, Madoff was giving up $60 million on his $15 billion in assets each year.

Consider the sheer scope of the fees Madoff was leaving on the table just from Fairfield Sentry alone. By 2000, Fairfield Sentry had $3.3 billion in assets. In 1990, Fairfield Sentry was up 27 percent. In the ensuing decade, it returned no less than 11 percent in any year and sometimes as high as 18 percent. In 2000, Fairfield Sentry returned 11.55 percent. Assuming Fairfield charged the hedge fund industry's standard fees of 1 percent and 20 percent between 2000 and 2008, on an average $5 billion in assets, then between 2000 and 2008 Fairfield charged investors—and booked as income—fees of $1.2 billion. Why would a savvy investor like Madoff willingly give up that kind of money?

Something was off. "It was too good to be true," Christensen recalled thinking. "The big money obviously had started rolling in to Madoff from those funds of hedge funds and the feeder funds. And the people running them didn't have to work for a living. They only had to pay Bernie trading commissions and they got 2 percent of assets and 20 percent of all profits? C'mon! They had to know something wasn't right."

At the same time as hedge funds were gaining in popularity, Wall Street was building up its own industry catering to them. Large brokerage firms like Barclays, Bank of America, Bear Stearns, and Goldman Sachs all offered "prime brokerage" services to hedge funds, which included something called "capital introduction." Capital introduction meant they helped hedge funds raise money and get exposure at conferences and even lent them money to make wagers in the stock and bond markets. "That's how they entice you to become a client. They say, 'This is what we can do for you,'" explained Tom Lauria. Having a prime broker gives a hedge fund "some credibility. It gives them a blue-chip name to show to investors as part of the infrastructure." It also gives investors somewhere to go to check the hedge funds' holdings, he explained. The prime brokerage industry is pretty up front about the fact that it charges hedge funds a fee for these services—a fee for raising money, a fee for appearing at a conference, a fee for borrowing money, and so on.

But Madoff did not have a prime broker, which should have served as a huge red flag to those in the hedge fund industry. Neither he nor his family attended Wall Street's popular prime brokerage events—the casino nights in New York, the conferences in Florida and Los Angeles, and the hedge fund networking events in the Caribbean or Monaco. They attended and hosted plenty of other industry parties for the legitimate broker-dealer side of the business—for the Security Traders Association and other traders' groups—but not events for hedge funds.

Madoff never had a prime broker because he never had a real hedge fund.

Instead of borrowing money from banks (which would have demanded he disclose his books to their oversight), Madoff was borrowing from ordinary people—the casualties of his pyramid scheme. "Most times hedge funds borrow money from banks or their prime broker at 3 percent and then pay back that loan over time and invest it in things they think will return some larger amount, like 10 percent. Madoff wasn't even borrowing the money," Lauria added. He was just stealing it.

In 1997, Rob Picard was working for RBC, the Royal Bank of Canada. The Canadian bank was mulling over investing some money in what was considered the holy grail of hedge funds: a low volatility fund. "Low volatility" meant the returns on the fund weren't always very high but they were consistent, as smooth as the Sargasso Sea every year, predictable and calm. Picard and other executives flew to New York to meet with Madoff in his midtown offices to see whether his guaranteed investment strategy was for real.

RBC had clients who wanted to borrow money from the Canadian bank to put into a feeder fund invested with Madoff. "Investors were coming to us asking for leverage, especially investors in the Tremont Broad Market Fund and Fairfield Sentry," Picard recalled.

Tremont was a huge believer in Bernard Madoff. Bob Schulman, who oversaw Tremont's alternative investments business with colleague Sandra Manzke, "insisted that we meet with Bernie. He was one of Madoff's biggest fans," Picard said. Tremont, founded by Manzke in 1985, started selling Madoff-managed investments in 1997 under the Rye Select Broad Market name, charging 2 percent of assets. Tremont's

Rye Investment Management unit eventually had $3.1 billion, or virtually all its assets, in Madoff's fund.

Once in from the airport, Picard and his group arrived at Madoff's nineteenth-floor office and were shown into an expansive conference room. Within about fifteen minutes, Picard realized he had logged hundreds of miles and countless meetings only to have stumbled into a fraud.

"Madoff stuttered when he tried to explain his options strategy, and right away I realized he either didn't understand it or he wasn't doing what he said he was doing," Picard said. RBC bank officials knew that Madoff was always taking in new money and that he had likely grown beyond the $8 billion in assets he claimed to be running. Picard figured it was closer to $20 billion or more.

Picard also knew that the world's top-earning hedge funds—Renaissance Technologies on Long Island, Citadel in Chicago, and Farallon in San Francisco, Julian Robertson's Tiger, Leon Cooperman's Omega, Highfields in Boston, Och-Ziff in New York—were showing up as major Wall Street players in *Institutional Investor* magazine or in other hedge fund rankings. Their returns, if they disclosed them, were closely tracked by hedge fund databases, such as MARHedge or TASS. Picard wondered why Madoff was never mentioned anywhere as one of the biggest hedge funds on Wall Street.

"We suspected something wasn't right," Picard said. After the meeting, some of the RBC investors redeemed out of the Tremont feeder funds. "Until Madoff was arrested, some of our investors wouldn't believe it. They said there was no chance he could pull off something like that."

Hedge funds, Picard had concluded, weren't about technical indicators or strategies. They were about people and access to those people. "It's all about people—Bernie, the people he surrounded himself with, and his investors. Every investor had similarities. What they were looking for and expecting, in their heart of hearts, was all behavioural finance." How to explain irrational investor decisions using psychology—especially using the theories of Daniel Kahneman, a psychologist at Princeton University, and Amos Tversky of Stanford University—is the basis of behavioral finance.

Charles MacKay, in his book *Extraordinary Popular Delusions and the Madness of Crowds*, perfectly summed up the aura of greed surrounding Madoff's hedge fund: "Money, again, has often been a cause of the delusion of multitudes. Sober nations have all at once become desperate gamblers. . . . Men, it has been well said, think in herds; they go mad in herds, while they only recover their senses slowly, and one by one."

Madoff's fraud was likely a multibillion-dollar version of the notes scam that Frank Avellino and Michael Bienes had been running with Madoff's help in the 1960s, '70s, and '80s.

The tight circle of family surrounding Madoff at his firm "acted like a wall of enablers," Picard said. "But it ran deeper than that." Once Madoff had gained the confidence of key investors like Carl Shapiro, the Swiss bankers Notz Stucki, Edgar de Picciotto's UBP, and Edmond Safra's Safra Bank, then others followed, such as Syz & Co., and other discreet Geneva private banks. "They were all deep into Madoff because Notz Stucki liked [Madoff]" as a fund manager, Picard explained.

"They looked at the returns and said to themselves, 'We have to give Madoff money.' The European investment community trusted the numbers. They took Madoff's word." Everyone seemed to be falling for Madoff's velvet rope trick. "Bernie's attitude of turning away money, of not needing the money, worked every time. There was nothing more exclusive than a velvet rope, even in a small way."

Harry Markopolos testified to Congress that by 2002, at least a dozen or more Swiss and French private banks were invested with Madoff—all thinking they had special access. None had any idea that their peers too had been sucked in as well, as they had become "mad in herds," all buying into Madoff. After Madoff's arrest in December 2008, Notz Stucki admitted that over the years it had steered over $730 million into Bernie Madoff via feeder funds set up for clients—one fund called Pendulum and another fund, Plaza. Notz Stucki denied that it had taken any juicy commissions to send money Madoff's way, and instead had taken "only a 1 percent fee, with no performance fees," citing the "low volatility" offered by the American financier. Bank executives had seen Madoff's alleged magic formula—his track record of double-digit returns every year—during sales pitches by the Fairfield Greenwich Sentry fund, which had a track record that dated back to 1990.

Besides promising returns that never failed, Madoff's best sales pitch was all word of mouth. Other funds of hedge funds also had products with returns linked to Madoff. Arden and FRM "would show you a page, a piece of paper with such and such of their funds, and underlying it would be Bernard Madoff," Picard said. "They were all in awe, saying things like, 'This is noncorrelated to the stock market,' meaning it didn't move in tandem with the Dow or S&P 500, and so was a good way to diversify. Or they would say, 'This can't lose money.'"

Picard didn't buy it. At RBC board of directors meetings, he had seen track records like these before. He wasn't sure exactly when the Madoff fraud spun out of control, but he believes it could have been during or after the 1987 stock market crash or during a market correction in the ensuing late 1980s.

"Madoff must have lost a lot of money at some point and was too embarrassed to face his friends and family," Picard suggested, since all those people were clients. Other hedge fund managers had done the same thing, like Michael Berger in 1999 with Manhattan Investment hedge fund, Sam Israel with Bayou in 2005, Arthur Nadel in 2009. (Nadel told investors his $350 million in hedge fund assets were posting gains when in fact there was less than $125,000 in the accounts.) The first month of losses, they tell a little lie, figuring they'll make it back. The second month, they lie some more. Eventually, they figure they're guilty no matter how much money they lose, so they continue to lie more and lose big.

Strangely enough, all these red flags did not sway Tremont or Fairfield Greenwich from investing.

Sandra Manzke had introduced Madoff to the Tremont folks, and then in 2007 Bob Schulman took over Tremont's single-manager business, the feeders. Schulman became one of the biggest advocates of Madoff's strategy. He "was one of Bernie's biggest salesmen. He would tell us [when we questioned Madoff's returns], 'You guys don't know what you're talking about,'" said one AMEX executive who worked with Schulman.

Schulman had an options background and had joined Tremont in 1994. So his former colleague was stunned that Schulman was taken in by Madoff. The AMEX official explained, "For someone with an options background, I don't know how he was able to justify and explain" how Madoff was trading his strategy, an options strategy buying calls and selling put options on the S&P 100.

There were those who suspected Madoff's magic was just an

illusion. Among Wall Street options traders, the conventional wisdom was that Madoff's strategy could not be replicated by anyone in the marketplace—at least not so it generated the double-digit returns he claimed. People leave tracks in the marketplace. When stocks rise or fall, there is always someone, somewhere, who knows why. But Madoff left no footprints. His activity did not appear in the marketplace; it was as if he didn't exist. None of the big trades he supposedly executed in the now-dwindling S&P 100 index options trading pit could ever be found. Trading in the S&P 100 was dying; more investors instead were using the popular S&P 500 index or NASDAQ index options, especially during the dot.com and technology boom.

Ken Nakayama, former head of equity derivatives at Deutsche Bank, would have seen Madoff's trades—had there been any. So would have the head of equity derivatives at Salomon Smith Barney, Goldman Sachs, Merrill Lynch, and other big "wire houses" on Wall Street. None of them ever saw Madoff's trades. Alex Jacobson from the Chicago Board Options Exchange had heard that Madoff's option trading on that exchange had stopped in the early 1990s.

The red flags were there, but still plenty of people ignored them to keep their money with Madoff. Some sociologists would argue that Madoff investors ignored the old saw "trust, but verify." Others said Madoff's investors simply allowed laziness or greed to overwhelm their good judgment since they viewed Madoff as a safe, conservative investment, like a Treasury bill or a money market account. After all, who do you ask for a referral for a good doctor, a dentist, a babysitter? Friends and family. Yet the same people did more research on buying a car than they did on the man who handled their money.

Madoff was a master of gaining trust without giving up a lot of information. Social psychologist Robert Cialdini, author of the bestselling book *Influence*, has highlighted six "weapons of influence" that ordinary people use to gain trust, including returning favors, commitment and consistency, being an authority figure, and being liked. "The trouble is that all of these can be faked, which is just what Madoff did," wrote Len Fisher, author of *Rock, Paper, Scissors: Game Theory in Everyday Life*. Some of his investors suspected that Madoff was cheating, but they continued to invest because they thought they were benefiting from his cheating, Fisher added. In other words, "they took Madoff for a different sort of cheat"—a savvy Wall Street type who was using information from his market-making operation to earn illegal profits on their behalf.

Fisher suggests that game theory could have helped investors stay away from Madoff. In game theory, each party demonstrates "credible commitment" to prove they can be trusted. "If Madoff's investors had looked for this sort of proof of commitment, in the form of proper auditing and a transparent portfolio of investments whose value could be checked, they would not have been caught out in so spectacular a fashion," he wrote.

Clients ignored the fact that Madoff printed on an old dot-matrix printer, and that despite his technological edge on the trading side, they couldn't check their own accounts online. "Why did investors fail to check? It can only have been because they thought that they would do better by not looking." By colluding in the cheating—believing in the Madoff magic, whether it was by illegal front-running or some inexplicable Midas touch—Madoff's investors proved the perfect example of one of game theory's most important and least-heeded lessons. Fisher concluded: "Cheats can prosper, but only when the other side isn't cheating as well."

Joe Gieger, a managing director at fund of hedge funds shop GAM, said representatives from the $39.2 billion asset management firm visited Madoff's operations early on and decided against investing with him. "We reviewed him twice. Once in 1998 when David Smith, chief investment director of GAM's funds of hedge funds group, who at the time was an analyst, went to visit him," he told the asset management trade publication *FINalternatives*. GAM couldn't triangulate the returns with what Madoff claimed was his strategy. Then, in 2001, GAM made another visit and again rejected Madoff.

Other big investors in hedge funds tried to understand the feeder fund vehicles funneling money into Madoff, but they were barred from asking too many questions and didn't bother probing further.

"I was introduced to a feeder into the Madoff fund and after being told about this rare opportunity to get invested with a manager of very high regard (to many), low fees and producing consistent returns," James Newman, vice president of operational due diligence at Ermitage, a fund of funds, wrote in a letter to clients. "From the outset I was denied the opportunity to perform a detailed due diligence review. We take a very dim view on any fund, regardless of size, industry status, or 'it's good enough for them' type reasons that restricts our due diligence process." He declined to invest.

Among others who avoided Madoff was Aksia, which in 2007 penned a letter warning clients away from Madoff feeder funds. Aksia was concerned that Madoff's comptroller was based in Bermuda, whereas most mainstream hedge funds had their own in-house comptrollers. In addition, Madoff's auditor, Friehling & Horowitz, operated out of a strip mall in New City, New York. This was highly unusual in an industry where most billion-dollar hedge funds were audited by one of the Big Four accounting firms, Ernst & Young, Deloitte Touche Tohmatsu, KPMG, or PricewaterhouseCoopers. Aksia reviewed the stock holdings Madoff was reporting quarterly with the SEC and concluded the holdings appeared to be too small to support the billions of dollars in assets Madoff claimed to be managing.

But Madoff did just fine without the support of these firms and relied on fund-raisers and feeder funds to build his client base. Feeder funds offered by firms like Tremont and Fairfield Greenwich also allowed Madoff to outsource all the regulatory headaches and the paperwork, said Lita Epstein, an Orlando, Florida–based forensic accountant and author of several books on financial statement analysis. "Madoff paid them to be the front door, the registered investment adviser, while he operated the underlying strategy. Madoff could even claim he was never a hedge fund. He knew there was a gray area that existed. He found the regulatory holes and he exploited them," she added.

Even Madoff's eerily consistent returns did not worry his believers. "Con artists know people's mental roadblocks and ways around them. To most people, Madoff couldn't be a get-rich-quick scam because he was offering 8–12 percent returns a year, which are certainly in the realm of possibility" and not outlandishly high, explained Pat Huddleston, founder of Investor's Watchdog, which conducts risk analysis of investment opportunities. Huddleston, who compiles safety rankings for investors who want to examine a money manager before investing, said Madoff would have only earned a 40 out of a potential 80 ranking. Why? "He had custody over all the assets. Self-custody and self-clearing of securities are immediate red flags."

Investors were hypnotized by the perceived exclusivity of investing with Madoff and believed that not investing would be foolish.

As Jason Zweig opined in the *Wall Street Journal*, "Mr. Madoff emphasized secrecy, lending his investment accounts a mysterious allure and sense of exclusivity. . . . If you did get invited in, then you were anointed a member of this particular club of 'sophisticated investors.' Once someone you respect went out of his way to grant you access . . . it would seem almost an 'insult' to do any further investigation."

The awkward revelations for funds of hedge funds have spurred some industry changes to head off another hedge fund manager cum criminal. Union Bancaire Privée had invested with Madoff, but, according to an outside spokesman for the firm, UBP has since instructed all underlying hedge fund managers in which it is invested that they are required to give custody of their assets to an independent third party and use an independent administrator.

"An independent administrator maintains the official books and records of the fund and produces the investor statements," said Reiko Nahum, the founder of Amber Partners, which conducts operational certifications on hedge funds.

According to Sarah Allen, head of hedge fund research and executive director of investment solutions at Ermitage, a fund of hedge funds based out of London, the balance of power will change, tilting more toward the investor, giving them more of a say in the structure, governance, and liquidity profile of the hedge funds in which they invest. It will also give investors the ability to demand fairer fees, perhaps based on liquidity factors or a longer-term performance structure. Larger investors should demand better governance and control, hence the increasing popularity of managed account platforms.

In Washington, D.C., hedge fund experts are still divided between mandatory registration of hedge funds with the SEC and demanding position information from prime brokers, which usually have decent transparency as to what their hedge funds are holding in portfolios. Regulate the lenders to hedge funds such as banks and prime brokers, and you will have more control over the industry, say some.

Others like Leon Metzger noted in congressional testimony that even hedge fund registration didn't prevent the Madoff pyramid scheme. Instead, Metzger supports mandating independent custodians. Most Wall Street clients with their own advisers still have brokerage accounts with, say, Charles Schwab or E-Trade holding the underlying securities. Custody by a third party prevents self-dealing. Metzger is an adjunct professor and lecturer at Columbia, NYU, and Yale, where he teaches an overview of the challenges of launching and operating alternative investment management firms—particularly hedge funds. He worked at the Paloma Partners fund of hedge funds for eighteen years, most recently as vice chairman and chief administrative officer. "Best practices calls for the trader, whether an employee at a hedge fund or an investment adviser directing a managed account, to have authority only to initiate" trades, not to actually execute them or to handle the hedge fund client's cash, Metzger told Congress.

Indeed, Aksia's CEO Jim Vos repeated that same warning. The Fairfield Greenwich, Tremont, and other feeder funds may have all used top-shelf auditors and accounting firms, but the bulk of their assets were held in custody by Madoff himself. Vos noted the lack of an independent custodian at Madoff. "Madoff Securities, through discretionary brokerage agreements, initiated trades in the accounts, executed the trades, and administered the assets. This seemed to be a clear conflict of interest and a lack of segregation of duties is high on our list of red flags."

Despite the wide array of warning signs, it wasn't always good business to turn down the "opportunity" to invest in Madoff. Sometimes, in fact, messing with Madoff could cost a person his job. The head of Lehman Brothers' alternative investments division found this out the hard way.

Ehrenkranz & Ehrenkranz, a law firm run by brothers Joel and Sanford Ehrenkranz, was well known on Wall Street. Not only did they have high-profile clients like the heirs to the Estée Lauder cosmetics fortune, but their firm had slowly evolved into a huge player in the hedge funds business. Joel Ehrenkranz in particular was considered a heavy hitter in New York social and philanthropic circles, serving on the board of the Whitney Museum. Joel and his wife, Anne, had endowed a professorship, the Joel S. and Anne B. Ehrenkranz Professor of Law, at New York University.

As early as 2002, Ehrenkranz and Lehman struck a joint venture to invest in hedge funds; Lehman Brothers partnered with Ehrenkranz & Ehrenkranz (also called E&E in Lehman's regulatory filings) and together they managed about $3 billion.

The Ehrenkranz brothers knew plenty of wealthy people, and they knew how to present fund of hedge funds to audiences where wealthy people would be listening. In 2007, for instance, an Ehrenkranz &

Ehrenkranz partner made a presentation to Tiger 21, which calls itself a "peer-to-peer learning group for high-net-worth investors" but which the *New York Times Magazine* dubbed "a support group for multimillionaires."

Now Joel Ehrenkranz was set to bring a new fund of funds he liked to Lehman Brothers.

Joel Ehrenkranz brought a man to the meeting named J. Ezra Merkin to pitch his fund of hedge funds to Lehman Brothers. The man who reviewed the funds for Lehman was skeptical—he had seen a similar strategy pitched to the Swiss bank he had worked at for a decade, and he quickly figured out that Merkin's outfit was just a feeder into Madoff.

The Lehman guy fired first.

"C'mon, Ezra. You know what's behind Madoff's operation, don't you? Don't act like you don't," he said.

Merkin and the man nearly got into a fistfight. Joel Ehrenkranz and Merkin left Lehman Brothers in a huff. Not long after this meeting, the man at Lehman Brothers lost his job.

There was another, less well-known Madoff gatekeeper: a woman named Sandra Manzke.

A straight-talking blowsy blonde, Sandra Manzke was unique for a few reasons—one being that she was a female in an industry dominated by men, the other being that she had one of the longest-running relationships with Bernard Madoff on Wall Street.

Manzke had created a few valuable highways to Madoff over the years. The first was Tremont, which she opened in 1984 with the backing of mutual fund manager Mario Gabelli. The second was Maxam Capital, set up by Manzke in 2005 also with the backing of another well-known money manager, Art Samberg of Pequot, and his right-hand man, Peter Decker. Art Samberg and Decker were listed in SEC filings as major shareholders in Maxam Capital as of 2009. The third entity Manzke helped set up as a gateway to Bernard Madoff was Kingate. Kingate was an outfit run by FIM Advisers, which was based in London and overseen by two Italian businessmen, Carlo Grosso and Federico Ceretti. Manzke sat on the board of directors of Kingate.

In an interview on PBS's *Frontline*, Manzke claimed she met Madoff sometime "in the early 1990s." But it was likely much earlier. As far back as 1990, the Kingate Global Fund, partly overseen by Tremont, was up and running with Madoff as the portfolio manager.

According to SEC filings, Manzke's Tremont was paid a retainer from Kingate based on the amount of assets her firm brought in. According to Tremont's 2000 10-K filing with the SEC, Tremont was paid a fee based on the amount of assets held by investors who were brought in to the Kingate funds. In 2000, that amount was $211 million and Kingate's net assets were $1.2 billion.

Manzke had an unusual background for a Wall Street hedge fund manager. Prior to establishing Tremont, Manzke toiled quietly in Wall Street's backwater. From 1969 to 1974, she worked at Scudder Stevens & Clark developing performance-measurement and reporting systems while attending film school at night. From 1974 to 1976, she worked as an independent consultant at Bernstein Macauley, where she was responsible for reviewing the firm's investment products. She would become a principal at Rogers, Casey & Barksdale, a pension fund consulting firm, from 1976 to 1984. While there, she served as the senior consultant to a number of corporate and ERISA (Employee Retirement Income Security Act) clients.

Finally, in 1984, Manzke struck out on her own. Her dream had been to put together a women- and minority-owned business that targeted American pensions, but her real talent was spotting exceptional hedge fund managers ahead of the pack. She managed to build up assets, and by 1987 Tremont Capital Management was overseeing about $650 million.

At this time two important men entered the picture: Mario Gabelli, the high-profile mutual fund investor, and Christopher Wetherhill, a shadowy Bermuda banker.

Gabelli was a showman on Wall Street. He had a buyout vehicle called Lynch Corp. that he used to buy up most of Tremont's stock. A few years later, in 1992, Gabelli spun out Tremont as a brand-new public company and a penny stock. (A penny stock typically trades for under a dollar a share, but there's no strict definition.) The Tremont stock price did well, rising from forty cents to ten dollars a share by 1999. Tremont moved from the over-the-counter market to trade on NASDAQ and by 2000 was reporting tremendous growth in three core businesses: consulting, information, and investment products for the global alternative investment industry. Tremont had bought TASS Investment Research, which owned an early database of twenty-five hundred hedge funds. This database allowed Manzke and partner Bob Schulman a window into the ever-expanding hedge fund industry, as a way to monitor which funds were doing well and which were losing money. The database itself would become one of Tremont's most valuable assets.

By that point, Tremont consulted on more than $7 billion in alternative investments and monitored more than $700 million of client assets in its proprietary funds. It oversaw more than $100 million in insurance policies too, with hedge funds as the underlying investment.

In 1998, Manzke and Schulman developed one of the first hedge fund indexes. The index, which was known as the CSFB/Tremont Hedge Fund Index, operated similarly to the Dow Jones or the Standard & Poor's 500 stock indices. It was supposed to track and compare hedge funds' returns and performance against other investments, like the five hundred public companies in the S&P 500, or against a basket of commodities or private equity, to name a few. The index soon became one of the standard benchmarks of hedge fund performance on Wall Street.

In 2001, Gabelli, who still owned 20 percent of the shares of Tremont, helped negotiate a sale of Tremont to a big investment bank and insurance conglomerate. After shopping the firm around, Oppenheimer bought the Tremont for nineteen dollars a share.

That sale to Oppenheimer alone netted Gabelli at least $20 million, and a similar take for another investor: Christopher Wetherhill. Wetherhill was the man behind another major Tremont shareholder, Mutual Risk Management. Both men, as well as Tremont principals Manzke and Schulman, reaped a small fortune in the buyout of Tremont by Oppenheimer.

Manzke and Schulman had incentives not to ask too many questions about Madoff, their cash cow. Madoff had become one of the key hedge fund managers in Tremont's stable, and the consistency of his returns helped seal the deal with Oppenheimer. In the merger agreement, Oppenheimer, their new parent company, insisted that Tremont hit certain revenue targets in the ensuing years until 2006—also known as "earn-outs"—so that Manzke and Schulman could share in the bonus pool down the road, according to SEC filings by Oppenheimer and

Tremont. In order to qualify for bonuses in later years, one of the only ways Tremont would be able to hit these targets was by sticking with Madoff. And because Tremont depended on Madoff's consistent returns, Manzke and Schulman never publicly questioned how Madoff made his money.

In short, Manzke and Tremont had to hit those performance targets to get their bonuses—and they would only be able to do that by sticking with Madoff.

The fees generated by sending money to Madoff warranted special mention: the Madoff–Tremont relationship was so significant that the investment bankers on the merger deal made note of Tremont's relationship with one special money manager. Putnam Lovell served as Tremont's financial adviser and was also the party Oppenheimer first contacted to express an interest in Tremont in 2000.

As part of its work on the acquisition, Putnam Lovell pointed out in its analysis of the "significant contribution to Tremont's revenues from a single relationship it has with an investment manager to its proprietary investment products." This "single relationship" could only have been with Madoff, with whom Tremont had already invested approximately $1 billion.

By the time Oppenheimer and its Boston-based insurance parent, MassMutual, took over Tremont, the fees from Tremont's Madoff-linked investment funds constituted the firm's fastest-growing revenue stream. Tremont's June 30, 2001, quarterly report, filed with the SEC before Oppenheimer and MassMutual took over Tremont, reveals the money trail: fees from Tremont's proprietary investment funds increased 45.6 percent just in the first six months of 2001 because of the relationship with Madoff. The filing read: "Fees from the Company's proprietary investment funds increased 45.6% during the first six months of 2001 to $8,008,200, up $2,509,500 over the first six months of 2000, and 46.6% in the second quarter of 2001 to $4,215,700, up $1,339,400 over the second quarter of 2000 due to the growth of the funds' net assets arising from additional investor capital contributions and overall positive investment performance."

Much, if not most, of this 45.6 percent increase was directly attributable to fees taken from Madoff investors. Each of the three Tremont hedge funds Oppenheimer took over as part of the merger deal—American Masters Broad Market Prime Fund, Kingate Global Fund, American

Masters Broad Market Fund—constituted a "significant percentage of [Tremont's] consolidated revenues," according to Tremont's SEC filings. They were funds set up to invest exclusively with Madoff.

It was only years later that Madoff would confess his fraud, and it would emerge that Tremont's fees and other feeder fund fees were based on phantom assets and imaginary investment returns. In Madoff's "cash in, cash out" Ponzi scheme, early investors' money was taken out to pay later investors

Under Tremont's Rye Select brand, Tremont had placed an additional $3.1 billion with Madoff. But Manzke was also reaping profits from Maxam and Kingate. She had helped establish Kingate Global, a joint venture between Tremont and Kingate Management. Manzke sat on the board of Kingate, which became one of Madoff's biggest single feeder funds, raising $2.75 billion for his firm, starting as far back as 1994. As late as 2005, Manzke was listed as a "manager" of Kingate as well as a board member.

Kingate was overseen by the London-based firm FIM, run by Federico Ceretti and Carlo Grosso. Kingate Global served as a feeder fund into Madoff and invested $3.5 billion in assets on behalf of clients such as BBVA (Banco Bilbao Vizcaya Argentaria), Pioneer Alternative Investments, and Union Bancaire Privée. Kingate represented about 70 percent of FIM's assets. FIM marketed the funds to many wealthy Italian families and collected a 5 percent fee for access to the funds and a management fee of 1.5 percent of assets. Since its inception in March 1995, Kingate claimed an overall return of 354.47 percent.

"There was a whole network of feeder funds all over Europe," the chief executive of one prominent fund of hedge funds in London told the *Sunday Times* after Madoff's arrest. "There were the three big ones: Fairfield, Kingate and Tremont. Anyone who asked to get in was told that they would have to wait for someone else to come out. Then there were the private banks, which offered access through their own funds. There were other ways in. The family offices of wealthy people from places like Switzerland and Luxembourg would occasionally let people invest in Madoff through their funds. It was always presented as a great opportunity."

It's unclear exactly when Kingate started doing business with Madoff, but Kingate used its brand name to sell several different feeder funds with access to Madoff. John Bruhl, an investor in Kingate Global, alleged in a 2009 lawsuit that Kingate initiated a fund of funds account feeding into Madoff in 1994.

Another Kingate fund was operating as far back as 1992. In a document issued by a Swiss private banking outfit, ALTIN AG, Manzke is listed as part of the money manager "team," which included Charles D. Sebah, Christopher Wetherhill, and Keith R. Bish, overseeing Kingate.

"The trading activities of Kingate are directed by a highly regarded, long-established U.S. broker-dealer," described one fact sheet on the firm released by ALTIN AG. "The portfolio is managed by an experienced team within the organization, based on the split-strike conversion options trading strategy. The inception date of the fund: January 1992."

That U.S. broker wasn't named, but clearly the board members such as Manzke and FIM's principals knew who it was: Bernie Madoff. Moreover, the "team" listed on the fact sheet were not portfolio managers. They were simply handing the money over to Madoff to invest in his supposed trading strategy.

Through European feeder funds such as Kingate and Tremont's offshore fund, the people who raised billions of dollars in assets for Madoff were able to market access to this Wall Street guru through Swiss banks. One of them was Banque Syz & Co. SA in Geneva, for example. Founded by Eric Charles Max Syz, a Swiss citizen who served as chairman of his own private bank, Banque Syz & Co. SA in Geneva specialized in asset management for high-net-worth individuals. Syz marketed Kingate funds under the brand name ALTIN, and he had many connections in the discreet world of Swiss banking. Before founding Banque Syz & Co. SA in 1995, Syz spent ten years with Lombard Odier Darier Hentsch & Cie in Geneva, and from 1990 to 1993 he was with the merchant banking arm of Lombard Odier.

In America, Sandra Manzke had one other powerful backer in a man named Art Samberg, the founder of the billion-dollar hedge fund Pequot Capital. Samberg was well known in the hedge fund industry and interviewed annually for *Barron's* Roundtable forum, a discussion with Wall Street's savviest professionals.

Together, Manzke and Samberg had a virtual lock on managing the pension money for Fairfield County, Connecticut, a suburb of New York comprised to a large extent of commuters that ranked among the wealthiest counties in America. In the early 2000s, pension plans began to seek access to hedge funds, and Manzke took advantage of the trend. By 2005, pension funds had a full-on love affair with these "alternative" investments, accounting for roughly 40 percent of all institutional money in hedge funds. While most pension plans had only modest stakes in hedge funds, others had invested more than 20 percent of their assets.

According to the late Greg Newton, who covered the hedge fund industry on his blog, NakedShorts, Fairfield County originally invested in Madoff in 1995, through Sandra Manzke. Eventually the county contributed around $20 million to Manzke through Tremont's Rye Broad Market Fund. "So that would probably be who town attorney Richard Saxl has in mind when he said, 'Officials will pursue other legal actions to try to recoup as much money as possible.' Assuming Fairfield's chief fiscal officer Paul Hiller can find the relevant documents in his filing system," Newton wrote after Madoff's arrest and Fairfield's discovery that Sandra Manzke—two times over nearly a decade—had directed the county to put all their money into a fraud.

In 2005, Manzke left Tremont. After Manzke had a falling-out with her partner, Bob Schulman, she then set up her own firm, Maxam Capital. Again, this new firm aimed to have a particular focus on finding minority- and women-owned hedge fund managers. According to the *Wall Street Journal*, Maxam instead proceeded to park $280 million—all of her personal wealth—with Madoff.

It's hard to know whether Manzke lost everything to Madoff, particularly since she and the feeders she helped set up had been earning tens of millions of dollars in fees every year from not only Maxam, but also Tremont and Kingate.

It's shocking how many successful—and, therefore, supposedly intelligent—people were so susceptible to Madoff's duplicity. "There were many seasoned market professionals, whom one would otherwise describe as intelligent and rational, who were taken in," said Christopher Miller of Allenbridge HedgeInfo. "Some of them may have thought they understood the split-strike strategy, but no one else was doing anything similar they could compare with. So instead of concentrating on the red flags, we looked for reasons why such people could be duped."

He came up with a few groups. The first was comprised of investors who did due diligence, knew that there were concerns surrounding Madoff, and so allocated only a relatively small percentage with the firm. For them, it was worth the risk if they could get the returns. "These people have a high level of tolerance for things they don't understand, or for being lied to," Miller said.

Another group were investors who did due diligence, knew that there were questions, but since Madoff had been running so long, was known to give money back instantly, and was so well regarded, they figured such allegations must be baseless. "These people have found the red flags, but then they start looking for reasons to ignore them. They want a money manager who is a profit-seeking type." Then there were investors who knew someone else had done due diligence and invested but who didn't know the concerns. "These people were cheapskates. It's all right to use a third party to do due diligence, but they invested even though they had not read the reports." This group includes investors through feeder funds, who did no due diligence because they were sold investments by regulated firms audited by big-name auditors who hadn't asked enough questions. Fairfield Greenwich, for one, shopped for three separate auditors over a period of three years. Auditors accepted the documentation they were given and the opinions from the tiny auditor that Madoff used.

"This is not just a hedge fund issue, this is a global auditing issue. There is no suggestion that big-name auditors did anything illegal," Miller said, but perhaps their terms of reference need to be looked at.

What common denominator was there between all the people who suspected Madoff had problems but looked the other way? Shared greed is the natural first answer. Police investigating a crime always ask, "Who benefits from the crime?" Merkin, Noel, Piedrahita, Manzke, Schulman, and others all shared a common interest. They all stood to lose a lot if they looked too closely and found something about Madoff that was inconvenient.

Chapter Five

I n the summer of 2007, a young hedge fund manager making a presentation to Walter M. Noel noticed that the septuagenarian had
fallen asleep.

The young man was in Noel's office seeking money. That's what
Noel did for a living. As a partner in the Fairfield Greenwich Group,
he gave money out—he seeded hedge funds. If the hedge funds made
a profit for the investors that Noel brought into it, he usually got 10
percent or more of those profits. Noel had some large and wealthy
clients—university endowments, pension funds—but most were just
men and women who either made or inherited a lot of money. In U.S.
stock markets, 2007 had been a decent year, at least through the early
summer, although by July storms had begun to brew in the credit markets. The U.S. housing market boom had crested and was now heading
for a crash. All the bonds and other complex instruments Wall Street
had constructed around bad-credit homeowner mortgages were beginning to unravel. A true crisis was gaining steam, in which banks, wary
of bad loans on each other's books, would stop lending to one another
and to businesses.

Having won the audience with Noel, the young man sat down at an
expansive conference room table. He launched into his sales pitch, explaining his investment strategy. He hoped that Noel's fund of hedge
funds, would give his start-up hedge fund some cash.

Things had started off reasonably well, but about a half hour into
the manager's presentation, Noel's eyes drooped, he began to nod his
head, and finally he dozed off for good. The young manager didn't
know what to do. He had waited ages for this meet and greet to discuss
the strategy. He looked at his colleague, who was sitting in on the

meeting, with his eyes quiet and wide. Should they wake Noel? Should they just keep talking? Was he ill?

Finally, the young man decided to drop some heavy papers on the table—*blam!*—to stir the sleeping Noel.

Noel's head snapped up and his eyes blinked. "Dammit!" he yelled in sleepy exasperation. "Why can't you be more like Bernie Madoff?"

Overall, 2007 was a fabulous year for Walter M. Noel and his partners in the Fairfield Greenwich Group, Jeffrey H. Tucker and Andrés Piedrahita.

Piedrahita, a short Colombian money-raiser married to Noel's oldest daughter, received a total salary of $46 million for that year alone. Walter Noel and Jeffrey Tucker paid themselves $31 million apiece.

These payments came almost entirely from one of the investment funds that Fairfield Greenwich ran for its investors, a fund called Fairfield Sentry. Fairfield Greenwich—named for the county and town where it was located in Connecticut—also ran other funds of hedge funds, but this one was by far the oldest and most popular among investors. Sentry had been in existence since 1990. The assets under its management were running into the billions of dollars by 2007. Despite its extraordinary size, the fund managed to produce some of the best returns in the industry. Fairfield Sentry had had only a few down months in its seventeen-year history. In 2007, the fees coming in from Sentry made up for losses in FGG's other funds of hedge funds, which were having a horrific year.

Noel, Tucker, and Piedrahita had no reason to worry about the health of Sentry because they knew the manager in charge. Bernie Madoff was an old friend of the firm's, like a brother, according to those who worked at Fairfield Greenwich.

In fact, it was easy to just keep raising money for Sentry precisely because the fund never had a down year. It was, undoubtedly, a statistical marvel. A few months here and there the fund might be off a bit, but for years—almost decades—Sentry had been churning out double-digit returns—12–15 percent every year, like clockwork, even when the rest of the stock market was suffering. Since 1990, Bernie Madoff had been a boon to Fairfield Greenwich and everyone who worked there. The business depended on him.

Walter Noel founded Fairfield Greenwich without much fanfare in 1983. Before this, he had worked for seven years at Chemical Bank, where he headed the International Private Banking Department. He worked in a similar area at Citibank from 1974 to 1977, according to his official biography from Fairfield Greenwich offering documents. He had begun his international private banking career at Bahag Banking in Lausanne, Switzerland, from 1972 to 1974. Earlier, for twelve years, he had been a consultant in the Management Services Division of Arthur D. Little, Inc.

Noel had graduated from Vanderbilt University in 1952, where he was president of the Christian Student Association. He went on to earn a master's in economics from Harvard in 1953 and an LLB from the Harvard Law School in 1959. Soon after, he married his wife, Monica, a Brazilian from a prominent family in Rio de Janeiro.

Noel was attractive to Bernie Madoff because he was an outside, third-party spokesman—a sort of aristocratic personality blessing Madoff's business. He was a WASP who legitimized Madoff's Wall Street firm in exclusive social circles, such as at the Round Hill Country Club in Greenwich, Connecticut, on the ski slopes of Europe, at the beach resorts on the private Caribbean island of Mustique. In addition, the entire Noel family would become a marketing machine for Madoff's fund-raising efforts. Walter Noel had five daughters with his wife Monica. Four of them would marry men who ultimately went to work for Walter Noel and FGG.

After Madoff's arrest, Noel family friend George Ball compared Walter to Jimmy Stewart's character in the movie *It's a Wonderful Life*. "He's a very decent person, very caring person, perhaps naive in some ways, but far from a fool," Ball told the Associated Press. And he likened Noel's longtime relationship with Madoff to that of an old truck in the barn that the owner assumes is reliable: "Familiarity leads to comfort," he said.

By all appearances, the Noel family was living the American dream. It was a dream, however, that Walter and Monica worked assiduously to promote. The Noels were rumored to have employed a publicity agent in the 1980s, when it was still fairly unusual for private citizens to pay for public exposure.

By 2002, the Noels had succeeded in achieving the desired high visibility. That year, all five of the Noel daughters, their children, and the matriarch Monica were photographed for a multipage spread in *Vanity Fair*. They were also featured in several other society magazines in New York City and the luxury summer spot the Hamptons. Marisa Noel Brown appeared on the cover of *Town & Country* magazine with her toddler son; the glossy also featured her four sisters, the family's Caribbean retreat on the private island of Mustique, and their parents, Walter and Monica Noel.

For the Noel daughters, living well was what life was all about. Corina, the eldest, "came out" in society as a member of the 1981 Junior Assembly and was presented at that year's Debutante Cotillion and Christmas Ball in New York. *Vogue* magazine profiled the "fashionable and athletic Marisa Noel Brown, a lacrosse champion as well as an excellent water-skier and tennis player." Wearing flip-flops, beige Urban Outfitters jeans, and an Allegra Hicks Indian-style shirt, Marisa recounted to *Vogue* a conversation with her father, "the hedge fund potentate Walter Noel, in which they extolled the virtues of their annual family ski trip out West, where they share sport on the same mountains by day and enjoy meals under the same roof at night." Marisa, a Harvard graduate who majored in multilingual Romance studies, told the magazine, "If you know the rules and etiquette of sport, if you learn this when you are young and you continue it into your adult life, you're at a huge advantage." Associating with the right people at the right stores and buying the right kinds of expensive products was all part of that. In 2008, Marisa, her sister Alix, and their mother, Monica, cohosted an invitation-only party hosted by hair stylist Frédéric Fekkai to celebrate the opening of Fekkai's salon in Greenwich, Connecticut.

It seemed that the Noels bred their daughters to help advance both a social agenda and a family business. The girls all earned top-flight degrees (Yale, Harvard, Georgetown, and Brown) and four of them wed husbands who would eventually go on to work in the family business. The Noel sisters also boasted social prowess. They rubbed shoulders with other wealthy Americans and internationals, and that made them and their husbands perfect hedge fund marketers. *Town & Country* magazine highlighted those with whom the Noel family socialized in its article on the Caribbean getaway Mustique. "Who goes: The same mix of rock stars and royalty has been coming since Princess Margaret had a house here. The Christmas crowd includes Mick Jagger, Tommy Hilfiger, Pierce Brosnan, Maguy Le Coze of New York's Le Bernardin restaurant, investment adviser Walter Noel and his family and the Guinness and Shannon families. 'This is the one place all of our children agreed that they would want to return to year after year,' says Monica Noel, whose five daughters are scattered in Brazil, London, Italy and the United States. 'So we bought a house, and wherever they are, they come for Christmas and New Year's.'"

The Noel "house" on Mustique was actually a huge estate that the family named Yemanja, after a Brazilian goddess of the sea. The Noels owned several other luxury properties, including a pied-à-terre on Park Avenue, a house in Southampton, and their main $6 million home on Round Hill Road in Greenwich, Connecticut.

To Madoff, this wealth and these social connections amounted to pedigree. Walter Noel was a "mediocre private banker," according to one headhunter who interviewed him for a job. But one of the qualities that may have made him a less-than-spectacular private banker was just the thing that made him most attractive to Bernie Madoff: he didn't ask a lot of probing questions.

Whether or not it was warranted, Noel had a reputation for sometimes acting oblivious. According to a friend of one of Noel's neighbor's, Noel often couldn't remember names. Some days Noel would pull out of his driveway and wave at the man next door, and say, "Hi, neighbor!" Other days Noel would drive out and say, "Hi, Jim!"

The neighbor's name was Richard.

Andrés Piedrahita married Corina Noel, the eldest of the Noel daughters, in 1989, and eventually merged his own firm, Littlestone Associates, into FGG in 1997. "Littlestone" was an English play on Piedrahita's last name.

As a result of the merger, Piedrahita became a partner in FGG, a managing director, and the highest-paid member of the firm. However, Andrés Piedrahita's biography, which was included in Fairfield Greenwich's marketing materials and the firm's Web site (prior to Madoff's arrest) left out some key periods of his life. According to these official biographies, Piedrahita founded Littlestone Associates in 1991. Prior to Littlestone, Piedrahita worked as a financial consultant at Prudential-Bache Securities, from 1981 to 1987. He was then at Shearson Lehman Hutton from 1987 to 1990. He had received his bachelor's degree from the Boston University College of Communication.

All of this is true, but what the biography failed to mention is that Andrés Piedrahita had worked on Wall Street just after graduating college. According to National Futures Association records, in 1982 and 1983 Piedrahita worked at a Wall Street firm called Balfour MacLaine, a commodity futures trading company that has since withdrawn from that business. Piedrahita was reportedly selling a money-losing futures fund called TAPMAN to rich individuals, such as Fernando Botero, son of the famous Colombian artist and sculptor.

Andrés Piedrahita grew up in an upper-class family in Bogotá, Colombia, the son of Gladys Arocha and Samuel Piedrahita, who was also a commodities trader. Andrés was the youngest of three children, and he attended high school at The English School in Bogotá. Local newspapers in Colombia quoted acquaintances after Madoff's arrest saying that "although he was the most popular . . . none of his classmates thought that he could become the most successful businessman of his generation. In high school, Piedrahita began to show some of his main characteristics: audacity, a way with people and ambition."

Andrés Piedrahita's life took a turn in 1989 when he married Corina. She was an American society girl and a graduate from Yale. Her mother, Monica Noel, was a member of a prominent Brazilian family and had met Walter Noel when he finished studying law at Harvard. The Noels were synonymous with elegance and sophistication.

Over the years, Walter Noel's lifestyle as well as that of his partner, Jeffrey Tucker, became increasingly swanky—in direct correlation with the growth of Fairfield Greenwich's assets in Madoff's hedge fund. In 2006, the Fairfield Greenwich cofounders bought a shared interest in a Cessna 560XL private jet, and in 2004 the Tuckers bought a showstopper horse farm in upstate New York.

And as FGG brought in billions of dollars, they handed at least half of those billions directly to Madoff. By 2008, roughly $7.5 billion of FGG's $14 billion in assets was invested, through various fund vehicles, with Madoff's phony hedge fund.

Also in 2006, the Noels paid $4.6 million for a home in Palm Beach, not far from the Madoffs. CitiMortgage offered them a $3.68 million mortgage for 243 Tangier Avenue, a three-bedroom, 4,186-square-foot house built in 1940. Many of Madoff's other major fund-raisers also congregated in Palm Beach, within a few blocks of each other in the same swanky neighborhood. Robert Jaffe had a house a few doors down from the Madoffs and from the Noels' house, as did Frank Avellino and his wife.

Everyone was getting rich, it seemed, all off Bernie Madoff.

This was all a long way from the beginnings of Fairfield Greenwich. The firm was fairly humble in the early years after its inception in 1983. Then, in 1989, it merged with Fred Kolber & Co., a broker-dealer firm.

Fred Kolber, a longtime specialist trading options on the American Stock Exchange, gave the firm credibility. A natural at the business, Kolber once said, "Trading options was like a game I understood and no one else did." Kolber, who had previously traded convertible bonds, said options "was like playing blackjack and looking at the dealer's cards."

"Way back then, Walter had been surviving as a modest money manager with just a few large accounts, mostly Brazilians who wanted to save their money from the country's hyperinflation. Walter set up shop in an office building and sublet the space to Fred Kolber & Co., a small company made up of partners Fred Kolber, his brother, Mark, Ed Berman, and Jeffrey Tucker, a former SEC lawyer," said Sherry Shameer Cohen, who worked at FGG in the early years.

According to Cohen, Walter's money management strategy was "basically following Friday's Value Line picks and investing in Berkshire Hathaway [then about $2,000 per share], Zweig International, and Mario Gabelli." Fred Kolber had set up the Greenwich Options Fund, an onshore hedge fund. "Walter fed a few domestic clients to Fred, whose trading yielded rather impressive returns." Noel then told Kolber "that if he would take his funds offshore, he would raise the capital. Fred did, and Walter brought in more money."

With Tucker and Kolber onboard at FGG, Walter Noel had two savvy Wall Street men backing his operation. At some point, however, Kolber had a falling-out with FGG and left, although the circumstances behind his departure remain unclear.

"Kolber left for philosophical reasons conflicting with Noel, and it's understood that many in the firm didn't entirely trust Noel," said one source who did due diligence for a firm considering purchasing Fairfield Greenwich. "Noel was never a partner in the options trading business and grew less and less enamored with it. He wanted to build out the other business." In 1991, Kolber left to found a real estate firm, BGK Properties.

But Jeffrey Tucker stayed with Fairfield Greenwich. After several years as a regulator, Tucker, a former attorney with the SEC, had entered the securities industry, in 1987, as a general partner of Fred Kolber & Co. At Kolber, Tucker was responsible for the development and administration of the firm's options company. Then, in 1989, Tucker and Kolber merged with FGG. Throughout FGG's development, Tucker was responsible for directing its business and operational development and had been a director or general partner for a variety of its investment funds.

Noel's daughter Corina ran the office. Intelligent, ambitious, and multilingual, she worked the social scene the same way her parents did. In the process, she met Andrés Piedrahita, her future husband.

Corina Noel Piedrahita worked full-time for her father and with her husband at Fairfield Greenwich Group until she stepped down in 2007. According to Cohen, "She was involved in almost every administrative detail, from setting up accounts, accepting wire transfers, arranging for commissions to be paid, establishing components in the weekly net asset values of the funds, and traveling back and forth between the firm's headquarters [then based in Greenwich] and the Citco Group, in Tortola [part of the British Virgin Islands], where the offshore funds were officially set up and administered. She was no passive stay-at-home mom, but an active member of FGG."

Jeffrey Tucker was savvy when it came to the inner workings of the financial world. Tucker had joined the New York Regional Office of the SEC in March 1970 as an attorney in the Small Issues branch. In December of 1970, he was assigned to the Legal Interpretations branch, and in August of 1972, he was assigned to an enforcement branch. Unusual for an SEC lawyer, Tucker had training in finance and a head for numbers. He had received an undergraduate degree in accounting from Syracuse University in 1966 and a JD degree from Brooklyn Law School in 1969. During his tenure with the SEC, Tucker lectured part-time at the Paralegal Institute, an educational institution in New York City.

Tucker had also married well. His wife, Melanie, was the daughter of textile tycoon Norman Schneider. Like Madoff's first investor, Carl Shapiro, Schneider was a garment industry icon. He and his brother Wharton founded Allison Manufacturing, a children's apparel manufacturer headquartered in Allentown, Pennsylvania, where it employed tens of thousands of local workers. The Schneiders had become very wealthy. In 1970, Norman and Wharton sold the firm to Beatrice, the U.S. conglomerate, which, in turn, began licensing Walt Disney cartoon characters on T-shirts produced by the Schneiders. This earned them even more money.

It was very likely through Melanie or her family connections that Jeffrey Tucker met Bernie Madoff. It isn't clear when the introduction was made, but in 1990 Noel and Tucker opened accounts with Madoff and began an investing relationship that would last until the day Madoff was arrested in 2008. By the time it was over, Fairfield Greenwich would send Madoff more than $7 billion.

What Noel and Tucker were offering investors was something no one else had—direct access to Bernie Madoff. Although Madoff needed greater and greater inflows of funds to keep his Ponzi scheme going, he continued to cultivate the notion that he would accept only an exclusive list of fortunate investors. People had to wait and pull strings to get in with Bernie. So what Noel and Tucker offered was a clear path to easy entry. No waiting for the green light, no begging or wheedling, no calls to Bernie's wife or brother—just a jet stream into the steadiest money machine on Wall Street.

This access brought enormous amounts of money in to FGG, and its partners made hundreds of millions of dollars in fees over the years. John Donachie, one-time head of compliance for Fairfield Greenwich Group in London, believes the feeders became so enamored with Bernie that hundreds of millions of dollars in assets grew to billions—and none of them, Walter Noel, Jeffrey Tucker, or Madoff, could stop it. "Likely Madoff then got swamped by the money coming in and decided 'I want to play in the forbidden world, go close to the edge and see how long it takes before they catch me. I'll play dangerously.'"

Fairfield Greenwich's arrangement with Madoff was particularly lucrative because Madoff didn't charge them any fees. Normally, hedge fund managers (like the young man whose presentation put Noel to sleep) would take 20 percent of whatever profits they made for investors. After the hedge fund manager took this fee, the feeder fund, such as FGG, would then charge its underlying investors another 10 percent. The feeder funds also often charged investors an assortment of sales fees and an annual management fee.

But Madoff was charging FGG nothing. He was giving up a massive amount of money. It was a bizarre choice for a Wall Street trader who is in the business of making money and would have been a red flag for anyone who wanted to see it. FGG was reaping *all* the fees from the investors' money put with Madoff. All they had to do was keep raising money and turning it over to him. This helped FGG earn at least $100 million a year in management fees alone during 2006, 2007, and 2008.

According to those who knew him, Jeffrey Tucker was a "hardworking guy who wanted to make a billion and saw a shortcut." He found that shortcut in Bernie Madoff, and as FGG put more and more of its money with him, its assets started rising from hundreds of millions of dollars up to billions. At the same time, the partners' lifestyles started getting more lavish.

By 2006, Jeffrey Tucker was practically retired, leading a second life on the horse-racing circuit. A group bidding for the New York Racing Association's state franchise even elected Tucker as their chairman. Empire Racing Associates, a group of New York horse owners and breeders, elected Tucker in 2006 in the hope he would help them secure the exclusive right to operate the state's three thoroughbred racetracks (Aqueduct, Belmont, and Saratoga) and their related gaming businesses.

Tucker had a residence in New York City, but he spent much of his time in Schuylerville, New York, a twenty-minute drive from the Saratoga Race Course. Racing enthusiasts from around the world came to the area to breed and race horses. In 2007, Sheikh Mohammed bin Rashid Al Maktoum, the ruler of Dubai and a horse-racing enthusiast, purchased a 106-acre horse farm adjoining Saratoga Race Course for $17.5 million.

As the chairman of Empire Racing Associates, Tucker also rubbed shoulders with the horsey set as a result of Equine Advocates, a charity for rescuing slaughter horses. He hosted the annual charitable awards dinner and silent auction at his horse farm, Stone Bridge Farm. The event took place during Travers Week, the height of the Saratoga thoroughbred racing season. Allaire du Pont, owner of five-time horse of the year Kelso, was honorary chairwoman. The highlight of the evening was an award presentation to the founders of the Thoroughbred Charities of America.

In addition to Stone Bridge Farm, which was 426 acres, Tucker bought other farms. By itself, the primary Stone Bridge horse farm and training facility in Schuylerville was worth $10 million. The neoclassical estate boasted a 7,720-square-foot Georgian-style residence, a Cape Cod guest home, three other houses, a nearly mile-long synthetic racetrack, a riding arena, stalls, barns with an office, paddocks, a maintenance building, and a starting gate with a clock. The property also included the Burgoyne Hotel building in Schuylerville, where the farm's staff live. "It's a masterpiece," a local real estate agent said.

More and more, Tucker became a figurehead back at FGG. He still went on the road sometimes and even traveled to China with other executives in 2006 to raise money for the hedge fund business back in America. "It is only a matter of time before hedge fund investing becomes a reality in China," Tucker said as he toured Beijing and Shanghai, visiting government officials to market hedge fund investing. "I would say that the most important idea for those new to this area is that, traditionally, hedge funds were created to protect capital and to diversify and thus help to control risk. To 'hedge' means to protect from loss," Tucker added. "A misconception about hedge funds is the idea that all of them seek huge returns and do so by taking huge risks."

Although Tucker retained a 17 percent ownership stake in FGG, equal to Walter Noel's, it was Noel's family that increasingly populated the business. In addition to Andrés Piedrahita, three of Noel's four other sons-in-law went to work using their social connections to raise money for the firm, mostly in Europe and Latin America. Piedrahita was the largest equity owner as well, with a 22 percent stake.

Noel's daughter Lisina was married to Yanko Della Schiava, who marketed FGG funds throughout southern Europe from his base in the Lugano representative office. The couple lived in Milan. Alix Noel's husband, Philip Toub, handled Brazil and the Middle East. He and Alix lived in Greenwich, Connecticut, although at one point they lived in Brazil for a few years. Marisa Noel married Matthew Brown, who also eventually took a marketing position at the firm. Piedrahita headed up the European and Latin American operations from his bases in London, Spain, and Brazil.

None of Noel's sons-in-law had any formal background in investing but were well trained in marketing. "This is not a serious group. They are pretend serious. They're not exactly going to walk in and pitch Harvard," said one person familiar with the Noel family. Indeed, in investing circles, the European money that fed into FGG was known as "dumb money" because it followed whatever funds had been hot last quarter or last year. It was the American funds, particularly the endowment funds run by David Swensen of Yale and Jack Meyer of Harvard, that were considered "smart money." Notably, none of these universities had invested with FGG.

Much of the marketing done by Noel and his sons-in-law was based on social status and connections. In Madrid, Andrés and Corina bought an elegant home in the Puerta de Hierro neighborhood from the banking family Juan Herrera and Martínez Campos. Emilio Botín, president of Banco Santander, was one of Andrés's good friends. So was Michael de Picciotto, nephew of Edgar de Picciotto, the founder of the Swiss bank UBP. Fairfield Greenwich Group would even go on to name two of the firm's Madoff-managed funds after the neighborhoods in which Andrés owned homes. The Chester Global Strategy Fund was named after his house in London's Chester Square, and Irongate is the English translation of Puerta de Hierro in Spain.

Piedrahita lobbied hard to keep up his society image. "I am a person who has a great ability at public relations. I'm a very friendly person. I love people. I am known for being fun. . . . I did well in life. I'm not ashamed of it," he told the *Wall Street Journal.*

Andrés Piedrahita was not shy about his wealth. The Piedrahita family also had an apartment in the Sherry-Netherland in Manhattan, plus a house and a 150-foot yacht kept off the coast of the swanky island of Mallorca. He leased a Gulfstream III jet, which he parked on a military base near Madrid, where he also has a house in a fancy section of town, along with a chauffeur and a butler. Piedrahita's Gulfstream was mainly used for commuting between Madrid and London. In fact, he became so used to traveling by private plane that he once admonished a friend's wife for flying commercial. Andrés was the life of his party, entertaining so many royals and titled aristocrats that it caused one rich friend, Fernando Botero, to joke at a particularly memorable dinner party that the "only dukes not there were the Dukes of Hazzard."

After his accountant friends Michael Avellino and Frank Bienes were issued a cease and desist order by the SEC in 1992, Madoff had to turn elsewhere for money. For a while, Madoff was able to rely on others, like Maurice "Sonny" Cohn and Richard "Dick" Spring, his travel companions from the seaplane out on Long Island who had a lucrative business raising money for Madoff through the Cohmad entity.

For Madoff, the introduction to Fairfield Greenwich Group was just the ticket he needed. The two firms were suited perfectly for each other. Fairfield Greenwich was a fund of hedge funds that needed a hedge fund with low volatility and steady returns, and Madoff desperately needed a steady stream of incoming money.

There was another, less obvious reason why Madoff was so appealing: his supposed hedge fund churned out returns as regularly as bonds paid interest. Few hedge funds were able to match that. In general, hedge funds logged big gains some years and big losses in other years— but 10 or 12 percent a year, *every* year? No one seemed to be able to do what Madoff did.

Madoff's returns were too regular. A hedge fund like George Soros's, which had up years with returns of nearly 50 percent followed by steep down years, was highly volatile and, therefore, not as secure an investment. Unpredictability made investors nervous. But that was and is the nature of hedge funds.

The smoothness of Madoff's returns were what set tongues wagging about getting into his fund. "Every fund of funds sought out a low volatility hedge fund," said a partner at a public hedge fund firm. ("Low volatility" is industry jargon for steady returns.) As long as a hedge fund's returns didn't fluctuate much, that was good enough for investors. The regularity of Madoff's returns should have made investors suspicious. But instead, they came to view him as a sort of money market account, or a certificate of deposit at a bank, paying low but steady and sure returns. "Everyone who looked at the data on volatility would look at Madoff, because everybody who was piling into hedge funds in the 1990s and after 2000, they all had to have a slice," the partner added.

But there was a catch: hedge funds like the one Madoff said he had just didn't exist. Maybe—just maybe—there were a few limited opportunities in the market where savvy investors could find secure, low volatility investments that paid double-digit returns, but if there were any, there weren't many. Even if the market had been sluggish and there wasn't much competing money, there weren't enough of them to support a fund the size that Madoff claimed his to be. And in boom and bust years like the 1990s and 2000, with so much money piling into and out of the stock market and into mutual funds, the results that Madoff was reporting were simply impossible.

But since Madoff was running a Ponzi scheme and not a hedge fund, he desperately needed new money to keep the scam working. Madoff had been involved in a similar scam with the Avellino and Bienes notes gimmick. But now Madoff's growing pyramid needed something bigger, in the billions of dollars. He needed consistently larger piles of money, and to get them he needed a legitimate front, an SEC-registered investment adviser—not a two-man accountant team inherited from his father-in-law.

Madoff needed a real hedge fund outfit as his marketing agent to act as the front office, the sample store, someone to take care of the paperwork, the investors, the questions the investors and the public might ask, and the endless due diligence requests.

Fairfield Greenwich Group fit perfectly.

What made the partnership even more appealing to Madoff was that Fairfield Greenwich sourced its cash from a completely different social circle than Madoff's. Where Madoff operated mostly within northeastern Jewish society, Noel hailed from Tennessee, was Christian, and was married to the daughter of the Haegler family, Swiss-Brazilian cocoa farmers. The Noels were avid cultivators of connections in the wealthy society of Waspy Greenwich, Connecticut, where they lived.

Another factor that made Bernie Madoff so appealing to investors was that while many of them may have thought he was doing something not quite legal, at least he was doing it on their behalf.

Union Bancaire Privée (UBP), the Geneva-based bank founded by

Swiss hedge fund godfather Edgar de Picciotto, was part of the Fairfield Greenwich network. It too invested with Madoff, both through FGG funds and on its own. In mid-December 2008—after Madoff's arrest—UBP issued a detailed letter to clients explaining why it had blown $700 million of their money on the Madoff scam. What the letter failed to mention was that UBP's own research department had raised many concerns about Madoff earlier that year and had recommended that he be stricken from the firm's list of approved managers. These concerns had been shared with UBP's senior management, but the firm kept investing with Madoff anyway. The letter also didn't mention the fact that one of its officers who was informed, Michael de Picciotto—Edgar's nephew—was a friend of Fairfield Greenwich's Andrés Piedrahita.

In an e-mail exchange that took place in February and March 2008, UBP's then–deputy head of research, Gideon Nieuwoudt, listed a number of concerns about Madoff. One of them was the lack of basic information available on Madoff's firm, including how much he had in assets, how many feeder funds there were, and how his investment strategy—which produced such amazingly steady returns—worked.

Nieuwoudt wrote that he had spoken to more than one hundred funds that were invested or had invested with Madoff, but none of them could explain how his strategy produced such consistent returns. "It all seems very opaque," Nieuwoudt worried. Nieuwoudt recommended that Madoff be taken off UBP's list of approved funds and stop investing with him. Among those cc'd on the e-mail discussion were at least two members of UBP's executive committee: Christophe Bernard, who headed the asset management business, and Michael de Picciotto, head of the bank's treasury, according to Nieuwoudt's account, which was reported by the *Wall Street Journal*. Despite Nieuwoudt's concerns, UBP remained invested with Madoff via four different feeder funds, including one run by Fairfield Greenwich Group. In early 2008, Madoff was among UBP's top five holdings.

Aside from its investments, UBP had other close ties to Fairfield Greenwich. These included providing advisory and other services to the management company of Fairfield's fund of funds division. Beyond that, three Fairfield funds invested in UBP's own Madoff feeder fund, called M-Invest Ltd.

Together, UBP and Fairfield were making a lot of money working with each other and with Madoff.

Only after Bernie Madoff was arrested did UPB admit to having suspicions about how he operated. In the letter to clients, dated December 17, 2008, UBP, which had $700 million invested with Madoff, said that "in essence, the perceived edge was Madoff's ability to gather and process market-order-flow information to time the implementation of the split-strike option strategy." In other words, Madoff, UPB believed, might be using information from the trading orders of its brokerage clients to generate profits for its investment clients.

The feeder funds like Fairfield Greenwich had an easy pitch with Madoff behind it, explained British gossip columnist Taki Theodoracopulos, who lost money to Madoff. A feeder fund manager would approach a bank or a rich person in Europe, "announce how regretful it was that the Madoff fund was closed, but drop hints that, if an opening came up, the 'mark' could become a member of the 'club.' The con was on, and sure enough the 'mark' would soon get another visit and hear the good news that finally they could join the club." The supposed exclusivity of Madoff's fund was the chief selling point among the Swiss and other European and non-U.S. investors. "When the 'mark' or 'marks' would ask for details, the answer was automatic: 'We cannot reveal anything of Bernie's moves or investments because they might be leaked, and all of Wall Street will follow suit.' Or words to that effect. It was a good con, and they all fell for it," added Taki. "The question is, of course, did the feeders know it was a con, or had greed got in the way of common sense?"

Werner Wolfer is a Swiss banker who manages a fund of funds at Geneva-based Banque SCS Alliance. Like Gideon Nieuwoudt at UPB, Wolfer also had some doubts about Madoff, but his fund invested in Fairfield Sentry anyhow. He mitigated the risk that Madoff might be front-running by sharing his suspicions with clients who put money into the Sentry fund.

Wolfer knew that traders everywhere were trying to match Madoff's consistent returns. But for all their efforts to replicate the supposed split-strike conversion strategy Madoff used—buying shares of top-ranked U.S. companies and entering into options contracts to limit the risk—they could not produce the consistent double-digit returns that he posted. He had also heard the talk in the investment community about how Madoff might be using his brokerage firm to buy and sell stocks ahead of his clients—front-running. A broker who engages in illegal front-running is, in effect, stealing from clients.

The rumors of front-running apparently did hurt the brokerage side of Madoff's business. Brokerage clients wanted a firm that would obtain the best prices available for them when buying or selling stocks. The front-running rumors, however, did not dissuade potential Madoff investors from buying in to his hedge fund. In fact, it worked in his favor. Many potential investors suspected—perhaps even hoped—that Madoff was doing something not quite legal on their behalf, whether it was front-running customers on the other side of his firm or some other secret formula. They figured a slap on the wrist from regulators would just be the cost of doing business.

"They were convinced that the risk was only that the Securities and Exchange Commission would do something," Wolfer said in an interview with *Bloomberg Markets* magazine. In the worst case, he added, "the SEC could say stop." And with every year the SEC failed to act, "the worries were a little bit less."

In 2001, most of the big investment banks and many of the commercial banks doing business on Wall Street had a derivatives desk, which was usually led by someone who had been a floor trader or a strategist or had dealt with some of the bank's most important clients. Derivatives are contracts that derive their price from some underlying asset—a mortgage, for instance, can change in value based on the market price of one's home.

Ken Nakayama was one of these people. After graduating from the University of Pennsylvania in 1991, he got a job at Bankers Trust, which had a reputation for hiring financially rigorous minds. Ken was thrilled. He was doing what he loved and, even after Bankers Trust was bought by Deutsche Bank in 1998, he got to stay on and ultimately head up the entire desk. He was trained to do business discreetly and smartly. At Deutsche Bank, an enormous German bank, Nakayama was the head of research for equity derivatives, or instruments that fluctuated in price according to the value of public companies' shares. A strategist for Deutsche Bank has an important job. Deutsche Bank's midtown office building, which was carved out of pinkish gray granite and loomed over the Museum of Modern Art on Fifty-third Street, featured a trading floor that spanned roughly the size of two football fields.

Nakayama recounted that he was once asked to run some figures on behalf of a client who was thinking of investing with Bernard Madoff. The returns on the Madoff funds were so good that Nakayama himself was thinking of investing through a feeder fund. He had already had a successful career on Wall Street, and now he wanted to branch out and invest part of his personal fortune in hedge funds.

Nakayama finally got his hands on some feeder funds' marketing materials. He'd come across one that claimed to have a familiar strategy—trading S&P 100 index options—named Fairfield Sentry fund.

He flipped through the marketing material. It sounded bland enough. "FGG is introduced to several hundred potential managers in the course of each year. A relevant subset of these leads are pursued and background information on promising potential relationships is collected and shared among FGG's professionals for initial assessment. The nature of FGG's manager transparency model employs a significantly higher level of due diligence work than that typically performed by most funds of funds and consulting firms. This model requires a thorough understanding of a manager's business, staff, operational practices, and infrastructure."

FGG promised to do "due diligence," or background checks, on its hedge fund investments. First, FGG said it reviewed a manager's past performance obtained from independent sources, in addition to conducting a series of manager interviews and reference calls. "Particular attention is paid to the extent to which each manager's controls are reasonably suited to maintain operational, market, and credit risks at an appropriate level and as represented by the manager," the document explained. "During this period, FGG personnel also have an opportunity to evaluate a manager's attitudes and receptiveness (as opposed to his proclaimed intention) towards providing FGG with full transparency of its security level trading activity and access to its investment thought process."

Nakayama figured there were plenty of other potential investors who looked at Fairfield Sentry's trading strategy in detail. So he started calling around. He was trying to figure out who the prime broker was for the underlying managers, but it wasn't clear who was actually running the money for Fairfield Sentry. The marketing materials claimed they checked everything. A multipoint list of measures taken to check potential funds included: "Conducts detailed interviews to better understand the manager's methodology for forming a market view, and for selecting and exiting core positions"; "Analyzes trading records"; "Conducts a number of qualitative and quantitative tests to determine adherence to risk limits over time"; "Confirms portfolio loss risk controls, diversification and other risk-related control policies, as well as any experience regarding unexpected or extreme market events"; and "Reviews the risk and return factors inherent in the strategy."

Nakayama compiled details about Fairfield Sentry. Eventually, he spoke with a salesperson at FGG's offices who finally admitted that the underlying strategy was run by an outside money manager—Bernard L. Madoff Investment Securities. Nakayama started questioning everyone he knew on the Street as to whether they knew Madoff or knew anyone who had ever invested with him. Most either had heard vaguely of Madoff or knew of his broker-dealer firm, which was known on Wall Street as one of the first to make the leap from paper to computerized trading in NASDAQ stocks.

"I felt like I had been around when that split-strike was invented. Back then it was called a 'reverse conversion' and it peaked around 1995," Nakayama recalled. After that time, the options Madoff claimed to be trading started to die off in volume and popularity. Normally, when big option trades hit the crowds down on the trading floor, somebody would have to buy or sell stock in corresponding amounts to offset the risk in the options. But with Madoff, no one was seeing those orders in the marketplace. Because with Madoff, the trades weren't happening.

In the early 2000s, Walter Noel "really began stepping up his life and getting involved more and more on the big-money charity circuit," said a person familiar with the firm. And even though he and his partners were making excellent money, the bull market beckoned. It was a big temptation lurking out there: Noel was debating whether to sell Fairfield Greenwich to a big bank or some outside firm, or perhaps even going public. The bigger the business grew the more the partners were interested in cashing in on the success. Other hedge fund firms had done so already, such as Blackstone and Fortress. Morgan Stanley had bought Avenue Capital, and quantitative hedge fund AQR was filing to go public.

One banker who looked at the FGG sale on behalf of a potential acquirer didn't like a lot of what he saw. There were internal squabbles, for one. Walter Noel's sons-in-law got paid much more, for the most part, than other nonfamily partners at the firm. Noel got $30 million in 2007 and was to make $18 million in 2008. Same for founding partner Jeffrey Tucker. The total compensation (bonus and base) that Andrés Piedrahita, managing partner and first son-in-law of Noel, received especially irked nonfamily partners. He received $45 million in 2007 and was to make $28 million in 2008.

When visitors stopped by the gleaming FGG offices, both in Greenwich and on Third Avenue in Manhattan, they were not disappointed by the growth and sparkling reputation of this fund of hedge funds. The place was gorgeous, guests were served drinks in crystal, there were fresh flowers in every vase and beautiful art to look at on the walls— not to mention beautiful receptionists in the chairs.

Charles Murphy, cohead of the European Financial Institutions Group at Credit Suisse, was another tapped to spruce up FGG for sale. Hired in 2007, Murphy received a hefty compensation. In 2007, he made $4.8 million for not even a full year there. In 2008, even with the economy heading south, he was on track to make $4.25 million. He had also squeezed equity in the firm out of Andrés Piedrahita, much to the chagrin of other employees there who had worked much longer without being compensated with ownership.

Murphy snapped up the mansion of Seagram heir Matthew Bronfman—of the billionaire beverage and entertainment Bronfman family—for a whopping $33 million, the highest paid at the time (2007) for a town house on the Upper East Side. In 1994, Bronfman had paid $3.5 million for the limestone mansion near Central Park, which came complete with ionic columns, a four-story glass atrium, six bedrooms, eight baths, six fireplaces, a library with polished wood paneling, a full basement with gym, a sauna, and a wine cellar.

Murphy obviously expected to do well from a sale of Fairfield Greenwich.

There had been bites from a buyer before. In 2004, a buyer approached Fairfield Greenwich about purchasing the firm. At this point, FGG had about 85 percent of its assets invested with Madoff. One of the prospective buyers hired a banker to do due diligence on Fairfield Greenwich Group. The banker spoke about his experience examining the firm's books and the principals working there. "It seemed Jeffrey

Tucker had got a whiff of the big money and that changed his constitution," said the banker. "When I asked him to walk me through the basics, the strategy, the paperwork, he flat out said no."

The banker did see some trading statements that Madoff had sent to Fairfield Greenwich, but they were simple statements, detailing a handful of trades every month. They were the same statements Madoff's individual clients received in the mail. And they were all phony.

The banker did the same digging that Deutsche Bank's Nakayama and other derivatives experts had done and asked for proof of all of Madoff's trades. "Then they produced the blotter of all the trades," said the banker. "I was allowed to look at it. I checked in open market, and these trades Madoff said he was making were 82 percent" of all the volume in the S&P 100 index options. In short, what Madoff was showing Fairfield Greenwich indicated he represented almost all of the trading in these options. That was the first red flag. He was trading so many that he would have had a monopoly on these options—and yet no one had heard of Madoff in the trading world of options.

"I called my friend in the trading pit in Chicago and asked a friend about Madoff. He said he'd never heard of this guy." That was the second red flag for the banker.

The banker called Goldman Sachs, where he knew the head of the trading desk. Again, no one had heard of Madoff. Goldman Sachs didn't even do business with the firm. "We will not trade with them," said the man at Goldman. "To me, that was the kiss of death," said the banker.

The next day, after lunch, Tucker and the Fairfield Greenwich staff explained away the curious news that no one on the trading floor had heard of Madoff. They told the banker the trades must have taken place elsewhere. "These transactions were in the OTC market," they told the banker. The OTC market is more open and wild, but when the banker called his friends who did over-the-counter trades, he still came up with nothing. No one was trading with Madoff.

"Does Bernie Madoff have a broker here?" he asked the biggest independent broker on the over-the-counter trading floor. Nobody had ever heard of anyone by that name.

The banker had options trading experience, although he left the trading floor in Chicago in 1995. The OEX strategy Madoff claimed to be using had fallen out of fashion by 2004. The S&P options

Madoff had once traded were a dead product. The NASDAQ was the hot index.

Computers were taking over the trading floor, and everyone else on Wall Street had caught up with what Madoff had built as his "edge" in trading stocks. "It was like an invasion of nerds: Timber Hill, Interactive Brokers, O'Connor . . . all of them started using computers," the banker recalled. Still, while computers had taken over the trading business, some things had not changed. For instance, everyone in the options business knew each other. "There's no way Madoff could have conducted those transactions and not have people know about it," the banker declared. "He could have gone to the Kabul exchange! It would have come right back to Chicago."

As for FGG, the banker said that, in his opinion, "they bought into positive returns and got seduced by it. They put the blinders on." He particularly blamed Jeffrey Tucker. Tucker, as an SEC-trained lawyer and partner in an options hedge fund, should have recognized the missing data in the options market. "He built a mental wall and said, 'I'm not going to engage in overt knowledge.' The whole theme of FGG was, they look great on the surface, everybody had the right pedigree and right suits."

The banker wrote up his memo for his bosses, who were looking to buy Fairfield Greenwich in 2004. He gave a recommendation that they should stay away. As a courtesy, he also gave a copy to Jeffrey Tucker and Robert Blum, another senior executive at Fairfield Greenwich.

Meanwhile, greed kept the top partners clinging to their equity in Fairfield Greenwich. Harold Greisman, a junior partner at FGG, "was the green-eyeshade honest decent guy who they needed around the firm. He did most of the work. He promised to become a full partner. Andrés Piedrahita stuffed him in a corner. Rob Blum was trying to get the firm well operated to sell it." Blum, whom the banker believes was unaware of Madoff's fraud, was forced out by Andrés Piedrahita.

As for Jeffrey Tucker, "he knew what real due diligence was being done and not done. He's the one who oversaw . . . their team of inept analysts." As a result, the banker said he is sure that, as far back as 2004, Fairfield "knew there were big questions [that weren't being asked about Madoff]. I'm certain they proactively ignored those questions. At the very least they're guilty of gross negligence. I'm 100 percent certain they knew that this was not a legitimate strategy. But they weren't going to question it."

Since Madoff's arrest, the banker argued, "They're playing stupid right now, playing the victim. FGG full well knew of multiple questions about Madoff's operation, reporting, accounting. The firm made conscious and proactive decisions to avoid responding to specific inquiries by potential investors. They deliberately avoided probing Madoff, his auditors, and *anyone* else in the exchange—and off-exchange, OTC—options world that could question the Madoff strategy or returns. They did near *zero* real due diligence on both Madoff and many of their international clientele. Ultimately, that will come back to haunt them."

In 2007, AIG decided to take a look at buying Fairfield Greenwich and sent its own banker over to take a look at the fund of hedge funds. The banker who examined FGG on behalf of AIG said Walter Noel and Jeffrey Tucker had hired lawyers to give them an opinion on whether front-running by Madoff would ever get them into trouble.

"They waved some sort of legal opinion in front of me, saying that if Madoff was ever caught for front-running, it wouldn't get Fairfield Greenwich in trouble," this banker said. Fairfield Greenwich was careful to concede that Madoff had access to and could see a lot of flow, or customer orders, on the legitimate side of his firm, the broker-dealer business. And that was his perceived edge for his illegitimate hedge fund. "So he buys ahead of it—*wink, wink, nudge, nudge*—and investors think they're getting one over on the SEC. That was the ploy to get people in," this banker said. "Investors thought they were getting a real Rolex for twenty bucks." A onetime insurance giant, AIG didn't end up buying Fairfield Greenwich, and then faced its own troubles and had to be bailed out by the U.S. government.

Finally, a third person said he personally warned Walter Noel that Madoff's profits were suspicious. Over coffee one day at a corner table in one of Greenwich's chicest breakfast spots, Versailles, a French pastry shop, this hedge fund executive said he told Noel that Madoff's returns were simply false—there was no way he could produce those returns year after year. "Stay away," he told Walter Noel. Noel wouldn't listen to his warnings.

Chapter Six

Sonja Kohn is an unusual player in the world of big money. A sixty-year-old Orthodox Jewish grandmother, she wears wavy auburn red wigs and large pieces of jewelry and appeared so in love with Bernie Madoff that one observer thought she was his mistress.

Kohn had good reason to be in love with Madoff, but their affair wasn't romantic. It was financial. Kohn channeled billions of dollars, mostly from Europe, to Madoff's hedge fund and received millions of dollars in kickbacks and fees from him.

Kohn met Madoff around 1990 when she was living in New York. She had moved to America from Austria with her husband, Erwin Kohn, a longtime banker for Commerzbank, and they settled in Monsey in Rockland County, outside of New York City. In 1987, according to records with regulators, she set up a brokerage firm called Windsor IBC, with offices at 67 Wall Street, Suite 2507.

"I was introduced to Mr. Madoff years ago," when he was a fund manager, Kohn told the *Wall Street Journal* after Madoff's arrest. "In the 1990s, he was one of the few hedge funds with any liquidity. His firm looked solid and was endorsed by people and companies who were the gold standard of the financial community."

By the early 1990s, after the stock market crash of 1987 and the closing down of Avellino and Bienes in 1992, Madoff was eagerly searching for new money. He needed to expand his network of feeders and was starting to look more overseas. He and his brother became a constant presence on the international exchange networking circuit. For example, Madoff attended an event hosted by the NYSE in June 1990 in Bermuda. Teams representing about a hundred members from the Cincinnati and New York Stock Exchanges, as well as a dozen or so other stock exchanges around the world, took part in this first annual golf and tennis tournament.

Bernie Madoff traveled all over the world, mixing pleasure and business in an effort to raise money. He and his brother, and usually Ruth and some close friends, made frequent appearances at industry events for global stock exchanges like the Interbourse. "He was there every year without fail," said Doug Engmann, who with his brother, Michael Engmann, were West Coast–based options traders who became a force in the industry. (Their business was later purchased by ABN Amro.) The Interbourse was a lavish weeklong ski trip, usually on the slopes of Europe, where brokerage and exchange officials from around the world mingled.

In an interview with a securities trade magazine, Madoff said that this was strictly a social event where professionals from stock exchanges around the world would get together for a week of fun and games and "meet face-to-face with the people we do business with." The second year, the event was held in Morocco, hosted by the Frankfurt Stock Exchange, and the 1991 winter event was held at Grindelwald, Switzerland, hosted by the Geneva Exchange.

In 1990, the year after the wall between East and West Germany came crashing down, Sonja Kohn opened up Eurovaleur. With offices in New York and operations in Europe, Eurovaleur was a sort of multimanager European fund overseen by star money manager Felix Zulauf, a Swiss who was well known in U.S. investment circles. While Zulauf, in Zurich, made broad asset allocation decisions, such as how much to invest and where, eleven different money managers in as many countries ran portfolios for Zulauf in fourteen European stock markets. "It's a unique way for Americans and Asians to invest in European equities," Zulauf said at the time. "You don't have to go to ten or fifteen individual countries or managers." The minimum investment with Eurovaleur was $5 million. An investment of $20 million won the right to have the funds independently managed, but only so-called institutional investors were allowed this privilege—no individuals.

It isn't clear how much business Kohn was directing to Bernie Madoff in the 1990s. But in 1994, she left the United States and returned to her native Austria with her family. There, in March 1994, she incorporated Bank Medici, which was to play a key role in the coming years in expanding Madoff's business across Europe.

Bank Medici did this through other banks, which would market her funds to retail investors. All over Europe, Sonja Kohn's Bank Medici funds began popping up in portfolios of European retirees. Most had no idea that the underlying fund manager was Madoff.

The Medici name was a fanciful one that evoked images of old wealth and power. The Medicis had been the most powerful family in Florence during the Renaissance, and they managed to amass a vast financial and political empire for themselves. There was, of course, no connection between the Medicis and Kohn's bank, but Kohn didn't highlight this.

"Kohn is no Medici," wrote Anthony Weiss, a staff writer for the Jewish newspaper *Forward*. "In fact, she's a Viennese-born Jew who became a *ba'al teshuva* in the 1980s and lived in the heavily Orthodox town of Monsey, New York." The term *ba'al teshuva* is Hebrew for "master of return (or repentance)" and is used to describe a person who is secular, not particularly religious, who then embraces their lost faith in an extreme form. "Monsey is actually home to both a declining Modern Orthodox population and a growing ultra-Orthodox population," Weiss explained. Ultra-Orthodox Jewish women cover their hair, and Sonja Kohn covered hers with wigs. But even Weiss was stumped about "where she falls on the Orthodox spectrum." Weiss wrote, "The [*New York*] *Times* describes her as ultra-Orthodox, apparently based on the fact that she wears a *sheytl*, or wig, and lives in Monsey. The wig suggests she's probably not Modern Orthodox, but high-flying women in the world of international finance are, indeed, anomalies in the ultra-Orthodox world."

Kohn played up her maternal side as the mother of five and a dutiful wife to her banker husband. "We have lived together in a happy marriage for over forty years. My husband was one of the youngest directors of Commerzbank. We started as a family business, started trading and after that moved into the finance businesses, which has been successful. We have five children and twenty-four grandchildren," Kohn told *Industrial Gazette*, a Russian newspaper, in July 2008. "I hope that from my employment in business my family has not suffered."

In December 2003, Kohn arranged for Bank Medici to get a full banking license from the Austrian Financial Authority. Bank Austria Creditanstalt, Austria's largest bank and a member of the Italian financial conglomerate UniCredit Group, was listed as a minority shareholder.

Although William Browder, who ran a Russia-dedicated hedge fund, described her as "strange, rather eccentric," the grandmotherly Kohn wasn't just a banker but a smooth operator and a name-dropper. Kohn was always handsomely dressed, wearing a perfectly coiffed wig and large gems.

Sonja Kohn carried two business cards. One read EUROVALEUR, with an address of 767 Fifth Avenue and a 212 phone number. Her other card read MEDICI FINANCE, with the same address and telephone number. One of her businesses was a feeder fund, the other a brokerage. "Kohn was wearing two hats," said Robert Picard, a former banker with the Royal Bank of Canada.

Picard bumped into Kohn in 1997 just as she was leaving Madoff's offices in midtown Manhattan. Kohn couldn't help herself. She introduced Picard to a man named Charles Fix and gushed, "We were together with Bernie!" Picard recalled. "She was pretending to be Bernie's closest confidante, and what she was doing was positioning herself" as an access point to Madoff, he said. Madoff was notorious for turning people away, and Fix, who was an asset manager with an inherited fortune, "was using her to get access to Bernie. She was meeting us as well and looking to see if we could set up an account with Bernie. She'd get a commission on that. Our position was, 'Screw you, we can get to Bernie anytime.' I had no intention of investing in Madoff through her fund" at Bank Medici, Picard added. "But I suspect she was getting doubly paid, by both acting as a feeder fund to Madoff and as a broker to Madoff."

"She acted as if she were absolutely in love with Madoff. The way she talked about him, I thought she was his mistress," said Picard.

As it turned out, Picard was right about Madoff paying Kohn. After Madoff's arrest, regulators in Massachusetts found records showing that Kohn had received $526,000 each quarter over a period of years from Cohmad for bringing in new money to Madoff. Other estimates are that she received $800,000 or more quarterly from Madoff.

Kohn larded the Bank Medici board with Austrian politicians. She even called herself an official adviser to the minister of economic affairs of Austria from 1996 to 2000 and claimed also to have advised the Austrian minister of foreign affairs and the Vienna Stock Exchange, according to Medici's Web site.

Her presentations carried a crestlike seal of twin lions, implying an affiliation with royalty. She even allied the bank's private foundation with the Vienna University of Economics and Business and the University of Pennsylvania's Wharton Global Family Alliance, "a private forum whose mission is to enhance the marketplace advantage and social wealth creation contributions of global families," according to Kohn's marketing materials for Bank Medici. "Together, the Foundation and these prestigious institutions are applying breakthrough academic research and Bank Medici's decades of real-world experience to identify the key financial and personal needs of family business dynasties."

Kohn's relationship with Bank Austria Creditanstalt gave her an imprimatur of legitimacy. For Bank Austria Creditanstalt was more than just a bank: it represented the combination of political parties—the socialists and conservatives—in Austria. On her board at Bank Medici were highly placed politicians such as Johann Farnleitner. A conservative, he had overseen the merger and privatization of Bank Austria and Creditanstalt.

Sonja Kohn also capitalized on the fact that Austria was fast becoming a close cousin to Switzerland in terms of banking secrecy and a country for the rich to hide ill-gotten gains or shelter assets from taxes. Bank Medici was tailor-made to service such clients.

Kohn even pointed out that Austrian national law requires banks to apply strict banking secrecy. The country is also unique in permitting banks to keep accounts that do not carry the depositor's name, the so-called postbook account, she told *Director* magazine in late 2008. She believed that Austria's tax and inheritance laws gave her firm a competitive advantage over its competitors in Switzerland and Liechtenstein by allowing it to attract wealth investors from the Middle East, China, and Russia.

Starting in the mid-1990s and continuing through 2008, Sonja Kohn marketed a number of funds that handed money over to Madoff to manage (although that was rarely if ever disclosed). For the banks offering Sonja Kohn's hedge funds, the funds were an easy sale—especially to the little people, the retail investors and others who wanted to put their small savings into something that, on paper anyway, rang up returns like a bond. Kohn's offerings promised 10 percent a year in returns and were among those whose innocent-sounding funds were listed by banks all over Europe and the United Kingdom. They were picked out of obscurity by individuals who simply saw the straight, 45-degree line of returns climbing across the page. These mom-and-pop investors had no idea that the graph was the signature of a monster financial scam artist.

Glenn Gramolini, a Geneva-based asset manager, told Bloomberg his first visit from Kohn took place in the mid-1990s. She explained Madoff's split-strike strategy, he recalled, by contending that as one of the U.S.'s biggest market makers—claiming to handle 10–20 percent of New York Stock Exchange order flow at the time—Madoff had an edge. "She was very pushy but very convinced and very confident," Gramolini said. "It looked to me at the time that she already had a very strong financial interest in it."

Once Sonja Kohn got Bank Medici in place, she began to use it as a platform for marketing the Madoff-linked funds. Kohn may have acted the part of the concerned, earnest banker. But she and her bank were little more than feeder funds for Madoff: the Herald, Primeo, and Thema funds, which each sought funds directly from investors and delivered, or fed, the money to Madoff.

In 2002, Gramolini invested 3 percent of his assets under management in Bank Medici's Dublin-based Thema International Fund. It was one of many funds controlled by Kohn's Bank Medici, including the Herald USA, Herald Luxemburg, Primeo Select, and Primeo Executive funds. Primeo Select, which was distributed by a Bank Austria unit, was Kohn's earliest fund that fed to Madoff. "Sonja Kohn was marketing the Primeo fund more like a conservative family holiday on a farm and not like a dangerous expedition to the Arctic," another investor told Bloomberg. "They didn't promise spectacular returns, but good and consistent ones."

Behind all the sales claims, we now know, was the Madoff-created steady stream of returns. Eventually, at Madoff's insistence, Kohn never mentioned his name in any of her literature. But the consistent performance reports that showed ever-increasing assets made investors flock to the funds. So easy was it to sell Madoff-linked funds that by 2008 Bank Medici had directed more than $3 billion worth of client money to Madoff through feeder funds. "In the last decade an average annual return of 12.01 percent was achieved with positive returns in each of even the most difficult years," Kohn crowed to a Gibraltar government newsletter in 2005, just as she had opened a Bank Medici branch in Gibraltar.

Kohn's ties with the Italian banking community helped as a marketing outlet as well.

Bank Medici, incorporated in Austria in 1994, was granted a full banking license by the Austrian financial authority in 2003. She kept ownership of 75 percent of Bank Medici, and the rest she sold to UniCredit, an Italian bank. Through UniCredit's subsidiary Pioneer, Bank Medici controlled the Primeo funds and transformed them into feeder funds for Madoff, to the tune of $3.2 billion.

The relationship helped her earn double commissions as well.

On one side, Pioneer's Dublin-based alternative investments division was paying her commissions of more than €800,000 in 2007 alone for referring investors to Pioneer's Primeo Select Fund, which was totally invested with Madoff. The fund's assets were reported as $280 million. The Herald (Lux) U.S. Absolute Return Fund, created in March 2008, was a 100 percent feeder fund into Madoff.

On the other side, she was being paid by Madoff to bring money into his firm. Austrian prosecutors now believe her contribution may have been even higher than the $3.2 billion alleged, and that she funneled as much as $8 billion Madoff's way.

Kohn was helping Madoff expand around the world—even as far away as Moscow. Interviewed by a local Russian paper, Kohn said she specialized in estate planning, particularly for the newly rich Russians, who needed creative ways to get their money offshore. Executives at some of the large Russian oil companies—for instance, Yukos—had heard of Madoff as early as 2005.

So regular were Madoff's returns for Bank Medici that customer banks were able to sell products that merely mimicked their performance. Paris-based BNP Paribas, for instance, issued a so-called tracker certificate for Bank Medici that mimicked the performance of Bank Medici's Herald (Lux) U.S. Absolute Return Fund, according to a document on BNP's Web site. The BNP certificate allowed people to deposit as little as a hundred euros into them.

By November 2008, Bank Medici was winning prizes across Europe for "amazing" performance. The flagship Herald USA Fund, started in 1996, reported a return of 6.5 percent for the year through November 28, 2008, with assets of more than $1.9 billion. Competitors couldn't match that: most had fallen an average of 17 percent as the global credit crisis bit into returns.

It was true, on paper at least, that none of Bank Medici's funds had had a single negative quarter. Herald (Lux) U.S. Absolute Return, opened in March 2008, has been "solid as a rock," Bank Medici said in a corporate statement in September 2008, adding that the fund's year-to-date return was 3.9 percent.

Sonja Kohn's reach stretched from the UK through Europe to Moscow, where she marketed herself as a great friend of Russia and Bank Medici as the perfect discreet private banker for Russia's new rich. "I believe that the majority of Russian businessmen, when they understand their business partners and trust them, are very reliable, but I'm not sure that it is the opinion of the rest of the world," she told *Diplomat* magazine.

Sonja Kohn had built a lucrative niche business—even though not many people understood exactly how she made money. Over just twenty years, Kohn had gone from being a penny stockbroker in 1987, registered under Windsor IBC brokerage firm, to running a $3.7 billion bank, partly owned by Bank Austria and UniCredit of Italy.

In a lawsuit against Kohn and her funds filed in U.S. District Court in the Southern District of New York, one investor, Horst Leonhardt from Austria, said that Kohn didn't disclose that the client's money was being funneled to Mr. Madoff and that "Madoff forbade the fund managers from naming him as the actual manager . . . in their marketing literature." He also charged that Kohn ignored the red flags: the returns were too smooth; Madoff didn't use a bank or prime broker to borrow money to make his wagers like other hedge funds did. He also noted that Sonja Kohn's bank was paid €875,000 in 2007 alone by the mutual fund company Pioneer for referring investors to Madoff.

A group of Bank Medici clients from Israel, Russia, and the Ukraine filed a complaint in Vienna's criminal court accusing the bank and Kohn of fraud and breach of trust. They claimed they had invested €80 million in the bank's Herald USA Fund without knowing it was being invested with Madoff, Gabriel Lansky, the lawyer representing the clients, told *Format*, an Austrian magazine.

Today, Bank Medici no longer exists; its license has been revoked. Sonja Kohn is in hiding. There were rumors that she was afraid of some of her angry Russian clients. Two of Bank Medici's largest funds had all of their assets with Madoff. Bank Medici's total balance with Madoff had been more than $3 billion.

In May 2009, new details about Kohn surfaced. Luxembourg public prosecutors suspected Kohn of money laundering, specifically in an account of Herald Asset Management, which is headquartered in the Cayman Islands. In the days following Madoff's arrest, Kohn allegedly made two transfers to Herald Asset Management, the entity which took in her commissions, totaling some €11 million.

Sonja Kohn and Bank Medici were among Madoff's biggest investors in Europe, but there were other European investors who played critical roles.

Among the most important of these were Notz Stucki, a private bank and asset manager founded by Beat Notz and Christian Stucki, and private banks founded by Edmond Safra and Edgar de Picciotto. Their investments with Madoff, which aided Madoff in bulking up the investment advisory side of his business, helped him to gain assets, and more important, the reputation that he would need to keep his scam up and running.

Madoff was able to pull off his scam for so long only because investors trusted him. Potential investors who did due diligence and looked closely at Madoff often decided to steer clear, as has been shown. But despite his suspiciously consistent returns and the heavy cloak of secrecy he wrapped around his operations, loyal investors continued to pour billions of dollars, and euros, into his coffers. If their friends and acquaintances trusted "Uncle Bernie" and invested with him, why shouldn't they?

In this way key European investors such as Notz, Stucki, Safra, and de Picciotto played a critical role in enabling Madoff. Once these and other kingmakers were in his network, Madoff knew that others would clamor to get in. Aside from Carl Shapiro, who lifted Madoff into wealthy social circles in America and gave him his first dose of solid credibility, some of Madoff's first big clients came from Europe. These were French and Swiss bankers who served international sheiks and royalty. Through them, hundreds of millions, and then eventually billions, of dollars started coming in during the 1990s.

Among Madoff's first European investors was the Notz Stucki investment firm. After Madoff was arrested, the firm, which was based in Geneva, would report that it had $737 million in investments with him. Separately, its founders had helped create two of the world's first funds of hedge funds before they joined forces to form Notz Stucki.

Beat Notz and Christian Stucki were among the first to develop the concept of funds of hedge funds. A fund of hedge funds is essentially a money dispatcher, farming out millions of dollars to different hedge fund managers to see who makes the best returns. Notz Stucki was one of the earliest managers of these funds of funds, handing over their Swiss francs to money managers they thought would pull away from the pack. By 2006, Notz Stucki's fund of hedge funds had $3 billion in assets alone; the entire investment firm ran about $16 billion. Two of Notz Stucki's funds, Plaza and DGC Pendulum, were invested with Madoff.

Beat Notz, who had a master's degree from the University of Geneva, once worked at Lehman Brothers International in Paris. In 1968, he cofounded Haussmann Holdings with Groupe Worms in Paris. His partner, Christian Stucki, graduated with a law degree from the University of Zurich. In 1968, he cofounded the Leveraged Capital Holdings fund with the Rothschilds, a French banking family that dates back to Napoleon. Both of these were among the world's first funds of funds. In 1969, Georges Karlweis, managing director of the private bank to Edmond de Rothschild, was the first to implement the idea of a joint-investment fund. That investment fund, called Leveraged Capital Holdings (LCH), still exists today, and Alexander Ineichen, in his tome *Absolute Returns: The Risk and Opportunities of Hedge Fund Investing*, lists it as the world's first fund of hedge funds.

In 1971, the hedge fund industry was tiny: probably less than $1 billion. Today, hedge funds control nearly $1.5 trillion—meaning the business has grown a thousand times over in under forty years. But back then, hedge funds were like the private clubs of the investment world. In the beginning, hedge funds were offered strictly to the ultra-wealthy and sold by private bankers to their favored clients. It was a club based on referrals, who knew whom, and a circle of trust built upon those referrals. In Switzerland, the hedge fund world was a fraternity of the wealthy and well connected. All these advantages gave the Swiss hedge fund investor community a perceived edge on finding good money managers ahead of everyone else. Moreover, the investors and the managers they gave money to also developed a special bond. A hedge fund's first investor garnered a special status as someone who believed in the hedge fund manager as a person and as a business.

Haussmann Holdings played kingmaker to many future titans of the hedge fund industry. Haussmann gave the then-unknown money manager George Soros his start in the 1970s and later, Julian Robertson's Tiger fund, Paul Tudor Jones, Louis Bacon, and others. Its initial $5 million investment in Soros's first hedge fund became worth $250 million twenty-five years later. Haussmann was seen as a leader among what Wall Street referred to as "smart money," or those who got in early on smart investments. Haussmann would seed other new hedge fund managers before the rest of the world even knew what a hedge fund was.

Not unlike Wall Street, most Swiss and other European funds of funds traveled in packs—as they competed for wealthy clients, no one wanted to appear as if they weren't smart money. So receiving a blessing from a member of the industry's nobility, like Notz Stucki—as Madoff did—was akin to receiving the hedge fund equivalent of the Good Housekeeping Seal of Approval. Madoff could not have asked for better references.

Then two very key and important Swiss banks became early investors with Madoff as well. These Madoff investors were discreet. In addition to being secretive in banking, "The whole structure of the Swiss asset management industry is designed to hide where the money came from," said one American fund of hedge funds consultant.

Madoff also won the blessing of these two important banks: Union Bancaire Privée, run by Edgar de Picciotto, and Safra Banking Group, founded by Edmond Safra and his father. Not surprisingly, the two banks are fierce competitors, founded by once-longtime friends. But after a falling-out between the friends, the banks became rivals. De Picciotto and Safra shared similar backgrounds. They were both Sephardic Jews whose families had emigrated to Switzerland or elsewhere in Europe and settled in to become low-profile financiers.

But to people like Madoff and other hedge fund supplicants looking for new money, Safra and de Picciotto were more than just bankers—they were gatekeepers to billions. They had social connections. They attended the best, most expensive, and carefully vetted European boarding schools (as did their children and their grandchildren), and they kept quiet about who their wealthiest clients were. To have them as investors was a coup. Once these men had signed off on someone as a new talent, the rest of the Swiss private banking world would line up to invest, practically without question.

"It was shorthand due diligence, using the reference of another person whom they all knew and trusted," said an investment banker who declined to invest in Madoff. Lombard Odier and other Swiss banks "were all deep into [Madoff], because Notz Stucki liked it," noted Picard.

In the case of UBP, Edgar de Picciotto went against the best advice of his employees and invested with Madoff. He may have been influenced by his nephew's friendship with Andrés Piedrahita, a partner in Madoff booster Fairfield Greenwich Group.

Started in 1969, UBP was very successful very quickly. The Geneva bank went global in 1971, when it began to invest with and outsource money to managers that the de Picciottos thought had a competitive edge. From the outset, UBP was trying to compete with other Swiss banks. To help itself stand out, the bank turned to hedge funds. In 1986, UBP launched D-Invest Total Return, a fund of hedge funds, which, like Haussmann, acted as a vehicle for farming out money to other hedge fund managers.

In return, UBP would accept fees from these managers for bringing investors to the game. UBP's fund of hedge funds was also the beginning of UBP's alternatives business, under which it would allocate its clients' money not just to plain vanilla investments like stocks and bonds, but to alternatives such as hedge funds, private equity, or hard assets like timber and precious metals. UBP had three different pools of money to invest in hedge funds and other so-called alternative investments— Geneva, London, and the United States. The American office was considered something of a sideline, and de Picciotto decided to build it up only in the 1990s. The strategy worked amid a historic bull market in America. By 2008, the U.S. office had more than $50 billion in hedge funds and the firm had $125 billion in assets. UBP had become one of the world's largest allocators, or distributors, for its clients' money into hedge funds.

"UBP wasn't reckless," said a former employee who helped construct the due diligence team at the bank. This person has since left to start a due diligence firm investigating hedge funds. "I know the [de

Picciotto] family well, and I know the due diligence that was done on Madoff. Ultimately, somebody had to make a decision about investing with him—the person who made that call was de Picciotto himself." There was no better explanation as to why UBP invested in Madoff, to the tune of $700 million.

De Picciotto, this former employee said, "was one of the pioneers to give access to wealthy Europeans to hedge fund managers like Soros" in the 1970s. But at the time, there was little or no due diligence. Nobody investigated or asked probing question of the accountants, administrators and other functionaries in the back office, which actually did the paperwork and transferred money for hedge funds. Hedge funds were given money based almost solely on trust. "You invested because you identified talent; if you shared his views about the world, then you gave access to this money manager to your clients, to invest with the best and brightest," the former UBP employee said.

Only in the 1990s did UBP begin formalizing its research process. Today it is one of the world's largest allocators to hedge funds.

But Madoff already had de Picciotto's confidence. And that personal legacy of trust carried over even after UBP started performing more formal digging on new hedge fund managers. By the late 1990s, UBP had developed a formalized process, but there were certain clients, like Madoff, whom de Picciotto exempted from these checks. "Let's face it, investing is not science. You make a call," the former UBP employee said. "In hindsight, Madoff was the wrong call. There were a lot of red flags. In the case of UBP, of course they did due diligence but they decided based on their relationship that they wanted to invest" with Madoff.

After Madoff's arrest, UBP told investors that it identified some concerns: nonsegregation of investment, brokerage, and custody functions was a risk, but it "found comfort" in Madoff's status as a reputable broker-dealer subject to regulators' audits, according to e-mails shown by UBP's then–deputy head of research, Gideon Nieuwoudt, to the *Wall Street Journal*.

UBP's defense of its Madoff investment was that the money lost had "been within its investment guidelines." To be fair, UBP had a point. Even after investing $700 million with Madoff, UBP's total loss for 2008 was 18 percent. The loss from Madoff accounted for 5–6 percent of that. And $700 million was only a fraction of the $125 billion UBP was overseeing. "They never went over the top," said the head of UBP's U.S. operations, who pointed out that UBP instructed all its underlying hedge funds that they would pull their money out unless the hedge fund provided complete and total transparency, and in the wake of Madoff's arrest, he assured clients that they were getting it.

But for some UBP clients, the combination of Madoff and the worst stock market declines in generations prompted them to withdraw money from the bank. Among those who withdrew assets from UBP was the Qatar Investment Authority, which invested the country of Qatar's $60 billion in oil riches on behalf of the state. Qatar Investment Authority was just the latest breed of investor in hedge funds, known as the "sovereign wealth fund." Russia had one, as did Singapore, China, and some OPEC nations. These took receipts from oil and commodities profits and invested them in hedge funds on behalf of the government.

After Madoff's arrest, the Qatar Investment Authority's executive director, Hussain Ali Al-Abdullah, did not mince words, saying Madoff had "killed the hedge fund." Other investors like Ithmar Capital's Faisal bin Juma Belhoul in Dubai also blamed institutional investors such as UBP for being too willing to take cash without asking questions. "They were given a lot of leeway," he told a local Arab news outlet. "A lot of flexibility in structures that were like black boxes. . . . Madoff is a classic example of where institutional investors did not bother to truly understand what was the underlying practice being done, as long as Madoff delivered a 10 percent consistent return over the years."

After Madoff was arrested, it emerged that dozens of funds of hedge funds and so-called feeder funds held a total of $20 billion or more with Madoff. These included UBP; Banco Safra out of South America; Banco Santander, the Spanish bank; and Pioneer Alternative Investments, part of Italian bank UniCredit.

At first, Safra denied it had invested any of its client money with Madoff, until Brazilian investors in Zeus Partners Limited said they had come to Madoff through Safra Bank. The Brazilian branch of Safra group was led by Joseph Safra, the brother of the late Edmond Safra, who died in a fire in his apartment in Monaco in 1999. Safra Group controlled a dozen banks in Latin America, the United States, and Europe. In a follow-up, the *Financial Times* noted that in the offering and sales documents of Zeus, the Bank Jacob Safra of Gibraltar was listed as the custodian of funds.

Safra quietly tried to make good to its clients after it was revealed that Madoff was a phony. Customers were offered a refund of up to a third of the money lost, through perpetual bonds returning 2 percent a year, or about 30 percent of their initial investment. In return, the customer had to agree to waive the right to sue. In response to this offer, a lawyer for one client fumed that he was "angry, to be polite."

Then, in April 2009, Irving Picard, a Baker Hostetler lawyer entrusted to liquidate Madoff's assets, went after Bank Jacob Safra for money Madoff had sent to the bank just weeks prior to turning himself in. Picard sued Safra for $150 million, which he alleged Madoff wired to the bank in the months leading up to his arrest. In particular, Picard went after an account opened by Bank Jacob Safra through the island of Gibraltar. Bank Jacob Safra had an account with Madoff, with designated account number 1FR083, opened around December 2001 under the name "Banque Safra–France as Custodian for Vizcaya Partners Ltd," which between 2002 and 2008 had deposited roughly $327 million into Madoff's JPMorgan Chase Bank account.

About six weeks before he confessed and was arrested for securities fraud, Madoff wired back $150 million to this Bank Safra account, apparently for the benefit of whomever was the shareholder behind Vizcaya.

Banco Santander, for its part, chose to avoid tangling with the Madoff trustee: the Spanish bank settled with Irving Picard in mid-June 2009 and paid $235 million to the Madoff victims' trust.

The Santander settlement represented money withdrawn just before Madoff's fraud was revealed in December 2008. But Swiss prosecutors will likely keep Santander in the headlines: a few days after Santander settled with Picard, Geneva's public prosecutor launched a criminal investigation into allegations that Santander's hedge fund unit Optimal misled investors when it funneled their money into Madoff's Ponzi scheme.

Aside from UBP, Safra, and a host of other European investors, there was another well-known investor in Madoff by the name of EIM.

EIM was really a one-man operation. Arpad "Arkie" Busson was Europe's ultimate jet-set playboy. Born in France in 1963, he had wealthy parents and attended the exclusive boarding school Le Rosey, the Swiss equivalent of Exeter, where he rubbed shoulders with sheiks and heiresses. Known as the "school of kings," Le Rosey counts among its alumni the duty-free-shopping heiress Marie-Chantal Miller; heirs to the Johnson & Johnson fortune; an heiress to the A&P supermarket fortune; the late Shah of Iran; the late Prince Rainier III of Monaco, the husband of actress Grace Kelly; and children of movie stars (David Niven, Elizabeth Taylor, Roger Moore) and rock stars (John Lennon, Diana Ross). For Busson, Le Rosey was the beginning of a social network that became a potential gold mine for investors in hedge funds years later. Busson skied at expensive mountain resorts and dated stunningly beautiful women. He had two children with Australian supermodel Elle Macpherson and reportedly once dated actress Farrah Fawcett. He is currently engaged to actress Uma Thurman. Busson and Thurman would sometimes have dinner with Bernie Madoff, according to Bernie's secretary. Ruth didn't want to attend, saying she was intimidated by Thurman's height and beauty.

Busson was both envied and emulated. He began in the hedge fund industry in the mid-1980s auspiciously, working to raise money for the then-unknown young American commodity trader Paul Tudor Jones. He raised money by cultivating his social networks and wealthy friends. The year the American stock market was crashing Tudor generated a stunning 201 percent return for its investors. That sealed Busson's reputation as a hotshot in the hedge fund world. Busson raised money for four more years—eventually raising funds for the famed hedge fund managers Louis Bacon and Julian Robertson—successfully enough that he then went out on his own, setting up EIM first in Switzerland and then in London and New York.

Busson's business grew rapidly, and EIM started sending investments to a variety of hedge funds. By 2009, Busson's firm had $10.9 billion of investors' money in a hundred client accounts, many of them large institutions like university endowments, pension funds, and retirement plans for corporations as well as municipalities.

But Busson also had a reputation for ending up at the scene of some big accidents in the hedge fund industry. EIM also invested in the dot.com-era hedge fund fraud Manhattan Investment, run by a young Austrian named Michael Berger. Berger created phony account statements for his hedge fund between 1996 and 2000 and was able to raise more than $575 million from investors by overstating the performance and market value of the hedge fund's holdings until he went bust with a bearish bet on Internet stocks. After a tip from Berger's prime broker, Busson ended up redeeming out of Berger's fund ahead of most other investors—prompting a lawsuit claiming Busson had inside information that Berger was lying about his returns and stealing investors' money. Investors ultimately lost roughly $450 million with Berger. Berger was convicted but then didn't show up for sentencing and fled the U.S. in 2002. He was released from prison in 2009 in Austria.

More than any other finance figure in Europe, Arkie Busson personified the excesses of the late twentieth century, the excess of rising stock markets, exploding house prices, and a mad rush of "sophisticated" investors piling into hedge funds without actually knowing anything about what they were getting into.

Busson was not embarrassed about his riches. He gave generously to charity and received favorable treatment in the press. After a fundraiser for his own philanthropy, ARK (Absolute Return for Kids), he bragged, "We've shown people that the hedge fund industry is a force for good in the world. In the past, my industry has been accused of everything from greed to carelessness to downright dishonesty. Now I feel a very different picture is emerging of us: working for others." Busson's mentor, both in the hedge fund business and in philanthropy, was Paul Tudor Jones, the American commodity trader who had started the Robin Hood Foundation, one of the hedge fund industry's first philanthropies. Busson founded his charity in 2002 with like-minded City of London financiers and raised nearly $50 million for local schools.

In an interview in October 2007, just as the U.S. stock market was cratering again—this time as a result of a worldwide credit crisis—Busson took part in a hedge fund roundtable published by *Barron's* magazine. There, he talked about the importance of vetting hedge funds before investing in them. "In looking at managers to invest in, one of the biggest parts of our homework is to understand the relationship between the hedge fund and the banker," he said. "Who is the banker? It's the prime broker. When we invest in hedge funds that use leverage, we have to understand a very complex relationship between both parties, including the terms of financing, how they collateralize, and how can they pull financing."

Busson, nonetheless, placed $230 million of his wealthy clients' money with Bernard Madoff, even though Madoff did not even have a prime broker. The week after Madoff's arrest, the *New York Post* cornered Busson to ask about the Madoff scandal and his choice to invest in the fraud. "For the amount of money and number of accounts, it's practically impossible that he was doing this alone," said Busson. "What's mind-boggling is the amount of assets and the amount of time he was doing it." EIM's exposure was through three outside hedge funds that EIM invests in and that had accounts with Madoff, Busson told *Bloomberg Markets* magazine. Not one of EIM's accounts had more than 5 percent of its assets with Madoff.

"The truth was, Arkie didn't do the due diligence on Madoff," said a rival of Busson in an interview, after Madoff was arrested. This competitor had heard about Madoff as far back as the early 1990s, when he worked for GAM, a hedge fund of funds unit of Julius Baer, with total assets under management of $66.8 billion. "My boss told me never, ever put money with Madoff. That he was a crook. From then on, I never did." At a succession of jobs in the hedge fund industry, this fund of funds investor had opportunities to invest with Madoff and stayed away. In 2008, he had risen to the head of all alternative investments at one of America's largest banks, and still he kept clients from investing with Madoff. "Either Arkie had no process or he ignored the process."

Busson contended that when someone wants to steal your money, there is no protection against willful fraud. "Catching a fraud is practically impossible," Busson told *Bloomberg Markets* magazine. "There's only so much due diligence you can do." Madoff, he added, "was not an obscure little manager in the boondocks. He seemed like a very experienced, knowledgeable, trustworthy man—like the best con artists always are."

In a sense, Arkie Busson was the type of hedge fund customer who bridged generations. He represented the new generation of young investors in hedge funds who might be expected to be more computer savvy. But they were often investing their parents' or inherited old money that represented a world that still relied on old-style social networking over new-style computerized investigation. Madoff played on the generational split, appealing to older people in European and American banking circles who took a person's word as his bond. They didn't ask questions. They didn't want or feel they needed to verify a money manager using newly available technology that made it easy to see whether the fund manager was actually doing what he or she claimed.

"They took Madoff's word. These strategies were sophisticated enough that the older generation didn't understand them, these trading strategies—they just assumed the manager knew what he was talking about," said Robert Picard, previously of Royal Bank of Canada and now a senior adviser with the restructuring team at Navigant Capital Advisors. "A lot of it had to do with age. But also it had to do with Bernie's attitude of not needing the money. That worked every time. There's nothing that sounds more exclusive than saying you don't need someone's money. That was his shtick. He would rope them in, taking a small amount of money at first, and then hundreds of millions."

Other European investors caught up in the Madoff scam included Britain's Merseyside and Hampshire pension funds; Italy's UniCredit and Deutsche Bank Italia pension funds; Danish and Dutch retirement giants PFA Pension and the Shell pension funds; and Switzerland's St. Galler Kantonalbank.

Britain's Merseyside and Hampshire pension funds shared the same intermediary, Bramdean Asset Management. Bramdean, run by one of London's best-known portfolio managers in high finance, Nicola Horlick, said after Madoff's arrest that it was "deeply shocked" that Madoff was a fraud. In late December 2008, Horlick said that her fund, known as Bramdean Alternatives, would lose only 4 percent of its assets if Madoff collapsed completely—which it did. The fund, which was very high profile and was quoted on the London Stock Exchange, had about 9 percent of its money invested with Madoff. It was managed by Horlick and RMF, part of Man Group, one of the largest advisers to and investors in hedge funds in the world.

But the relationship was convenient for both parties. Nicola Horlick and her company Bramdean used Madoff just as he used them: her fund of hedge funds treated Madoff much like a money market account, and could "redeem" or cash out of Madoff accounts with just ten days' notice—almost unheard of in hedge fund circles. That gave Bramdean the opportunity to stay liquid, or have ready cash at hand, by investing with Bernie Madoff.

Bramdean had had some portfolio winners in 2008, including in currency markets. But mostly the firm was the talk of London for having invested in Madoff. Horlick angrily told BBC Radio, "Even if we had to write off the total whole Madoff exposure, the fund would only be down 4 percent. The entire stock market is down 35 percent. What makes me really angry is the coverage isn't clear at all. Even after this the investors in that fund would have done extremely well."

Horlick defended her ignorance by trying to pass the buck to other, bigger investors and regulators in America. "If we should have known better, and RMF, one of the biggest hedge fund managers in the world, then what about all these banks? HSBC, for example, lent $1 billion" to investors using Madoff as collateral. "The SEC was responsible in America for regulating it, and in 2005 and 2007 gave us a clean bill of health. How would we feel if this had happened in the UK? That's the major question we should be asking."

Strangely enough, Madoff's supposed hedge fund strategy was very simple. He was meant to be buying options that made money that went up or down, depending on his call, and moving the money into U.S. Treasuries at the end of the year. One of the things that made it so easy for people to ignore the red flags was that the returns were actually relatively low compared to most hedge funds. "It was the opposite of a get-rich-quick scam!" Nicola Horlick insisted. "That's what's so terrible—all these risk-averse investors have lost money—foundations, individuals—all risk averse—pensions, who've lost all their money in this."

Even though RMF had teams of people looking at Madoff's trading records, both they and Bramdean missed the warnings. "Now it's very difficult for people to invest in things meant to be regulated in America," Horlick added. "They've fallen down on the job. This is the biggest financial scandal probably in the history of the markets."

But there was another important reason why older, experienced European bankers did not see Madoff's flaws: fees.

Haussmann Holdings' own documents lay out exactly why investing in hedge funds was so enormously lucrative. In a 2007 offering memorandum, Haussmann spelled out the rules for investing in its hedge fund: minimum investments in class A shares, $50,000; class B shares, $100,000; class C shares, a minimum euro equivalent of $50,000.

In return, Haussmann charted a tidy 1.5 percent to subscribe to the fund and another fee of 0.50 percent if you came in through a broker or middleman. On a $100,000 investment, Haussmann charged a $1,500 commission just for the privilege of investing and another $500 to whomever introduced the investor to the fund. And that was before someone like Madoff—or other real hedge fund managers like Soros—made their profits for the year. Soros returned profits of more than 35 percent annually for decades, and eventually his Quantum Fund grew to $20 billion in assets. A fund of hedge funds firm such as Haussmann's would take 10 percent of Soros's profits.

Haussmann also revealed one of the hedge fund industry's dirtiest little secrets: rebates. Haussmann charged investors just for managing their money. And Haussmann casually said that "standard business practice" allowed payment of a portion of those fees to whoever brought a new customer in (e.g., broker-dealers, investment advisers, banks, etc.). "Under certain circumstances, the investment manager and its affiliates may rebate a portion of the fees that they receive to third parties," according to the 2007 offering documents.

"It works like this with rebates," explained one American hedge fund manager. He had just been forced to "redeem," or given money back to, one of his investors, Sandra Manzke of Tremont Capital, after she lost $270 million in Madoff's Ponzi scheme. She was forced to cash out of the rest of her hedge funds.

"A private banker works for a bank in Geneva, say, for a decade. He or she builds up a client base—wealthy people, people they meet at their clubs, playing tennis, skiing in the Alps, or socially—and by the end of that ten years they have a valuable list of clients."

One day, the private banker walks out and sets up his own shop. He approaches an up-and-coming hedge fund manager and says, "I have a list of wealthy people who I can introduce to you. They'll invest in your fund"—say, $100 million. On that, the hedge fund manager charges 2 percent a year just for managing the money and 20 percent of the profits after a year. The private banker sticks his hand out: "What are you going to give me for bringing them to you?" The hedge fund manager offers him 1 percent of his 2 percent management fee for bringing in new investors. That amounts to a rebate of $1 million just for the introduction by the private banker.

Just for acting as the middleman or matchmaker between investors and hedge funds, a hedge fund intermediary can end up being paid very handsomely.

Chapter Seven

M adoff never called his off-the-books side business a hedge fund. He never even gave it a name. He swore investors to secrecy, making them promise not to tell anyone he was managing their money. That's because, technically, Madoff wasn't running a real hedge fund even though the amount of money he was controlling was so enormous it rivaled other billion-dollar hedge funds in assets.

America's original "hedged fund" was started by sociologist Alfred Winslow Jones in 1949. He made bets on stocks and other securities he believed would go up in price ("long" positions) and at the same time wagered on stocks going down in price ("short" positions). The idea was that the "longs'" and "shorts" would offset one another, and the portfolio would be a "hedged" fund. More recently hedge funds were lumped in with venture capital and private equity as "alternative" investments—meaning alternatives to stocks, mutual funds, and long-only funds—or funds that only made bets on prices going up.

Perhaps hedge funds are best compared to betting at the horse races—investors can wager on one horse winning and another losing or coming in second or third—and still make money. A hedge fund aims to make money betting on winners and losers.

Madoff let people believe that his "advisory" business was a hedge fund, perhaps because it gave him a cover of secrecy and exclusivity that he needed. Hedge funds weren't required to register with the SEC until 2006, so for decades Madoff was able to operate under the radar without anyone questioning what he was up to.

Moreover, Madoff paid other people to act as the storefront and money-raisers—such as his old friend Sonny Cohn, Cohn's daughter, Marcia, Robert Jaffe, and Alvin Delaire, who all worked within Cohmad, respectable Connecticut and European feeder funds such as

UBP or Fairfield Greenwich, and Sonja Kohn and her quiet Austrian bank. To the outside world, Madoff positioned himself as nothing more than a broker, even though he was running enough money to rival Julian Robertson's Tiger funds, George Soros's Quantum funds, and in the past decade, more than a hundred hedge funds boasting at least $1 billion in assets.

Madoff's "advisory" operation wasn't structured like a hedge fund: he didn't use a prime broker like other hedge funds did, nor did he borrow from banks or publish his returns. Most important, Madoff was a fraud because he never actually invested his clients' money.

But, if he had wanted to, Madoff could have run a real hedge fund without raising any eyebrows.

It was not unusual for well-known Wall Street traders to cross over to the more profitable asset management business, which in the late 1990s and early 2000s was becoming the Street's new profit center. Running other people's money, instead of trading, was where the big money was. Everyone wanted in on the game, including those who had previously run staid mutual funds.

Hedge funds were the hottest thing going, and many successful Wall Street traders left the security of their day jobs and struck out to start a hedge fund. Anyone who had a good track record from his or her own P&L, or profit and loss track record—usually from running a proprietary trading desk—and the gumption to leave could persuade the boss to hand over some seed money to help get a fund started. Sometimes their old employers, such as Morgan Stanley or Goldman Sachs, even bought a piece of the new outfit or gave them some start-up cash to run a hedge fund in-house. Behind many new hedge funds were incubators like FrontPoint Partners and SkyBridge that would seed hedge funds with their own money and take equity, plus a portion of the manager's fees going out into the future.

And if you didn't have the opportunity to leave the trading desk and start a hedge fund in-house, then you could always defect—abandon your big Wall Street firm and form a start-up hedge fund.

The example of Fidelity was one that many on Wall Street watched carefully. For years, the Boston-based mutual fund giant did not let any of its mutual fund managers short stocks, or bet a share price would go down (hedge funds are free to do so). Nor were Fidelity's portfolio managers also owners in the business (hedge fund managers are often

MADOFF, BERNARD L.
Varsity Swimming Team, Locker
Guard, 80% and 90% Cert.
After: Alabama U.

Bernie Madoff signed Judi Asch's yearbook upon his graduation from Far Rockaway High School, near where he grew up in Queens, New York. *(Courtesy of Judi Asch)*

Madoff returns home after a court appearance in New York on December 17, 2008, just days after his arrest. Three months later, he would plead guilty to eleven criminal counts but refuse to implicate anyone else in the Ponzi scheme. *(AP Photo/Jason Decrow)*

Ruth Madoff, Bernie's wife and high school sweetheart, is escorted by private security after visiting her husband in jail just a few weeks after his guilty plea. Throughout their marriage, Bernie placed many of their assets in Ruth's name. *(AP Photo/Mary Altaffer)*

Peter Madoff, Bernie's brother, arrives at court in New York in April 2009. Peter, who was trained as a lawyer, started working for his brother in the 1970s and served as chief compliance officer for the legitimate broker-dealer firm. *(AP Photo/ Louis Lanzano)*

Robert Jaffe, a onetime Boston stockbroker, married Ellen Shapiro, heiress to Ruth and Carl Shapiro's multimillion-dollar fortune. Jaffe drew investors to Madoff from exclusive country club golf courses and funneled their money through Cohmad. *(Chris Ford/PatrickMcMullan.com)*

Walter Noel, cofounder of Fairfield Greenwich Group, and his wife, Monica, traveled in elite, jet-setter social circles and helped Madoff reach a new level of international investor money. *(Patrick McMullan/PatrickMcMullan.com)*

Ezra Merkin, pictured here at a ceremony in Jerusalem, was revered in the modern Jewish orthodox community. Through his Gabriel and Ascot funds, Merkin invested large charity and university endowments with Madoff. *(AP Photo/Eliana Aponte, Pool, File)*

Even Hollywood celebrities lost money in Madoff's massive hedge fund scam. Kevin Bacon and Kyra Sedgwick invested through Ezra Merkin's fund of hedge funds, on the recommendation of her stepfather, Ben Heller. *(AP Photo/Franck Prevel)*

Sandra Manzke founded or helped set up three different "feeders" into Madoff, including Tremont, Kingate, and Maxam funds. *(Chuck Fishman)*

Married to the Noels' eldest daughter, Andrés Piedrahita was the biggest owner in Fairfield Greenwich, which fed over $7 billion into Madoff's phony hedge fund. *(Matt Carasella/ PatrickMcMullan.com)*

Harry Markopolos, an options expert and certified fraud examiner, became the main whistleblower who uncovered Madoff as a fraud in 1999, but his multiple warnings to the SEC went unheeded. *(AP Photo/Susan Walsh)*

René-Thierry Magon de la Ville-huchet felt so guilty about losing his investors' money through his Access International fund of funds that he committed suicide shortly after Madoff's arrest. *(David X. Prutting/Patrick McMullan.com)*

The City of London's famed "superwoman," Nicola Horlick, head of Bramdean Asset Management, blamed the SEC and other U.S. regulators for not catching Bernie Madoff sooner. *(Geoff Pugh/The Daily Telegraph)*

After confessing to a $50 billion financial fraud, Madoff spent months under house arrest in his sumptuous Manhattan penthouse apartment—infuriating his thousands of victims and the public. *(Patrick Andrade/The New York Times/Redux)*

Once owned by the Pulitzer family, the Madoffs' Palm Beach house, worth an estimated $11 million, was located just blocks from Robert Jaffe's mansion and Walter Noel's house. *(AP Photo/Jon Way)*

Bernie and Ruth Madoff's villa in Cap d'Antibes, France. After Bernie's arrest, the French government tried to seize the estate, worth an estimated $1 million. *(Nora Feller/The New York Times/Redux)*

the largest equity partners in the fund). One former Fidelity alumnus, now a hedge fund manager, calculated that while at Fidelity his mutual fund added $3 billion in equity capitalization value to the firm, but he got no equity.

Among the first to leave Fidelity and form a billion-dollar hedge fund was Jeff Vinik, who ran Fidelity's well-known Magellan mutual fund, and Larry Bowman. (Vinik set the bar high: Vinik Asset Management returned 52.9 percent net of all his fees between opening in 1996 and 2000.) Then Brian Posner left Fidelity in 2000 to form Hygrove Partners. In the ensuing years, so many mutual fund honchos left Fidelity that in 2001 Eric Kobren, founder of *Fidelity Insight* newsletter, launched a fund of Fidelity hedge funds called Alumni Partners. Its sole purpose was to give money to former Fidelity mutual fund portfolio managers who had started their own hedge funds.

The wave continued. Dan Benton had already left Pequot to start Andor Capital. Others from Dresdner Kleinwort left to join Pequot. Brian Stack, who managed about $5 billion in mutual fund and institutional assets for MFS Investment Management in Boston, quit to launch his own hedge fund. Rudy Kluiber, a former manager of State Street Research and Management's Aurora Fund, also in Boston, defected to found the GRT Captial Partners hedge fund with two other managers from State Street. Aetos Capital, founded by James Allwin, former head of institutional investment management at Morgan Stanley, hired two pros from billion-dollar endowments: Anne Casscells, onetime chief investment officer for Stanford University, and Jeffrey Mora, who had managed alternative investments for Northwestern University.

Banks began buying hedge funds outright. The Bank of New York bought fund of funds operation Ivy Asset Management; John Nuveen acquired alternative investment shop Symphony Asset Management. In 2002, magazines like *Institutional Investor* began annually tracking the hundred largest hedge funds and best-paid hedge fund managers.

Once the trend began in the late 1990s, the first decade of the twenty-first century gave rise to "star" traders who left trading desks to start their own hedge funds, often with the backing of their old employers. Goldman Sachs, for instance, had already spawned several hedge fund managers out of its proprietary trading desks, most notably Leon Cooperman's Omega Advisors, Inc., hedge fund.

Then came Eton Park. Eric Mindich, known as a gifted trader on

Goldman Sachs' risk arbitrage desk, and the youngest partner in Goldman's history, left in 2004 to start Eton Park Capital Management and immediately raised more than $3 billion. His hedge fund charged a 2 percent management fee and 20 percent of the profits, and demanded investors leave their money in the fund for as long as three years (much like a certificate of deposit at a bank, this requirement is known as a "lockup" in the hedge fund world). Before Eton Park had even opened the doors on the new hedge fund, Mindich's starting point for earnings was $60 million—or 2 percent of $3 billion in assets raised. That 2 percent was his flat fee whether or not the fund earned money. It was the talk of the Street for months.

The success of Eton Park signaled the beginning of a hedge fund bubble. By 2004, the dot.com bear market was over, and a post–Internet bust, Alan Greenspan–inspired bull market was again in full swing. In 2004 alone, more than fourteen hundred new hedge funds started up. By 2005, an estimated eight thousand hedge funds were overseeing total assets of around $1 trillion. Fifteen years earlier, by comparison, there had been perhaps eleven hundred hedge funds managing a total of about $50 billion. Morgan Stanley market strategist Barton Biggs loudly warned the investing public of the impending hedge fund bubble, then left Morgan Stanley and started his own hedge fund.

Madoff could have easily joined the ranks of Eton Park, Julian Robertson's Tiger funds, or Jim Simons's Renaissance Technologies funds, overseeing billions if he had wanted to. He had the assets, the broker-dealer operation as a legitimate business and trading platform, and he had the reputation. By 2000, rumor was he was one of the biggest billion-dollar hedge funds on the Street. Despite that, his so-called hedge fund was nothing but a fraud.

Although hedge funds' popularity was growing, very few people knew exactly what one was. Even Congress had a hard time defining the term. In 1966, Carol Loomis of *Fortune* magazine profiled the original "hedged fund," started by Alfred Jones in 1949: Jones would buy and hold stocks he thought would go up in price (his "long" positions) and then "hedged" those holdings with stocks he thought might fall in price (his "short" positions).

There is no definition under U.S. federal securities laws as to what a hedge fund is. Rather, hedge funds are blandly dubbed "lightly regulated private investment vehicles" in the mainstream press. They "try to maximize risk-adjusted returns for investors—as compared to simply beating some index or the market as a whole," wrote Troy A. Paredes, then a professor at Washington University School of Law in Saint Louis, Missouri, in a May 2007 draft of his paper "Hedge Funds and the SEC: Observations on the How and Why of Securities Regulation." (In 2008, Paredes was appointed an SEC commissioner, a sign that hedge funds may have some understanding and support in Washington.)

Hedge funds are usually structured like some other types of businesses, corporations, or law firms: as limited partnerships or limited liability companies. Investors put money in and become limited partners. If you are "qualified" or "accredited"—generally meaning rich enough to afford losing all your money in the fund—you buy into a hedge fund under an exemption, a private placement that doesn't need the registration requirements under federal securities laws.

Perhaps most important to understand is that hedge funds are not mutual funds. Consequently, unlike mutual funds, hedge funds have wide flexibility in trading, including shorting securities, using leverage, or borrowed money, to make bigger bets (as Long-Term Capital Management did in 1998), and charging an incentive (or performance) fee tied to the hedge fund's returns.

In his paper, Paredes noted that critics have characterized hedge funds as "shadowy" investment vehicles that escape regulation by "exploiting loopholes" in the federal securities laws in order to freewheel in the equivalent of a "wild west" financial frontier. There is some substance to the bad reputation that hedge funds have received. In 2003, then–New York State attorney general Eliot Spitzer implicated hedge funds in a massive mutual fund market-timing scandal, alleging that both hedge funds and mutual funds engaged in illegal after-hours trading that cost their shareholders billions of dollars. (Spitzer didn't go after the hedge funds, instead focusing on charging the mutual fund companies.) Regulators questioned whether Wall Street firms who serve as prime brokers for a particular hedge fund were conflicted—noting that they could steer investors to hedge funds in part because the hedge funds agree to use the firms for other profitable services like trading or stock lending.

It is no wonder investors are skeptical of hedge funds. Often they do not understand the strategies these funds use, or the complex models that underlie them. Others argue hedge funds are un-American or unethical because, unlike mutual funds, hedge funds are allowed to short, or bet the price of, say, an ailing U.S. automaker like General Motors, will go down.

Concern flared that hedge funds might be manipulating takeovers when they bought or sold shares in a target company. One German billionaire even took his own life after losing "hundreds of millions" by wagering in volatile short selling of Volkswagen. His bet and that of many hedge funds lost money when sports car manufacturer Porsche revealed it was quietly buying up shares and taking over Volkswagen.

The SEC has brought a few enforcement actions against hedge funds in recent years. In early 2005, the SEC sought to stop an alleged $81 million fraud involving a number of hedge funds run by the KL Group in which the fund manager was creating phony account statements. Later that year, the SEC was alerted to a nearly $500 million fraud at Bayou Management, and since the Madoff scandal broke out the SEC charged an $8 billion hedge fund fraud by Stanford Financial in Texas.

With suspicions surrounding hedge funds, some have posited that hedge funds manipulate the energy markets to their advantage. "I can't tell you how many times I get phone calls from reporters asking me if hedge funds are manipulating the energy markets on the days that the price of oil starts to spike up," said Mitch Ackles, who represents the Hedge Fund Association, a lobbying group for small start-up hedge funds. "How come they don't call me for comment when the price of oil is going down?"

Then there are the dazzling paychecks. According to *Institutional Investor*'s annual salary review of hedge funds, the average compensation of the top twenty-five hedge fund managers was around $250 million in 2004. In 2008, more than a dozen hedge fund managers made at least $1 billion.

Hedge funds have become so popular that the saying on Wall Street seems to ring true: all it really takes to make millions in hedge funds is "two guys and a Bloomberg." (A Bloomberg terminal is the stock quote machine invented by billionaire financier Michael Bloomberg to distribute securities data and news.)

In the midst of this frenzy for true hedge funds, Madoff's scam was able to thrive.

Madoff was able to exploit investors' desire to get in on the hedge fund craze by offering low-risk, consistent returns year after year with no losses. His clients were so glad to be a part of his fund that they didn't bother to ask questions or wonder how Madoff was able to generate these returns using a supposed strategy—buying shares of large U.S. companies and entering into options contracts to limit the risk—that no one else could duplicate. If Madoff was front-running and predicting market swings, no one seemed to care. If anything, it confirmed his mystical prescience.

UBP, the Geneva-based Union Bancaire Privée, chaired by Edgar de Picciotto, admitted as much in his December 17, 2008, letter to clients explaining the bank's involvement with Madoff.

Not everyone knew about Madoff's rumored front-running edge, nor did they look closely enough at the holes in Madoff's operation.

Pacific West Health Medical Center Inc. Employees Retirement Trust, which invested with Madoff through the Fairfield Sentry feeder fund, argued in a lawsuit that Fairfield and its employees should have recognized Madoff's misconduct when Fairfield Greenwich Group partners met in 2000 with Bernard Madoff and Credit Suisse Group. At that meeting, Oswald Grübel, who at the time headed Credit Suisse's private banking unit, and two other Credit Suisse executives raised concerns about Madoff's hedge fund auditor.

Sandwiched between two medical offices, Madoff's auditor operated from a small office in the Georgetown Office Plaza in New City, New York. Its staff consisted of Jerome Horowitz—a partner in his late seventies who lived in Miami—one secretary, and one active accountant, David Friehling. The accountants Friehling and Horowitz weren't peer reviewed and had no other clients.

Unusually, Madoff served as the custodian of his clients' assets. Supposedly, Madoff traded through his own broker-dealer operation, which also executed and cleared these trades, and assets were custodied and administered within his organization, which also produced all documents showing the underlying investments. It made the fraud so much more possible since Madoff was handling the entire operation—cash in, cash out, producing statements, and handling the assets—on his own. According to a report on the Madoff scandal by finance professors at the French business school EDHEC, there were no third parties "independently confirming the legal ownership of the fund's securities."

In a managed account, the hedge fund manager may control trading decisions over the account but doesn't actually touch the assets. The client's bank or custodian normally oversees the money, conducts administration, and periodically provides the client with the net value of the assets. But Madoff was a broker-dealer running thousands of managed accounts. The absence of independently calculated net asset value to his clients seemed normal—with a broker, investors only get brokerage statements.

"Madoff was not structured like a typical hedge fund," said Reiko Nahum, who runs Amber Partners, a London-based due diligence firm that vets hedge funds for investors. "If you were an investor with Madoff, you didn't buy shares in a Madoff L.P. You opened up a brokerage account through Bernard Madoff Securities. There was no entity in which shares could be purchased," unlike in real hedge funds. Onshore funds usually offered investors shares in a limited partnership; offshore funds part of the profits distribution. In Madoff's case, there was no entity. Just belief in the man himself.

Nor did Madoff's fund have an independent administrator to calculate the net asset values.

"Investors take a lot of comfort from a good administrator, which is an outside firm that maintains the books and records of a hedge fund and produces statements that are sent to investors separately," Nahum said. "We make sure they are being generated independently— not by the manager. The duties must be segregated." To vet a hedge fund manager—"and to do it well"—requires, Nahum estimates, 250 man-hours.

Other hedge funds on Wall Street, such as Renaissance and S.A.C. Capital, are also "self-clearing," as Madoff's was. In the wake of the Madoff scandal, some are changing their practice. For example, Millennium, run by former AMEX floor trader Israel "Izzy" Englander, is no longer self-clearing its trades.

Madoff also kept the amount of money he managed a secret. He wouldn't tell Grübel the amount, saying only that he had twelve people working with him to manage the strategy, along with six senior traders. Based on that meeting, Credit Suisse urged clients to withdraw cash from Madoff's firm because "the bank couldn't determine how he made money," Grübel told Bloomberg. Credit Suisse clients proceeded to redeem about $250 million from Madoff-run feeder funds.

Because his so-called hedge fund had been around for so long and had so many investors, Madoff was able to tell people that he could afford to turn people away. But this aura of exclusivity and "I don't need your money" attitude was just part of the sales hook. Sometimes Madoff even acted downright rude with potential clients. In the mid-1990s, a Julius Baer banking client had a meeting with Madoff and one of his sons (though the Baer banker could not recall which one) at Madoff's offices to hear more about the strategy of the hedge fund. The meet and greet had been set up by Fairfield Greenwich. As the Baer client began taking notes, Madoff walked around from behind his desk, ripped the man's notebook out of his hands, and threw it on the floor.

"No notes! No fucking notes!" Madoff yelled and stormed out of the room.

"The guy was so rude, he was a bastard," said the former Julius Baer banker. Even so, the Julius Baer client gave Madoff money six months later. "It just goes to show how people were hypnotized by his steady returns."

The sudden increase in the popularity of hedge funds can be explained by a number of factors—many of them political.

In part, Congress's 1999 repeal of the Depression-era Glass–Steagall legislation, which kept commercial depositor banks and investment banks separate, allowed the resulting supermarket financial institutions cum banks to start, seed, or lend money to hedge funds. It was more profitable for a bank to do business with hedge funds, instead of just everyday lending against their depositors' accounts.

The Economist put it succinctly in a 1992 article: "Bank lending is inherently more expensive than securitization." Banks employ costly specialists to monitor default risk, one human being and borrower at a time. The regulatory cost of banking was justified when banks got credit information more cheaply than investors who had no direct relationship with a borrower. But advances in technology cut the cost and enabled the mass production of risk assessment for the securities markets. "Credit-rating agencies already did the job of bank credit officers for big companies with widely traded debt. Investors had already started trading pools of credit-card loans because they believed they could judge the collective risk of default without knowing the credit-worthiness of each borrower. Banks fondly believe that small-business and personal loans are safe from the ravages of securitization," the magazine added.

Even without the impending U.S. housing and mortgage bubble and the glut of subprime borrowers, safe lending alone by banks just didn't pay as well. Wall Street's newest industry of securitizing bad loans by suspect borrowers did pay; lending to wealthy clients so they could invest in hedge funds did too, as did seeding hedge funds. Commercial banks wanted in on the game.

Lending to hedge funds was a favorite new line of bank business, as was underwriting securities such as derivatives backed by American subprime borrowers. Fairfield Greenwich had a cottage industry offering leveraged notes financed by JPMorgan Chase, Nomura, and other banks; all the notes were investments in Madoff, his returns magnified a few times by borrowed money.

By 2006, the interest in hedge funds was so explosive that a few had already done initial public offerings, or IPOs, while other private capital pools like private equity giant Blackstone and AQR, a quantitative hedge fund, one that uses computers rather than human judgment to pick securities, geared up valiantly to do the same just as the stock market began to slide in the fall of 2007. AQR partner Cliff Asness went so far as to allow *New York* magazine inside the hedge fund's headquarters—an obvious ploy to drum up interest in the IPO. Not long after the story ran on the cover, AQR confirmed it had filed to go public.

In truth, the bubble in hedge funds was just the latest example of excess in financial markets—the young men, and a few women, who led these hedge funds were chasing unbeatable incentives that prodded them to take risks for a potentially enormous upside. And the only downside was that they were losing other people's money. So in essence, there *was* no downside—for those in charge.

Hedge funds did fill a funding gap that had emerged after the dot-com collapse between 2000 and 2003 amid the demise of smaller regional investment banks such as Montgomery & Co. and Robertson Stephens. Banking supermarkets and finance giants, such as Citigroup and Bank of America, and top-tier investment banks, such as Goldman Sachs, had little interest in lending to small companies.

As a result, hedge funds became influential enough lenders that they were in essence, if not by law, functioning as a "shadow banking system." This was a phrase popularized by mutual-fund bond guru Bill Gross, who headed the giant California-based mutual fund company PIMCO. Though dramatic, Gross's phrase pointed out that hedge funds were not regulated as banks, which had certain capital requirements. Nor were they as monitored as broker-dealer securities firms, which had to file with Wall Street watchdogs and undergo regular audits.

Madoff managed to exploit these regulatory cracks perfectly. He knew the loopholes, since he ran a legitimate trading operation as a broker-dealer on two floors of the Lipstick Building, and he knew he could probably get away with the phony advisory business one floor below, as long as it stayed out of sight. He literally operated right under the noses of market regulators.

In a sense, hedge funds were America's new banks, intent on financing the country's icons of industry. Cerberus Capital Management, a hedge fund run by Ezra Merkin's friend and business associate Stephen Feinberg, had become one of the major shareholders in GMAC, the finance arm of Detroit's Big Three automaker General Motors. Cerberus then installed Merkin as the head of GMAC, where he served until the White House insisted Merkin step down as part of the automaker's 2009 government bailout. Eddie Lampert of ESL hedge fund had pushed for a 2005 merger of Sears and Kmart as a real estate play and had stuck around to start directing the stores' retail strategy.

Hedge fund managers rose up to emerge as the new masters of Wall Street. Just as the Internet had transformed computer geeks into billionaire rock stars, cheap money and a rising stock market transformed once-secretive hedge fund managers into America's new big shots, gambling with other peoples' money without accountability to anyone.

Until recent years, hedge funds weren't well known outside Wall Street. However, in the wake of the credit crisis of 2008, which prompted the failure of Bear Stearns' internal hedge funds and investment bank Lehman Brothers and unmasked Bernie Madoff's phony hedge fund, it's fairly certain that hedge funds will make headlines for years to come. Even industry insiders admit hedge funds are in need of more regulation—or at least oversight. Just as mutual funds grew in popularity a generation before—as Americans invested in 401(k)s or IRAs— hedge funds will likely grow in the twenty-first century.

The Madoff scandal was a product of several bubbles: the bubble in hedge funds, in housing prices, in credit cards, in Americans living beyond their means. Cheap credit whetted society's appetite for the next get-rich-quick scheme. These bubbles were aided and abetted by Federal Reserve chairman Alan Greenspan's cheap credit policies, a concurrent breakdown of federal regulations over derivatives in 2000, which permitted gambling with credit default swaps—the same type of gambling in bucket shops outlawed after the Panic of 1907—and the subsequent washout in which hundreds, if not thousands, of hedge funds shut down.

From 1949 to the mid-1980s, hedge funds were highly obscure and largely restricted to the ultrawealthy. In the early days, hedge fund investors paid a fee of 15 or 20 percent on any gains the fund made. An additional management fee—now traditionally 2 percent of assets—was added later. These enormous fees are the major difference between a hedge fund and other types of funds, such as mutual funds. In addition, mutual funds are highly regulated by the SEC because so many Americans now own them: Americans hold nearly $7 trillion of their savings in mutual funds. That's compared to $14–$15 trillion in banks and $1.4 trillion in hedge funds.

Given Madoff's billion-dollar fraud, the SEC's failure to police him, the collapse of so many hedge funds after the market crisis of 2007–08, and the public's appetite for alternative assets besides mutual funds, hedge fund regulation in the United States will likely be a reality in the next decade.

Sandra Manzke's career perfectly illustrates the explosion of the hedge fund industry and why, today, these funds are in need of some serious oversight. Manzke's hedge fund investing career started in 1985, when there were just sixty-eight hedge fund firms in existence (as opposed to about ten thousand in 2008). Today, there are roughly 8,500 hedge funds, more than all the public companies currently trading on the NYSE. Manzke, who fed more than $6 billion to Madoff through various feeder funds, claims she lost everything to her favorite hedge fund manager.

Unlike with mutual funds, however, investors can't trade in and out of hedge funds as quickly or easily. Nor can the average mom-and-pop investor easily divine what hedge funds currently hold in their portfolios. This information is classified as the "edge" of any good hedge fund.

What set Bernie Madoff apart from other hedge funds is that he even asked his clients to sign confidentiality agreements saying they would not talk about the firm or even reveal that they were invested with him.

By the time Manzke met Madoff, she had been a longtime investor in hedge funds, first working closely with Bob Schulman at Tremont, then leaving to start her own firm, Maxam Capital, in Darien, Connecticut. By 2008, however, Manzke admitted she was officially "disgusted" with hedge funds. It took a lot for the doyenne of a highly secretive industry to speak out publicly against the very business with which she had become so intimately connected. Just days before Madoff's arrest, Manzke went on a tirade against the industry, writing an open letter to other hedge fund investors urging them to form a group—she suggested it be called the Hedge Fund Investors United Forum—to highlight specific hedge funds that were not acting in the best interest of clients. It sounded like a rich person's trade union with the budget of the World Bank.

The stock market was down 47 percent, even more than its worst year, 1931. Everyone was losing money—bleeding cash—and wondering when the crisis would end. Hedge funds were facing their worst year on record. Since the beginning of 2008 until Manzke's December 2008 letter, more than seventy-five funds had liquidated, suspended client withdrawals, or limited redemptions. Others had instituted questionable-sounding "side pockets," which placed money-losing securities in a separate account so they could not be sold.

In short, Manzke alleged, hedge funds were grabbing money from their investors. "Every day, I get a notice from another manager who is side-pocketing investments or suspending redemptions," complained Manzke, who is normally known for her calm demeanor. "It's outrageous. . . . While we all recognize the difficulties of the current market environment, I am appalled and disgusted by the activities of a number of hedge fund managers," she fumed in the letter.

It seemed hedge funds—once touted as gold mines that rewarded investors with double-digit or even triple-digit annual returns—were now threatening to not return the money at all. The grim joke circulating on Wall Street was that investors would be lucky "to get not a return *on* capital, but a return *of* capital." One hedge fund suspended redemptions a week before the withdrawal deadline, even though they had given clients a six-month notice to pull their money. Other funds began fiddling with fee formulas, saying they would charge lower fees as they liquidated a fund over three to five years. According to Manzke, they shouldn't charge anything.

Some try to keep investors' money locked up, or simply take their 20 percent fee and then shut down without explanation. "We have managers who have received millions of dollars in incentive fees, walking away and leaving investors with nothing," Manzke ranted. "Further, management fees have crept up to outrageous levels and hedge fund organizations are paying employees lucrative wages, while investors are bearing these costs, unjustified by mounting losses."

Another glaring example of how shamelessly lovesick investors have acted over hedge funds can be seen in the flurry surrounding Old Lane Partners and Vikram Pandit. For decades, Pandit had worked for Morgan Stanley, then left to found Old Lane Partners, a hedge fund named after the road where he lived in Connecticut. In the summer of 2007, Citigroup was so eager to bring Pandit onto its staff that it bought Old Lane for $800 million and happily paid Pandit $165.2 million, pretax, for the privilege. Pandit invested $100 million of this, after tax, back into Old Lane. Former U.S. Treasury secretary Robert Rubin, who had become chairman of Citigroup, issued a glowing welcome: "Vikram and his colleagues are world-class professionals of achievement who will bring enormous capabilities and experience. . . . This combination will be of significant strategic importance and will create a robust organization of great value to our clients."

In December 2007, however, all hell broke loose at Citigroup. The board had ousted CEO Charles Prince over massive losses from the mounting global credit crisis. Pandit was then enthroned in Citi's top spot. There was just one embarrassing detail: Pandit's Old Lane fund was sucking wind. Citigroup executives either had to inject more cash into the troubled hedge fund or shut it down. Old Lane had made very little money and its returns had flatlined for the two years that Pandit ran it. So many investors bailed out of Pandit's hedge fund that the bank had to take a $200 million write-down. Citi eventually dissolved Old Lane in 2008. At about the same time, Citigroup started laying off nine thousand employees, on top of the forty-two hundred job cuts it had made in 2007. And that was just the beginning of the layoffs.

By 2007, amid a thundering international financial crisis, nearly $2 trillion had accumulated in hedge funds, but the industry was under fire like never before. Hedge funds were even starting to inspire class warfare. Not long after two Bear Stearns hedge funds collapsed, bringing down the investment bank, the Federal Reserve Board promised $30 billion to backstop the sale of Bear to JPMorgan. Protesters showed up in Bear's lobby, chanting, "Help Main Street, not Wall Street."

"The financial schemes didn't just create money for Wall Street movers and shakers and their investors," wrote editor Richard Weissman in *Multinational Monitor*. "They made money at the expense of others. The costs of these schemes were foisted onto workers who lost jobs at firms gutted by private equity operators, unpayable loans acquired by homeowners who bought into a bubble market (often made worse by unconscionable lending terms), and now the public."

Madoff's fraudulent hedge fund might have continued had the stock markets not collapsed around the world. But with the crashing economy, all of a sudden all his investors wanted their money back—and they wanted it now. The stock market collapse of 2008 squeezed his investors all at the same time—and they came running to him for money. It was not unlike the bank run in the classic movie *It's a Wonderful Life*—except, unlike Jimmy Stewart's character, Madoff wasn't offering to pay everyone back.

Panicky investors were also frightened by other hedge funds imploding. Bear Stearns' collapse in early 2008 began with revelations that two in-house hedge funds were filing for bankruptcy. Two star traders were running mortgage-backed securities hedge funds, and Bear Stearns was running dry trying to shore up these in-house funds. The failure of these hedge funds ultimately fed into worries that Bear Stearns was losing its credit lines, and soon after the company had to accept a government-orchestrated takeover by JPMorgan Chase. Both hedge fund managers at Bear Stearns were criminally charged and pleaded not guilty.

Madoff too was charged criminally, but the difference between Bear Stearns and Madoff was that Bear Stearns' hedge funds were actually trading real securities for investors—albeit securities that later proved to be worth only pennies on the dollar. And Bear Stearns wasn't asking investors to keep secret who was overseeing their assets.

The 2008 market crash also turned hedge funds against their investors.

The wealthy people who had begged for entry into these exclusive clubs now couldn't wait to sue for damages. Ultrawealthy hedge fund clients—and now, more and more, America's university endowments and pension funds—pay copious fees when hedge funds do well but bear the brunt when they suffer big losses.

One investor, Raoul Felder, a prominent divorce attorney, even went public over his hedge fund fiasco. Felder claimed he had made clear to his hedge fund "that he earns substantial and sufficient, for him, sums of money, and that as far as the money entrusted to defendants, his stated goal was the preservation of capital." He told the *New York Post*, "I said, 'I don't care about making money, I just don't want to lose money. I want to make sure it's secure and safe. Secure, secure, secure.'"

Worse, Felder was in a hedge fund that had made the same bets as lots of other Wall Street hedge funds. So many hedge funds had sprung up that they were all buying and selling the same holdings—a phenomenon known as a "crowded trade." Like a fire in a movie theater, when one starts to sell and the stock price drops, all the hedge funds run for the exits to sell too, driving the share price down even further. All the funds lose money. Thousands of clients in hedge funds lost trillions of dollars around the world—corporations in Australia (BT Financial Group), public pension clients in Ontario (the Ontario Teachers Pension Plan), and even average individuals such as doctors, lawyers, and retirees who put their money in hedge funds.

Felder, whose divorce clientele has included Martin Scorsese, Lawrence Taylor, and Patrick Ewing, sued his hedge fund manager, alleging the fund was a gamble when he wanted to play it conservatively. "My instructions were very simple," he said. The so-called Duke of Divorce filed a $5 million suit, saying he was misled into investing $750,000 in a riskier hedge fund that brought the firm more fees and commissions out of "greed and self-interest." Felder's court papers say he asked to get out of the fund in April 2008, but they urged him to stay in until June 2008.

"It's like the owner of a restaurant who tells the waitstaff, 'Push the chopped liver,' even though it's spoiled. It may make the customer sick, but they get their money. Anything for money," Felder fumed to the *Post*. The suit stated that firm bigwigs "tried to minimize his concerns" by noting $750,000 "represented only a minor portion" of his portfolio. "They said, 'What does it matter to you? You have a lot of money. So what?'" Felder said.

Felder took all of his money (totaling somewhere between $9 and $10 million) out of the hedge fund, called Global Diversified Strategies Hedge Fund B, run by AllianceBernstein. Though he was in better financial shape than most, mom-and-pop investors should pay heed, he cautioned. "This kind of fraud is being duplicated all over America. They didn't listen to me. If they don't listen to me, how are they going to listen to a retired druggist?"

He had a point. The boom in hedge funds meant that these private, unregulated investment pools no longer attracted just the superrich; now they took in John Q. Public and John Q. Public's pension fund—like the New York State pension fund, which invested $5 billion in hedge funds, and the California Public Employees' Retirement System (CalPERS), which invested $11 billion in hedge funds in 1999, and was one of the first to invest on such a large scale. Hedge fund feeders, acting as the front for Madoff, took in Repex and Pacific West Health Medical Center and hundreds of other retirement plans, which are now suing for their lost savings.

Meanwhile, the 2008 financial crisis unmasked those hedge funds, which had not actually hedged, or protected investors from losing their capital.

In a rout, hedge funds haven't conclusively proven they can help diversify a portfolio during bear markets—which is exactly when investors need protection. Only a few billion-dollar hedge funds capitalized on the carnage in the U.S. housing market, chief among them Paulson & Co., managed by John Paulson.

And still, the frenzy among investors for alternatives to plain vanilla mutual funds continues to the present day. Many investors in hedge funds show the same traits as mutual fund investors: they fall victim to "performance chasing," simply placing their money in whichever hedge fund was best in the past quarter or year—a highly risky strategy. One trader described the risk of investing in a hot hedge fund this way: "Here's the analogy: you win a date with the hottest girl in America in exchange for paying her 20 percent of your annual salary. And then one day both of you are disfigured in a horrible car wreck, you wake up in the hospital—and you're married."

Dramatic, maybe, but this perfectly illustrates what makes hedge funds such a gamble: investors pay outrageous fees when hedge funds do well and make money, but when the funds collapse, those investors bear the full brunt of the losses.

Even a hedge fund expert like Sandra Manzke, among the best and brightest of investors, was caught in the ultimate swindle. A week after she mailed out her rant of a hedge fund letter, Madoff was arrested. Manzke claimed to the *Wall Street Journal* that she was "wiped out," having invested her personal fortune—$280 million—with Madoff.

Chapter Eight

The wild decades of the 1990s and 2000s in financial markets around the world provided the perfect environment for Bernie Madoff to operate his scam. So the question remains: how did Bernie Madoff manage to pull it off for so long?

There were many signs—even inside the walls of the firm itself—that something was awry. For one, the environment at Madoff's broker-dealer firm—the legitimate trading operation that occupied the eighteenth and nineteenth floors of the Lipstick Building headquarters—was vastly different than the one downstairs on the seventeenth floor. On the eighteenth and nineteenth floors, Bernard, Peter, and Mark and Andrew operated a top hundred market-making operation, a registered broker-dealer that had heavy trading volumes every day and employed go-getter young men and women trying to make their names with big trading wins. They were regulars at industry networking events sponsored by the Securities Industry Association or the Security Traders Association.

Before computers took over a bulk of the trading operation, the atmosphere had the feel of a loud, somewhat nerdy fraternity. This was where Madoff matched buy and sell orders for important big-name customers, institutions like Bear Stearns, Charles Schwab, Fidelity, and Lehman Brothers. There were dozens of other big broker-dealers all over the Street, and hundreds of other firms like Madoff that had started out strictly as trading firms.

The eighteenth floor was also home to secondary staff, such as Ruth Madoff, who had an office just below Peter's on the southwestern side of the building, and Shana Madoff, Peter's daughter, who had been hired out of law school as the rules compliance officer for the firm's market-making arm. Also on the eighteenth floor was the IT crew, which occupied a large chunk of floor space on the western side of the floor.

Maurice "Sonny" Cohn had an office next to Ruth's. The northeastern quarter of the floor was for Cohmad, the firm that he and Bernie owned. Though many people didn't know it, Cohmad's primary business was to raise funds that were funneled to the seventeenth floor, where Madoff operated his so-called advisory business. Cohmad was totally enmeshed inside Madoff's offices in the building, and Cohn's daughter, Marcia Beth, sometimes sat on the trading floor as well. She was also listed as Cohmad's compliance officer.

Bernard Madoff used the Cohmad entity as a sort of friends-and-family ATM, to write checks and send out payments for money-raisers—payola for everyone from Sonny Cohn himself to Robert Jaffe to Richard "Dick" Spring to the eccentric Austrian Sonja Kohn who acted like a schoolgirl whenever she was around Bernie Madoff.

For example, Cohmad was paying its most successful money-raisers like Spring $500,000 a month. Cohmad as an entity paid referral fees for accounts referred, much like a real hedge fund would pay a third-party to market itself. But instead of calling the payments what they were, Madoff characterized the fees as trading or brokerage fees, thus giving the impression that Cohmad was doing lots of trades for Madoff clients. In other words, Cohmad brokerage was just window dressing for the fraud.

The dollars Madoff paid to Cohmad were based on something real—the money the fund-raisers brought in and kept under Madoff's umbrella. Copies of Madoff-issued checks made out to Cohmad Securities were in some cases signed by Enrica Cotellessa Pitz, Madoff's controller. In small ways such as this, the two businesses, the legitimate broker-dealer and the fraudulent hedge fund, sometimes intermingled.

There were even subtle differences in the overall appearance of the eighteenth and nineteenth and seventeenth floors. For example, the lobby on the seventeenth floor was hushed and quiet and dark—a vast difference from the lobbies on the eighteenth and nineteenth floors, which were open and light and separated by a glass-walled entryway leading to Madoff's expansive trading floors, alive with ringing phones and human voices.

Madoff's phony hedge fund, which some knew as his advisory business, occupied the southern side of the seventeenth floor. (The northern side of the floor housed Muriel Siebert's office. She was renowned as the first woman to own a seat on the New York Stock Exchange, and she still operates out of the offices there today. She had nothing to do with Madoff's operation or the fraud.) The premises of Madoff's advisory business were off-limits to most employees from the broker-dealer side. Generally, the hotshot traders on eighteen and nineteen and the people working on seventeen didn't mix or socialize much, except for the annual staff party in Montauk, Long Island, which Madoff hosted for his U.S. employees.

The seventeenth-floor offices looked nothing like the icily modern black and grey offices upstairs. The eighteenth and nineteenth floors were generally immaculate, as Madoff didn't allow broker-dealer employees to keep paper on their desks and he was obsessed with making sure all equipment was arranged in a meticulously ordered fashion. On these floors, phones rang and employees shouted.

The seventeenth-floor offices, on the other hand, were a shambles. There were papers and printouts everywhere. People were dressed more casually, and there was no hint of the obsessive-compulsive order that Bernie demanded elsewhere in New York and also at his London office. Even the entryway on the seventeenth floor was almost hidden. Left of the elevator bank was a dark mahogany brown wooden wall from floor to ceiling. There was no obvious door, no signage, nor even a break in the paneling. A small abstract sculpture was situated next to the east-side window and didn't appear to belong to anyone.

At the broker-dealer, Madoff and his market makers and proprietary traders were regularly visited by outsiders, such as the SEC or other regulators and agencies such as FINRA, the NASDAQ, the NYSE, or commodities and futures regulators. People visiting the brokerage business on eighteen and nineteen had no idea that Madoff had another set of offices one floor below, or that he was running an outright fraud there.

The broker-dealer was subject to annual audits, at least once every two years, and officials from the SEC and FINRA reviewed Madoff's brokerage books and records to verify compliance issues—whether trades were executed promptly, whether stock quotes matched those in public markets, whether payments were made in a timely fashion. They examined his cash flows, statements from clearing firms detailing which stocks Madoff bought and sold, trade confirmations from counterparties, banking records, etc. The audits were overseen for the firm by Bernard Madoff and his brother, Peter.

In truth, the proprietary and market-making arms of Madoff Securities served dual purposes.

The first was to make money, and at that it was very successful. A Lazard valuation report of these businesses—which the investment bank used to shop the Madoff brokerage around Wall Street for auction in April 2009—revealed that the BLMIS broker-dealer grossed $67 million in trading revenues in 2006. Of this, $52 million came from proprietary trading, or individual traders taking bets and handing over a portion of their winnings to the firm. Net trading revenues in 2006 totaled $72.5 million, while expenses—including salaries—stayed roughly around $30 million. All told, in 2006 the firm's net profit was $41 million, a handsome take.

In 2008, the proprietary trading operation went into the red, when the trading desk appeared to go "long and wrong" with the stock market. Its loss of $10.9 million was an offset of the $35 million in revenues from market making. Madoff's gross trading revenues also slumped in 2008 to $26 million from $67 million in 2006. But 2008 was a bad year for everybody on Wall Street. Generally, over the years Bernie Madoff's brokerage business made good money.

The second—unstated—purpose of Madoff's broker-dealer was to lure wealthy investors into the Madoff fold: Hollywood celebrities like Kevin Bacon and Steven Spielberg, politicians like New Jersey senator Frank Lautenberg, sports team owners like Fred Wilpon of the New York Mets and Norm Braman of the Philadelphia Eagles.

Many, perhaps even most, employees at Madoff's broker-dealer were unaware that there was a billion-dollar fraud being orchestrated, literally, right under their noses. "We knew there was a hedge fund downstairs, we just didn't know much about it," said one former trader from the broker-dealer. Many of these employees had even handed over their and their families' retirement funds to Madoff's advisory operation. After Madoff's arrest, many of these employees—some of whom still worked at the firm—lost their entire retirement savings.

"I am still stunned that Bernie would do this to his own employees and friends," the trader said bitterly. He noted that Madoff's statement at his guilty plea indicates the Ponzi scheme "started as an attempt to make up for one year's bad performance and continued indefinitely."

Like a gambler doubling down on a losing bet, Madoff was likely "hoping to make it back the next day."

So how did Madoff pull it off?

Enter Frank DiPascali, Jr., Marlboro smoker and high school graduate who often sported Puma sneakers, pressed jeans, and T-shirts, and an old-fashioned slicked-back "duck's ass" hairdo.

For many investors, DiPascali was their only point of contact with the Madoffs over the years, or even decades, during which they were invested. And generally, DiPascali was not a pleasant person to deal with. "I talked to him a few times, and my mom would call him too," said one investor in San Francisco. "But over time, I tried not to call them. It was so offensive to me, that customer service was being conducted like that. Frank was rude all the time. It wasn't personal and it was very unfriendly." Nearly every investor who called in and spoke with DiPascali had a similar experience.

DiPascali joined Madoff's firm in 1975, the year after he graduated from Archbishop Molloy, a Catholic high school in Queens. He had been recruited to work at Madoff's firm by Annette Bongiorno, Madoff's longtime personal assistant.

Bongiorno and DiPascali were kindred spirits: they were both from Howard Beach, a tough, working-class neighborhood in southeastern Queens. (In the 1980s, Howard Beach gained infamy after the so-called East Coast Watts Riots, which were spawned by the death of a young black man at the hands of several local white teenagers.) In fact friends from the neighborhood, Bongiorno introduced DiPascali to the Madoff firm, and afterward DiPascali's brother-in-law Robert Cardile came to work there. He, like Bongiorno and DiPascali, stayed at the firm for many years.

Over the years, Bongiorno began to perform other duties for Madoff in addition to her role as his secretary. For instance, she often handled client problems, like when an investor discovered that the Social Security number on his or her statements was incorrect. Over time, Bongiorno even began acting as a fund-raiser for Madoff. She apparently recruited family members and others from her Howard Beach neighborhood, according to the 162-page list of Madoff investors released by the victims' trustee. At least five investors lived in the same Howard

Beach neighborhood as Bongiorno (before she moved elsewhere) or within blocks of the former homes of Bongiorno and Frank DiPascali.

Bongiorno and DiPascali were also investors in the firm themselves. According to investor lists, documents filed by the Madoff victims' trustee, and the Massachusetts state regulator currently suing Madoff, Bongiorno and her husband, Rudy, had even been paid by Madoff to bring in clients, under the account name RuAnn, marked so that they could be paid for the assets they raised.

Before joining Madoff, DiPascali had never worked on Wall Street, and he inflated his résumé to make it appear as though he was doing much more substantive work for Madoff than he was. In 2002, DiPascali and his wife moved to the affluent town of Bridgewater, New Jersey, where he sought an appointment to a vacant seat on the board of the Bridgewater–Raritan Regional School District. As part of the application, he submitted a résumé that said he graduated in 1974 from Archbishop Molloy High School, then took classes at St. John's University and Brooklyn College from 1974 through 1976. DiPascali never finished college. He joined Madoff's firm in 1975 and spent five years as assistant to the managing director and then six years as director of research, according to the *Wall Street Journal* and Bloomberg, both of which obtained copies of his résumé.

On the résumé, he also listed a position as director of Madoff Securities International in London, and another position as former chairman of the NASDAQ stock market options committee. These, however, were complete lies. There was no such thing as the NASDAQ stock market options committee. Moreover, the NASDAQ didn't launch trading options until 2007.

DiPascali's style and demeanor also set him apart from the people at the broker-dealer operation. For one, he didn't look at all like a typical Wall Street Master of the Universe. "Frank didn't fit," said one former employee. "I would see him in the hallways and say hello, or at the Montauk annual [staff] party," but otherwise DiPascali had little to do with the staff working upstairs.

Robert McMahon, who worked at Madoff for two years as a computer systems contractor covering all three floors of the firm, didn't know who DiPascali was when he started at the firm in 2004. "I thought he was the electrician or the phone repair guy." In reality, DiPascali was responsible for overseeing half a dozen or so employees at the seventeenth floor hedge fund.

McMahon had read an article about Madoff prior to starting his job there, which mentioned that Madoff might be running a big money management firm to the tune of $7 billion. When McMahon started at the Madoff firm in 2004, he asked about the advisory business. "Someone told me, 'It's none of your business. Don't mention that article if you want to keep working here. Bernie runs another company. We have nothing to do with that business. Don't go asking around about it.' I said, 'Fine, okay,' and forgot about it. In hindsight I realized we just were not supposed to ask questions. I assumed it was something they did for high-net-worth people. It wasn't part of our domain and we didn't work for that side."

In an interview with the Daily Beast, a news Web site, one employee described DiPascali as "a very off-putting man . . . rough, not very friendly. He had a thick New York accent, not a very cultured manner. When we were at one of the Montauk beach parties, his son was there and he used the word 'Guinea' to describe him."

DiPascali sat in the southwestern quadrant of the seventeenth floor, and next to him were a cluster of longtime Madoff employees: Robert Cardile, his brother-in-law, who had been with the firm for twenty-four years at the time of Madoff's arrest; Eric Lipkin, who handled payroll for the entire firm, as well as some client service duties; JoAnn "Jodi" Crupi, who processed client requests and handled money coming in and out of their accounts; and Erin Reardon, who was named by a longtime investor as a point of contact at the firm.

Investors recall DiPascali well. In some cases, he was the only person with whom they ever spoke at the Madoff operation. Sometimes he even served as the point man who explained Madoff's investment strategy to clients. Lawrence R. Velvel, dean of the Massachusetts School of Law and a Madoff investor, recounted that Frank DiPascali had been the person delegated to explain to him Madoff's split-strike conversion strategy. After a description filled with all the technical terms and jargon of a real money manager, Velvel recalled on his blog that DiPascali told him, "Madoff was swinging for singles, not homers." The strategy was designed to be consistent and safe, not a huge risk.

DiPascali, however, was not always so obliging with curious investors.

Others reported that he was often blunt with investors who questioned Madoff's strategy. According to the *Chicago Tribune*, DiPascali even once told an investor who asked why Madoff's statements appeared so different from those of other firms, "Look, if you don't want your money here, just tell us and we'll send it all back to you."

DiPascali, Bongiorno, and Crupi appear to have been the most important figures working on the seventeenth floor. That doesn't directly implicate them as having knowledge about the billion-dollar fraud, but it does mean they were likely handling the paperwork and cash flows of the fraudulent operation.

DiPascali was the one who investors usually talked to when they wanted to put in or take out money. Although DiPascali was the main point person for Madoff's hedge fund clients, sometimes Peter Madoff took over this role. The family foundation of Senator Frank Lautenberg of New Jersey, which had invested with Madoff, sued Peter personally after Madoff's arrest, contending that he was a "control person" at the firm. Peter Madoff indeed signed the SEC filings on a quarterly basis. These filings claimed that Madoff advised fewer than twenty-five clients with $17 billion in assets, which was obviously false when you take into account the huge number of clients being provided from the feeder funds alone.

But DiPascali was the real authority on the seventeenth floor, sometimes referring to himself as both director of options trading and chief financial officer. In addition to speaking with clients, DiPascali supervised a group of employees involved in taking and keeping clients' orders and account balances. According to an SEC memo, DiPascali "responded evasively" to questioning by investigators following Madoff's arrest.

Madoff's method of operation was to have individual investors open a brokerage account—which wasn't really a brokerage account since it wasn't with the broker-dealer side of the business—so he held custody of their cash. Then, instead of putting their money into a hedge fund, Madoff simply took the money, used some of it for himself, and paid off old investors with the newer investors' money—a classic Ponzi scheme.

Investors would write checks or sometimes wire their money directly into his JPMorgan Chase (previously Chase Manhattan) bank account, number 140081703. This bank account was where Madoff, or sometimes his brother, would do the "cash in, cash out" transactions for investors of the phony hedge fund.

This was nothing like a real McCoy hedge fund—in which investors fill out mountains of paperwork ensuring they are accredited, or wealthy enough to invest, and actually receive shares in a limited partnership. Most Madoff victims didn't know that, however, or if they did, they were coming in through an outside third part, like a feeder fund.

The Ryans were a perfect example of longtime Madoff investors who saw the Madoff family and the Madoff business intertwined. Their case demonstrates how the Madoff fraud dated back for generations.

In 1985, Theresa Ryan and her husband, Lawrence J. "Larry" Ryan, had set up a joint trust through his accountant to invest their savings. After her husband died, Theresa, or Teri, became the trustee. She taught at a middle school in California and had a son, Daniel, who worked as a software salesman in New York City. After Madoff's Ponzi scheme was outed, Teri was wiped out financially. Her son also lost $450,000 as a result of his investment with Madoff. Currently, she is searching for substitute teaching jobs. In her mind, the fraud had been a lifelong family affair. According to Teri Ryan, the whole Madoff family is to blame—starting with Madoff's father-in-law, Sol Alpern, who had initially referred his accounting firm clients from Alpern & Heller.

Teri and Larry Ryan became involved with Madoff through a family friend who had referred them to Sol Alpern, who by 1985 was living in Palm Beach. Through Alpern, the Ryans joined an investment pool that put money with Bernard Madoff under Sol Alpern's name. The Ryans sent their first check for $100,000 to Sol Alpern. Larry Ryan handled most of the communications with him.

In 1977, Frank Avellino and Michael Bienes took over Alpern's accounting firm's roster of clients and formed their own company. Bienes bought a place in Florida in 1980 and shifted his focus from accounting to raising money for Madoff for a fee. Avellino did so as well. In the early 1980s, Madoff wanted to put a stop to all the individuals who were opening accounts. There were simply too many of them. Instead, they were instructed to join one of the many investment pools organized by Avellino and Bienes, which in turn provided account statements and investment tax accounting services. For tax purposes, Avellino and Bienes treated the annual returns as interest income, and investors were told that the high interest was earned because the account was an arbitrage.

When, in 1987, Sol Alpern transferred all his Bernie Madoff investments accounts to Avellino and Bienes, they in turn managed the Ryans' trust through the late 1980s. Periodically, the Ryans received trade confirmations from Avellino and Bienes. Then, in 1990, Avellino and Bienes instructed the Ryans to cash out of Alpern's fund and invest directly with Bernard L. Madoff Investment Securities. Their new primary contact was Frank DiPascali.

The Ryans still sent IRA contribution checks, made out to Bernard Madoff and cashed by him. In return, the Ryans were mailed phony trade confirmations each month, as well as monthly account balance statements. Teri and Larry Ryan even met DiPascali once in person, in 1990, around the time that Avellino and Bienes transferred their account directly to Madoff. Over the years, they had numerous phone calls with Frank DiPascali and letters about their account.

After speaking with DiPascali, the Ryans put more money in— the proceeds from selling two properties and a lump-sum retirement payment.

To Teri and Larry, there was no reason to be suspicious. After all, Madoff was well known for his brokerage firm. From 1991 to 1993, Madoff was serving as chairman of the board of NASDAQ and was a founding member of the board of the International Securities Clearing Corporation in London. Less well known was that he oversaw an advisory business for high-net-worth people on a separate floor of his operation. Madoff kept that quiet—claiming that since he had fewer than fifteen clients, so that by law he didn't have to disclose the advisory business to the SEC.

To the letter of the law, that may have been true. But in 1992, the SEC was turned on to one side of the Ponzi scheme—the fund-raisers Avellino and Bienes. They were busted in 1992 for raising about $440 million without being registered for licenses. Avellino told investigators the money was managed by a broker promising investors 13.5–20 percent a year. If Madoff fell short of those, the accountants made up the difference. Accepting this explanation, the SEC settled with Avellino and Bienes and shut down their accounting firm. They underwent an audit and paid a fine.

Ryan also received a card along with her account statements saying, "Our accountants are making a regular examination of our financial records. If this statement does not agree with your records, please report any differences to our accountants." The card bore the name F&H and included a self-addressed envelope to Friehling & Horowitz. She assumed the accounting firm was aware that investors like her were relying on the auditors to accurately verify Madoff's statements. Trades were small and the trade confirmations always matched the statements.

Initially, the Ryans' investment returns were stable and steady, ranging from 7 to 22 percent a year. After 2001, the returns never again surpassed 13 percent annually. Today, Teri Ryan thought she would have about $6.3 million saved over a period of twenty-three years, stretching from 1985 to 2008. She had retired and was going to live off the savings.

To Teri Ryan, there is no separating the Madoff family members from the scandal, all of whom worked for his fraudulent scheme. "Madoff's inner sanctum included recruiters and fund-raisers—like Avellino and Bienes—who pitched his services as entry into an exclusive club. Investors sought him out at country clubs and charity dinners. Trust, personal relationships, and reputation was a key component of his marketing," Ryan alleged in a lawsuit against Frank Di Pascali, Madoff accountants Friehling & Horowitz, Frank Avellino, and Andrew, Mark, and Ruth Madoff. Teri's trust in Madoff's family had bankrupted her.

A huge cultural divide separated the people in the legitimate and illegitimate Madoff operations. On the eighteenth and nineteenth floors, Bernard, Peter, and Bernie's sons, Andrew and Mark, hired and worked alongside exceptionally bright and well-educated people. Many had undergraduate degrees from Ivy League universities, and some even held advanced degrees. Andrew Madoff had a degree from Wharton, the University of Pennsylvania's business school. Neil Yelsey, who had helped create the original computerized trading system established by Peter Madoff, had a PhD. Both Peter Madoff and his daughter, Shana, had law degrees from Fordham. Everyone was required to dress in suits and ties at work.

"The people on nineteen were on Mount Olympus, they were gods, the big-time prop traders," said Robert McMahon, the computer systems contractor. "The guys on eighteen were tasked to keep the systems running." But the people on seventeen, McMahon said, were "lower-skilled. That's being kind. Some of them would have been unable to find a job anywhere else on Wall Street. Some were unemployable." The seventeenth floor was "Bernie's world," he added, with many of the employees clocking nine-to-five days for hefty paychecks. Most had never worked anywhere else on the Street. Despite this, they were paid enormous salaries. "Clearly they were ignorant about the things they were doing. They were archetypes, just following orders," said McMahon. "They were like mushrooms. Well fed and kept in the dark."

Madoff was able to keep the fraud going by compartmentalizing information. Few employees on seventeen were qualified to ask why they were completely separate from the broker-dealer on eighteen and nineteen—and they were well paid, so it wasn't really in their interest to connect the dots.

In addition to the compartmentalization of duties, Madoff didn't allow employees to archive e-mail on their hard drives or elsewhere, despite SEC regulation that required all Wall Street firms to do so. Instead, he ordered that all e-mails be printed out and then deleted from computers. Cohmad fund-raisers too were ordered not to use e-mail at all, not to call investors, or distribute written marketing materials.

Salaries were large because Madoff wanted to keep people happy. Two brothers who worked doing trade reconciliations were sons of Dan Bonaventuri, one of Madoff's most long-standing employees. Each of the brothers made up to $400,000 a year, doing reconciliations or matching up trades with records of the transaction for each client. That is unheard of, even on Wall Street, for clerical work. Typically back office employees are paid salaries similar to those of secretaries or other administrative workers.

"Nobody left because they could never get another job that paid as well as this one. Some people, after his arrest, speculated that it was kind of like hush money; nobody asked any questions because the Madoffs were nice, protective, generous," recalled one employee in an interview with the Daily Beast.

Madoff did have a reputation for treating employees well. One former employee recalled in an interview with the *Sunday Times* that after his father died, Madoff sent company cars so executives could attend the funeral. Treatment like this was yet another way in which Bernie garnered the loyalty—and cooperation—of those around him.

On the west side of the seventeenth floor, Annette Bongiorno had her own office across the room from Frank DiPascali's group. Bongiorno also had two assistants, Winnie Jackson and Semone Anderson, with offices on either side of her. Jackson and Anderson were responsible for researching what prices Madoff's portfolio shares were trading in recent weeks and months. Since Madoff listed only blue-chip stocks in his clients' portfolio, it wasn't difficult to get trading data going back in history, even for decades.

Investigators believe this is how Madoff was able to engineer his fake trades. Once he had decided that in November 2008, for example, all his clients' accounts would be up 1 percent, then he would have to work backward—figuring out which stocks he would have had to trade in order to make 1 percent in the month of December.

He would enter trades that never happened, with real prices, into the old IBM AS/400 computer he used for his advisory business and— *voilà!*—Madoff had created a track record.

Using a simple spreadsheet such as Excel, the more than twenty-three hundred clients' accounts were likely updated automatically— dividing among all the accounts the gains from the "trades" that amounted to "profits" of 1 percent in December.

Once these "trades" had been made, however, there had to be a paper trail—even if it was a phony one. According to federal investigators, regulators, and Irving Picard, the trustee appointed to liquidate Madoff's assets, Anderson and Jackson also helped generate phony stock trade confirmations for client accounts, which purported to show gains. The confirmations are now believed to have been fictitious. It's very possible that the team on the seventeenth floor created the phony confirmations unwittingly, and were not complicit in the fraud. Neither DiPascali or Bongiorno, or anyone from the seventeenth floor, has been charged.

Annette Bongiorno directed her assistants to research daily stock prices, at times dating back several months. They would then use the stock price data to produce trading tickets that would reflect the famously consistent returns that made Madoff a legend. Over the years, Madoff sent out thousands of these confirmations claiming to justify trades that never occurred. Madoff hadn't made any trades in customer accounts for at least thirteen years, and likely not for decades. For the most part, the people who got these statements had no reason to suspect that anything was wrong. After all, they showed these statements to their accountants, and their accountants signed off on them. Why should they be suspicious?

In an increasingly wired world like Wall Street, where today everyone has access to stock price data instantly on Yahoo! Finance or MarketWatch's BigCharts, the same tools available to traders and analysts, it seemed impossible that Bernie Madoff would be able to get away with reverse-engineering stock prices to retrofit his amazing returns. But Madoff was able to do this by using the IBM AS/400 computer, an archaic piece of technology that allowed him to manipulate stock price data.

Robert McMahon thought it was odd that the Madoff firm insisted on building almost all of its own information technology infrastructure. But then again, Peter Madoff had built the automated trading system practically from scratch, and the firm continued updating its capabilities, even as late as 1999, when Madoff's trading system was becoming obsolete. For their super-high-tech trading floor on nineteen and to keep trading data secure on eighteen, the Madoff firm had purchased a package by Stratus Technologies, a top-of-the-line computer system. Stratus delivered stock and other security price data to traders linked through the company's network. Stratus specializes in fault-tolerant systems for the securities industry. Stratus's other customers have included Bear Stearns, Deutsche Bank, Merrill Lynch, Prudential Securities, and the Vancouver Stock Exchange.

Though the broker-dealer firm was equipped with state-of-the art technology, the engine behind Madoff's fraud was the aging IBM AS/400. Every day, the Stratus system upstairs would automatically update Madoff's trading operations with the latest settlement data—the dollars and cents prices at which stocks closed at four p.m., when the U.S. equity market closes for the day. But the AS/400 was not so advanced.

"I was always told the AS/400 was Bernie's—nobody touches it," McMahon said. Other times he was told the IBM AS/400 housed the "books and records of the company." Still, no one touched the AS/400 but Bernie Madoff.

In any case, at the end of every day someone had to send a computer file to update the AS/400 with the latest stock price data. All the data, however, had to be entered manually. Entering the data by hand, McMahon noted, meant that the person doing it could put in whatever they wanted.

McMahon said he realized in hindsight why Madoff had locked himself into a cumbersome and expensive-to-maintain IT system: he couldn't risk being found out as a fraud. "He would have had to hire a consulting firm—outsiders—to help migrate away from the systems he had," McMahon said. Newer computers would have had their own reporting capability and there would be no need for the AS/400 computer. "All that data would have been migrated and stored to a new system—but again, outsiders doing the work would uncover the disparity of trading data."

And an outsider looking into the old IBM AS/400 would have been able to discover—and document—the who, what, where, why, and how of the entire process.

Internally this separation of computer systems—the Rolls-Royce of computers upstairs and the Ford Model T downstairs—also helped hide the fraud from the majority of Madoff's staff. Besides, they were acculturated to not ask questions of senior leadership—and they were well compensated for doing so.

The Stratus system helped facilitate the upstairs broker-dealer operation. "This is where all orders and indications of interest to trade would be routed, executed, and generally facilitated," explained McMahon. The Stratus is a highly fault-tolerant supercomputer, but in today's age of software and remote servers, it was overkill, even for Madoff. "You're essentially using a Rolls-Royce as your commuter car. You can boast about having the 'best of the best of the best,' but what you're using it for is something that today's technology has rendered pedestrian. Would you hand your neighbor's kid the Waterford scotch tumbler to use as their lunch glass?"

During the day, there were three or four master security files running all the time that kept track of everything—every trade Madoff had on the books, whether a stock had split or had issued a dividend. "It's your telephone book of securities data," McMahon said. But the Madoffs' upstairs and downstairs systems were very disparate—on purpose. "People on seventeen sat at a dumb terminal—not even a PC—a dumb terminal" with a securities record full of missing information. To update it, two people had to enter the data manually to propagate each field.

In order for the fraud to happen, there had to be this separation of the two entities, with one set of real data and one set of fictional data. Madoff couldn't allow them to share the same stock price data, because the prices were the essence of the fraud. For example, Madoff's November 2008 statement showed he bought Apple shares at $100.78 on November 12, about a month before his arrest. But Apple's stock on that day never traded above $93.24. He also said he bought shares of chip maker Intel Corp. at $14.51 on November 12, but Intel's highest price on that day was $13.97.

A professional trader would have caught such an error. But employees on seventeen weren't professional traders—nor were they incentivized to ask questions. Madoff and other employees on seventeen punched in the stock prices on the IBM AS/400 and would just enter stock prices that would square with his fake returns. Then Bongiorno and her assistants could print up any statements they wanted, send them to clients, and bet that the client wouldn't check.

Madoff's broker-dealer operation was one of the most active trading firms in the country, but not a single share of stock was ever traded on seventeen. An industry-run regulator found no record of Madoff's investment fund placing trades through his brokerage operation.

"Our exams showed no evidence of trading on behalf of the investment adviser, no evidence of any customer statements being generated by the broker-dealer," Herb Perone, a spokesman for FINRA, said in a statement after Madoff's arrest. FINRA had regularly examined Madoff's upstairs operations as had its predecessor, the NASD, every two years since it opened in 1960. But the examiners had never seen—had never even known about—the seventeenth floor.

Madoff's London office also played a large role in helping hide his fraud. London may have started out legitimate, but over the decades it morphed into a financial outpost for the Madoff family, a place where they felt comfortable stashing what they considered their personal money—roughly £113 million, by 2008.

Madoff Securities International Limited, as the London operation was called, opened its doors in 1983. The business entity was owned by Madoff, his wife, their sons, and a longtime friend of Bernie's, Paul Konigsberg. Konigsberg's accounting firm showed up hundreds of times on the list of Madoff victims, since he too was often referred by Madoff as a good accountant for handling securities.

The London office had electronic terminals that allowed Madoff employees to log in directly to and trade on the NASDAQ exchange from overseas. As usual, the Madoffs were among the first to make use of these market-making terminals outside the United States.

During this time, Madoff was reportedly eager to trade ADRs, or American Depositary Receipts. (ADRs give companies outside of the United States access to the American capital markets. ADRs are dollar-denominated securities that trade, clear, and settle like any other U.S. security, either over the counter or on one of the major U.S. exchanges. Finland's Nokia and Brazil's Petrobras have ADRs that trade in the United States.) The office in London allowed the Madoff firm more flexibility at a time when traders in the United States could make trades only during the hours that U.S. markets were open.

By 1989, however, the NASDAQ extended its hours and traded several hundred over-the-counter stocks during the predawn hours in the United States, thus allowing firms there to trade during London hours— part of the gradual globalization that would one day overtake securities trading. This may have made the London Madoff office less essential to the daily operations of the broker-dealer and proprietary trading business.

Over time, however, the Madoffs' London branch would become the family bank teller. It was offshore as well, so Madoff could wire money from his U.S. operations to London, invent transactions worth hundreds of millions of dollars to replicate fake trades, or simply wash the funds out of his American accounts, then spend them on luxury items like the Leopard speedboat he purchased in France. (This is also known as money laundering.)

Although Mark and Andrew Madoff were located in New York, they held ownership and titles as directors in the London operation.

Ruth and Peter Madoff also held shares, and Sonny Cohn also originally had shares as well. Paul Konigsberg was another director. Charles
Stillman, an attorney for Konigsberg, said Konigsberg received the non-
voting shares when he did work for the London operation when it first
opened in the 1980s. Konigsberg, he added, didn't have any "meaningful business role" in the London operation, which suggests he didn't
have any say in how the business was run.

Konigsberg, however, was a major fund-raiser for Madoff's New
York hedge fund since at least 1998, according to Madoff investor
Steven Leber. Leber filed a $4 million lawsuit in Florida against Konigs-
berg and his accounting firm, Konigsberg & Wolf, charging negligence
and professional malpractice with respect to a Madoff account opened
by Leber in 1998. In that suit, Leber alleged that Konigsberg offered to
act as a conduit into Madoff for Leber's $4 million or so in family
money—but only if Leber started using Konigsberg's accounting firm
as well. Konigsberg Wolf & Co. has offices in New York and is listed
on the Madoff victims' trustee list. Konigsberg himself, as well as his
firm and some of his family members, also appear on the victims' list
more than three hundred times—sometimes on his own behalf, other
times on behalf of accounts set up for others, such as the Norman
F. Levy Foundation.

It's possible the London operation was a way to repay Konigsberg
for his fund-raising services without the commission money being
traced. After all, through Madoff Securities International, Madoff was
able to handsomely compensate other family members. In 1998, for
example, directors of the London operation received emoluments, or
payments, totaling £688,570 while the operation reported profits of
£1.03 million, according to the *Wall Street Journal*. In 2007, Madoff
directors altogether received emoluments of £1.09 million, with the
highest-paid director receiving £301,437 alone.

Meanwhile, Madoff had two primary bank accounts set up for him
in New York. One account was with the Bank of New York Mellon,
account number 866-1126-621 (referred to as BONY 621). This account was supposed to be the broker-dealer's primary cash account. He
also had an account at JPMorgan Chase, account number 140081703
(referred to as JPM 703), which investors used to wire money or send
checks to the fake advisory business. This was also the account investors used when they withdrew funds. Many were able to withdraw

funds within days, and Madoff always had the money ready, no matter how large the amount. It was one of his biggest selling points.

After his arrest, Madoff would claim in court that the legitimate brokerage firm and the criminal hedge fund were completely separate. However, in 2001 money began to slosh back and forth between the two bank accounts regularly. This continued up until the day Madoff turned himself in. For example, money was transferred from both the Bank of New York and the JPMorgan Chase accounts to the London office. Madoff personally wired roughly $500 million over to London and then back again between 2001 and 2008, according to copies of the documents filed by the Madoff trustee, Irving Picard. Over those seven years Madoff also withdrew cash from the broker-dealer's account with Bank of New York, sometimes as much as $2 million in a single day.

Madoff Securities International in London also "traded for Bernard Madoff's personal accounts and members of his family," said Picard. The trustee's revelations didn't stop there. In a filing with the U.S. bankruptcy court, Irving Picard laid out how the London bank accounts had been used as Madoff's personal piggy bank. Madoff began regularly wiring money to the London office to pay for expensive items.

He purchased the $7 million Leopard yacht in the south of France by sending cash through his UK office. The yacht, named *The Bull* like his other cruiser in Palm Beach, was built for Madoff in 2006. The boat was also registered in Ruth Madoff's name, as were many of the couple's high-priced trophies. The twenty-seven-meter (eighty-nine-foot) Leopard, built by French luxury boat builder Rodriguez Group, was moored at the Port Gallice in France, where the annual fee to keep a yacht of this size costs nearly $50,000. Madoff told employees in London to transfer money to the shipyard, reasoning that the builders already had euro-denominated bank accounts, which would make the transaction easier—or at least, that was the explanation he gave. The London employees sent the money after receiving an invoice from the boatyard, and Madoff later transferred cash to the London firm's accounts to make up the difference. At least $250 million was allegedly wired back and forth between Madoff's New York and London offices for such purchases.

In November 2008, Madoff phoned Chris Dale, the finance director of Madoff Securities International in London, and told him to sell an entire portfolio of British bonds. Madoff then instructed Dale to transfer the money—$165 million—to his New York business, so he could buy U.S. Treasuries on London's behalf. Madoff claimed he was worried about the return because of the pound sterling currency's fall against the U.S. dollar. "He was worried about the British economy and said he preferred his investments in U.S. treasuries," Dale told *The Independent on Sunday*, a British newspaper. "This seemed perfectly realistic at the time because of the banking crisis and the pound's weakness."

Madoff's London employees didn't think to question the wires, what they were for, or any other transactions—after all, he was the boss. One employee told the London *Times:* "He was the chairman of the company and it was his capital in the business. If he phoned up and told us to move money for him, we did it." Employees in London claimed they had no clue that Madoff was using his British outpost as a money launderette.

The Friday after Madoff was arrested in the United States, Stephen Raven, chief executive of Madoff Securities International, was still unwittingly defending the office against Madoff's larger fraud. He issued an indignant statement: "We only became aware overnight of the news relating to our chairman, Bernard Madoff. His major shareholding in our firm is a personal investment. MSIL in London is a small proprietary trading firm—we are not client-facing and we trade only with the firm's own money." That was true, but the ultimate purpose of the London outpost was very different: it was where the Madoffs washed their investors' money and then spent it on expensive furnishings, yachts, automobiles, and other luxuries.

Julia Fenwick, another employee at Madoff's London offices, was a good friend with Shana, Peter's daughter. Because of their friendship, Fenwick sometimes vacationed with the extended family. She even attended Bernie's seventieth birthday party—held just months before his arrest—and became intimately familiar with his and Ruth's love of Fleet Street tailors, Boots brand face cream, and the jet-set lifestyle.

When Madoff visited London, Fenwick said in an interview with *The Mail on Sunday*, he was often accompanied by his interior designer. The designer was charged with the task of polishing Madoff's appearance and selecting Ruth Madoff's clothes. Bernie collected watches through vintage dealers in London's Piccadilly shopping district and sported wedding bands that matched each watch. During his two or three visits a year to London, Madoff would patronize Savile Row and have his tailors from the upscale shop Kilgour pay a visit to him at the firm's Mayfair "Hedge Fund Alley" offices. While he was being measured for high-priced suits in the boardroom, his wife would pass the time knitting.

While in London, Madoff stayed at the Lanesborough Hotel, among the most expensive in the world. Guests pay up to £8,000 per night and are provided with their own private on-call butler. Madoff would leave a trunk of clothes at the Lanesborough, which the hotel stored, cleaned, pressed, and hung in his suite for the next stay.

As her friendship with Shana grew, Fenwick spent more time with the Madoffs outside the office. Fenwick happened to be in the United States in 2002 for the Madoffs' annual beach party in Montauk, Long Island, thrown for all his U.S. staff and their families. When the chairs and towels were set out on the beach, they were arranged with the Madoff family at the center and places for the others arranged according to their importance. Top traders sat close to Bernie and lesser employees were seated farther out. After the beach there was a party at a yacht club. "It was like going to a lavish wedding," Fenwick recalled.

In 2007, Fenwick attended Shana Madoff's wedding to Eric Swanson, a lawyer with the SEC. Other SEC people also attended, including Swanson's boss, Lori Richards. (Because she attended this wedding, Richards awkwardly testified in front of Congress after the scandal broke that she was recusing herself from the SEC's Madoff investigation.) What struck Fenwick as odd was a joke Bernie Madoff privately made to her. At the wedding reception at the Bowery Hotel in New York City, Bernie leaned in and pointed to other SEC employees among the guests. "Look over there," he told her. "That's the enemy."

Despite Madoff's unwillingness to answer questions from investors and employees about his advisory business, the Madoffs were always open to being interviewed, especially about their stock trading systems, or for general market commentary.

David Gaffen, then a reporter at WSJ.com, the *Wall Street Journal's* Web site, is one of a new breed of bloggers constantly updating commentary about the markets. Blogging is demanding and time-consuming, and the Madoffs were always ready to lend a quote or some commentary.

In October 2008, Gaffen visited the Madoff operation and described the offices as "antiseptic," with gunmetal gray walls and charcoal carpeting. Gaffen got off on the eighteenth floor to interview Mark Madoff in person and was shown onto the trading floor. Gaffen had seen Madoff's operation once before—a decade earlier as part of a Securities Industry Association press tour, in which financial journalists visited various Wall Street firms, the floor of the New York Stock Exchange, and trading floors as part of a meet and greet campaign. Bernard Madoff was there the first time. "He was affable, like your uncle," Gaffen recalled.

Still, Gaffen needed comment. The stock market was rollicking in the midst of several major bank failures, such as Bear Stearns in March 2008 and Lehman Brothers just the month before. "Yesterday's markets were characterized by a lack of buyers rather than a significant selling," Mark Madoff told Gaffen in that interview. Mark was still head of listed trading for Bernard L. Madoff Investment Securities, and he was sitting with Gaffen in the firm's hexagon-shaped conference room in the middle of the eighteenth-floor office. "Today felt like the opposite," Mark Madoff added. He continued pontificating, saying that the market was gapping up as buyers looked for offers that were not there. "I think everybody is confused and nervous and that's why you're seeing the market just jump all over the place," he said.

A week before Bernard Madoff was arrested, Gaffen again spoke with Mark Madoff by telephone. "At least you're seeing a tug of war, which is good," Mark said of the trading atmosphere, which was abysmal in 2008. "The market is down 40 percent—you can't forget that. The economic picture is not great . . . but a good bit of that economic news is priced in."

While Mark Madoff was trying to put an optimistic face on the market for Gaffen, some big Madoff investors were starting to get spooked. One in particular was JPMorgan Chase.

By September 2008, JPMorgan Chase may have had indications, or actually known, that Madoff was a fraud. How might they have found out before everyone else?

JPMorgan Chase is an enormous bank, which on one side— JPMorgan—operates an investment division and on the other side— Chase—runs a typical commercial bank with loans and deposits. On this commercial banking side, Chase was handling Madoff's billion-dollar bank account, the JPM 703 account. Earlier in 2008, JPMorgan Chase had taken over Bear Stearns' operations in a government-orchestrated bailout to save the firm from imminent collapse.

Madoff was close friends and business associates with longtime over-the-counter trader Aldo Parcesepe, a senior managing director and head of NASDAQ market making at Bear Stearns. He regularly traded with Madoff's broker-dealer firm. Between 2005 and 2008, Parcesepe served on the board of the National Stock Exchange (NSX), the electronic exchange for equities and options that the Madoffs had subsidized in the late 1970s. Peter Madoff served on the NSX board with Parcesepe, who retired from the board in 2008. Madoff owned 10 percent of the NSX, and Bear Stearns regularly traded through the exchange. The NSX was familiar stomping ground for the Madoffs, as it had once been known as the Cincinnati Stock Exchange, which the Madoffs had refurbished with their own money. It was the same exchange that had helped the Madoffs attract orders from Wall Street customer firms all over the country, and the hub of the Madoffs' payment for order flow.

Brokers who traded at Bear Stearns used the firm's automated equity order system to buy and sell stocks. A broker would enter the stock symbol and the number of shares he or she wanted to trade. The system was supposed to do the rest: work to find the best counterparty to trade with from among the many market makers that traded with Bear Stearns. However, for NASDAQ stocks, Bear Stearns had an unwritten code: the system automatically defaulted to trade with Madoff.

Madoff reportedly paid Bear Stearns substantial fees for this default setting on their equity order system, and he may have paid other customers to do the same as well. Between 2000 and 2008, Bear Stearns' four hundred or so brokers all used this system, and all their NASDAQ trades defaulted to Madoff. It was a big source of revenue for Madoff and vaulted Bear Stearns to the largest counterparty trading with Madoff. The arrangement was in place when Bear Stearns went under in early 2008, and it continued under JPMorgan Chase until Madoff's arrest in December 2008.

Madoff also had a strong relationship with Chase Bank, and starting at least in 1992 all the money he lured into his phony advisory business— any check or wire handled by the seventeenth floor—was deposited into Chase Bank. The accounts swelled over the years, and by 2006 he had billions of dollars in cash on deposit in Chase Bank. These were "demand" deposits, meaning Chase had full use of the funds until Madoff withdrew them. All the funds were commingled in a single account and Madoff could withdraw the money as he saw fit, without any limitation.

Between 2006 and 2008, Chase Bank's accounts from Madoff averaged several billion dollars. However, in 2008, as the stock markets began dropping precipitously, so did Madoff's cash balance. Between September 2008 and December 11, 2008, the Chase account often dropped near zero. In November, the balance dropped close to zero several times, forcing Madoff to transfer roughly $160 million from his Madoff Securities International in London to the Chase Bank account. He was juggling payouts to investors demanding their money back and moving money around from different offices and bank accounts around the world.

And he continued to take in new investors. In the month of November, investors deposited $300 million worth of new cash in the Chase account while Madoff withdrew $320 million. Meanwhile, he was hitting up his old friend Carl Shapiro for a new investment—of $250 million.

Chase, meanwhile, was doing other business with Madoff besides banking. In 2006, JPMorgan Chase developed a derivative product for its wealthy clients. It was linked to the Fairfield Sentry Fund offered by Madoff feeder Fairfield Greenwich. The bank offered investors—mostly in Europe—a note that paid three times the earnings, or returns, of the Sentry Fund. The note matured in five years. To hedge against the risk, JPMorgan Chase deposited three times the face value of the Fairfield notes into the Sentry Fund. To hedge its risk on the derivative product, the bank invested in the Sentry Fund itself. This way, if the Sentry Fund did well, the bank's returns would offset its obligation on the notes.

By the summer of 2008, JPMorgan Chase had deposited $250 million with the Sentry Fund. With the financial meltdown on Wall Street and around the world in full swing, most of the markets were down 30 percent or more, and yet the Sentry Fund reported gains of 5 percent. JPMorgan Chase began to grow suspicious.

Chase representatives from the commercial banking side met with Madoff. They wanted to discuss his cash flows and to know what percentage of his portfolio was leveraged, or invested using borrowed money, and with whom he traded options contracts. The simple math was just as many others had concluded: the options market was too small to handle the size and capacity Madoff was claiming to manage in his supposed options strategy. Moreover, it was implausible that Madoff could be generating substantial positive returns when the S&P 500 index was down 30 percent.

Madoff wouldn't tell Chase any of the key information, such as amounts held in cash, his borrowings, or who his counterparties were. Managers from Chase's London office and colleagues in New York decided they would go through the back door.

Parcesepe's trading desk had people who regularly traded with Madoff, and they knew the number of trades executed through Madoff. On its trading side, JPMorgan learned that Madoff's trades with Bear Stearns—by then a part of Chase, now Madoff's largest counterparty— could not possibly sustain a portfolio returning 10–12 percent a year on what the bank knew from the deposit side had to exceed at least $7 billion. The Chase team had access to Madoff's account records, which showed huge cash positions until the middle of 2008, when the stock market went into free fall. It was obvious: Madoff was a fraud.

In September 2008, JPMorgan Chase quietly liquidated its entire $250 million position in the Sentry Fund, even though it remained liable on the derivatives it had sold to the wealthy clients. At the time, the Fairfield Sentry investment notes were showing a 5 percent gain for the year. The bank had concluded Madoff was a phony, and the only way to protect itself was to liquidate anything connected with Madoff.

Not only that, but by September 2008 Chase may have known that if Madoff's hedge fund was a fraud, he was likely diverting his advisory side funds. Still, Chase continued accepting wires and checks from Madoff's latest round of investors. Throughout the fall of 2008, according to one lawsuit filed against Chase (*MLSMK Investments Company v. JPMorgan Chase & Co. et al.,* SDNY 2009), the bank "continued to work in partnership with Madoff despite being privy to information that the fraud was collapsing and therefore consuming more and more of the victim proceeds."

Up until the final months of 2008, Madoff's legitimate broker-dealer business was making money steadily. The firm had enough capital to support its trading activity, and the income it produced provided a financial cushion for Bernie to support his scam.

But equally important as the funds the broker-dealer brought in was the cover that the two dozen traders working on the nineteenth floor unwittingly provided for the scam. Often the market-making business was the backdrop to meetings Madoff held with potential investors. Madoff met with potential casualties in his conference room on the nineteenth floor, and behind him the new prospects would see the activity on the trading floor. There he would pitch individuals like Fred Wilpon of the Mets, institutions like HSBC and Santander, nonprofit corporations like the American Jewish Congress, and state or local municipal pension plans. He bragged that he never had a losing quarter, and promised returns of 10–12 percent a year.

Madoff also used the legitimate market-making traders and the volume they generated each day to disguise the fact that there were no trades—no trading at all—on behalf of his seventeenth-floor investment advisory clients.

Madoff supposedly kept meticulous records of his investors' phantom investments. Each month the investors received a detailed account statement, produced by Frank DiPascali and Annette Bongiorno's crew, showing the supposed stock and option trades of the past month together with the returns based on their account value. But it was all faked.

"It was sleight of hand. A sort of kabuki theater," said Robert McMahon. "The eye sees, the ear hears, and the brain believes."

Chapter Nine

On the morning of Wednesday, February 4, 2009, Harry Markopolos, a tall, wide-eyed man with a patrician nose and an earnest bearing, took his seat in front of the U.S. House of Representatives Committee on Financial Services for his day of vindication.

Markopolos had been called in front of the committee to provide his insight into Bernard Madoff's fraud. A certified fraud examiner, he had spent almost ten years trying to unmask the titan of Wall Street for what he really was—a liar and a thief. And after nearly a decade of living like Greek mythology's Cassandra—seeing disaster looming in the future but doomed never to be believed—Markopolos had finally been proven right. He had been right all along.

To most on Wall Street, Bernard L. Madoff had been a man beyond reproach. Bernie Madoff was a trusted counselor to the SEC, even helping to train young SEC lawyers when they first started working at the agency, schooling them on the ways of Wall Street. Questioning Madoff's veracity seemed almost unthinkable.

Harry Markopolos, however, was never a believer. For almost a decade, he was sure that Bernie Madoff was a fraud, and he told a lot of people exactly that—including a number of SEC officials. But no one ever followed up vigorously on his allegations. Over the years, a few investors and journalists, including myself, would question Madoff's unusually steady performance, but only Markopolos pursued the story.

Markopolos came to view Madoff as a domestic enemy, an antipatriot who would unravel the very fabric of America's market system. And his skepticism proved true, if too late. In February 2009, roughly a decade after he had first fingered Madoff as a fraud, Markopolos had members of Congress interrupting one another for airtime. The hearing had the atmosphere of a petting zoo, with starstruck politicians eagerly questioning this blunt, well-spoken, curly-brown-haired whistle-blower from Boston.

But it wasn't always this way.

Harry Markopolos first came across Bernard Madoff in 1999 when he was working at Rampart Investment Management, a Boston-based firm that specialized in U.S and international index and stock option strategies. At the time, Rampart was losing clients to Madoff, and Markopolos's boss, Ron Egalka, and colleague Frank Casey asked him to do some calculations and reverse-engineer how a competing strategy like Madoff's was making money. Rampart, which used the same split-strike conversion strategy that Madoff claimed he used in his hedge fund, could not match Madoff's steady numbers. This was especially perplexing considering that Madoff was not trained in the sophisticated options trades like the ones used at Rampart.

After four hours of number crunching, Markopolos knew one thing: the figures just didn't add up. Either Madoff was a genius who could devise a strategy so brilliant that Markopolos and his colleagues—all of whom were trained in quantitative finance—couldn't duplicate, or he was a fraud. Markopolos concluded that Madoff was doing one of two things: faking his trades or making them by front-running the orders that came through his broker-dealer. Either way, Madoff was breaking the law.

In his congressional testimony, Markopolos recalled his theories about Madoff's fraud: "Fraud hypothesis 1 was that Bernard Madoff was simply a Ponzi scheme and the returns were fictional," he told Congress (Markopolos declined to be interviewed for this book). Fraud hypothesis 2 was that the returns were real but they were being generated by front-running the broker-dealer order flow and the split-strike conversion strategy was a mere front. "Either way, Bernard Madoff was committing a fraud and should go to prison."

A year after his boss asked him to crunch Madoff's returns, Markopolos contacted the SEC's Boston Regional Office and spoke with SEC staffer Ed Manion. Before joining the SEC, Manion had worked in money management at The Boston Company, a local Massachusetts financial firm. Under head of research Dick Kroll, The Boston Company had been at the forefront of marrying investing and technology. When computers were just beginning to play a role on Wall Street, Kroll started hiring math and computer science graduates from top schools like MIT and Harvard. When options began being listed and actively traded, The Boston Company was on the cutting edge of investing in options as well. Kroll had his mathematically inclined minds start applying quantitative techniques—high-end number crunching—to the business of investing. At the time, the idea was considered revolutionary, although today quantitative investing is standard practice on Wall Street.

Under Kroll's mandate, coheads of research Fran DeAngelis and Charles Clough hired a number a quantitative analysts and trained them. Ron Egalka was one of the quantitative analysts. Options trading came naturally to Egalka, and after a successful career at The Boston Company, he left in 1983 to found his own shop, Rampart Investment Management. Rampart specialized in U.S. and international index and stock option strategies. All of these people worked there when Ed Manion was working as a portfolio manager.

Fran DeAngelis, who started at the firm in 1968, recalled that Manion "wasn't a company man. He was stubborn. He had worked at Fidelity and didn't follow the herd. He didn't go to research meetings, he and another PM, Gerry Zukowski, were always around the Quotron [an early stock quotation computer]. He was tough and smart. If he's in your corner, he'll go to the wall for you. He was an independent person." By 1995, Manion had left The Boston Company for the SEC. "Knowing Ed Manion, if Harry Markopolos went to him, unlike other guys in the SEC Manion would be smart enough to say, 'There's something to this.'" DeAngelis said. Indeed, Ed Manion, one of the few Chartered Financial Analysts in the SEC at the time, did think something was wrong and supported Markopolos's campaign to expose the fraudulent financier.

In 2001, Markopolos sent a report titled "Madoff Investment Process Explained" to Manion. Manion forwarded Markopolos's updated warning up the chain of command at the SEC, to the Boston Regional Office's director of enforcement, an attorney named Grant Ward. In the 2001 report, Markopolos estimated that the suspected Madoff pyramid scheme had grown to as much as $7 billion.

But Manion's superiors at the SEC didn't listen to Markopolos or Manion. Manion became frustrated with the SEC's unwillingness to take the fraud seriously and look into the allegations. Still, after Madoff was arrested, Markopolos told Congress that Ed Manion had been the only SEC staffer to take his claims seriously.

Harry Markopolos grew up in Erie, Pennsylvania, served in the military as an Army intelligence officer, and after his discharge trained as a chartered financial analyst. He later lived with his wife and children in Whitman, Massachusetts. He was a straightforward American guy who liked numbers. In 2004, he left Rampart to start his own firm, hiring himself out as a certified fraud examiner and expert for attorneys who were suing companies that had defrauded the government. He socialized with other "quants," like Dan diBartolomeo, Herb Blank, Donna Murphy, and Andrew Lo, a hedge fund expert and professor at MIT, who examined how numbers, finance, and computer science intersected. Herb Blank had even helped found an informal group called QWA-FAFEW, where finance nerds could get together, drink a few beers, and swap deep-thought strategies and theories, whose Boston meetings Markopolos would sometimes attend. (QWAFAFEW stood for Quantitative Work Alliance for Applied Finance, Education, and Wisdom. Most of the people who joined had some training beyond an MBA, and many had PhDs. All shared a common interest in quantitative solutions to understanding markets.)

On their own time, Markopolos and his old colleagues from Rampart kept tracking Madoff for almost ten years. Despite the SEC's failure to investigate his claims, Markopolos was determined to out Madoff, but the longer his warnings were ignored, the more disheartening the effort became.

Over the years, Markopolos escalated his warnings to the SEC. On the advice of Manion, he began contacting Meaghan Cheung, the branch chief of the agency's New York office. In a November 2005 e-mail to Cheung, Markopolos sent a twenty-one-page report outlining "why I believe that Madoff Investment Securities LLC is the world's largest Ponzi scheme." By this time, Markopolos believed the scam had grown to about $30 billion. He included a list of twenty-eight red flags that pointed to Madoff's guilt. Among these was the fact that Madoff's operation wasn't organized like a typical hedge fund and he didn't charge typical 20 percent performance fees, only trading commissions. He also pointed out that third parties raised all the money and handed it to Madoff in exchange for the consistent returns, yet most of the end investors didn't know Madoff was the money manager. Madoff swore investors to secrecy, requiring them not to reveal he was their portfolio manager.

Although this document would be widely circulated around Wall Street after Madoff's arrest, at the time it was ignored by the SEC.

About a month later, in December 2005, Markopolos had a twenty-minute phone conversation with Zoe Van Schyndel, a onetime SEC employee who warned him not to expect too much from the agency. Van Schyndel, like Markopolos, was also a Chartered Financial Analyst and knew something about numbers. She had left the SEC as a New England branch chief and was now living in Key Biscayne, Florida, teaching finance part-time at the University of Miami. She was also a contributing writer for *Barron's* and *Institutional Investor* magazines and the online stock Web site the Motley Fool.

She told Markopolos she would love to take on his hedge fund case as a story idea someday, but she warned that the SEC was a bureaucratic institution that often overlooked major cases for fear of stepping on the wrong toes. He shouldn't expect too much from them, no matter how persistently he protested. Markopolos wrote a memo to himself after his conversation with Van Schyndel that detailed her career and interest in Madoff: "Spent 10 years at the SEC, left there as a Branch Chief. Says the SEC is bureaucratic and political and turns down slam-dunk cases all too often."

Markopolos was also in touch with Michael Garrity, the Boston branch chief of the SEC. Like Manion, Garrity saw the irregularities in the Madoff operation but referred Markopolos to the SEC officials in New York since Madoff's firm was headquartered there. Markopolos said he was warned by the Boston branch: "New York does not like to receive tips from Boston. Truer words were never spoken." In his testimony to Congress, a bitter Markopolos argued that the SEC overlooked Madoff's fraud because the agency is "captive to the industry it regulates and it is afraid of bringing big cases against the largest, most powerful firms."

Markopolos was increasingly frustrated. Everyone was ignoring his warnings. He had reached out to Zoe Van Schyndel in the hopes that she would encourage him. But instead, her story merely reaffirmed his worst fears. "Clearly the SEC was afraid of Mr. Madoff," he recounted to Congress.

Part of the SEC's problem was that it didn't employ many people who had been trained in finance or banking—those who knew how Wall Street ripped people off. Instead, the SEC had the odd tradition of hiring mostly lawyers, many very smart and competent, others just clocking time at the government agency so they could then go work as Wall Street attorneys. The good ones left because they were overworked, underpaid, and discouraged from making big cases. And some SEC lawyers—some just as greedy and ambitious as those on the Street they regulated—worked at the government agency just to make their bones. They would graduate law school, work at the SEC for a few years, rotate out, and go work on Wall Street for ten times more money—sometimes a hundred times more money. That was the SEC in a nutshell.

Markopolos had even given then–New York State attorney general Eliot Spitzer information on Madoff, but Spitzer—despite his reputation for being a pit-bullish and aggressive Wall Street cop—did nothing. And like the SEC, none of the other securities agencies such as NASD, or its successor, FINRA, that were supposed to investigate financial fraud took a look.

Markopolos had first heard of Bernie Madoff in 1999 when a coworker, Frank Casey, returned to Boston from a marketing trip in New York. Casey reported that investors there were raving about Madoff. Not only was Madoff a respected broker-dealer, but he ran a side business, a hedge fund with unbelievably consistent returns.

Casey's news was met with irritation by his boss. "We were losing a tremendous amount of business as a result of Madoff," Ron Egalka recalls. Egalka loved mathematics and logic, and everything at his firm was based on those ideas. He wanted to use math to mint money, and one of the strategies he and his staff came up with was something called a "split-strike conversion."

But Egalka was frustrated: he had popularized the strategy, but instead of winning clients, he was losing them to Madoff, who claimed to be using a similar index options strategy. So Egalka tasked Markopolos with analyzing how Madoff made his returns and trying to replicate them. "We wanted to see if we could deconstruct what they were doing or improve on what we were doing. The more we looked at it, the more we realized there was something wrong," Egalka said.

Casey, Markopolos, and their lead research assistant, Neil Chelo, puzzled over some fund of hedge fund marketing materials and the returns it claimed to generate. It was a fund they hadn't heard much about, called Broyhill, but the firm outsourced the managing of its money to the famed broker-dealer Bernie Madoff. He claimed to be doing the same complicated trades that Egalka's firm was doing, yet Madoff's numbers were very different. His monthly numbers were almost uniformly positive—even when the stock market was falling. It didn't make sense: the strategy itself involved buying stocks in the Standard & Poor's 100 index and buying and selling options against those same index stocks.

"The reason I was immediately suspicious was that I had run a slightly similar, but actually functional, product," Markopolos said in his prepared testimony. "As good as this product was, it often lagged the market, whereas Bernard Madoff's was always doing well under all market conditions." This was the most glaring red flag that Madoff had to be a fraud: he reported only three losing months out of eighty-seven, or seven years. Meanwhile, the S&P 500 index was down twenty-eight months in that same time frame. Madoff had to be cheating.

Based on the Madoff-linked fund marketing data he'd seen, Markopolos estimated that in 1999 Madoff's scheme involved roughly $3 billion. But how exactly was Madoff cheating?

Markopolos, Casey, and Chelo also did what many others had done; they checked Madoff's purported trading history. They called around other firms but couldn't find anyone—at places like Deutsche Bank, Merrill Lynch, Goldman Sachs, and others—who had actually traded S&P options with Madoff.

"I thought maybe he was doing the trades in the over-the-counter market," which is essentially unregulated, Egalka said. "There was nothing. We started getting suspicious. Harry thought maybe Madoff was front-running." This was a plausible theory considering Madoff did have a very active, very legitimate broker-dealer business.

Rampart had a greater interest than most in figuring Madoff out, as well as a greater ability to do the analysis. Rampart had generated a lot of interest among sophisticated investors in the split-strike conversion strategy—but Rampart people kept bumping into Madoff wherever they went. Like a bad penny, Madoff was the competitor who wouldn't go away, and was stealing business from Rampart at every turn.

"It wasn't uncommon for one of us to be out visiting with potential clients, and they would say, 'Give me a Madoff strategy, we'd love to do that,'" Egalka said. "But there was no way to deliver that." Over the long term, "we could get the same returns he did," but not with the consistent, low volatility. Madoff seemed to have discovered the equivalent of cold fusion in finance with the strategy he claimed to be using. The team at Rampart concluded, correctly, that this was because it simply didn't exist.

Unlike most traders and investors, the people at Rampart really knew how the complicated split-strike conversion strategy worked, how the underlying elements interacted. They understood derivatives, how they traded, what they were worth, and what they typically returned in a month or a year. Only quant jockeys like those at Rampart and big investment banks really studied them. Madoff knew this obscure-sounding strategy would deter most people from asking questions.

The striking thing about Madoff's performance was not that he generated unbelievably high returns. At 10 percent annually his returns really weren't that high. In fact, what Madoff was marketing wasn't a cowboy strategy. He claimed it was a steady-Eddy fund, not a get-rich-quick scheme. The other amazing thing was the consistency. Madoff's supposed hedge fund would crank out gain after gain for the month, a 1 percent or so return like clockwork. To investors, an investment with Madoff appeared almost as reliable as a Treasury bill. Plus, Madoff offered clients the option of withdrawing money with just thirty days notice, sometimes even less. No hedge fund on Wall Street offered that.

Rampart was generating the same returns as Madoff, but Madoff was doing so with less volatility, which meant less risk. Wall Street cares about volatility because unpredictability, by definition, makes it difficult to gauge how the market will fare. We often hear or read about "the volatility of the market, which drove many investors away" and the tendency to big ups and downs scares people. Madoff capitalized on that fear.

Hence, Rampart was up against not only Madoff, but Wall Street's innate hatred of volatility.

Egalka uses a baseball analogy. It was as if two Red Sox sluggers had the same batting average of, say, .333. The difference is that one hitter had big up months and big down months, as most players naturally would, while the other cranked out one hit per every three at bats without fail, like a robot. No ballplayer could ever do that.

In 2002, Harry Markopolos flew to Europe on an eye-opening business trip. He had a theory about Madoff, and this trip was a chance to prove it.

Markopolos's host and fellow traveler was a French aristocrat by the name of René-Thierry Magon de la Villehuchet, the head of Access International, a feeder fund into Madoff. De la Villehuchet and his cousins were descendants of Napoleon's marshals, and he used his impressive address book to recruit clients for Madoff. Among his marketers for Access were Patrick Littaye, François de Flaghac, Prince Michel of Yugoslavia, and Philippe Junot (ex-husband of Princess Caroline of Monaco). De la Villehuchet traveled several times a year to Geneva to raise money for Access. Ultimately Access would invest $1.4 billion in Madoff's scheme.

De la Villehuchet typified the Old World European who capitalized on his family and social connections to help benefit his business. It was the same world populated by wealthy jet-setters like Arpad Busson, Andrés Piedrahita, Edgar de Picciotto, and Prince Michel of Yugoslavia, who accompanied Markopolos and de la Villehuchet on their first meeting in London. While in London, Prince Michel went to a polo match to meet his cousins, Prince Charles of Wales, and his two sons, Princes William and Harry. Markopolos believes royal families of Europe may also have been investors through Access as a result of Prince Michel's family ties. This was the old generation of hedge fund investors—the ones who didn't do heavy-handed due diligence. They invested based on relationships.

After London, Markopolos and de la Villehuchet traveled to Paris and then to Geneva to meet with potential investors. Each time they sat down for a meeting, de la Villehuchet explained to the prospects, "Harry's strategy is like Bernie Madoff's, only with more risk." Markopolos could barely hold his tongue. Privately, he knew that his firm's profits were real and Madoff's were fake. "If I had said this, and if they had known that I had reported Madoff twice to the SEC, Access would have dropped me at the nearest curb," Markopolos testified. So he kept quiet and decided to use the trip to gather information, becoming a self-styled mole among Madoff investors.

During the trip Markopolos met with more than a dozen French and Swiss private client banks and funds of hedge funds, which farmed out money to managers they thought were winners: among them Barclays Bank, HSBC, JPMorgan, Oddo Asset Management, Dexia Asset Management, and Fix Asset Management. All bragged that, even though Madoff had apparently closed his hedge fund to new investors, they had special access and he would take money from them. "It was during this trip that I knew," Markopolos said, having connected the dots that this was not simple front-running but a Ponzi scheme and an all-out fraud.

The velvet rope Madoff carefully drew in front of his European clients served as the perfect hook. All of them had been sucked in by Madoff because each thought they were getting special VIP treatment. Only Markopolos knew they all were in Madoff's fund at the same time. De la Villehuchet succeeded in bringing in well-known names from the *Forbes* 100 list to Madoff, including Liliane Bettencourt, the world's wealthiest woman. The octogenarian heiress to the L'Oréal cosmetics fortune invested part of her $22 billion through Access.

Just after Madoff's arrest in December 2008, de la Villehuchet became despondent over the loss of his clients' money to Madoff. On the evening of Monday, December 22, he locked the door of his office on Madison Avenue in New York City, a few blocks from Rockefeller Center. He swallowed some sleeping pills and then slit his wrists with a box cutter. He was found dead the next morning.

A few years after Markopolos and his team figured out that Madoff was a fake, Egalka lost interest in the investigation. By then, Rampart had struck a major deal with Merrill Lynch and another large mutual fund firm to run closed-end funds and other portfolios. By 2008, Rampart had grown exponentially to oversee more than $12 billion in assets.

Today Egalka uses the same logic to examine the why of the Madoff fraud, as he was examining the how ten years ago. "Madoff truly is a menace and probably a sociopath, which would argue that he could have done the fraud from the beginning. [But] in my heart of hearts, I don't think Madoff started out with the idea of screwing the public, of doing a Ponzi scheme. I think he started out doing the split-strike conversion successfully, but at some point in time, maybe a month or two, he lost money. Maybe it wasn't as attractive as he wanted. And then, there was so much money coming in that he took some to supplement the performance. It became easy to do."

As long as the stock market was rising, investors didn't demand their money back from Madoff. "The whole thing became easy to manipulate without anyone getting nervous. But then with the credit crisis in 2007 and 2008, the markets dropped," Egalka explained. "As long as the markets are going up, people are satisfied. They don't have a need for the assets. The whole thing became easy to manipulate without anyone getting nervous. But when markets [are] moving down strongly . . ."

Markopolos, however, had not lost interest, and neither had some of his former colleagues. Although each of them went on to work at different firms, they continued their obsessive Madoff investigation. Neil Chelo, also a Chartered Financial Analyst, continued to check every formula, calculation, and modeling technique presented to the SEC in the nine years until Markopolos's final submission. Beginning in late 2003, Chelo worked as director of reseach for Benchmark Plus, a Tacoma, Washington–based fund of funds worth $1 billion–plus. While there, he interviewed several managers at Madoff feeder funds and even looked at Fairfield Sentry's audited financial statements for 2004 through 2006. He noted that these statements showed that Fairfield Greenwich had used a different auditor nearly every year.

Frank Casey, a former U.S. Army airborne ranger infantry officer with intelligence-gathering experience, left for a new job as North American president for UK-based Fortune Asset Management, a $5 billion hedge fund advisory firm. According to Markopolos's testimony, Casey closely tracked Madoff's feeder funds, collected their marketing documents, and figured out Madoff's cash situation. "He determined that Madoff's Ponzi was unraveling in June 2005 and May 2007 and in need of additional funds to keep the scheme going, and tabulated Madoff's likely assets under management," Markopolos testified.

By November 2005, the fraud was growing so huge, Markopolos realized, that Madoff had everything to lose—$30 billion or more—if he were to be exposed. By this point, Markopolos reasoned, Madoff would be willing to do anything to protect his secret and keep from going to jail. Markopolos and his associates began to worry for their personal and professional safety. "If Mr. Madoff was already facing life in prison, there was little to no downside for him to remove any such threat. At various points throughout these nine years each of us feared for our lives," Markopolos testified. "We also concluded both the fund and the secrets that assisted its growth and development were of unimaginable size and complexity. . . . He was one of the most powerful men on Wall Street and in a position to easily end our careers or worse."

Given the warnings from Markopolos and the obvious red flags all around Madoff, why was the SEC so resistant to investigating him? The answers range from incredulity that a respected Wall Street figure and trusted friend of the agency might be a crook to incompetence and bureaucratic bungling to political favoritism and fear of stepping on the wrong toes.

Bernard L. Madoff Investment Securities had a history of being one of the longest-operating brokerage firms on Wall Street. He and his brother played prominent roles in the industry, volunteering for every advisory committee they could. In addition to serving as chairman of the NASDAQ, Madoff also acted as an adviser to the SEC on market structure and other issues.

Madoff's name was so well known around the SEC that he was easily able to influence SEC policy in his favor. In 1990, the NASD, the securities industry's self-regulatory organization, assembled a panel and suggested experts to study payment for order flow. Madoff, who was named chairman of NASDAQ that year, played a key role in lobbying to keep payment for order flow legal—it was an enormous boon to his business. Eventually the SEC followed suit. To some, payment for order flow equaled a legal kickback scheme, and it seemed Madoff had cast a spell over the SEC. As long as it was disclosed to clients, the SEC said, they didn't even have to consent.

After Madoff got the SEC to approve payment for order flow, his business exploded. He accumulated roughly 10 percent of all the volume in New York Stock Exchange–listed companies almost overnight. His competitors were partly righteously angry and partly envious. In a

1993 letter to the SEC, the New York Stock Exchange protested that such payments amounted to bribes and prevented discovery of the best price for stocks by routing orders electronically to a preferred firm instead of having them exposed to the auction process on the exchange floor.

The AMEX also criticized Madoff's payment for orders, saying it encouraged brokers to route orders based on what was best for them rather than the client. The AMEX compared payment for order flow to kickbacks in the defense industry and questioned how ethical it was.

In 2001, Madoff gained another victory with regulators in what became known as the "Madoff exception."

Madoff wanted an exemption from a rule that had been in place since the 1930s barring short selling when a stock's price was falling. (Short selling is a practice by which investors borrow shares from someone else and then sell them. They do this because they think the price will go down and they will be able to buy the shares more cheaply later and return them to their owner. Short selling puts downward pressure on prices.) The rule, known as the "short-sale rule," was designed to be a circuit breaker of sorts—a way to break the momentum of a share price falling too swiftly. Instead, the stock had to be moving higher, under the so-called uptick rule.

"Market makers like Madoff wanted an exemption from the rule," explained Egalka, who also supported the exemption. "If you restrict market makers' ability to [sell short], then you impact liquidity."

Despite its name, the Madoff exception benefited many other firms on Wall Street, but since Madoff was so prominent and had lobbied so vociferously for it, Wall Street took to calling the rule after him. Madoff argued that the SEC's Division of Market Regulation should grant a limited exemption to registered market makers and specialists. Since the new process of decimalization had taken hold, trading in pennies had made life difficult and cut into profits. In a letter to the SEC dated February 9, 2001, Madoff argued that he and other registered market makers and specialists should *not* be subject to the ban on selling short—regardless of whether the stock price was falling. The ban on selling short would prevent brokers from trading in an orderly fashion.

These short sales would be noted as "sell short exempt." Shortly afterward, the NASD followed suit and incorporated the exemption into its own rule book.

In 2004, when the SEC once again considered revising short-sale rules, Madoff and his brother sent the SEC a letter reiterating how important the special exemption was to business. The Madoff exception would allow market makers to "sell short out of their inventory at a price that would otherwise be prohibited under the various short sale rules. It is critical to note that these are 'passive' exemptions, invoked only in response to a customer's 'buy' order. It is these exemptions that allow market makers and specialists to provide their rightful and beneficial role in the marketplace—to provide liquidity when demanded and maintain fair and orderly markets."

President Franklin D. Roosevelt created the SEC during the Great Depression to mop up after the stock market crash of 1929, to investigate financial scandals, and to rebuild investor confidence. During the Depression, Congress had formed the Pecora Commission to study the causes of the crash, whose investigation led to the creation of the SEC. In the early days of the commission, Ferdinand Pecora grilled top Wall Street financiers and set the stage for stricter regulations, which would come in the form of the Securities and Exchange Acts of 1933 and 1934 and the creation of the SEC.

In a 1934 memo, Pecora wrote: "If the system of private property is to be a reality for all the people who save money as a protection against sickness and old age, there must be a discontinuance of past practices by which a few men have been able, for their own aggrandizement, to destroy the savings of hundreds of thousands—even millions—of our people." This was the mandate on which the SEC was founded. And for three-quarters of a century, the SEC was aggressive, waging high-profile investigations against insider trading, corporate bribery, and fraud. Accomplishments ranged from a 1970s overhaul of stock trading commissions to the conviction of junk bond king Michael Milken.

In the last few decades of the twentieth century, however, the SEC had begun filling its ranks with lawyers instead of traders, analysts, bankers, or other people with Wall Street experience. The SEC was established for the sole purpose of regulating the financial industry, yet it was hiring people with no financial background. The young lawyers might have been versed in the law, but they knew nothing about how the financial markets operated. So they were often ill equipped to ferret out unfair and dishonest dealing. In fact, one of the things that Bernie Madoff did to build his reputation and get close to the people who ran the SEC was to teach the new hires about the ways of Wall Street. Madoff was the person telling the people at the SEC what constituted fair and normal business practices.

The prime candidates for SEC jobs, moreover, were for the most part not interested in building careers at the agency. Many were recent law school graduates, most of whom would join the staff for a few years and then leave to work for the very firms they had been regulating. The opportunities for conflicts of interest were rife. But the practice was accepted. It simply became a part of the culture. The low salaries at the SEC played a crucial role. Not everyone at the SEC was incompetent, and some of the lawyers were extremely bright. But they were desperately underpaid.

Ron Geffner graduated Benjamin N. Cardozo School of Law and began working for the SEC in the New York branch in 1991, making $40,000 a year. Geffner was SEC "class of '91," as lawyers refer to their first year at the SEC, under regional director Richard "Dick" Walker, but not a single member of his class stayed on at the SEC. Geffner, an ambitious enforcement attorney, said the SEC jobs were sought after. "It was a tough job to get out of law school. I came in early and I stayed late. I thought it would be great training," he said. A securities lawyer like Geffner made ten times that amount in private practice, and with twins on the way, Geffner left for a private law firm that now represents many hedge funds as clients.

In the last decade, the SEC backed away from taking on high-profile cases. Harvey Pitt, who served as SEC chairman from 2001 to 2003, admitted in an interview he gave to *Securities Industry News* that the SEC had a road map to Madoff, provided by Markopolos. But, he explained, Markopolos "was not an employee; he was an outsider. The fact that the SEC didn't [listen] has to be attributed to human failure. There are a number of inquiries going on as to why this occurred. The folks who got tips were not capable of having them lead to some form of government action."

The commission, he claimed, also moves very slowly. "Once a problem has been unearthed, it can take more than five years to investigate and bring an action." He pointed to the investigation into telecom giant WorldCom as the ideal SEC action. "The best example is the WorldCom case. We learned about misconduct and within twenty-four hours we were in court. It was the way real-time enforcement was intended to work." The WorldCom securities fraud case led to the conviction of its one-time CEO, Bernie Ebbers, as well as the Public Company Accounting Reform and Investor Protection Act of 2002, commonly referred to as Sarbanes-Oxley. The legislation was motivated by a series of corporate scandals, most notably WorldCom and Enron.

Although the SEC had been becoming more bureaucratic and less aggressive for some time, under Chairman Christopher Cox the SEC morphed into a weak, defanged shell of itself. Cox, appointed by President George W. Bush, took over as SEC chairman in August 2005 after seventeen years serving as an affable California congressman representing Orange County. A Harvard-trained lawyer, Cox was an enthusiastic supporter of Newt Gingrich's Republican revolution. He helped enact the GOP's Contract with America that restricted investor lawsuits against companies accused of securities fraud. The view at the SEC was that the White House under President Bush was antiregulation, and Cox set that tone at the agency. The Cox years would come to be known as one of the most dysfunctional and inept periods in the commission's history.

One of the most glaring examples of Cox's antiregulation attitude involved the case of Gary Aguirre. Aguirre, a former public defender, had worked for the SEC's Washington office starting in 2004, but was fired in 2005 after trying to go after Art Samberg, the manager of the Pequot Capital hedge fund. In the course of his investigation, Aguirre learned that Samberg had been tipped off to a potential merger by John Mack, a top Wall Street executive who was about to become chairman and CEO of Morgan Stanley. Aguirre wanted to interview Mack personally, but SEC higher-ups began stalling his requests. Aguirre said his attempts to question Mack were undermined by senior enforcement staff. Then a supposed smear campaign against Aguirre began.

In 2005, the same day it was reported that John Mack was being considered for the top spot at Morgan Stanley, senior SEC enforcement officials began cooling to Aguirre's insider trading investigation involving Mack. Not long afterward, Aguirre was fired. Aguirre claimed he was fired because he had accused senior SEC officials of giving Mack special treatment and that his superiors were afraid that the investigations would jeopardize their job prospects at the big law firms representing Pequot and Mack—in particular, at Debevoise & Plimpton.

Several former SEC lawyers had already joined Debevoise, including former U.S. attorney Mary Jo White. Not long after Aguirre opened the case, White contacted Aguirre's supervisor, Paul Berger, on behalf of her client, Morgan Stanley's board of directors. Thereafter, Berger blocked Aguirre from deposing John Mack. Berger reversed Aguirre's merit pay and evaluation—which he had received just eleven days earlier—and then fired him. Then, according to an internal e-mail between Berger and the law firm, within a few days Berger was soliciting for a job at Debevoise. "From the day that the SEC was contacted by Mary Jo White of Debevoise, Berger blocked the investigation," Aguirre said in an interview. "When I questioned the decision I was told it was for political reasons."

In 2006, the Aguirre firing made headlines. The Senate held hearings to determine what had happened, and Aguirre's testimony was damning. He was vindicated. Aguirre moved back to San Diego to work with his brother Michael Aguirre, a city attorney. A subsequent U.S. Senate report stated that the SEC showed undue deference to Wall Street power brokers in the probe. In 2009, Pequot Capital's Art Samberg shut down, citing the burden of the government investigation.

Another incestuous relationship that Madoff had with the SEC was the 2007 marriage of his niece, Shana, to SEC staffer Eric Swanson. Not only was Swanson now part of the Madoff family, he was also part of a team at the SEC that championed electronic trading—the very sort of trading that had made Madoff famous.

Swanson had a history of encounters with the Madoffs. In 1999 and again in 2004, Swanson, an assistant director in the inspections division of the SEC, was part of the team, led by Lori Richards, conducting routine examinations of Madoff's brokerage firm. Richards, Swanson's boss at the SEC, would later attend Shana and Eric's wedding. During these exams, the teams found nothing suspicious—certainly no indication of the Ponzi scheme that Markopolos was alleging.

In addition to his position on the Madoff investigative team, Swanson had also overseen an NYSE floor trader investigation in which some specialists were convicted. As a result of this probe, the NYSE ended up losing ground to the NASDAQ—yet another win for Madoff, who was chairman at the time. It was also a victory for BATS, a new electronic exchange where Swanson currently serves as general counsel. "He should have been barred from joining a company that benefited from his regulatory activities," wrote Charlie Gasparino in a column for the Daily Beast Web site.

Swanson had a reputation as a straight shooter and a decent guy, but his marrying into the Madoffs and then leaving the SEC to work on the Street left room for questions about whether he had sold out to the Madoff empire. And to Madoff's rivals, it seemed as though Swanson's earlier NYSE investigation was an early attempt for him to crack down on future competitors. Swanson's new employer, BATS, had filed in 2008 to become one of the country's newest electronic stock exchanges. BATS, based in Kansas City, hired Swanson as its general counsel in early 2008 to steer the new exchange through the SEC's jungle of regulatory issues. Swanson had worked at the SEC for ten years, quickly rising to assistant director in the office of compliance inspections and examinations.

But Swanson wasn't the only friend Madoff had among industry regulators. Madoff's profound knowledge of markets had a way of inspiring confidence and respect among SEC staff members. "The guy had the SEC eating out of the palm of his hand," according to a specialist from the NYSE who was a rival to Madoff.

Madoff's competitors were seething. Mostly they were upset about what seemed to be an SEC agenda: promote electronic trading over old-school auction-style trading on the AMEX and NYSE—at any cost. A cadre within the SEC—Lori Richards, Eric Swanson, Richard Colby—"wanted electronic trading to succeed, period. That was their agenda," said one former AMEX official, "even if it was wrong." It was an agenda that helped Madoff and hurt his rivals.

In December 2005, as the Pequot scandal and Aguirre's charges were moving toward public disclosure, the SEC finally began digging further into Madoff's operation. The SEC scheduled an interview with Fairfield Greenwich, Madoff's largest feeder fund and client, and Madoff set up a phone call to help prep Fairfield for the meeting. It appeared that the SEC was finally looking into Madoff based on concerns brought to them by Harry Markopolos, although he would not find that out until nearly four years later. Markopolos had served up a major scandal on a silver platter to the SEC. But the SEC wasn't hungry. In 2006, the SEC wanted all hedge funds to register so the government could keep track of this secretive, once-underground business. Didn't the agency want to bag a big hedge fund case to demonstrate they were fit to regulate the industry?

Finally, the SEC was taking action.

Mark McKeefrey, Fairfield general counsel, and Amit Vijayvergiya, Fairfield's chief risk officer, based in Bermuda, were on the phone call with Madoff to prep for the SEC interview. According to a complaint filed against Fairfield by the state of Massachusetts, Madoff gave McKeefrey and Vijayvergiya explicit instructions to understate Madoff's role in Fairfield's investment operations. Then he instructed them to make it seem as though Madoff was not managing the investments but just executing trades at their request.

"Obviously, first of all, this conversation never took place, right, Mark?" asked Madoff.

McKeefrey didn't answer. Amit, however, replied, "Yes, of course."

"All right." From there, Madoff began a rambling series of instructions telling McKeefrey and Vijayvergiya what to say and, more important, what not to say to the SEC.

He instructed Fairfield to give answers that would steer the SEC away from the idea that Madoff was a money manager. Fairfield should help perpetuate the false idea that Madoff was not acting as an investment manager—after all, hedge funds were supposed to register as investment advisers with the SEC. Madoff had not registered with the SEC—if the agency came looking and found out he had so many thousands of clients, surely his fraud would be discovered. He had to give Fairfield a script to follow that made it sound like *they* were the investment manager, not Madoff.

"We're not the one that's operating the fund. . . . The investment manager is the one who tells us how much to add . . . or subtract," Madoff instructed. "And that's done basically with a phone call. Okay?"

"Okay," said Vijayvergiya.

"Because that's the way we've always responded to any of those questions," Madoff prompted. "We get a phone call from the investment manager and change the allocation." He urged them not to offer the

SEC anything in writing. "Anytime you say you have something in writing they ask for it." A phone call was "the way pretty much everybody operates," Madoff coached. Fairfield agreed to going along with tailoring its story to the SEC to suit his needs, according to the Massachusetts complaint, filed by Secretary of State William Galvin.

Madoff advised Fairfield that the SEC was likely going to be interested in potential front-running of his clients. "You don't even have to make the statement that there's no front-running possibility, that's assumed."

"I know because of my relationship with the regulators," Madoff told them after a brief pause. Hedge funds "are 50 percent of the marketplace and . . . it's just changed the landscape, and the commission has no idea what the hell is going on."

He warned the two men not to be drawn out or to give the SEC additional information, and they should just stick to the script. "The less you know about how we execute . . . the better you are. Your position is, Madoff has been in business for forty-five years . . . we make the assumption that he's—he's doing everything properly."

Madoff repeated over and over: "We're just the executing broker. We don't market you. We don't know who your clients are." He also instructed Fairfield that if asked by the SEC who Madoff's other clients were, to answer: "You can say, yeah, we know—you know, that there are funds that execute this strategy through Madoff. But you don't know the size, you don't know the arrangement."

Madoff felt he had prepped them well. He even mentioned toward the end of the call the revolving door between the SEC and Wall Street. "They ask you a zillion different questions, and we look at them sometimes and we laugh. . . . They work for five years for the commission and then they become a compliance manager at a hedge fund."

But Madoff had a final instruction: Don't act like you care too much.

"You don't want them to think you're concerned about anything. . . . Just be, you know, casual."

Long before the 2006 SEC investigation, Fairfield had been given several warnings about Madoff. According to a former brokerage trader for Madoff, the article I wrote for *Barron's* in 2001 was the "talk of the trading floor." Jeffrey Tucker scheduled a visit to Madoff's office not long afterward. Madoff and DiPascali showed Tucker what they described as the purchases and sales blotter, a record of each trade. Madoff let Tucker thumb through the pages and opened up another journal that he claimed was the stock record for Madoff Securities. He told Tucker to pick two stocks.

Tucker picked AOL–Time Warner and turned to a page that supposedly listed each client's holdings in that company, according to Tucker's testimony to Massachusetts state regulators. Then, Tucker testified, either Madoff or DiPascali turned on a screen that they said would let them access their Depository Trust Company (DTC) account, a sort of central utility where Wall Street holds records of all of its transactions. They moved the screen down and scrolled until they reached AOL. Tucker compared Madoff's supposed stock record with the alleged DTC computer account, and the two numbers "tied."

It had been a magic trick, a sleight of hand, on Madoff's part. Tucker never double-checked with DTC to find out if Madoff was telling the truth. He had never seen a DTC computer screen before, nor did he ask for a printout to compare with anyone else. The screen Madoff showed him was nothing more than a dummy.

Surprisingly, neither Tucker nor Noel, nor anyone else at Fairfield, had ever seen the seventeenth-floor offices in the Lipstick Building. They, like most people, had only visited the nineteenth floor. Nor did they know the names of anyone besides Madoff and DiPascali, who actually put the strategy into effect.

In effect, the Fairfield-Madoff-SEC information circle formed a feedback loop, manipulated by Madoff himself. Madoff schooled Fairfield on what to say. When the SEC asked how Fairfield became comfortable with Madoff, they consistently pointed to SEC oversight of the broker-dealer. Then Madoff instructed Fairfield to tell the SEC that "Madoff has Chinese walls between the various business lines of his firm." Fairfield claimed it had no reason to believe otherwise, other than the fact that it was what Madoff told them to believe. The SEC then relied on that information from Fairfield.

———————

Right up until the end, Fairfield was raising money for Madoff. Tucker even wrote a letter, dated December 10, 2008, the day before Madoff confessed and turned himself in to the FBI, that Fairfield Greenwich was busy defending against redemptions and investors pulling their money out. Fairfield began setting up two new funds—BBH Emerald and Greenwich Emerald—to funnel more money to Madoff. Tucker and his wife personally invested $14.8 million, even though they had never seen any documents or done any due diligence on Madoff beyond an occasional visit or phone call.

After Madoff's arrest, Fairfield employees worked furiously to produce evidence of the due diligence they had never actually done. An e-mail from Manuel Gomez to Kim Perry in Fairfield's UK group, dated two days after Madoff's arrest, read:

> You mentioned that Fairfield used to get copies of some trades done by Madoff. In order to cover my ass, can I get some copies of those trades?

> I need to show people who invested in Sigma [another class of Fairfield funds funneled to Madoff] that I was doing due diligence in what is the largest scam in financial history.

In 2006, the SEC finally opened an investigation into Madoff's operation, but eventually closed its investigation the same year. In its conclusion, the SEC claimed it found no evidence that Madoff was running a Ponzi scheme, as Markopolos had alleged.

But with a fraud of this magnitude, one wonders how it was possible for the SEC to overlook it. Why did the SEC investigate Madoff and never find the fraud? Perhaps for the same reasons others didn't either—they were simply too lazy to look.

Former SEC officials and others who have examined the SEC case documents point out that the examiners never used their most potent weapon with Madoff: the power to subpoena his records. And even if they had, he might have given them the same phony documents he had shown to Jeffrey Tucker. Still, the SEC's inquiry was puzzling. First, it never reached the level of a formal investigation.

"When you look at the closing documents, it seems clear that the

Markopolos allegations of Madoff being a Ponzi scheme were never even investigated," said Thomas Gorman, a former SEC staff member who worked for its Enforcement Division and Office of the General Counsel and is currently a partner at Porter Wright in Washington, D.C.

Despite finding out that Madoff had lied to them about how many clients his broker-deal business had, in November 2007 the agency concluded they had "found no evidence of fraud," according to copies of the SEC closing documents. "All files have been prepared for closing. Termination letters have been sent to Bernard L. Madoff Investment Securities LLC, Bernard L. Madoff and Fairfield Greenwich Group," the SEC stated. "The staff has no objection to the eventual destruction of the files and has no knowledge of any impediment to such a disposition."

In the case of Eric Swanson, Peter Madoff's son-in-law, the question was whether he influenced the SEC's oversight. But the larger question is whether Madoff himself was able to gloss over any SEC inquiry. "It clearly appears so," Gorman said.

What the SEC did find out was that Madoff had never registered as an RIA, or registered investment adviser. "They solved that issue. What they never really looked at was the substantive fraud issue. And there were certainly more than enough facts," Gorman added.

But SEC attorneys Meghan Cheun, Doria Bachenheimer, and others who had examined Madoff in earlier years—including Eric Swanson— never examined the trading for Madoff's advisory clients, despite Markopolos's increasingly insistent pleas.

"It appears that once Madoff agreed to register [as an adviser], they were satisfied and walked away," Gorman said.

Gorman said it is standard operating procedure at the SEC and other regulatory bodies to ask for trading records, especially among hedge funds of funds like Fairfield Greenwich, Tremont Capital, and other big feeders into Madoff. Gorman has seen fake trade blotters like the one Madoff created and showed to Jeffrey Tucker. "Yes, normally fraudsters like Madoff falsify trading, but not over long periods of time. It's an incredible amount of work, especially given the strategy he claimed using stocks and options. Frankly, they could have easily said, 'We'd like to see the records.' They're supposed to be sophisticated people."

Other securities attorneys contend that the SEC examiners would not have done that type of detailed checking—such as adding up positions in AOL–Time Warner and double-checking with the DTC to see whether the stock was really there. "That's not what they do," said Rick Stone, a former Lehman Brothers lawyer for ten years, now in private practice. "The SEC comes in and they tick off boxes on a check-list," such as whether trade tickets are time-stamped; does the broker send out monthly statements; a log of customer complaints. "They rarely or never look at big-picture fraud."

As for Madoff's family, Madoff's brother, Peter, as well as his wife, Ruth, may have known there was something fraudulent going on on the seventeenth floor of the Lipstick Building. Peter Madoff deposited clients' checks into the advisory side of the business. Ruth kept track of invoices and did bookkeeping.

"It's difficult to believe other people weren't involved," Gorman said. "My question is: what did he think he was doing in the beginning? He opened up the fund . . . with the idea of stealing? Or was it a legitimate business that went bad?"

Markopolos knew that the people who worked at the SEC were not very sophisticated about the workings of Wall Street. In an e-mail to his circle of friends and colleagues in 2006, Markopolos suggested that if the SEC had not caught Madoff by then, "they never will until he blows up." Earlier in the summer, Markopolos had visited with Leon Gross, Citigroup's global head of equity derivatives. Gross is a brilliant options strategist who, Markopolos recalled, told him that "Bernie is a fraud and there's no way his purported stock and options strategy can possibly beat Treasury bill returns. [Gross] also can't believe the guy hasn't been exposed yet."

In his testimony to Congress, Markopolos said he believed that most SEC staffers suffered from "ineptitude and financial illiteracy." The SEC "has too many lawyers and not enough auditors with industry experience who know finance and can easily spot when the numbers don't add up or are too good to be true."

Markopolos said he had submitted the same evidence on Madoff, bolstered with additional names and leads, several times between 2000 and 2008—and the SEC didn't catch Madoff.

He pointed out that almost every securities analyst on Wall Street knew how to use a Bloomberg terminal, a computer that is the lifeblood of the industry. But SEC examiners and attorneys weren't even trained on how to use one—to punch in a stock symbol, to examine the quarterly earnings or balance sheets, or to chart the performance of the share price, or a bond or other securities.

Further, SEC staffers like Ed Manion and Gary Aguirre, who tried to investigate frauds, were either stifled by bureaucratic infighting and turf wars or silenced by colleagues fearful of upsetting a lucrative job in the offing. Markopolos said he was even fearful that Ed Manion would face retribution within the SEC.

Later, after Madoff's arrest in 2008, Cox admitted that under his regime, SEC staff brushed off "credible and specific" reports of fraud committed by Madoff over the previous ten years and did not marshal the ability to seek subpoenas, one of the SEC's most powerful tools to unearth fraud, or bring whistle-blower tips to the attention of commissioners.

If Pequot raised difficulties for the agency, "Madoff added the finishing touches," Gorman noted. "Here the SEC had multiple opportunities to discover at an earlier time what appears to be the Ponzi scheme fraud of the ages. The agency was even given a road map to the fraud—but lost its way."

Even at the end of Markopolos's hearing in February 2009, SEC officials were refusing to respond to questions about the Madoff investigation posed by Representative Gary Ackerman, a New York Democrat. "You've told us nothing!" Ackerman shouted at the table full of sheepish SEC officials. "You have totally and thoroughly failed in your mission, don't you get it?"

Markopolos had ideas for fixing the SEC, such as setting up a paid whistle-blower program similar to the one at the IRS and moving the headquarters of the SEC out of Washington, D.C. He had already gotten some laughs earlier in the day on the SEC's talent for missing frauds: "If you flew the entire SEC staff to Boston, sat them in Fenway Park for an afternoon, they would not be able to find first base."

To be fair, those who invested directly with Madoff played their parts in perpetuating the fraud as well. To stay in Madoff's game, they agreed to cooperate with his deceptions. They honored his request to not talk about him or tell others that he was managing their money. They didn't do due diligence. They continued to invest in the face of many red flags.

Some investors even put money in with the knowledge that Madoff did not allow outside performance audits. According to Markopolos, one London-based fund of hedge funds asked if they could send a team of accountants to conduct an audit on Madoff. They were told that only Madoff's brother was allowed to audit the firm. Peter Madoff also signed BLMIS's quarterly filings to the SEC for the advisory business, which only registered in 2006 following the SEC investigation.

Still, there was a psychology to being part of something special, something different, that many investors couldn't resist. As the university professor and Madoff investor Robert Chew, who lost his entire savings with Madoff, confessed in a column in *Time* magazine: "We knew deep down it was too good to be true. . . . We deluded ourselves into thinking we were all smarter than the others."

Chapter Ten

Bernie Madoff's pyramid scheme spanned the globe—reaching from New York to Hollywood to London and Paris and beyond.

Many of Madoff's European investors were ultrarich. Prince Michel of Yugoslavia traveled across the continent raising money for Madoff through René-Thierry Magon de la Villehuchet's Access Fund. The royal families of Europe and even London's House of Lords were infiltrated. Lord Jacobs of Belgravia was bitten, losing part of his £128 million fortune. Lady Victoria de Rothschild, a distant relative of Nathaniel Rothschild, the Atticus Capital hedge fund executive, was also on Madoff's casualty list.

In America, however, Madoff's investors were more diverse. They were plumbers in upstate New York; retired prison guards in Arizona; movie stars like John Malkovich, Kevin Bacon and his wife, Kyra Sedgwick, Hollywood producers like Steven Spielberg and David Geffen; and mom-and-pop investors in Wisconsin and Minnesota. In the weeks after Madoff's arrest, once-merry Christmas and Hanukkah parties—from Greenwich, Connecticut, to Palm Beach, Florida—struck a somber note.

"Anyone who was crowing about being in Madoff in 2007 was in hiding by 2008," said one money manager.

Madoff's scam cut a swath across all social classes and almost all the fifty states, and like real hedge funds Madoff's scheme had wormed its way into many IRAs and 401(k)s without most knowing he was there. Some had invested through feeder funds, or through feeders into other feeder funds. Others became directly invested through social connections with the Madoffs at their country clubs, via their family lawyers, their rabbis, even their priests.

Notably, one out of every six Madoff casualties hailed from Florida.

"It was like an atomic bomb went off," said lawyer Richard Greenfield, who now represents many of Madoff's victims in the especially hard-hit Palm Beach area.

Palm Beach is so rife with Madoff investors that, sitting at an upscale café on Royal Palm Way, the main thoroughfare on the island, Greenfield can literally point to them as they walk by. One investor, Ira Harris, a former Salomon Brothers partner and member of the Palm Beach Country Club, walks by Greenfield's table.

Greenfield calls to him: "Hey Ira! How are ya?" Harris waves and then scurries away.

Greenfield currently represents some once-wealthy Palm Beach widows whose husbands had put all or much of their retirement savings into Madoff's firm, thinking their wives could live comfortably on the steady returns each year. Greenfield has filed a lawsuit against the NASD and the SEC's new chairman, Mary Shapiro, who had served as the head of FINRA during its biannual examinations of Madoff, which yielded no evidence that Madoff was doing anything illegal.

Madoff had followed the money to Florida. His father-in-law, Sol Alpern, had retired to Florida and was still actively recruiting new investors for Bernie in the 1980s. In addition, Madoff's longtime patron Carl Shapiro and his family divided their time between homes in New England and Palm Beach.

Palm Beach is an extraordinarily insular wealthy community, which is still starkly divided between old-money WASPs and the nouveaux riches. In Palm Beach, social segregation between Jews and non-Jews is talked about today as openly and offhandedly as if it were 1930s Berlin. Despite token members of the opposite creed, the country clubs are divided by religion. Jews frequent the Palm Beach Country Club, where Madoff and many of his investors and colleagues were members, while non-Jews tend to people the Everglades Club, Bath & Tennis, Beach Club, or others on the opposite side of town.

Entering the grounds of the Palm Beach Country Club, a cab driver nonchalantly tells a passenger, "This is where the Hebrews go, to their club." She adds, "The Christians go to the other clubs," waving at the opposite end of town. The divide feels not only accepted, but encouraged.

In the 1890s, Henry Flagler, a cofounder of Standard Oil along with John D. Rockefeller, built a railroad to open up Florida as a winter retreat for those who lived up north. He also built two large hotels in Palm Beach, the Royal Poinciana and The Breakers. According to the 1939 book *Florida: A Guide to the Southernmost State*, Flagler "was one of the first of a long line of retired millionaires who came to Florida to play and remained to work."

Palm Beach wrestled with class warfare well into the late twentieth century. Schools there didn't integrate until 1971. The Everglades Club was notorious for its policy denying membership to blacks and Jews, who were not welcome as guests. (Socialite C. Z. Guest once brought cosmetics queen Estée Lauder, a Jew, to the club for lunch. Though Lauder denied being Jewish at the time, Guest's tennis privileges were temporarily revoked as punishment.)

More recently, there has remained an ingrained prejudice among old-money social circles against new money like the Shapiros, the Jaffes, and the Madoffs, the generation who came to rule Palm Beach in the past fifteen years. The newcomers were cultured, they gave money to charity, and as a result got their pictures in the local newspaper, known as the "shiny sheet" because it highlighted the new millionaires and their donations just as much as the Waspy longtime residents. Resentment among the old guard lingered.

Bernie Madoff began circulating more regularly in Palm Beach around 1996. Carl Shapiro sponsored him as a member at the Palm Beach Country Club. Jaffe and Sonny Cohn were listed as references. Madoff was also known to spend time at The Breakers, the historic hotel on the coast, as well as the Atlantic Golf Club. In 1996 alone, Madoff spent roughly $40,000 in dues at those three clubs. All told, Madoff spent roughly $950,000 on country club memberships between 1996 and 2008, according to Irving Picard's records.

But the dues were a small price to pay for the business relationships Madoff formed through these clubs. He used his connections there to solicit investors. Ruth also played a part in recruiting clients for her husband, schmoozing at cocktail parties and social events.

Palm Beach Country Club has the aura of a retirement home mixed with the opulence of a Helmsley Hotel. Once you've handed your car keys to the parking valet there and announced which member has invited you, you are ushered inside the expansive white sandstone building's richly appointed lobby, complete with Oriental rugs and a quiet gift shop selling $300 sweaters. In the ground floor lobby, golf scores are updated on a chalkboard. Upstairs, beyond the dining room, men sit at sumptuous wooden tables in cane-backed chairs playing bridge in a room overlooking the golf course; women play bridge in another sunlit room nearby overlooking the Atlantic.

A golf caddy down on the greens named Andy said he often walked the course with Madoff—at the Palm Beach Country Club in winter and at the Atlantic Golf Club in the summertime. "He usually golfed nine holes, and he was always on the phone," said Andy. Sometimes Ruth golfed with him.

There were several men in particular who helped Madoff infiltrate Florida's monied social circles. Two of them, Carl Shapiro and Jeffry Picower, were retired billionaires who had set up some of America's most generous charitable foundations. Robert Jaffe, Shapiro's son-in-law with a reputation for being a playboy, raised money on the golf courses. The others were accountants, such as Frank Avellino, Michael Bienes, and Michael D. Sullivan.

Nearly all of these men had been tied to Madoff for decades. Picower built a lucrative career as a lawyer and investor in biotechnology companies, and had a checkered past for allegedly creating tax shelters. Sullivan, the youngest of the Florida connections, took over the Madoff fund-raising for Avellino and Bienes after they were busted by the SEC for their illegal notes scam.

To this day, Bienes claims he was unaware they were doing anything illegal and blames their misconduct on bad advice from Madoff himself. Through his lawyer, Bienes declined to be interviewed for this book. "We were just a couple of accountants with a fund," Bienes said in a 2009 interview on PBS's *Frontline*. "We had a group together, and we were doing the accounting and bookkeeping and record keeping and tax 1099s for the group. We didn't consider ourselves brokers or dealers. We didn't know. We were naive, yes. Whether you believe it or not, we were unsophisticated and naive."

Bienes also claims that it was Madoff who had advised them against registering their operation with the SEC. After the 1992 SEC run-in, Avellino and Bienes insisted on meeting with Madoff. Once inside the impressive Lipstick Building offices, Bienes's fear and anger over what had happened overtook him. Bienes blamed Madoff for the mess and insisted it was his fault for advising them to not register.

"You son of a bitch—it's over now," Bienes said. "We went through it. It cost us a lot of money and a lot of grief. And it's all your fault, Bernie. Goddamn you, it's your fault. Because we asked you, 'Should we be registered? Should we get registered?' We were willing to do it. We were willing to pay any lawyer any fee. And you said, 'No, no, no, no, no, no, no.' And now you're looking at us as if we did something wrong?"

Madoff listened coolly. Bienes collected himself, realizing he may have cost his family and his partner a shot at keeping their account with one of the best money managers on Wall Street. "He had a big trading operation. He was a market maker. He was one of the top market makers on the street. He traded all the stocks on the NASDAQ. Why would he need us?" Bienes said. "I believed we were his only feeder. We were a small component of his huge business. He could lop us and say, 'Forget it,' or just make some calls and get other people to do what we were doing."

Bienes apologized for his outburst, and tempers cooled. Madoff told the two accountants that from then on, the annual returns were going to be much lower—probably half of the original 20 percent guaranteed returns. He said it was because he had been "burned on the margin." Bienes said he was not swayed by the warning of lower returns. He was just thankful he was allowed to stay. Madoff had let Avellino and Bienes reinvest, but only if they did so not using their own names.

"'You effin' guys. You effin' guys,'" Bienes quoted Madoff as telling him and Avellino. "'You're lucky. You're lucky I take you back. You effin' guys.'"

Bienes claims he stopped fund-raising for Madoff after the SEC shut his and Avellino's firm down, and he claims to have fallen out of touch with Avellino. But this is not the whole truth. According to the Florida Secretary of State's corporate database, Avellino and Bienes Accounting Services was registered in Florida in 1993—just one year after the SEC closed its case against the firm. The entity then changed its name to Mayfair Bookkeeping Services and reregistered as recently as 2008. Both men are listed as partners in Mayfair's 2008 annual report. In 1996, Avellino, Bienes, and their wives signed a Grosvenor Partners, Ltd., partnership agreement as general partners of Mayfair Ventures. It was one of several new entities Madoff asked Avellino and Bienes to create if they wanted to stay invested in Madoff's hedge fund.

There is also evidence that Bienes may have used his connections at his local church to help raise money for Madoff. Bienes and his wife, Dianne, were close with senior church officials in the Miami archdiocese. Bienes had been named a Knight of St. Gregory, and his wife a Dame of St. Gregory, by the local archbishop to honor them. (In Catholic churches, clergy can award ecclesiastical honors to laypeople, such as an "order of knighthood" for personal character, reputation, and notable accomplishment.) Bienes even reportedly convinced Monsignor Vincent T. Kelly to invest some of his church funds with Madoff at one point. Kelly, whose name is on the trustee's list of Madoff investors, told the *South Florida Sun Sentinel* that in the mid-1990s he opened a personal account with Madoff and another for his family's foundation. He declined to discuss whether he lost money, calling it a "personal matter."

Today, in the wake of Madoff's arrest, Bienes's $6.7 million home in Fort Lauderdale is in foreclosure. He paid the $2.5 million promised to St. Thomas Aquinas High School, where Monsignor Kelly is the principal, for an arts center built in Bienes's name. But he can't honor all his commitments, such as the full $4 million he pledged for a diagnostic imaging center at Holy Cross Hospital in Fort Lauderdale.

"Madoff is the enemy. He's a swindler. He's a crook," Bienes told the *Sun Sentinel*. "He stole our money."

After the SEC shut down their operation, Avellino and Bienes told their old clients to call Madoff directly. Most A&B clients did and opened their own separate accounts with Madoff's brokerage. Bienes claims he left his and his wife's money in Madoff's account and stopped raising money for Madoff altogether. He and his wife traveled, spending lots of time in London. They donated heavily to charity—upward of $35 million over the next fifteen years. Sometimes friends of Frank Avellino's or friends and neighbors of the Bieneses' would hear that the two men had access to Madoff. They would ask for a referral into Madoff—or they would ask how to get in, and Avellino would drop the name of Michael Sullivan, who had taken over some of Avellino and Bienes's accounts after the SEC probe in 1992 and attended the same church as Avellino.

"'There's a guy in my church with his partner, Greg Powell,'" Bienes said Avellino told him. "'They're terrific guys. They're accountants, former IRS, and they know about me. . . . We work on this committee and that committee. And they would love to get into this thing. And I could get them to Bernie. I could get them to get an account or two with Bernie.'"

Bienes warned Avellino not to make the same mistake as before and to make sure these men were licensed. Avellino insisted that they were, and he continued funneling money to Madoff through his own private account, called Kenn Jordan Associates. Even Avellino's housekeeper invested money through this fund. She is now suing Avellino in Massachusetts.

Michael D. Sullivan, another local accountant and a partner at S&P Investment Group, also drew investors in Florida to Madoff. These clients were either referred to Sullivan by Avellino or Bienes or through Avellino's and Sullivan's membership at Christ Church in Fort Lauderdale. Many of Sullivan's clients came from Bienes and Avellino, and for years Avellino, Bienes, and Sullivan shared office space. The three had registered their entities with the state of Florida at a shared address: 6550 Federal Highway in Fort Lauderdale.

"Like everyone else in the Madoff cast of characters, you can't believe a word that comes out of the mouth of Michael Bienes," alleges Jamie Peppard, an investigator and accountant based in Long Island, New York. "He is an unrepentant predator who is pedaling furiously to stay out of prison." A blogger for the Talking Points Memo who writes under the name Mrs. Panstreppon, Peppard researches fraudsters. She was one of many bloggers who leaped into coverage of the swindle after the Madoff arrest. Along with another online columnist, Jay Berkman, whose father had been seduced into giving money to Madoff by Maurice "Sonny" Cohn, Peppard regularly posted online about the case and the government's slow response, discussing the fact that many of Madoff's fund-raisers claimed innocence because they were also personally invested and how Florida was a haven for criminals seeking to whitewash their pasts and reinvent themselves. Bloggers such as these, along with some of Madoff's victims, used the Web to rally together despite being separated across the United States and the globe.

Michael and Dianne Bienes gave an estimated $30 million of the money they had earned through Madoff to local Florida philanthropies. The Bieneses' names were etched into the Broward County Library, the Broward Center for the Performing Arts, and Holy Cross Hospital. They also often threw lavish parties at their home, and even once hosted a *Great Gatsby*–themed soiree that seems chilling in hindsight.

Some of the larger feeder funds, such as Fairfield Sentry, Gabriel Capital, and Ascot Partners, which were headed by Ezra Merkin, were run by investment professionals. But many were not. For instance, Steven Mendelow and Edward Glantz, associates of Avellino and Bienes's in Florida, formed an entity called Telfran Associates, which acted as a feeder fund to Avellino and Bienes. Telfran raised approximately $88 million from eight hundred investors over a period of three years. Telfran sold investors notes paying 15 percent interest, which they in turn invested in notes sold by Avellino and Bienes that paid between 15 and 19 percent interest. Since Avellino and Bienes fed their funds to Madoff, the Telfran investors were also clients of Madoff, albeit indirectly. Others were companies or groups of people whose only purpose was to invest with Madoff. These consisted of feeder funds and leveraged funds that simply tracked Madoff's returns. There were also men and women who acted as feeders, like the Cohmad brokers, Stanley Chais in Los Angeles, and Sonja Kohn in Austria.

Since these informal partnerships and pools weren't mutual fund companies or stockbrokerages per se, and they didn't register as investment advisers, the SEC did not officially oversee them.

Florida attorney Mark Raymond described Madoff's crew of fund-raisers as "Bernie's fraternity." An attorney and partner of the Miami office of Broad and Cassel, Raymond now represents Michael Bienes. Raymond has handled victims of more than twenty-five financial and Ponzi scandals.

After the 1992 SEC investigation closed, Bienes "got religion," Raymond, Bienes's lawyer, said. "He said, 'Thou shalt not be involved in investments.' He never discussed investments with anyone. But it never looks good when the person you've been dealing with gets indicted. This guy [Madoff] was in the company of *machers*, kings and princes, the elite of the elite on Wall Street."

At the time of this writing, no one has sued Bienes over his ties to Madoff.

Avellino and Bienes inspired a series of copycats, including KLM Asset Management, which is listed as a Madoff customer. KLM is run by Norman Kantor, who operates a successful building supply company in

North Plainfield, New Jersey. Norman Kantor had invested with Madoff in the past, and in an attempt to duplicate the success of Avellino and Bienes, he established KLM, his own feeder into Madoff, roughly fifteen years before Madoff's arrest.

"Kantor was friends with Fred Wilpon," the owner of the New York Mets, one KLM investor explained. Through Wilpon, Kantor started investing with Madoff and receiving anywhere from 10 to 15 percent annually. "He was telling everyone about it . . . his sons, his family, his grandchildren. In fact, he was so happy, he started borrowing money from banks like JPMorgan Chase, roughly $19 million. He would borrow from the banks at a lesser rate," then take that money and put it in Madoff and pocket the difference in the returns.

According to this investor, Norman Robbins, Kantor had heard of what Avellino and Bienes were doing, so he decided to start taking money from people and investing it in Madoff. Kantor created KLM Asset Management as a "copycat scheme," said the elderly investor, whose wife and ninety-five-year-old brother also invested in Madoff. "Every November, he would take money from people, guarantee them a certain amount or rate of interest, of, say, about 8.5 percent annually for the following year, invest it with Madoff, and keep the difference."

Robbins put his money with KLM in 2005. He kept receiving payments from the company through the third quarter of 2008. On December 8, 2008, he decided to deposit more into his account. He wired $430,000 to Kantor's son, Steven, and asked him what the coming year's return was going to be. Madoff was arrested just three days later. Robbins is suing KLM in New Jersey court to get his money back.

Madoff's investors from Florida and from around the country came from all economic levels and were tied in with him through a variety of formal and informal networks. Some formed legal partnerships, like the 1973 Masters Vacation Fund, which was started by retirees who used their first decade's worth of gains to go on a cruise. Some were informal arrangements in which one person, like New Jersey building supply titan Norman Kantor, let other people deposit money into Kantor's feeder account with Madoff.

It's not clear who convinced local Florida politicians to invest with

Madoff's fund. The Democratic leader of the Florida House of Representatives, Franklin Sands, was one of the most high-profile public officials in that state to be a victim of Madoff's scheme. Sands, like most other Madoff investors, was referred to Madoff through a friend, although he later called the intermediaries "professional advisers." Other local politicians, like the mayor of Venice, Florida, were also invested with Madoff.

Even though Sands lived and worked in Florida, he was a successful Jewish businessman who had grown up poor in Brooklyn as the son of an immigrant and moved south, as many other of Madoff's prey had done. Sands had never even met Madoff, but about twenty years before the Ponzi scheme was revealed, Madoff's fund was pitched to Sands as a no-risk investment with steady results and an exclusive membership club that limited acceptance of new investors. Sands, who had made his fortune running and selling jewelry businesses, was lured by this impressive pitch. He told reporters that over the years he even moved his retirement savings into the fund. In the end, Sands and his wife, Leslie, invested—and lost—their entire $3 million life savings. In addition to his $33,000 yearly salary as a legislator, Sands now has a second job as a health-care salesman.

Robert Jaffe, the son-in-law of Carl Shapiro and one of Madoff's chief Florida fund-raisers, epitomized the unquestioning middleman. For years, he shilled for Madoff and didn't ask questions. Jaffe was the way into Madoff. At ninety-five years old, Carl Shapiro seemed bent on giving away most of the fortune he had accumulated. Rumors circulated that Shapiro had sold his company and made hundreds of millions of dollars—and that Madoff had turned it into a billion dollars or more. Everyone in Palm Beach couldn't wait to get some of what Madoff had done for Shapiro.

Jaffe had married Carl and Ruth Shapiro's daughter, and into a fortune. Jaffe did boast some credentials as a stockbroker. He had worked for the Cowen and Company investment firm in Boston, and Jaffe and his wife, Ellen, were fixtures on the Boston charity circuit. Like other rich socialites, they wintered in Florida, and in the late 1980s some of these wealthy donors (to Massachusetts General Hospital and other hospitals throughout New England, for example) began asking if fund-raising events could be held in and around Palm Beach. The "season" of charity balls and galas in Palm Beach was born.

That suited Robert Jaffe perfectly. This Madoff middleman had a regular one o'clock golf game with a group of buddies at the Palm Beach Country Club. Moreover, not only did the club require a steep entry fee, restricting access to all but the wealthiest, but its 120 or so members gave generously to charity—at least $250,000 a year, every year.

After Madoff's arrest, there was outrage at and little sympathy for Jaffe. "He lived an arrogant, affected life," Richard Greenfield recalled. "People would court Jaffe to get to Madoff." And worst of all, Jaffe had not disclosed to anyone who invested that he was being paid by Madoff through Cohmad. Madoff paid everyone to bring him money—but those individual fund-raisers, including Jaffe, conveniently neglected to disclose that to clients.

It was Donald Trump who finally broke the social divide in Palm Beach. He opened a club that didn't concern itself with religion or ethnicity—all you had to be was really, really rich. "Trump was the first to open up a club in Palm Beach for everybody," said Jose Lambiet, columnist for the *Palm Beach Post*. Everybody, that is, who could afford to pay. By 1999, Bernie and Peter had joined Trump's new club, The Mar-a-Lago, and Madoff even once tried to get Trump to invest but was unsuccessful.

It was at The Mar-a-Lago one night after Madoff's arrest that Jaffe had an unpleasant public confrontation with one of his most high-profile clients. According to the *New York Post*, Jaffe showed up at a black-tie birthday party for carpet tycoon John Stark. "Nobody could believe he had the balls to show up because about 25 percent of the guests were people who lost hundreds of millions of dollars with Madoff," reported Page Six, the gossip section of the paper.

Among the birthday party guests was Jerome Fisher. The founder of Nine West, the shoe and clothing manufacturer, had lost $150 million in the Madoff scam. Fisher, who was seventy-eight at the time, confronted Jaffe, screaming, "You dirty bastard! And on top of everything, you got a [bleep]ing commission to get me to invest!" The two men avoided each other all night. Fisher had already lost $200 million—with a different hedge fund, KL Financial—and now he'd been duped by Madoff for another $150 million. (KL Financial was another hedge fund investment scam cooked up by a young Florida-based money manager who was later arrested by the FBI.) Fisher was one of the biggest losers, but he wasn't alone: roughly a third of Palm Beach Country Club members were reportedly swindled out of a staggering $1 billion.

Just months after Madoff's arrest, the dust had already started to settle in Palm Beach.

At best, "people still want to believe Jaffe was a nice person, they just think of him as being duped, as not smart," Greenfield recollected in May 2009. "They say, 'It wasn't Bob Jaffe who ripped us off, but Madoff himself.' I have a couple of clients, people who came in to Madoff through Jaffe. I asked them, 'Should we sue Jaffe?' and they said, 'Oh, absolutely not!'" Greenfield said. "As much as people don't think very much of him, no one in Palm Beach wants to sue him." Greenfield believes this forgiving attitude among the rich "is a sociological thing." Palm Beach is so tightly knit that few people want to sue and then have to face Jaffe at their local country club. It would be awkward and distasteful.

The only party of note to sue Jaffe is the SEC, a suit that his lawyers called unfair and baseless in the law. In June 2009 the agency said he had his own accounts at Madoff generating returns of up to 46 percent, while the investors that Jaffe brought into BLMIS received annual returns of only 12 to 18 percent. Based on these outsized returns, Jaffe raised $1 billion for Madoff, then made withdrawals from his Madoff accounts totaling at least $150 million between 1996 and 2008, the charges alleged. The SEC said there was little chance that Jaffe thought Madoff was running a legitimate operation. "Jaffe knew or recklessly disregarded that the trades . . . in his accounts were fictitious," the agency said.

Even Jerome Fisher has not sued Jaffe. Instead, resignation has set in. During the spring of 2009, Fisher began selling his art collection to help recoup some of the $150 million he lost in the fraud. In May 2009, Christie's in New York put up for auction a 1968 painting by Picasso entitled *Mousquetaire à la pipe* (*Musketeer with a Pipe*). The painting, which Fisher had purchased in 2004 for $7.2 million, sold for $14.6 million. But Fisher's strategy didn't work for everyone. That same week, William Achenbaum, who runs the Gansevoort Hotel Group and was another Madoff casualty, tried to sell his own Picasso—a 1938 portrait of the artist's daughter Maya—at auction at Sotheby's. The pricier work, estimated at $16–$24 million, went unsold.

Rick Stone, another Florida attorney and former Lehman Brothers lawyer, agreed with Greenfield that the reason victims are hesitating to sue Jaffe is out of a desire to protect their social status. "These are people with no money who don't want to make waves or admit they have the loss or lose social standing." Stone said he believes there was a country club mentality that also encouraged people to invest with Madoff and then to stay quiet when they became victims. "I call it 'financial incest,' because he was dealing with an older crowd of people desirous of status," he said. "Madoff earned you not only good returns but status. It's like being a member of the Four Arts Club," an exclusive library and sculpture garden in Palm Beach. (Stone's wife went there to try and join when they moved to the area, and the director told her, "We have not allowed new members for thirty years.")

The fact that Madoff appeared to limit the number of investors he would accept, said Stone, played to the Palm Beach mentality in much the way it played to the Europeans, to royalty, to funds of hedge funds, and to others who thought of themselves as VIPs. "There were only 120 members at the Palm Beach Country Club. It was a status thing to be associated with this crew. It was secretive and better somehow. Investing with [Madoff] meant, 'You are average and I am not.' And that is what Palm Beach is all about."

Resolve has grown in Palm Beach that Madoff didn't do it alone. Richard Rampell, for one, doesn't believe that Madoff pulled off the biggest financial scam in history by himself.

"It's impossible," Rampell said in an interview at his offices in downtown Palm Beach. The longtime accountant has had Madoff clients over the years, and he was careful to read the trade and profit statements from Madoff's business at the end of each year. Rampell even had one client who was so suspicious he redeemed every year "just to test Madoff and make sure he could get his money back." Every time the investor redeemed, he got the cash—no problem.

Rampell believes Ruth Madoff played a role in luring investors to her husband's fraudulent operation—or at least in perpetuating the fraud. "I believe Ruth had to have had some part in this," said Rampell. "They spent a lot of time together. How could they not know he has all these assets transferred into her own name? This does not pass the smell test that she's innocent."

"You have to understand—people come to Florida to re-create

themselves," explained attorney Rick Stone. He pointed to Mark Foley, the former Republican congressman and a resident of West Palm Beach who departed Washington after he was caught flirting with underage congressional pages. "I fully expect him to run for office again," Stone said. "There is just no shame here."

An air of financial ostentation still reigns throughout Palm Beach, even in places as mundane as the grocery store parking lot. The main supermarket in Palm Beach is Publix, a grocery store chain in the Southeast. But here, the store offers valet parking for its privileged customers, some billionaires. The lot is generally filled with Range Rovers, Jaguars, Maybachs, and Bentley convertibles. Across the street from Publix, the local drugstore sells caviar, and a popular bakery owner on the same block speaks French with her customers. Here, shopping for groceries is as different from typical American Main Street as it could be.

On Worth Avenue—Palm Beach's equivalent of Fifth Avenue or Rodeo Drive—the fallout from the Madoff scandal is easy to see. On an afternoon ripe for shopping in early 2009, Worth Avenue attracted only a few young women, wearing clothes from Anthropologie and shoes from Coach. A few older ladies sporting obvious plastic surgery and tanned elderly men dined and drank in local upscale restaurants such as the mainstay Taboo; others slowly cruised the avenue in those Bentleys with their tops down. High-end stores like Chanel, Cartier, and Trillion men's clothing shop, where Bernie Madoff handpicked $1,000 shirts and sweaters, were mostly empty. A pair of pants Madoff ordered (prearrest) from Trillion was still being held at the store.

Palm Beach, often described as "God's waiting room," according to SocialMiami.com gossip columnist Allison Weiss Brady, had an air of desperation.

Bernie Madoff traveled all over the world mixing pleasure and business in an effort to raise money. He and his brother, Peter, along with Ruth and some close friends, made frequent appearances at industry networking events for global stock exchanges like the Interbourse. "He was there every year without fail," said Doug Engmann, who, with his brother, Michael Engmann, was a longtime broker in stocks and options.

"Madoff was a constant presence at these exchange events," said Engmann, who noted that Madoff also threw lavish parties at the annual Wall Street industry bash in Boca Raton, Florida. Many brokerage firms sponsored these events—it was just the way business was done.

But Madoff was absent from places he should have been—such as the hedge fund databases. Andrew Schneider is the founder of HedgeCo.net, one of many databases that act as a "dating service" between potential investors in hedge funds and the underlying managers who wanted to raise money. He had set up the Web site to help make these connections in a semitransparent way, and he also offered recommendations for services like lawyers, accountants, administrators, and infrastructure—"the pillars of a good hedge fund," Schneider said. "Madoff didn't have any of these things—an outside administrator, a well-known accountant, or an outside law firm that anyone had heard of," Schneider noted. "Immediately that should have been a red flag."

Despite the fact that he wasn't raising money in the usual hedge fund circles, Madoff was able to infiltrate the pension fund of the West Palm Beach Police. Its investment was small: only one half of 1 percent of its $161 million portfolio was invested with Madoff. It was made in October 2007, when the pension invested 5 percent of its assets into a Tremont feeder fund, the Rye Select Broad Market Prime Fund. A consultant, Collins Capital Low Volatility Performance Fund, allocated money to Tremont, which in turn allocated the money among twenty-one hedge funds including Madoff. All told, the police pension's exposure totaled $838,000 out of $161 million—but it shows how Madoff invisibly insinuated himself and his fraud even in the savings plans of law enforcement.

Madoff promised steady, positive returns to everyone, but it appears that his arrangements varied with different clients. According to the Madoff trustee lawsuits and federal prosecutors, Florida mainstays Carl Shapiro and Jeffry Picower were getting a better return from Madoff than many other investors. In their indictment, U.S. prosecutors allege that Madoff had promised returns of 40 percent or higher to some early investors, which was far above what most of his clients were expecting. Madoff trustee Irving Picard alleges that Picower had withdrawn up to $6.7 billion from Madoff since 1995 and had ordered Madoff to "target" returns of up to 950 percent a year.

Some investors might also have gotten Madoff to generate "phantom" losses for them. In particular, Jeffry Picower, a billionaire and well-known philanthropist, asked Madoff to do just this. If Picower had a big gain on another transaction, such as a real estate deal, then if he could generate a "loss" in his Madoff account, he could use the loss to offset the gain and reduce the net tax bill he owed to the IRS.

Although Picower received monthly or quarterly statements purportedly showing stock held in—or traded through—his accounts, as well as profits, the trades on these statements "were a complete fabrication," according to the trustee's lawsuit. Based on the trustee's investigation, and with the exception of isolated individual trades for certain clients, "there is no record of BLMIS having cleared any purchase or sale of securities."

Moreover, Picower was in a position to know he was ordering up trades and profits that were implausible—pure fantasy. For example, two of Picower's trading accounts—Decision Inc. #3 and Decision Inc. #4—earned rates of return of more than 100 percent for four consecutive years, from 1996 to 1999, and sometimes more than 550 percent. Picower's Decision Inc. #2 account earned more than a 950 percent gain annually in 1999. Indeed, in the years between 1996 and 2007, some Picower accounts enjoyed supposed annual returns of more than 100 percent.

The trustee argued that Picower was in a position to know better, as he is a sophisticated investor, accountant, and lawyer who organized buyouts of health-care and technology companies since at least the 1980s. He reportedly knew Madoff for decades and has been invested in Madoff since at least the 1980s. Not only that, but Picower and his assistant, April Freilich, had set up their own system to monitor their accounts inside Madoff—so closely that they were able to spot apparent inconsistencies with Picower's customer statements better than Madoff's employees.

Finally, Picower even went so far as to ask for fake trades to be made in one of his accounts—dated back to before the account was even open. This Picower account combined outrageous returns with backdating to create trades that supposedly happened before the account was even opened at Madoff. In April 2006, Picower opened a sixth account, Decision Inc. #6, with a wire transfer of $125 million. Madoff promptly began "purchasing" securities in the account, but backdated the vast majority of these purported transactions to January 2006.

By the end of April, just weeks later, Picower's account showed a value of $164 million—a gain of $39 million, or a return of more than 30 percent, in less than two weeks of trading. The reason for this massive gain: the April 2006 Decision Inc. #6 customer account statement reflected fifty-seven purported purchases of securities between January 10 and January 24, 2006, almost three months before the account was opened or funded.

Over the years, Picower took out about $6.7 billion from Madoff, and records suggest he knew Madoff was backdating the trades—in fact, Picower was requesting that he do so. And of that $6.7 billion, at least $5.1 billion was money Madoff and Picower created using phantom trades. That money, the trustee alleges, belongs to Madoff's true victims.

The Picowers' attorney, William Zabel, told the Associated Press his clients "were totally shocked by his fraud and were in no way complicit in it." They and their foundation were victims, he said.

According to a 2009 article in *Fortune*, Frank Di Pascali was trying to negotiate a plea bargain with federal prosecutors, a fact the FBI confirmed. According to the terms of the deal, in exchange for a reduced sentence DiPascali would testify that he manipulated returns for Madoff investors such as Avellino and Picower. If DiPascali does testify to helping, and he admits that he knew about the fraud—then Madoff could be charged with conspiracy. If it turns out these or other investors knew their returns were false, they too could be charged as part of a conspiracy.

Madoff is not the only Wall Street criminal that Picower has been tied to over the years. He invested $28 million in Ivan Boesky's arbitrage fund. (Boesky pleaded guilty to conspiracy charges as part of a plea bargain in 1987.) Picower also had a history of tax avoidance. Earlier, in the 1980s, Picower was sued along with his accounting firm for selling "shaky tax shelters" involving computer leases—a vehicle that helped its owner reduce their overall tax bill. When the IRS challenged the deductions, one client who had put $30 million in Picower's lease shelters sued. The suit in federal district court, naming Picower and his accounting firm, Laventhol & Horwath, was settled for $1.1 million.

In 2000, according to the *Palm Beach Post*, the Jeffry M. & Barbara Picower Foundation was the second-largest nonprofit in the state of

Florida. (The Carl Shapiro Foundation was number four.) In 1999, for example, the foundation gave $250,000 to NARAL (National Abortion and Reproductive Rights Action League) Pro-Choice America, $700,000 to public television station Thirteen/WNET in New York, $120,000 to the Children's Aid Society, and $107,000 to the Boys & Girls Clubs of Palm Beach County. But the foundation's largest grant was to the Picower Institute for Medical Research, for $5.5 million, or almost half of the total $13.3 million that year.

The following year, an investigation by the *St. Petersburg Times* explored a web of business relationships between it, the Picower Institute for Medical Research, and two for-profit pharmaceutical companies. The Picower Institute for Medical Research is a charitable medical research organization, but it can commercialize drug discoveries as a for-profit pharmaceutical company. And Jeffry Picower was the company's largest shareholder. "When the spinning was over, a for-profit drug company owned largely by Picower was left holding license to many of the most important discoveries of the Picower Institute. Humankind, it seems, would not be the only beneficiary of the spending and investments of the nonprofit Jeffry M. & Barbara Picower Foundation. Jeffry M. Picower would, too," Mary Jacoby wrote in the paper.

Congress has granted foundation donors the right to deduct the amount of their gifts from their taxable income, giving wealthy people an important incentive to set up charities. But the laws forbid self-dealing—that is, those who create or manage a foundation cannot profit, even indirectly, from the endowments. Picower, however, managed to circumvent this rule.

In its 2007 tax filing, the Picower Foundation listed many investments, approximately two-thirds of which were equities, including Johnson & Johnson, Caterpillar, and AT&T. About one-third of the assets were reported as United States Treasuries. All of these investments were entirely handled by Madoff.

So in 2007, when the Picower Foundation revealed that Madoff had served on three of its boards and that all of the foundation's money had been invested with one man, perhaps it should not have been entirely a surprise. The Picower foundation reported a $952 million investment portfolio on its tax return that year. It is unclear exactly how much of that money the foundation actually lost with Madoff. But days later, Barbara Picower announced that the foundation had been shut down.

The Picowers may still be forced to pay even more for cozying up to Madoff.

In March 2009 the IRS said in a Senate Finance Committee hearing that private foundations—including the trustees, directors, and officers—can be forced to pay a 10 percent penalty tax if they fail to exercise due diligence on an investment that jeopardizes the charity's finances. Under this rule, foundations with exposure to Madoff, such as the Picower Foundation, the Chais Family Foundation, led by Stanley Chais, in Encino, California, and many others could be charged for failing to heed red flags or improperly diversifying their foundations' investments.

Despite the frenzy in Florida to invest with Madoff, there were some people who refused to put their money with him. Salomon Konig was one of these people. Konig also hails from the Florida Jewish community. He lives near Miami, having emigrated from Venezuela. He started his career as a commodities trader and worked his way up to running a fund of hedge funds and investing in real estate. Konig is the head of Artemis Captial Partners, a fund of hedge funds named for the Greek goddess of the hunt. Artemis operates, like many feeder funds, by giving money to hedge fund managers Konig thought looked promising.

"Madoff was a black box," said Konig, who helps endowments and wealthy families select hedge funds. Unlike the Madoff feeders, such as Tremont and Fairfield Greenwich, however, Konig made a point to ask any hedge fund managers if they had any money with Madoff before he invested with them. Konig was so worried that he told funds of hedge funds he was not interested in doing business with them if they were involved with Madoff. He knew there was something wrong with Madoff's numbers, even if he couldn't prove it. Whenever he visited a new hedge fund, Konig gave the manager a questionnaire that asked, among other things, "Do you have any exposure to Madoff?" If they did, he didn't give them money. Madoff was so pervasive in the hedge fund industry that Konig wanted to inoculate himself and his firm from what he was sure was a fraud.

"We would always ask, 'Do you have any Madoff?' Because if the person said yes, that said something about their investigation skills,"

Konig said. "I would always ask people, 'Tell me what you know about Madoff, how he does it every year.' They inevitably would say, 'I can't.' We knew that he was a market maker on the brokerage side of his business. He started trading options, and I think that he decided to circumvent the law. He would take whatever profits he made from trading, and say, 'This month I'll allocate this percentage to the hedge fund.'"

Konig believes the fraud may have started in 1987, when the stock market crashed. If not then, he contends the fraud began in March 2000, just as the Internet bubble started to burst and the stock market plunged. But he admitted, "I really have no idea. Only Madoff himself knows."

In 2000, Konig had his own market maker operation, and its profits started to collapse too. Stocks were now being traded in decimals, which hurt profit margins for traders. Konig got out of the brokerage business, realizing he could cut his losses. "I knew Madoff ran a very similar business. We eventually sold ours, and that's when the rumors began about Madoff."

Mr. Konig should know. He ran a mini Ponzi scheme in Venezuela and had to leave the country in 1993. He cannot return and faces an outstanding arrest warrant in that country. One investor in Konig's firm in Venezuela, who was interviewed by phone, said he's not surprised that Konig has gone public with his criticisms of Madoff. "It takes a crook to smell another crook," said Carlos Vainberg, an investor from Venezuela. He and several others sent a letter to the SEC in 1998 asking that the agency take action against Konig, but they have not filed suit in the United States. "I am astonished to read Mr. Salomon Konig's comments on Madoff case," he said. "He along with his brother Harry ran a mini Ponzi in Caracas. They swindled many people of the Jewish community, including me. They had to leave the country at once. They cannot return unless they want to live in jail."

Madoff's arrest and admission to one of the greatest frauds in history came as a surprise to many people. The man many considered to be their closest ally and trusted family friend had fleeced them.

On December 11, 2008, Ellen Shapiro Jaffe was seated in her chauffeured Town Car when her cell phone alerted her that she had an incoming call. She had already been on the cell phone, as her driver cruised around Palm Beach, with a local caterer ordering caviar for a party at their house a few nights hence.

She put the first call on hold and answered the incoming one. It was her husband, Robert. He uttered a few words.

"What do you mean he's been arrested?" she screamed. *"But that's where all our money is!"*

Chapter Eleven

Lost along with this money is the crucial element of trust. The lesson for the public has been that neither companies nor the analysts supposedly assessing those companies' prospects can be trusted. Nor can people always trust the independent accountants who certify company reports. They cannot even always trust the financial cops of the Securities and Exchange Commission to catch cheaters in a timely fashion.

—Leon Levy's 2002 memoir, *The Mind of Wall Street: A Legendary Financier on the Perils of Greed and the Mysteries of the Market*

On the evening of Wednesday, December 10, 2008, Jacob Ezra Merkin held a benefit party at his expansive duplex apartment at 740 Park Avenue in Manhattan. The apartment consisted of eighteen rooms and eight bathrooms and was situated on the corner of the building. Merkin had purchased the apartment for $11 million in 1995 and considered it one of his best investments. His neighbors and other residents of the building past and present were famous and rich like himself. The roster included people such as Ronald Lauder, the Estée Lauder cosmetics heir and investor; John Thain, head of the New York Stock Exchange; Jacqueline Kennedy Onassis; and even John D. Rockefeller, Jr.

Ezra lived life on a gigantic scale and was known to view lavish purchases not as indulgences but as investments. In addition to his apartment, at one of the most exclusive addresses in New York, he also collected art. He had hired Ben Heller, an elderly statesman in the art world, to be his art adviser, and upon Heller's recommendation Merkin purchased several paintings by Mark Rothko, the abstract expressionist, over the preceding five years. The paintings too were a key investment in Merkin's increasingly elite portfolio, a portfolio that was filled not just with things but with people from New York's wealthiest and oldest families, where social connections turned into business opportunities, and back again.

Take Heller, for example. He invested most of his personal and charitable funds, including a $3.4 million trust and more than $10 million that he had planned to give to his six children and eight grandchildren, in Merkin's successful hedge fund, Gabriel Capital. Heller's stepdaughter, the actress Kyra Sedgwick, and her husband, the actor Kevin Bacon, also invested in Merkin on Heller's recommendation.

Merkin didn't particularly like the Rothkos, but he didn't buy them because he liked them. He bought them because they were valuable and likely to rise in price. And he had hired Heller because he was a well-known name in the art world, not because they shared the same aesthetic. Merkin was careful about how he spent his money. Despite his own personal wealth and that of his family, he wore the same few rumpled suits and drove an old minivan. (The habit of not appearing wealthy was bred into Merkin and his siblings by their father.) He rode the subway to work. He purchased expensive items as *investments*—cars and men's suits only depreciated in value, so why buy more? To him, they were pointless.

Still, the Rothkos displayed in Merkin's apartment, which served as their gallery, were among the largest and most spectacular in the world. Merkin owned two nine-by-fifteen studies for murals that Rothko executed for the Four Seasons restaurant in New York's Seagram Building and for the Rothko Chapel in Houston. He also owned a third Rothko study for a Harvard University mural. Heller, an early Rothko collector, even advised Merkin and his wife, Lauren, on which rugs and furniture they should buy to complement the paintings and what kind of dimmed lighting they should install to offset the enormous works. "It was my conception," Heller told Bloomberg. "I helped them learn about art and culture."

On the night of his party, everything seemed to be going Merkin's way. He had recently been asked to contribute his commentary on bankruptcies for a new edition of Benjamin Graham and David L. Dodd's classic book, *Security Analysis*. The book, which was originally published in 1934 in the middle of the Great Depression, had become a Wall Street bible, the text for generations of "value-style" investors such as Warren Buffett, who made money by picking cheap stocks and betting their price would go up over time.

To commemorate the seventy-fifth anniversary of the book's release, Merkin and other money managers, including Seth Klarman, James Grant, and Howard Marks of Oaktree Capital Management, had been asked to pen essays. Merkin's biography for the book release sounded suitably estimable: "J. Ezra Merkin, managing partner of Gabriel Capital Group in New York City, is one of today's leading investors in corporate bankruptcy and distressed securities. In his essay, 'Blood and Judgment,' Merkin lays out various bankruptcy scenarios using real examples, and analyzes the investment opportunities from a value buyer's perspective."

In the book, Merkin cautioned that "as long as investors remain human, and thus subject to greed, fear, pressure, doubt, and the entire range of human emotions, there will be money to be made by those who steel themselves to overcome emotion. Think of Graham and Dodd as embodying the spirit of Hamlet, Prince of Demark, who declared: "Blest are those/Whose blood and judgment are so well commingled, /that they are not a pipe for Fortune's finger/to sound what stop she please."

The December soiree at Merkin's apartment capped his slow but spectacular elevation into business circles and social leagues that even his father, Hermann, who had been a successful businessman and philanthropist in his own right, never would have dreamed of. The invitation-only event was raising money for the American Friends of the Israel Museum, which often threw fund-raisers in private homes where attendees would donate $10,000 to $25,000 apiece.

Merkin had made it past the credit crisis of 2007–08 intact—at least so far—even though the market was far different now than when he had started out. In 2008, the stock market had lost almost half of its value, wiping out trillions of dollars in assets. Luckily, Merkin's Ariel, Ascot, and Gabriel funds had survived. These hedge funds of funds had been his ticket to the prestigious address where he resided with his wife and their four children.

In fact, it seemed this was the wealth that provided many their tickets to the 740 Park Avenue building. The president of the building,

Charles Stevenson, also ran a hedge fund, Navigator Group. (According to the book *740 Park: The Story of the World's Richest Apartment Building*, Stevenson himself had gained entry to the building only after U.S. ambassador to France, Felix Rohatyn, made phone calls on his behalf to the building's cooperative board.) Other residents included Israel Englander of Millennium, Thomas Strauss of Ramius, and Steve Schwarzman of the Blackstone Group, who had thrown himself a $3 million birthday party the previous year. They were all hedge fund managers or private equity fund managers too.

It was not easy to gain admittance to 740 Park, and sometimes tenants were even forced to leave. In the wake of the financial meltdown, newspapers had been rife with stories of failed bankers and disgraced financiers like Bear Stearns' Jimmy Cayne or Lehman Brothers' Dick Fuld, whose investment firms had both collapsed. Many were likely to be kicked out of famous buildings—740 and 765 Park, 820 Fifth, the River House all made the list—because their fortunes had dried up. "They don't want you going belly up, they don't want you, your fabulous company . . . all of a sudden going facedown, and you have to sell apartments and you can't pay your maintenance," said Edward Lee Cave, a broker to the rich, in an interview with the *New York Observer*.

Merkin, however, had made a favorable impression on the 740 Park Avenue co-op board, which approved him immediately. Board members were so intimidated by Merkin that few of them even bothered to ask any questions about him or his business. Because of his authoritative and professorial bearing—not to mention his plain suit, beard, and reputed scholarship in the Torah—some even assumed he was a rabbi.

In October 2008, Merkin had met with New York University endowment officials in an effort to convince them that the stock market's recent collapse presented a perfect opportunity for them to buy low and that they should plow more money into the hedge funds he had selected for his fund of hedge funds.

The idea of college and university endowments trying to beat the market was not new. David Swensen had done so at Yale, managing the school's endowment money into the top ranks by returns of billions of dollars; Jack Meyer had hired professional managers to oversee Harvard's endowment. Even John Maynard Keynes, the famed economist, served as the investment manager for part of Cambridge University's endowment. During Keynes's fifteen years as endowment manager, from 1928 to 1943, he outperformed the stock market by a substantial margin.

In 2008, more than 10 percent of the assets managed by Merkin belonged to college endowments, including New York University, New York Law School, Tufts University, and Bard College. But that October, NYU turned down Merkin's offer, saying they didn't want to invest more money.

"What about investing with Bernard Madoff?" Merkin had asked the investment committee officers, thinking that, face-to-face, it might be harder for them to say no. But they resisted, saying they wouldn't invest with Madoff because he wasn't the right vehicle for the endowment, according to NYU's ongoing suit against Merkin.

Merkin stayed silent. Unbeknownst to the NYU endowment, Merkin had already handed NYU's money to Madoff.

Ezra Merkin established himself in society as an insider with an aura of both grandeur and secrecy and a tendency to think that he always knew what was best for other people. As the eldest son of Hermann Merkin, a successful Wall Street businessman and shipping magnate, Ezra, born in 1954, had large shoes to fill.

Hermann Merkin was a force of nature and came to overshadow almost every aspect of Ezra's life. Born in Leipzig, Germany, in 1907, Hermann fled the Nazis and took his family to New York in 1940. He served in the U.S. Army; afterward, he and his father, Leib Merkin, formed Merkin & Co., an investment bank and brokerage and member of both the American and New York Stock Exchanges. Hermann served as a trustee of Bar-Ilan University in Israel and Yeshiva University in New York, to which he reportedly donated millions of dollars. He even endowed a chair in Talmud and Jewish philosophy at Yeshiva's seminary.

Founded in 1886, Yeshiva was a classic Modern Orthodox institution that, in the words of its first president, Bernard Revel, was designed for *Torah U'Maddah*: "Torah and secular studies." Yeshiva promoted religiosity and scholarship and, not unlike many liberal Catholic universities, encouraged its students to study both theology as well as more worldly subjects, such as computer science or Victorian literature.

In addition to his donations to universities, Hermann also endowed the Merkin Concert Hall in Manhattan and was founding president of the Modern Orthodox Fifth Avenue Synagogue, in which he served for more than twenty years. His wife, Ursula, shared his communal and philanthropic outreach, as did their six children.

The Fifth Avenue Synagogue was not just a place of worship; it represented the heart of Modern Orthodoxy in America. The Modern Orthodox movement can be traced to the mid-1800s in Germany and Rabbis Azriel Hildesheimer and Samson Raphael Hirsch. As Daphne Merkin, Ezra Merkin's sister and a writer for *The New Yorker* magazine wrote, Hirsch was a theologian and leader who "admired [Friedrich] Schiller almost as much as Maimonides, cautiously embracing modernity while insisting on the obligation to observe Jewish law." She added, "His credo, *Torah im Derech Eretz*—Torah Judaism in harmony with secular culture—was a bow in the direction of both God and Germany."

Hermann Merkin was a shipping magnate, but that was not solely how he amassed his fortune. He hailed from a prominent family of furriers in Leipzig, and when they came to America they'd had some money salted away. Once in America, Hermann built a three-pronged business. One part was managing money inherited from or earned with his father and placing it with other fund managers—a sort of early fund of funds. Another was running Merkin & Co., the banking and brokerage firm he and Lieb had set up to trade in stocks and bonds. The final prong was a key holding in Overseas Shipping Group (OSG).

Hermann was one of the founding backers of OSG's predecessor, Maritime Overseas Corp., which was started in 1948 by Raphael Recanati. The Recanatis were an ancient Jewish family that traced its roots back to Roman times. According to *Hadassah* magazine, the Recanatis would be known as "the Rockefellers of Israel" after some family members emigrated there. Settling in Tel Aviv, the Recanatis established the Israel Discount Bank, which became one of the largest in the country. Under the umbrella of Overseas Shipping Group, Rafael Recanati eventually patched together several smaller tanker charting companies, turning the new organization into an American industry leader. Hermann Merkin acted as a director on OSG's management board and remained a shareholder in the company for decades as it grew to become one of the most well-known tanker owners in the world.

OSG, which went public in 1969, had a penchant for secrecy and favoritism to insiders. A March 1995 *TradeWinds* newsletter profile offered the following on the company: "OSG avoids publicity like the plague." Even though the company was publicly listed, it released only "the bare minimum of required information."

The longtime family owners of OSG, such as Recanati and Merkin, were a favorite target for Wall Street financial analysts who considered their fee arrangement with OSG a ruse to enrich themselves at the expense of shareholders. Between 1972 and 1981, pretax profits at OSG rose from $18 million to $107 million. But a small coterie of families, including the Merkins, at Maritime Overseas Corp., which acted as a private management company within OSG, was heavily compensated just for running the day-to-day operations of chartering vessels. According to OSG filings, executives at Maritime Overseas Corp. paid themselves vessel and voyage "commissions" of $6 million in 1993, $5.7 million in 1992, and $6.3 million in 1991. In 1998, OSG ended its unusual thirty-year management "contract" with Maritime Overseas insiders—a fee relationship that had long been viewed as a conflict of interest for the controlling families.

Today, Ezra Merkin, his siblings, and their children still hold about 37 percent of the shares of OSG in various trusts, which amounts to about 10.3 million shares. Between May 2008 and May 2009, that stake was worth anywhere from $205 million to $825 million, depending on the share price. According to OSG's filings with regulators, Solomon N. Merkin, Ezra's brother, took over their father's position at OSG and has sat on the board of directors since 1989. Sol Merkin appears to have taken over the family's investment banking and financial affairs as well, running Merkin & Co. out of offices in New Jersey. He and his brother Ezra don't appear to have any business ties.

Still, the siblings were expected to keep their wealth understated, and Ezra's younger sister, Daphne, would later say she grew up believing their father sold chairs on Wall Street—not shares. The "Merkin gene for excessive discretion" embraces frugality and disdains visible displays of riches, Daphne wrote in a 1999 *New Yorker* article titled "The Trouble with Growing Up Rich."

Bernie Madoff was a friend of Hermann Merkin's. "Madoff had a long friendship with Ezra's father, and he came highly recommended," said Michael Steinhardt, one of Wall Street's earliest hedge fund managers. Based on a friendship with Ezra Merkin, Steinhardt was also an investor in Ezra Merkin's fund of hedge funds.

Elie Wiesel, the Nobel laureate, Holocaust survivor, and now Madoff victim, attended the Fifth Avenue Synagogue with Hermann Merkin. Through Ezra Merkin, he became an investor with Madoff. In addition to his personal wealth, Wiesel's foundation, the Elie Wiesel Foundation for Humanity, put all of its assets—totaling $15 million—with Merkin, who eventually handed all of it over to Madoff.

After graduating from Harvard Law School and working briefly at a law firm, Ezra Merkin went to work as a financial analyst with Joel Greenblatt in 1985. Greenblatt was a follower of Warren Buffett and Graham and Dodd, deeply schooled in so-called value investing, a school of thought that aims to buy what are believed to be undervalued assets and betting the prices will rise. Greenblatt was also the founder of the New York Securities Auction Corp., a firm that created weekly auctions for thinly traded junk bonds, stocks, and warrants.

Ezra parted company with Joel Greenblatt in 1988 because Greenblatt had no intention of increasing the size of his fund. Merkin took his investors with him and started Gabriel Capital. Ezra's model was that of the fund of hedge funds—a fairly new animal on Wall Street that was becoming increasingly common given the nearly $1 trillion of assets that were being invested in hedge funds.

Funds of hedge funds raise money by attracting investors—but they don't actually invest the money. Funds of hedge funds then funnel the cash to talented managers in exchange for a fee. Merkin had a knack for spotting such talent. By 1992, he was raising money for Stephen Feinberg, whose private equity firm, Cerberus, later bought a controlling interest in Chrysler and GMAC, the big auto lender. By this time Merkin had also begun investing with Bernard Madoff.

After Hermann Merkin died, Ezra took over for his father in many capacities. On the Jewish community circuit, he adopted Hermann's role at the Fifth Avenue Synagogue, and he gave generously to Jewish charities. In 2000, Ezra took over his father's long-standing relationship with Yeshiva University, where Hermann had been a trustee for decades. Ezra also served on the board of the school's Rabbi Isaac

Elchanan Theological Seminary. In 2001, Ezra Merkin and his wife endowed the Merkin Family Chair in Jewish History and Literature at Yeshiva's Bernard Revel Graduate School of Jewish Studies.

Ezra also tried to match his father's business success through his Gabriel group of hedge funds. He also continued his father's penchant for secrecy and mixing social and business connections.

At close range, Ezra Merkin had intimate friends and many admirers. At Fifth Avenue Synagogue, for example, the Merkins "are revered. Ezra is revered. The old guard loved Hermann and they love his son," said one congregant. "He's an upstanding pillar in the community—period. They are a great family, especially Lauren. He shows incredible commitment and knowledge of the interworkings of the service." For example, at each service, before the reading of the Torah, certain congregants are selected to give a prayer between the chapters. Those who are selected have generally experienced a recent major event in their lives—such as a marriage or the birth of a child. Ezra would often help the assistant rabbis choose who would be given the honor of reading the prayers. "He called me up when my daughter was born," the same congregant said. "He takes care of the community by calling up the right people; he's interwoven in the community fabric in this way."

However, Ezra also used his connections at the temple to recruit investors. This was the same technique employed by other Madoff investors such as Michael Bienes and Frank Avellino at Florida churches, Robert Jaffe at Florida and New England country clubs, Arpad Busson at ski resorts, Walter Noel on the private island of Mustique, and Andrés Piedrahita at dinner parties around the world.

"Ezra held a unique place in the Jewish community," said one former derivatives trader who knew the family. "He embodies the ideals of a wise Jewish theologian. He was also incredibly successful, and still married to the same wife. That gives him a seal of approval, and a lot of trust. All the boards and endowments in the Jewish community short-circuited the normal due diligence process. They could hand their money over to someone they broke bread with."

According to an NYU lawsuit, Merkin began placing a portion of his Ariel fund into an account with Madoff around the year 2000. "Ezra knew Madoff through his father as a respectable person," Michael Steinhardt told lawyers for NYU. A New York hedge fund manager himself, Steinhardt estimates he lost $2 million investing with Merkin.

Certain friends and associates of Merkin's believe he was well intentioned in his decision to put charities' money with Madoff. "Perhaps he thought at first he was doing a good thing," the trader added.

By 2001, Merkin was overseeing roughly $2 billion in assets in his Gabriel Group family of hedge funds, which included Gabriel, Ariel, and Ascot. Merkin as well had made investments in Cerberus and others. And he was turning over a larger and larger portion of these assets to Madoff. By 2008, Merkin was overseeing $5 billion in assets and sending almost half—$2.4 billion—to Madoff.

With such a large amount invested, Merkin became one of Madoff's biggest sources of funds. Between 1993 and 2008, Merkin reaped a staggering $470 million in fees just from the money he sent to Madoff. There is no doubt that Merkin contributed mightily to perpetuating Madoff's Ponzi scheme, which was growing to $65 billion.

By this point, Madoff and Merkin sat on the board of Yeshiva University together, and Merkin made up to $35 million a year just from that relationship with Yeshiva alone.

During this time, however, Merkin grew increasingly imperious. In 2000, he was brusque with executives of a New York charity who met with him to discuss a potential investment. Laura Goldman, who now runs the money management firm LSG Capital in Tel Aviv, was present at the meeting as an adviser for the charity. In an interview with Bloomberg, she said that, after arriving more than an hour late to the meeting, Merkin became impatient when asked for details. The charity decided against giving him funds.

"Merkin had sway over people like crazy," Goldman said. "They were grown men and they barely got out of the meeting without signing over their lives. He's very arrogant, and when you ask questions, he makes it like, 'Why are you asking me a question?'"

Although she was unaware of Merkin's ties to Madoff at the time, Goldman, a twenty-year veteran of Wall Street, had met Madoff in the 1990s when they were both seeking potential investors in Palm Beach. She later published an online account in which she described the encounter.

After speaking with Madoff and getting no answers about his fund's strategy, she withdrew a small investment that she had made earlier with him and encouraged others in Palm Beach to do the same. She was promptly accused of being anti-Semitic by Palm Beach residents and other believers in Madoff. "And I live in Israel!" she noted.

Ezra Merkin had developed a close relationship with the Wall Street legend Leon Levy, who was known for being a savvy and innovative deal maker. Through Levy's mentorship, Merkin earned a reputation for being among "the wisest men on Wall Street." This was high praise coming from Levy, who was known as a kingmaker on Wall Street. He had trained many men and women in trading and asset management who then went on to have illustrious investing careers themselves— including hedge fund operators Michael Steinhardt of Steinhardt Partners, Bruce Kovner of Caxton Associates, Jeff Gendell of Tontine Associates, and John Paulson of Paulson & Co., among others. Levy was born in 1925, in Manhattan. His father, Jerome, a dry-goods merchant, considered himself an amateur economist and was an acutely successful investor. According to Leon's obituary in the *New York Times*, Jerome took credit for predicting the stock market crash of 1929 and sold much of his portfolio in stocks before the crash.

Leon's key partner, with whom he would work for nearly fifty years, was Jack Nash. Levy met Nash in 1951 when they both joined Oppenheimer & Co. Together, they built the brokerage house into a firm that was among the earliest money managers for institutions and leveraged buyouts. In 1982, Nash and Levy sold Oppenheimer for $163 million and opened a hedge fund, Odyssey Partners, which averaged an annual return of 27.7 percent before fees, earning it among the best long-term records in the investment business. The two men closed Odyssey, which grew to be worth $3 billion, in 1997 and returned all the capital to investors. "Basically, we think that the size of the firm has become too big relative to our ability to invest," Nash told the *Wall Street Journal*.

A student of Levy's at City College, Roger Hertog, also worked for him at Oppenheimer. Hertog explained that, although the firm was small, it was still a player in the field of leveraged buyouts, or when a financial sponsor borrows money in order to buy a share of equity in a company. According to Hertog, Levy and Nash "had a very good record and were thoughtful people."

Through Odyssey, Levy and Nash became pioneers in the hedge fund industry—and their blessing was worth its weight in gold. John Paulson, who made billions of dollars in 2008 by betting on the U.S. housing collapse and mortgage-backed securities crisis, said Levy structured complex long-term transactions while Nash focused on short-term trading. "Jack was the consummate New York trader. He was smart, fast, and fair. Leon was a master of the hundred-to-one long shot, and Jack was ground to the earth."

Levy and Ezra Merkin apparently kept in close touch and shared ideas, although people who worked with Merkin at his Gabriel and Ariel funds said that, in fact, Merkin was likely passing on the ideas from his managers and Wall Street friends—Joel Greenblatt, Steve Feinberg of Cerberus, and Victor Teicher.

Like Levy and Nash, Merkin and his money managers like Teicher had very different roles. Merkin was a consummate salesman. Compared with some of the other funds of hedge funds investing with Bernie Madoff, Merkin was a scholar. But those who knew him say that was part of the sales pitch.

"Walter Noel at least didn't pretend he was anything else other than a salesman," said one former employee of Merkin's. "Ezra held himself out as a wise man, all-knowing, writing the preface to the Graham and Dodd book. He was just smarter at selling himself."

In 1988, Merkin put Victor Teicher in charge of a substantial portion of the money he raised for Gabriel Capital. Merkin kept 20 percent of the profits from these funds and gave Teicher half of that. Ezra was not managing most of the funds; he spent the majority of his time raising money for Gabriel and its offshore fund, Ariel. Teicher had his own firm, Ithaca Partners, and separate from that he also ran money for Merkin. After a prison term, Teicher then came back as a consultant for Merkin. He couldn't work on staff because he was a convicted felon.

At this point, Merkin's role at his hedge fund group was clearly defined—he was the moneyman. "Wall Street is just twenty guys selling each other stuff, while some *schwartzer* in the basement does all the work," Merkin would joke privately. Publicly, however, Merkin acted like a Wall Street sage.

"Even Leon Levy thought Ezra was brilliant—he had everyone sold. He wasn't a scholar, or a genius," Teicher recalled. "That said, he didn't put on airs. He was a salesman, nothing more. He knew who he was."

In reality, by the 1990s Merkin's money managers were the idea men, the ones making most of the primary investment decisions for Merkin's hedge funds.

Teicher was talented, but his name became controversial. In 1991, the SEC filed suit against him, alleging he had purchased various stocks in the 1980s with inside information from three sources: a law firm (Paul, Weiss, Rifkind, Wharton & Garrison), an investment banking firm (Drexel Burnham & Lambert, which was forced into bankruptcy in 1990 after becoming involved in illegal activities in the junk bond market), and a broker-dealer (Marcus Schloss & Co.). All three were members of the so-called Yuppie Five group of insider traders.

Teicher was convicted in 1992 and sentenced the following year. He went to prison in 1994 and continued to help manage money under the Gabriel umbrella while serving his sentence. After he had served his time in a New Jersey jail, Teicher returned to working for Merkin on a consultant basis, from 1998 until 2000, earning a handsome $1 million per month.

Merkin and Teicher had ties that went back generations. Their grandfathers had known each other in Leipzig, Germany, when the Merkins were a furrier family and the Teichers ran a printing business.

During Teicher's absence, Merkin hired Nathan Leight to run the portfolio's day-to-day operations, but his performance was bumpy. In 1998, Teicher returned to running the portfolio. Teicher's name wasn't on the door anymore, but he didn't particularly care. He just wanted to run money—which is what he did best. After college, Teicher had started out selling insurance but was such a poor salesman that he once advised a potential customer, a friend of his mother's, that rather than invest the premiums in a policy, he was probably better off putting it in the bank. "He'd make more money," said Teicher, a ringer for a young Rutger Hauer, with glasses and wide-wale corduroy pants. "I could not sell. I was a terrible salesman."

Teicher went on to work at Salomon Brothers in the municipal finance division alongside John Meriwether, later infamous for his billion-dollar fund fiasco Long-Term Capital Management. Teicher then worked in the government bond department. He then moved to Junction Partners, an affiliate of Odyssey Partners. Located in the same pink granite building across from New York City's Museum of Modern Art, Teicher worked thirty feet away from Jack Nash and Leon Levy's operation. He came to know both men and spoke to Levy about bankruptcy investing. Teicher started Ithaca Partners in 1985 and joined forces with Merkin in 1988, meaning Merkin hired Teicher to manage money.

Like Levy and Nash, Merkin and Teicher worked better together than apart. The two men needed each other. Merkin needed Teicher's ideas, both to make money and to spin the ideas as his own in marketing pitches for Gabriel, and Teicher needed a salesman to raise assets to run. In 1988 they opened the Gabriel firm together and worked until Teicher went to prison in 1994. After serving his sentence, in September 1998, Teicher returned to Gabriel to manage the firm again until 2000. Together, they never had a losing year and earned roughly 22 percent a year after fees.

Socially, however, Merkin hid his relationship with Teicher. Ezra and Lauren Merkin didn't invite Teicher and his wife to their oldest son's bar mitzvah, which deeply hurt Teicher's wife. At the next Merkin son's bar mitzvah, the Teichers were invited but didn't sit at the head table, which was occupied by Merkin, Michael Steinhardt, and Bernard Madoff.

"I was lucky to meet Ezra. I wouldn't have made it without him," Teicher said. "I was lucky to hook up with him. He was a world-class salesman, he got the dough, and although there's a tendency toward elitism—that the people who are smartest are the most important thing—that's just silly. At the end, you get paid for executing, for getting things done."

Steven Feinberg was another idea man whom Merkin mined for brilliant investments. As he did with Teicher, Merkin farmed out money to Feinberg's Cerberus fund and started seeding other funds as well.

Feinberg named Cerberus after the three-headed dog guarding the gates of hell in Greek mythology. Feinberg identified with the idea that one of the dog's heads was always on watch—and equated it with how his firm would guard its clients' investments around the clock, Merkin told *BusinessWeek* magazine. As managing partner of Gabriel Capital Group, Merkin became Feinberg's partner in a number of funds and deals. Feinberg "thought he would be able to move from passively investing in securities to building a business and actively managing companies," Merkin said of Feinberg.

Hedge funds like Stevie Cohen's SAC, Ed Lampert's ESL Investments, and Ken Griffin's Citadel were beginning to make headlines by investing in American icons of industry—and Cerberus was among their ranks. In late 2005, *Business Week* estimated that Cerberus controlled companies with combined annual sales of $30 billion, more than 106,000 employees, and a bigger payroll than ExxonMobil Corp. Its holdings included 226 Burger King restaurants, the National and Alamo car rental chains, building products maker Formica Corp., and the old Warner Hollywood Studios.

The Gabriel-Cerberus duo also did deals together. In 2005, they outbid competitors in an auction to buy a 9.99 percent stake in Bank Leumi from the government of Israel. Its offer of $3.70 per share, or $532 million in total, was 16 percent above the market price.

They had gone up against serious competitor bidders like Frank Lowy, the Australian retail tycoon, and Lev Leviev, a Russian oligarch and investor in construction, rental property, hotels, energy, and diamonds. Even Israel's state finance minister, Ehud Olmert, welcomed the deal as a vote of confidence in Israel's economy. "This is good news for the state of Israel. It is good news for the citizens of Israel," he told the Associated Press in Jerusalem. "Something is happening in Israel's market, in Israel's economy."

The Bank Leumi deal was a sign that Merkin had arrived. He was playing in the big leagues, even if it was just riding on the coattails of Feinberg. "Ezra was basically an adjunct of Cerberus. They shared the same offices, they used Ezra Merkin on the board of GMAC [a key holding of Cerberus]," said one investor who came to know Merkin well over the years. "He was basically their satellite."

It was through this deal for Bank Leumi that Merkin met Mort Zuckerman, the owner and publisher of the *New York Daily News* and *U.S. News & World Report*, and the cofounder of Boston Properties, a public real estate investment trust. For years Zuckerman mediated between Israelis and U.S. administration officials. He had been part of a rival bidding group for Bank Leumi, and came away impressed with Merkin's negotiating skills.

In the spring of 2006, Zuckerman offered to back the Cerberus-Gabriel bid for Bank Leumi with $50 million of his own money if they gained control of the bank. In the meantime, according to a lawsuit Zuckerman filed after Madoff's arrest, Merkin continued to lobby Zuckerman to become an investor in Gabriel, and finally, in July 2006, Zuckerman relented.

The two men met over the course of several days to discuss Gabriel, Ariel, and Ascot, another Merkin fund. Zuckerman now says that Merkin described Ascot as a "diversified" fund of hedge funds, while Gabriel invested in distressed companies. Zuckerman had a charitable remainder trust that had already endowed $100 million for research at Memorial Sloan-Kettering Cancer Center in New York, and it was a portion of this trust that he would be investing with Merkin. Zuckerman didn't want to take any unnecessary risks.

"The first rule of managing money is, don't lose it," Teicher said. So Merkin advised Zuckerman that Ascot was the more conservative of the two hedge funds; Zuckerman put $25 million of the trust's money in Ascot and $15 million of his own personal money in Gabriel. Merkin handed all of this money over to his increasingly favorite money manager: Bernie Madoff.

By 2007, Zuckerman had opened up the kimono and allowed Merkin to see his entire portfolio of investments. Meanwhile, Merkin cultivated his reputation for being one of the smartest men on Wall Street. He was invited to join investment committees of prestigious national institutions, including that of Major League Baseball (MLB).

Peter Stamos, who once served as chief economist and chief of staff for former senator and presidential candidate Bill Bradley, introduced Merkin to the MLB. Stamos had founded Sterling Stamos, which manages about $4 billion in assets, in 2002, with the backing of Fred Wilpon, co-owner with Saul Katz of the New York Mets. Stamos came to know Merkin through Fred Wilpon and invited Merkin to sit on the investment committee for Major League Baseball.

The MLB investment committee was peopled with luminaries, including John Powers, who oversaw the Stanford University endowment; Abby Joseph Cohen, a Goldman Sachs investment strategist; and Nobel Prize winner Myron Scholes.

One afternoon, at a baseball game attended by several committee members, Ezra Merkin was discussing how he had decided to allocate money to the different money managers. "We were talking about diversification and so forth. Ezra said, 'Why would you want to diversify away from your best manager?' At the time it didn't seem important," recalled one board member. "But in hindsight it definitely was."

Merkin was in the process of building up his commitment to Madoff to 30 percent of all the assets in Gabriel and all of Ascot. Fortunately,

Major League Baseball's investment committee was barred from giving
money to current board members, so the pensions of American baseball
employees were spared from investing with Ezra Merkin by dint of the
fact that he was sitting on its committee.

"My gut reaction is that Ezra Merkin got rich, he was in love with
his role as a sort of philanthropic godfather, and he got busy and he got
careless," the committee member said. "He started to believe his own
bullshit." As for putting so much money with Madoff, he said, "It was
shameless and expedient, lazy and dishonest. It was easier [for Merkin]
to not dig, to just ship Madoff all the money than to engage in the hard
work he purported to do. He was guilty of trusting Madoff. He's a
smart guy, no question. Everybody else—the Palm Beach crew, the individual investors—they weren't sophisticated, they were socialites, not
investors. But Ezra? He's the one person who I thought afterward, 'Oh,
my god, I can't believe he was involved.'"

Before they lost a reported $300 million to Madoff, the Wilpons
were also stung by another hedge fund, in 2005. Sterling Stamos had
been an investor in Bayou Fund, another hedge fund Ponzi scheme similar to Madoff's. Bayou and Madoff shared some eerie similarities, both
using backwater accounting firms. While Madoff used the three-person
accounting firm Friehling & Horowitz, Bayou invented a fictional accounting firm. Both Bayou and Madoff used their own brokerage firms
to execute trades.

Jack Nash first met Madoff in 1991 and made a small investment into
his hedge fund. About a year later, Nash asked his son, Joshua, to review
the trading tickets and account statements, many inches thick, which
Madoff mailed each month. Joshua took a look. Neither he nor his father, despite their combined decades of experience on Wall Street, could
figure out how Madoff was making money. According to a lawsuit filed
against Merkin, they subsequently scheduled a visit with Madoff at his
offices, during which Madoff gave vague responses to questions about
his money management strategy. Troubled by this, Jack Nash pulled his
money out of Madoff, despite the fact that he had made an 18 percent
profit in less than two years.

Afterward, Nash warned Merkin that something wasn't right with

Madoff's returns. Later, Nash learned that Madoff purportedly held all his assets in Treasury bills at the end of each quarter, which Nash viewed as an important warning sign. Nash could see no reason for exiting the market and buying Treasury bills at every quarter end other than to reduce transparency in the strategy. Doing so meant Madoff would miss many trading opportunities stretched over days and weeks covering the end of a calendar quarter. Why would Madoff pass up the possibility of a quick profit?

Teicher also warned Merkin that "Madoff's returns smelled." He told Merkin that "the Madoff returns were not probable" and that trading statements had been "altered," according to his deposition by Beth Kaswan, a lawyer for New York University's endowment.

Having received the warnings, Merkin contacted Madoff. "Is it true?" Merkin asked. Madoff reassured him there was nothing to the rumors, and Merkin kept all his clients' money with Madoff. He did no other background checks on his own, according to statements in NYU's lawsuit against Merkin.

Nash and his son continued to warn Merkin numerous times about Madoff. Each time, Merkin would express confidence in Madoff.

Jack Nash asked Merkin, "Why does Madoff used an obscure auditor if that was the case?" Indeed, Madoff's auditor, Friehling & Horowitz, had Madoff as their only client.

Joshua Nash also bumped into Merkin on several occasions since they both served on the boards of several nonprofit organizations together. With each encounter, Joshua Nash would raise concerns about Madoff, and Merkin would point out that other nonprofits were making consistent 12 percent or more in annual returns with Madoff. Normally, Merkin would cut Joshua Nash off by saying he had already heard the same objections from his father.

Despite their objections to Madoff, Merkin never told the Nashes that a substantial portion of Gabriel's fund assets were invested with Madoff—as much as 25 percent by 2008.

In 2001, two news articles questioning Madoff's returns were published—one in *Barron's* and the other in a hedge fund newsletter called MARHedge. Gabriel's chief counsel e-mailed them both to Merkin, who kept them in his files.

These articles, in addition to Jack Nash's warnings, should've been enough to convince Merkin that something wasn't right about Madoff. But Merkin didn't listen. Indeed, by 2008, 100 percent of Ascot and 25 percent of Gabriel assets were parked with Madoff.

Between 1995 and 2008, Merkin earned $471 million in fees from the money he'd allocated to Madoff. These included fees based on false profits at Madoff's fund. From 1989 to 2007, Merkin's fees from Gabriel fund alone totaled $277 million.

In April 2009, New York attorney general Andrew Cuomo charged Merkin with civil fraud against state charities, alleging that Merkin had simply steered $2.4 billion to Madoff without performing adequate due diligence. Ascot's assets amounted to $1.8 billion of that total.

Zuckerman sued Merkin also, saying that in the early morning hours after Madoff's arrest, he received two faxes from Merkin. The first revealed that "substantially all" of Ascot's assets were invested with Madoff, along with about one-third of Gabriel's assets. All of that money was lost.

This was the first time, Zuckerman claims, he had heard Madoff's name connected with Merkin's funds. He was also shocked to find out that Ascot was not a diversified fund but had every single dollar invested exclusively with Madoff. After learning the truth, an incensed Zuckerman confronted Merkin, demanding to know how he failed to reveal that Ascot was turning over all its assets to Bernard Madoff.

"Diversification is the fundamental rule of conservative investing. How could you do this?" Zuckerman demanded.

Merkin didn't deny anything. He simply said: "It may have been connected to something I said several years earlier."

"That's preposterous," Zuckerman replied, according to a copy of his personal lawsuit against Merkin. Zuckerman too had received warnings about Madoff's unbelievable returns. One financial adviser who consults with wealthy families recounted a conversation he had personally with Zuckerman prior to Madoff's arrest. "I told him there was no way Madoff was making those returns without cheating, maybe even front-running." Zuckerman shrugged off the warning as well, but this conversation implies Zuckerman knew Merkin had invested some of his funds in Madoff (Zuckerman declined to be interviewed.)

Billionaires weren't the only casualties of Merkin's decisions. There were regular people as well. Daniel Goldenson, a publisher and conservationist from Maine, put his retirement savings in the Ascot Fund in 2001, on the advice of Launny Steffens, the former vice chairman of Merrill Lynch. All of Goldenson's investments in the fund came from Merrill Lynch or Smith Barney and were wired from Goldenson's regular account and IRA accounts to Ascot.

"All his money, we learned this week, went out the back door to Mr. Madoff," Goldenson wrote in a letter to U.S. District Judge Louis Stanton after Madoff's arrest.

Other investors began e-mailing Merkin the morning after Madoff's arrest.

> Dear Ezra,
>
> Over the years my family . . . developed a warm relationship with you and we learned to respect your insightful advice.
>
> In fact, our trust in you was so great that our family trust's largest holding in any single fund manager was with you and I personally invested my own funds in you. . . . As you can imagine the stories that are circulating . . . are grotesque with people we know in common claiming that you are at best a charlatan and at worst that you were totally in sync with Madoff.

On January 7, 2009, after meeting with Merkin, the same investor proffered a theory. What had Merkin truly done by parking billions of dollars in Madoff's phony hedge fund?

> You were nothing more than a glorified mailbox.

Teicher, for his part, colorfully described how he warned Merkin several times in the early 1990s that Madoff's consistently high profits were impossible to repeat year after year. The profits "were inconsistent with what could possibly take place in reality," he said. Teicher added that Merkin's former accountant, Andrew Gordon, also said that Madoff's investment scheme "looked like a fraud to him," according to NYU's lawsuit against Merkin.

On December 11, 2008, the night Madoff was arrested, Teicher wrote to Merkin in a late-night e-mail:

> The Madoff news is hilarious; hope you negotiate out of this mess as well as possible; I'm yours to help in any way I can; unfortunately, you've paid a big price for a lesson on the cost of being greedy.

Later Teicher wrote again to Merkin:

> I guess you did such a good job in fooling a lot of people that you ultimately fooled yourself.

Chapter Twelve

Throughout 2008, in the midst of the worst American economic crisis since the Great Depression, the Madoff family spent tens of millions of dollars on high-priced items such as luxury cars, apartments, private jet rentals, and investments in other funds.

Meanwhile, Madoff investors were tallying up how lucky they were to have invested with Bernie while the rest of the world was losing its shirt. Roughly one-third of the members of the Palm Beach Country Club had invested with Madoff—for a total of $1 billion—by 2008. Fairfield Greenwich had invested $7.5 billion; Sonja Kohn's Bank Medici upward of $3.5 billion; Sandra Manzke more than $6 billion through her Maxam, Kingate, and Tremont funds.

But in the year leading up to Madoff's confession, investors started to panic and withdrew $12 billion out of accounts at the firm. About $6 billion was taken out in just the three months before the financier was arrested in December. Fairfield allegedly withdrew $1 billion in November alone. Jeffry Picower had withdrawn $5.1 billion over the years. Harley, the fund vehicle for Charles Fix's family, withdrew $1 billion. In November 2008, just one month before Madoff's arrest, Ezra Merkin took out $2 billion, Stanley Chais $1 billion, and Sandra Manzke $300 million.

Had the stock market in the United States not collapsed, Madoff's scam would probably have continued. But by the autumn of 2008, the shaky economy was beginning to take its toll, investors were clamoring for money out of their last safe haven, and Madoff needed to oblige them to keep the scam going. He needed cash fast.

Madoff and his key lieutenant, Frank DiPascali, were meeting around the clock in person or on the telephone with key feeder fund chiefs such as Walter Noel and Jeffrey Tucker, Sonja Kohn, and Ezra Merkin.

In early December, Madoff hit up his trusted investors Robert Jaffe and Carl Shapiro, to try and stop the bleeding. Jaffe and Shapiro agreed to make additional investments. Bernie would try to keep the big money flowing in and use it to pay off some of his major clients. Shapiro wired $250 million to an abnormally impatient Bernie, who repeatedly called asking whether the wire had been sent.

By the end, the Shapiros, one of Madoff's earliest and most important investors, had $545 million with Madoff.

Bernie was facing a staggering amount of redemptions as more and more people cashed out. All of a sudden, everyone was pulling out their retirement nest eggs, their college funds, their money for their grandparents' assisted living, their vacation savings funds. They needed the money now because all their other investments were losing big.

The "sticky money" from individuals, from old friends and referrals on whom Madoff had relied for decades—the money that never left him—was now leaving. Even the big players were panicking. Investors wanted $7 billion of their money back from Madoff before the year's end. A worldwide panic had erupted.

In the past, Madoff had never had a problem giving money back—usually in thirty days or even less—to those who redeemed. The money had always been there because he had never had a problem getting more. But this was the first time everyone had come rushing into his office demanding money back at the same time. Now the redemptions were bigger than he'd ever experienced.

The global credit crisis and subsequent collapse in the U.S. stock market spelled the end for Madoff. Even he, with his manipulations and his ability to get practically anyone to trust him, couldn't escape the wave of fear that swept through the United States and the world. Even Bernie Madoff couldn't make people feel that their money was safe.

The crisis that had started with a crash in asset values in the U.S. housing market infected just about anything and everything—mortgage bonds, equity prices, U.S. Treasury bonds, and emerging markets. For years, U.S. retail banks and mortgage originators such as Countrywide had been making so-called subprime mortgage loans to people who could not afford to pay them back. The banks then repackaged and re-sold these loans to investors like hedge funds, insurance companies, and investment banks. Eventually, when U.S. homeowners began to default, the banks and other investors around the world were holding billions of dollars in bad loans. This led to a ripple effect throughout capital markets as once-major investment firms who held these mortgage-backed securities—beginning with Bear Stearns in March and Lehman Brothers shortly afterward—collapsed. The United States had already slipped into a recession, and suddenly all the rosy estimates for housing prices had evaporated. As the economist John Kenneth Galbraith observed of many great U.S. market crashes and ensuing economic slowdowns, "Recessions catch what the auditors miss."

The Madoff magic had run out. The family was "like the Sopranos, with Bernie at the center and the fund-raisers his consiglieres," said Herb Blank of Rapid Ratings, an independent ratings agency on Wall Street. "Bernie wound up with a scheme that worked, but he let it get too far, which is the weakness of most men. Had the stock market not crashed," he added, "Madoff might never have been revealed."

The staff at Bernard L. Madoff Investment Securities was surprised when, for the first time, Madoff decided to throw the office holiday party at Rosa Mexicana restaurant a week earlier than usual. This was December 10, 2008. Madoff was normally the life of the party, but this year he was low key, while Ruth played the role of upbeat holiday hostess. Bernard's secretary, Eleanor Squillari, would later report that he seemed not to have a care in the world.

Earlier that same day, Bernard, his sons, and his brother had left the office early, Squillari told *Vanity Fair*. Bernard had called them into his office and, Squillari believes, confessed what was going on. The four Madoffs left, and Bernie never came back to the office. Neither Andrew nor Mark went to the holiday party.

Squillari noticed that Madoff left his appointment book carefully positioned on his desk, even though he never left the office without it. FBI investigators found the book the next day, with unusual and prominent notes such as "remember to pay employees" written inside.

Squillari believes all the odd actions point to a meticulous plan by Madoff to orchestrate his arrest.

A few hours before the holiday party, Ruth came into the Lipstick Building offices acting squirrelly. She was withdrawing $10 million from a Cohmad brokerage firm account in her name. It had been her second withdrawal in less than three weeks. According to a complaint filed by state regulators in Massachusetts, she had already withdrawn the first slug of cash, totaling $5.5 million, in November.

In the 1990s, Madoff had begun transferring assets into his wife's name. Among them were the $11 million Palm Beach mansion and the $1 million home in Cap d'Antibes. The corporate entity that owned one of their yachts *The Bull*, which was valued at $7 million, was also registered in Ruth's name. The couple's house in Montauk, Long Island, was jointly purchased in 1979. Their Upper East Side apartment, which she and Bernie had purchased in 1984, was also in her name. All told, about $55 million worth of assets had been put in Ruth's name by her husband. In the weeks after his confession, while Bernie was under house arrest in his sumptuous penthouse apartment, he and Ruth also mailed millions of dollars' worth of watches and jewelry to their sons and other relatives.

Months later, Ruth Madoff would also claim that $17 million in cash and $45 million in municipal bonds held in an outside bank account was not part of the fraud but rather money she had inherited.

Lev Dassin, the acting U.S. attorney for the Southern District of New York and the lead prosecutor in the Madoff case, says Ruth's claim that all those assets belong to her is false. Dassin directed his office to seize Ruth's assets, including the three boats registered to her.

Ruth's mother, Sara Alpern, died in 1996, leaving behind just $2 million in three trusts. The money was left to Sara's husband, Sol, and their daughters Joan and Ruth each inherited just over $1 million after Sol's death, according to probate court records. That's a far cry from the $65 million she claimed are assets she inherited.

The night of the Madoff office holiday party, Madoff did not regale employees with praise like he usually would at such a festive year-end occasion. After all, it was bonus season, and everyone who worked for him had done well financially. On that night, according to William Nasi, who worked at the brokerage firm, Bernie was acting in an unusually distant manner, but Ruth was in fine shape, chatty and upbeat.

"Little did we know that just hours after the party ended the FBI would be knocking on the door of their apartment," Nasi told papers in the aftermath of Madoff's arrest.

Although Bernie Madoff admitted to the $65 billion Ponzi scheme, this was not the real figure. That $65 billion included phantom gains Madoff had been booking in client accounts over many years. Much of these billions in profits never existed at all, except on paper.

Assuming investors were making 10 percent annually over the life of Madoff's fraud, it's possible the amount of money investors placed in the Ponzi scheme equaled something much less—perhaps $10 to $20 billion, according to analysts who have done the calculations. The money investors put in—versus the amount Madoff paid out to third parties to keep the fraud going—depends on when the fraud started.

If Madoff began his fraud way back, perhaps at the start of the firm in 1960 or 1970, when his brother joined, then Madoff investors likely paid in around $4 billion, while Madoff himself paid out third-party fund-raisers about $16 billion to keep the cash flowing and the Ponzi scheme going.

If, however, the fraud began more recently—say, just a decade ago—then more of investors' money funded the Ponzi scheme, likely around $30 billion, while he paid outside fund-raisers around $15 billion.

But for the young people left with no college fund, the retirees all over the world forced to return to work now that their retirement savings had vanished, the elderly with no funds to take care of them into old age, none of this matters. The pain of losing everything is not a phantom. It drove Madoff's casualties to reevaluate their futures.

Madoff personified all that was false, all that appeared to be upside down in the world. Homes weren't worth what was once thought, stock prices stopped going up, all assets seemed to collapse in value at the same time. In the midst of the financial crisis, the Madoff scandal gave Americans—and people all over the world—just one more reason not to trust Wall Street or the government that was supposed to keep it in check.

News outlets raged against Madoff. There is "a general air of collapse in America right now, of the sense that our institutions are not and no longer can be trusted," Peggy Noonan wrote in the *New York Post*, dubbing it "the age of the empty suit."

Those who we trusted, who "were supposed to be watching things, making the whole edifice run, keeping it up and operating, just somehow weren't there." For if Uncle Bernie couldn't be trusted, who could? The government had overlooked him, just as it overlooked the subprime mortgages and the mountains of derivatives and other complex debts that would destroy America's oldest investment banks.

Three months after his confession and arrest, Madoff pled guilty to his crime but claimed no one else was responsible. He had done it all by himself, he claimed.

At his own guilty plea hearing, on his last day as a free man, Madoff even concocted a tale of his crimes, saying the fraud began only in 1993. It was an obvious effort to shield his family members, especially Peter and Ruth, who were with him from the beginning (Ruth had helped keep the books for the business since its beginning in 1960, and Peter joined the brokerage full-time in 1970). Madoff refused to cooperate with prosecutors, other than to admit to the eleven criminal counts. He did not cut a deal with the government to give details about the crimes in exchange for leniency. He would go down his way—alone and on his terms.

After Madoff's statement in court, acting U.S. Attorney Lev Dassin stood up in front of the judge, visibly frustrated. Madoff's guilty plea was only "one step in an ongoing investigation," he said. And the prosecutors weren't going to stop with him. "Despite speculation to the contrary," Dassin snapped, "there is no agreement whatsoever, public or otherwise, between the government and Mr. Madoff about his plea, his sentence, or the filing of additional charges against him or anyone else." The government's attorneys were furious: they wanted to implicate family members, or at least some other associates, but Madoff had other ideas.

Editorialists and commentators the world over screamed that Madoff was getting off easily. Madoff was "emotionless. Petulant. Bitter. And pathetic. And he proved, beyond doubt, that he's learned absolutely nothing," making "nothing but excuses for his pathological behavior," Andrea Peyser of the *New York Post* raged in her column the day after Madoff pleaded guilty. The *Post*'s editorial that day agreed that the case "cannot be closed until the enablers—unwitting or otherwise—have been brought to account, too."

The *New York Daily News* opined that even if he gets a life sentence, Madoff is already "seventy years old and will surely soon begin to slip into natural decline." Ultimately, he'll only serve about "two lousy, damn days" for each life he ruined and each charity he crippled. Columnist Michael Daly noted Madoff's lack of remorse "was accompanied by an assertive little nod of the head, and his voice carried no despair, no resignation, no obvious regret."

That day, March 12, 2009, Madoff knew he was headed to prison—he wasn't wearing his wedding band. After the handcuffs clicked around his wrists, Madoff was led to the Metropolitan Correctional Center, which houses vicious criminals and terrorists. There Uncle Bernie Madoff assumed a new nickname: prisoner number 61727-054.

Willard Foxton, whose father killed himself after losing his life savings to Madoff, wrote there was no way "the punishment for his serious fraud is stiff enough—even if Bernie gets the full 150-year sentence," he would end up in a federal resort-style prison. Madoff even consulted Martha Stewart's jail counselor, who had helped her to cut the best deal on which location to serve out her insider trading prison sentence a few years prior.

At the very end, some of Madoff's victims felt that he had cheated them not only out of their money but also out of a sense that justice could have been served.

Now that Bernie Madoff is behind bars, it is up to Irving Picard to sort through the debris and settle claims. Picard, a brilliant, patrician lawyer who is well regarded among his colleagues, was appointed the trustee of Madoff's assets in the wake of his arrest. Picard has the bearing of an overly tall basketball player, usually stooped, sometimes bearing wire-rim glasses and a slight imperiousness. He speaks with the authority of Dostoyevsky's Grand Inquisitor.

As is to be expected in such a highly charged, emotional situation, Picard has earned the contempt of many Madoff victims who want more of their money back, and faster. Picard and his legal team are also widely feared by the biggest beneficiaries of Madoff's pyramid scam, including Jeffry Picower, Stanley Chais, Robert Jaffe, Sonja Kohn, and Sandra Manzke.

Picard and his team have argued that some of Madoff's investors were more special than others. Picower, for example, who has a history as a tax cheat, and Stanley Chais, another feeder into Madoff, were allegedly ordering up not only fake gains, but fake losses. They could record those phony trades on their tax returns and pay little or no taxes on the money they made from Madoff or other investments. Picard also alleged that Picower and others actually asked Madoff to concoct phantom trades that were then backdated in an effort to avoid paying taxes. Some trades were even marked with dates earlier than when some of these accounts had been opened.

In the case of Picower and some other large Madoff investors, Picard believes they were aware that Madoff was lying *for* them—they just may not have believed he would then lie *to* them.

One of Picard's biggest antagonists among Madoff's more humble victims is a plucky divorcée named Ronnie Sue Ambrosino, who, at the time of Madoff's arrest, was living with her second husband in an RV in Arizona. Dominic and Ronnie Sue met and began their lives together late in life, after she had divorced Larry Leif, her first husband. Ambrosino had become invested with Madoff after Leif, a Palm Beach businessman, had left her a $1.6 million investment in the fund as part of their divorce settlement.

Six months after Madoff's confession, Ambrosino gathered together hundreds, if not thousands, of Madoff's fourteen thousand victims into a support group. She started the Madoff Victims Coalition group online and e-mailed different casualties of Madoff. She'd had her chance in court in March to speak at Madoff's hearing, but there was no trial because Madoff pleaded guilty and waived that right.

By April 2009, after making the rounds of television shows and congressional offices, Ambrosino and her husband, Dominic, were back in Arizona. They barely had enough money to fill up the RV's tank with gas, and now it was time to file tax returns. Her biggest disagreement with the government, in fact, was the taxes she had paid for years on the fake returns she was supposed to be receiving from Madoff's fund. The IRS had collected hundreds of millions of dollars from Madoff investors over decades on these false profits.

Worse still, Picard had determined that investors could not use the last statement Madoff had sent out to determine what they were owed. That allowed Madoff to be the decider of who won and lost, the trustee argued, of who was robbed and who had taken their money out of the Ponzi scheme early enough to get it all back—and perhaps had taken out even more.

Ambrosino didn't buy that line of reasoning. Neither did Dominic, who before retiring had invested his pension with Madoff, which he'd saved up working as a Rikers Island prison guard.

Ambrosino argued that she was entitled to the figure stipulated on her November 30, 2008, statement. Picard's line of reasoning was "utter nonsense," she said. The Securities Investor Protection Corp., Picard's agency, "has never before interpreted the statute in this way." Under SIPC's traditional interpretation, brokerage customers like Madoff investors were due back the amount of money from their last statement, which in Madoff's case was November 2008. Instead, SIPC wasn't using that as the cost basis for each victim's account.

"What SIPC and Picard are really saying is that to use the customer balance would be to allow Congress to determine how much investors get paid. SIPC does not want to follow the law because this would cost SIPC money and SIPC is only interested in saving itself money and covering up its own failure to properly assess its members for a sufficient amount to cover any potential liability," she wrote in her first manifesto on behalf of Madoff investors.

Some of Madoff's favorite billionaire investors, like Jeffry Picower and Stanley Chais, should have been savvy enough to have suspected it. But not the little people. Ambrosino pointed out that thousands of other average people were duped by Madoff and were not in any way complicit. These "are honest, law-abiding citizens who relied upon the SEC to properly patrol the securities markets," she said.

SIPC said it would pay up to $500,000 in insurance for each victim. Ambrosino, however, contends they used a flawed formula to decide how much of that amount each investor is due. Ambrosino pointed to the agency's own definition of net equity: the balance in the customer's account less any sums the customer owes the broker. "It is only by ignoring the law that SIPC and Picard can take the position they have taken," she protested.

The aftermath of Madoff's crime resonated around the world—and not just the finance worlds of Wall Street, the City of London, Hong Kong, Latin America.

Madoff's confession and arrest killed off many of his feeder funds. Fairfield Greenwich Group kept its doors open but fired most of its staff. Both the state of Massachusetts and the trustee have alleged that victims are owed money from the feeder funds like Fairfield Greenwich, Maxam Capital, Kingate, and others. Sandra Manzke of Tremont and

Maxam was promptly sued by investors from all over the world. Ezra Merkin was charged by the attorney general of New York with defrauding state charities and university endowments. As for Sonja Kohn, she disappeared from public view. In May 2009, the Austrian magazine *Format* estimated she had funneled a far larger sum to Madoff via her Bank Medici than was first thought, as much as $5 billion to $8 billion.

Madoff was a fraud. He wasn't running a hedge fund, even if he did operate his scam with a similar level of assets and discretion. As for the real hedge funds, many failed in the wake of the crisis: in 2008, a record 1,471 liquidated, or nearly 15 percent of all hedge funds. According to data from Hedge Fund Research, hedge fund investors yanked $150 billion of their money in the fourth quarter alone, triggering yet more selling. And more than 275 funds of hedge funds were liquidated, also a record.

Absolute Return magazine noted that three of the top ten funds that closed were Madoff feeder funds, including Fairfield Greenwich Group's Fairfield Sentry Fund, which had an estimated $6.9 billion in losses. Gabriel Capital Group and Ascot Partners, controlled by Ezra Merkin, lost $3.3 billion in assets connected to Madoff. Likewise Tremont Group's Rye family of funds lost $3.1 billion, and Kingate Management, another Sandra Manzke feeder fund that closed down, lost $2.7 billion.

The Jewish charitable community was decimated by Madoff, as were celebrities and business personalities. World Trade Center site developer Larry Silverstein, the estate of the late singer John Denver, actor John Malkovich, TV personality Larry King, the Jewish women's charity Hadassah, and even Madoff's lawyer, Ira Sorkin, all appear on the trustee's 163-page list of victims. The list includes hundreds of trust funds, charities, pension plans, and unions, as well as accounts for Madoff's grandchildren and his closest friends' grandchildren and widows. Roughly fourteen thousand brokerage accounts made up the "Swindler's List," as L.A.'s *Jewish Journal* called the trustee document. Of the total, one in six lived in Florida and one in seven on Long Island, with the largest cluster being six hundred people living in Great Neck, New York.

The effect on the American Jewish community was viral: 39 percent of American Jews said they were affected in some way, either because an organization or charity they supported had been affected by the

Madoff crimes (29 percent) or because someone they knew was affected (17 percent). Only 1 percent had been personally hurt, according to a survey conducted by J Street in a March 2009 poll of the American Jewish community.

Many Jews were livid simply because they feared Madoff had revived anti-Semitic stereotypes of greed. Jewish victims themselves pointed out that more than half of Madoff's investors were not Jewish and claimed all sorts of religious denominations and cultural backgrounds—a fact that had been overshadowed in the debacle. "No one had reinforced stereotypes more than he," said Burt Ross, the former mayor of Fort Lee, New Jersey, speaking in front of the courtroom at Madoff's sentencing.

The hedge fund industry will invite more scrutiny as a result of Madoff's fraud. By 2010, U.S. president Barack Obama has pledged to sign a package of sweeping financial and regulatory reforms not seen since the 1930s. SEC registration for hedge funds is already under way, although it's unclear the agency has the manpower or resources to regulate hedge funds in a meaningful way.

For Americans' pension funds, hedge funds could become as common an investment as a mutual fund someday. But if Madoff was any indication, they will have to choose much more skeptically. Three of the largest top twenty-five pension advisers—UBP, Man Group, and EIM Group, run by Arpad Busson—had career-jeopardizing exposure to Madoff. "If you had Madoff, you're out as a hedge fund of funds manager, no matter how small your investment. The career risk for an institutional CIO is just much too high to allow you to retain advisors and consultants who gave Madoff the green light," said Daniel Celeghin, director at consultant Casey, Quirk & Associates, in Darien, Connecticut.

If anything, the Madoff scandal transcends ethnicity, religion, class, and even international borders, and shows that even the savviest and most intelligent people can be duped into believing something that is too good to be true.

Epilogue

Tears flowed down many faces on the twenty-ninth of June, 2009, but Bernie Madoff was dry-eyed throughout his sentencing hearing, which began shortly after ten a.m. in Judge Dennis Chin's courtroom.

Madoff was indeed a record holder: he had stolen more money, over a longer period of time, from more thousands of people all over the world than any thief in history. And his punishment would be stiffer. According to Judge Chin, Madoff displayed "extraordinary evil," which set him apart from generations of criminals before him: bank robber John Dillinger, Wall Street's Ivan Boesky and Michael Milken, Bernie Ebbers of WorldCom, Jeffrey Skilling of Enron.

According to Judge Chin, "several hundred" jilted investors had penned letters and e-mails to him, asking that Madoff receive the maximum sentence in a maximum security prison. One letter had swayed Judge Chin, he said, in particular: a widow who said that after her husband's heart attack, she went to see Bernie Madoff. He put his arms around the widow and said, "Don't worry, your money is safe with me." Now she has had to sell her home and can't put her granddaughter through college.

But not a single person had written the court in Madoff's defense— not his sons, or his wife, or his many colleagues on Wall Street. Bernie Madoff's wife, Ruth, also did not attend his sentencing.

In the cavernous, cathedral-like courtroom, with dark wood benches, cornices, and baseboards, green granite and brass, nearly three hundred Madoff casualties, press, and curious onlookers crowded in to watch Madoff breathe his last hours of freedom.

Ronnie Sue Ambrosino, the plucky divorcée, and her second husband, Dominic Ambrosino, were the first Madoff investors to speak. Dominic was now too old to reapply for his prison guard job at Rikers

Island, which supplied him and his new wife with a small pension, now their lifeline. "As the guy on the right side of the bars" from Bernie Madoff, Dominic still wanted to know, "When will *my* sentence end?"

The Fitzmaurices, who were "not millionaires" to begin with, noted that Madoff showed no remorse. "He was scamming people just days before he confessed," Tom Fitzmaurice said. "He and his wife and two sons lived a life reserved for royalty, not common thieves. You have two sons who despise you . . . and a marriage made in hell. May God spare you no mercy."

Then Burt Ross, the former mayor of Fort Lee, New Jersey, moved to the microphone, with the assistance of his wife, Joan, and two walking sticks. Ross had been one of the lucky few who had already been paid $500,000 by SIPC trustee, although his total loss was $5 million. He and his wife had lost their retirement, and—he choked and struggled through his sobs—"the inheritance of my father, who worked his entire life." Madoff deserved a special level of hell. "Dante recognized fraud as the worst sin," Ross said, adding, "May Satan grow a fourth mouth where he spends eternity."

Next a thirty-three-year-old man testified that Madoff had stolen money set aside to care for a mentally disabled brother. "I only hope his jail cell becomes his coffin." The next woman told the courtroom she now survived on food stamps and at month's end scavenges for food. The following victim, the chief financial officer of Hadassah, testified that she and her family "are not anonymous. Madoff knows me, my husband, Ron, and son Eric." Her son had worked for Madoff one summer. "That beast has a name to me. Under the façade, he is a beast. He fed upon us to satisfy himself. He is an equal opportunity destroyer."

Madoff's longtime lawyer, Ira Sorkin, then addressed the judge. "We represent a deeply flawed individual," he said, and noted that most of the money from Madoff's "cash in, cash out" Ponzi scheme had gone to redemptions, according to the presentencing report.

Losses accounted for by the time of Madoff's sentencing totaled $13 billion. Of that $13 billion, $1.276 billion included Bernie and Ruth Madoffs' assets, such as the private jet, the yachts, the homes, the tens of millions of dollars in loans to family members; $1.225 billion had been recovered, another $735 million was sought by the trustee still; and finally $10.1 billion was being pursued by Irving Picard, the trustee, in "claw backs," or money paid out by Madoff to early investors. Still, that $13 billion did not include all the "feeder funds."

Madoff finally had a chance to speak, and stood up to face the judge. His charcoal gray suit hung on a thinner frame, his wavy pewter hair had grown longer, his eyes looked haggard behind rimless eyeglasses. His freakish grin from the previous December had vanished.

"I made a terrible mistake," he said softly, in a monotone, sometimes reading from a piece of paper, mostly looking at the judge. "I couldn't admit that I had failed." He believed he could work his way out, but the "harder I tried" the deeper he dug himself. "I live in a tormented state" knowing the suffering he had caused and the legacy he had left of "shame, to my family and grandchildren." His wife, Ruth, "cries herself to sleep every night."

Then he turned around and faced the benches of citizens in the courtroom behind him. "I apologize. I will turn and face you." Then he sat.

From the team of U.S. prosecutors, Lisa Baroni stood and remarked that the government didn't agree Madoff had made just a single mistake, a small loss from which he couldn't extricate himself. No. Instead, "This was not a crime of market conditions. It was calculated and orchestrated. For more than twenty years, he stole ruthlessly and without remorse, he used victims' money to enrich himself."

Judge Chin finally rendered his ruling. The courtroom grew silent. "Despite all the emotion, there has been no mob vengeance," he said, looking admiringly at Madoff's victims. The $65 billion figure, he added, was still disputed. And even though roughly $170 billion flowed in and out as a result of Madoff's scheme, "This is not just a matter of money."

Madoff had not been helpful in recovering assets, the judge noted. "He has not told all he could." Madoff transferred $15 million in BLMIS funds to his wife just weeks before his arrest. Madoff's crimes were not only "extraordinarily evil" but also an "irresponsible manipulation of the system" that took a "staggering human toll."

Judge Chin was choosing a "symbolic" sentence of 150 years in prison for three reasons: retribution, deterrence, and the fact that the victims came from "all walks of life—he struck at the rich . . . the middle class, the elderly." Screams and applause broke out in court chambers.

Madoff again did not show any emotion at just before twelve o'clock noon, when the judge sentenced him to a century and a half in prison, many times a life sentence for the now seventy-one-year-old criminal.

On the way out of the courtroom, Ronnie Sue Ambrosino was ebullient. She was headed over to a rally in Foley Square for her Madoff Victims Coalition, where they were fighting for back taxes paid to the IRS on Madoff's phantom profits. There would be lots of issues to grapple with in the future. But she couldn't stop smiling. "I think my heart just started beating again!"

Acknowledgments

In the spring of 2001, I interviewed Bernard Madoff for *Barron's* magazine in a story entitled "Don't Ask, Don't Tell." At the time, Madoff claimed to be running one of Wall Street's largest under-the-radar hedge funds. When I asked him questions concerning his investment strategy and his curiously consistent returns, he responded with double-talk. Yet his investors were enamored with his steady profits, never experienced a losing year, and didn't ask questions. They even honored Madoff's bizarre request: not to tell anyone he was managing their money.

I knew Madoff wasn't doing what he claimed, but I had no idea he was running a historic pyramid scam. In 2001, I also didn't know Harry Markopolos, the certified fraud examiner who had made it his personal mission to expose Madoff's scam, and starting in 1999, repeatedly sent the SEC warnings that Madoff was a fraud. Michael Ocrant of MARHedge industry newsletter, beat me to the punch in writing a story. Unfortunately, all of these sirens fell on deaf ears.

My endless gratitude to my parents, Julie Casey Arvedlund and Richard L. Arvedlund, who gave me their love, talents, and every advantage in life; to my sister and best friend, Maggie Arvedlund, who pushed me to write this book, offered Wall Street–wise edits, and who opened her home to me even when romantically inconvenient. Thanks, you guys— I love you so much! To my in-laws, John and Johanna Beattie, John and Olga Beattie, who gave me their son and brother, their encouragement, and who introduced me to a resourceful neighbor (go Princeton!), and finally, huzzahs to "the cavalry," my friend and researcher Caroline Waxler, I thank you.

I deeply, heartily thank my Penguin Portfolio editors Adrian Zackheim and Brooke Carey for their interest in the book, their patience with a first-time book author, their confidence and hard work; Will Weisser, Courtney Nobile, Alex Gigante, and Nancy Cardwell; my literary agent, Esmond Harmsworth, who waited for the right pitch; Colleen Rafferty and Kate Caulfield and the rest of the intrepid team at Zachary Schuster Harmsworth; and publicist Kate Pruss Pinnick.

My gratitude endures for bosses and colleagues at *Barron's*, especially Ed Finn (who published the original *Barron's* 2001 story on Madoff), Rich Rescigno and Randall Forsyth (who hired me), and Sandra Ward (who told me about the Striking Price columnist job); the *New York Times* (especially Bill Keller, Steven Lee Myers, Sophia Kishkovsky, and Glenn Kramon); the *Wall Street Journal* (Greg Zuckerman, Jeanne Whalen, Alan Cullison, and Tom Lauricella); TheStreet.com (Dan Colarusso, Peter Eavis, and Dave Kansas); the *Moscow Times* (Marc Champion, Jeff Grocott, and Geoff Weinstock); Dow Jones News Wires (Loren Fox, Maria Mooshil, Rick Stine, and Neal Lipschutz); *Philadelphia* magazine; and Tufts University newspaper *The Observer* (Neil Swidey and Matt Bai). Also, Mark Seal at *Vanity Fair* and Peter Trachtenberg and Christa Bourg at MediaBistro.com provided encouragement for a hedge fund book.

I could not have completed the calculations and analysis unraveling Madoff's fraud without the assistance of Nick Gleckman, Jay Berkman, and Doug Engmann, or the many Wall Street folks who helped my research for this book and over the years: Kevin Tierney, Peter Halloran, Hal Lux, Riva Atlas, David Winters, Mike Bickford, Chip Burke, Mike LaBranche, Dick Cummins, Doug Kass, David Bailin, Dan Wiener, John Bogle, Dr. Anna Wachtel, and "100 Women in Hedge Funds."

I had the support and love of friends even while I was absent, especially: the 350s crew, Heidi Porter, Mimi Villamor, Bonnie Kornberg, Meeta Anand, as well as Tufts alum Darcy Chamides Watson; *Moscow Times* comrades Natasha Mileusnic, Radhika Jones, Sujata Rao, and Bay Brown; Kimberly Fellingham, Adam Cassidy, Jackie McGowan, Kelly Mearkle, Shamik Cholera, and Barbara Leonardi; Dan Melkonian, Dale Carlson, and Kim Stevens and her sister Karla; and the Montauk crew.

Hugs to my oldest friend Stewart and her husband, Jay Joseph. Thanks to Ursuline Academy and Archmere Academy, especially Paul Villafuerte, Christina and Bob Sonchen, and Father Frances McLoughlin;

Delaware friends and neighbors, the Gallaghers and the Johnsons. To my family, who inspire me to keep writing, especially my aunts Frances, Liz, Olivia, and Kathy; my cousins John, Vaughn, Marianne, Cathy and Peter Stebbins, and Amy and Brian; Dino, Mette, Anna and Hans Hustinx. In memoriam—Mary Stebbins; John and Virginia Casey; Elizabeth and Svend "Dan" Arvedlund; John and Helen Beattie; John and Virginia Gaerste; John and Barbara Wyman; Evonne Rust; Rosemary Bennett; and William Beattie.

My fondest regards to the folks at Vision Capital Advisors; Sanford C. Bernstein hedge funds, especially Firth Calhoun and Charles Alvarez; Chuck McGivney and Jeff Kluger of the law firm of McGivney & Kluger P.C.; Steve Lapper, Steve McMenamin, Gregg Wirth, John Troland, and Jane Veeder; Ross and Caroline Nowak; Brett and Peggy Zola; Eric and Elizabeth Flaim; Matt and Tracy Sullivan; Kevin Glassco; Charlie and Leslie Bensley; Peter Rohrman; Cathleen and Stephen Montano; Matthew and Hanna Beattie; Raymond and Day Bank; P. D. and Kathryn Rust; Bonner English; David Rust; Paul and Sarah McKenzie; Lily Piel; Sofia Piel; Gary and Bia Lowe; Kerstin Piel-Lefavour and Willis Lefavour; Brendan and Nicole Chandonnet; the Honorable John J. Coyle, J.S.C.; Second Platoon, Delta Company, 2nd Battalion, 25th Marines, 1991; the brothers of the Delta Chi Fraternity, Hobart College class of 1989; Peter Farrell; Mark Paton; Paul Hawkins; David Crimmins; Jane Caughey; Kim Howard; Bob Beattie; Charlie Beattie; Ann Marie Snyder; Frank Friestedt; Patrick Finnegan; Paul Kerrigan; Michelle Doria; Cindy Schmidt; David Bogdan; and Courtney Drake. To those who helped with the 2001 *Barron's* story, and with this book, who did not wish to be named—my eternal thanks. To friends in the rooms who helped me, one day at a time.

Lastly, to my husband, Richard Patrick McEwan Beattie. I *couldn't* have done it without you—thank God sent you to me. I love you always.

Notes

Chapter One

11   "At just after eight o'clock on the morning of Thursday" Author interviews with federal officials and attorneys.

11   "famous occupants . . . range from Wall Street tycoons" Susan Dominus, "Madoff Apologizes to Neighbors for the Ultimate Co-op Crime," *New York Times,* 12 January 2009.

11   "the couple's $8 million, ten-thousand-square-foot home" Jennifer Gould Keil, Jeremy Olshan, and Dan Mangan, "Bernie Faces Boot: Apt. Brokers Told to Shop Penthouse," *New York Post,* 30 January 2009.

11   "sons of the man who lived in apartment 12A had contacted federal officials" Justice Department complaint, Agent Theodore Caccioppi, December 2009.

12   "Madoff answered . . . wearing . . . a pale blue bathrobe" Stephen Foley, "Bernie's billions," *The Independent,* 29 January 2009.

13   "Caruso-Cabrera, a pretty brunette news anchor on CNBC" CNBC, 11 December 2009, www.cnbc.com/id/15840232?video=960111409&play=1.

14   "Laurelton resembled other middle-class American towns" Author visit.

14   "its residents either spoke" "Brief History of Jews in Queens," prepared by Jeff Gottlieb, president, Queens Jewish Historical Society.

14   "Laurelton is still a neighborhood of immigrants" Gregory Beyer, "Living in Laurelton, Queens," *New York Times,* 26 April 2009.

14   "Madoff's paternal grandparents" U.S. Naturalization Records—Original Documents, 1795–1972, Pennsylvania, District Court, Petitions: #3146-3345.

15   "across the street from PS 156" "Memories of PS 156," www.laureltonnewyork.net/memoriesofps156.html.

16   "Life in Far Rockaway was lovely and clean" Author interview with Carol Salomon Marston.

16   "Rockaways were always safe and fun" Author interview with Nora Koeppel.

17   "Colomby was a favorite teacher" Author interview with Harry Colomby.

17   "Bernie was around" Author interview with Sanford "Sandy" Elstein.

17   "The Bernie I knew was a good-natured, happy-go-lucky guy" Douglas Feiden, "Rockaway Beach to Ponz Scum," *New York Daily News,* 21 December 2008.

19   "pretty, petite blond" Mark Seal, "Madoff's World," *Vanity Fair,* April 2009.

19   "Sammy, of all the frats" Author interview with Stan Hollander.

20   "nurtured a misperception that he had actually graduated from law school" Author interview with Michael Allison, president, International Business Research.

20   "Peter would come in . . . while he was still in college" Author interview with Michael Murphy.

21   "Ruth's paternal grandmother, Beile Alpern" The Statue of Liberty–Ellis Island Foundation, ships' manifest records, 1905.

21   "Far Rockaway High School's reunion Web site" www.farrockaway.com.

21   "respectable address of 10 East Fortieth Street" NYS Tax Commission in the Matter of the Petition of Joseph Mirsky for a Redetermination of a Deficiency or Refund of Personal & Unincorporated Taxes under Article(s) 16 & 16A of the Tax Law for the Year(s) July 31, 1959.

21   "a Laurelton-area sorority" Author interview with Phi Delta Gamma sorority sister Marion Sher.

21   "Ruthie, as she was known by friends" "Growing Up with the Ponzi King," *The Saratogian*, February 13, 2009; author interview with Jay Portnoy.

21   "Josie college" Steve Fishman, "The Monster Mensch," *New York* magazine, 22 February 2009.

21   "After graduation, Ruth enrolled at Queens College" David Segal and Alison Leigh Cowan, "Madoffs Shared Much; Question Is How Much," *New York Times*, 15 January 2009.

21   "a traditional Jewish wedding" Laurelton Jewish Center, www.laureltonnewyork.net/Laurelton_Photos.html.

22   "one-bedroom apartment in Bayside, Queens" Julie Creswell and Landon Thomas Jr., "The Talented Mr. Madoff," *New York Times*, 25 January 2009.

22   "the Madoffs were treated like rock stars" Author interview with Karen Klein Lutzker.

22   [Ruth Madoff] "graduated from Queens College in 1961" Mark Clothier and Oshrat Carmiel, "The mysterious Mr. Madoff," 19 December 2008 (Bloomberg).

23   "[Madoff] took a $50,000 loan from his in-laws" John Helyar, Katherine Burton, and Vernon Silver, "Madoff Enablers Winked at Suspected Front-Running," 27 January 2009 (Bloomberg).

24   "The broker-dealer firm was registered in Sylvia's name" SEC complaint filed against Bernie's mother, Sylvia R. Madoff, August 6, 1963, SEC Acts on Delinquent Broker-Dealers.

24   "the SEC struck a deal" SEC News Digest summary of actions (Issue No. 64-1-15) For Release January 23, 1964.

24   "Sylvia Madoff wound down her career" Nicholas Varchaver, James Bandler, and Doris Burke, "Madoff's mother tangled with the feds," *Fortune*, 16 January 2009.

25   "Sol Alpern . . . told everyone" Nina Mehta, "The End of a Sure Thing: Madoff's Long Bet," December 22, 2008, http://mehtafiscal.wordpress.com.

25   "sense of physical refuge" Phil Brown, "The Catskills Institute," Brown University.

25   "Cynthia Arenson, who inherited" David Segal and Alison Leigh Cowan, "Madoffs Shared Much; Question Is How Much," *New York Times*, 15 January 2009.

26   "Madoff had wormed his way" David Arenson, personal blog regarding his cancer and treatment http://clldiary.blogspot.com/.

26   "they hired two young accountants" Linda Sandler and Allan Dodds Frank, "Madoff's Tactics Date to 1960s When Father-in-Law Was Recruiter," 29 January 2009 (Bloomberg).

27   "accounting firm raised $441 million" Randall Smith, "SEC Breaks Up Investment Company That Paid Off Big but Didn't Register," *Wall Street Journal*, 1 December 1992.

27   "Heller died on December 8, 1967" *New York Times*, Death Notices, 12/8/67.

27   "Sol Alpern retired . . . 1974" Helyar, Burton, and Silver, "Madoff Enablers Winked at Suspected Front-Running.

27   "Arellino and Bienes, was sued for a shoddy audit" In the Matter of M. Frenville Co., Inc., Rudolph F. Frenville, Jr., and Rudolph F. Frenville, Sr., Avellino and Bienes, A Partnership, Appellant, *v.* M. Frenville Co., Inc., and Rudolph F. Frenville, Sr., and Charles Stanziale, Esq., Interim Trustee. No. 83-5789. United States Court of Appeals, Third Circuit. Argued June 15, 1984. Decided September 17, 1984.

28   " 'Sol, his father-in-law, had been doing it,' Bienes recalled" Interviews, Michael Bienes, transcript, www.pbs.org.

Chapter Two

31 **"this client was Carl Shapiro"** Shannon Donnelly, "Madoff Arrest Called 'Knife in the Heart,'" *Palm Beach Daily News*, 16 December 2008.

31 **"tiny companies . . . called the pink sheets"** Charles H. Kaplan, "Behind the Pink Sheets—Lie Undiscovered Small Companies with Big Values," *Barron's*, 28 September 1987.

32 **"(NASD) had passed a rule 'penalizing members'"** United Press International, 18 January 1969.

32 **"shares from the initial public offerings"** "NASD president Richard Walbert warns members not to execute sell orders of new . . ." *New York Times*, 27 March 1969.

32 **"co-founder of Herzog Heine Geduld"** Author interview with Buzzy Geduld.

32 **"postal strike in 1970"** Bill Keller, "Memories of Patco Haunt Post Office Labor Talks," *New York Times*, 5 August 1984.

32 **"notice 'by telegram'"** "SEC proposes new rule that would require immediate notice, by telegram, when . . ." *New York Times*, 21 April 1971.

33 **"Madoff did not invent the NASDAQ"** Gordon Macklin, "Talking Business with Macklin of Nasdaq O-T-C Trading: A Busy Field," *New York Times*, 17 March 1981.

34 **"Market Design Committee"** Jack Willoughby, "Generation gap," *Institutional Investor*, 1 February 1999.

34 **"Intermarket Trading System"** Ivy Schmerken, "The Bulls and Bears Come Out at Night: Electronic Trading," *Wall Street & Technology*, 1 September 1990.

35 **"create a so-called third market"** Robert H. Battalio, "Third market broker-dealers: cost competitors or cream skimmers?," *Journal of Finance*, 1 March 1997.

36 **"*Forbes* ran a glowing story"** Richard L. Stern, "Living Off the Spread: Bernard Madoff," *Forbes*, 10 July 1989.

36 **"more than three thousand companies had their share prices"** Vartanig G. Vartan, "Market Place; Pros and Cons of O-T-C Data," *New York Times*, 10 February 1983.

37 **"By the mid-1990s, the regional exchanges"** Kathryn E. George, "The Great Regional Battle for NYSE-Listed Order Flow," *Traders*, 1 November 1996.

37 **"We all knew Bernie"** Author interview with Dale Carlson.

38 **"Nasdaq price manipulation"** Scot J. Paltrow, "Probe Launched Into Nasdaq Stock Trading," *Los Angeles Times*, 19 October 1994.

38 **"thirty firms settled"** Price-fixing settlement, "Justice Department Charges 24 Major NASDAQ Securities Firms with Fixing Transaction Costs for Investors," 17 July 1996, www.usdoj.gov.

41 **"the chief threat to the old way . . . the Cincinnati"** Peter J. Brennan, "Regional Stock Exchanges: Fighting the Competition," *Wall Street & Technology*, 1 April 1993.

41 **"his own business niche"** Ivy Schmerken, "The Bulls and Bears Come Out at Night; Electronic Trading," *Wall Street & Technology*, 1 September 1990.

41 **"limited to so-called 19(c)3 stocks"** Ivy Schmerken and Jenna Michaels, "NASDAQ at 9:00 A.M.," *Wall Street & Technology*, 1 November 1992.

42 **"The politics of trading off the exchange floor"** Catherine Stevens, "The Regionals Shape Up," *FW (Financial World)*, 16 September 1986.

42 **"system designed by TCAM Associates"** Joshua Zecher, "TCAM at Your Service (TCAM Systems Inc. Offering Retail Firms a Sophisticated Order-Routing and Management Trading Network," *Wall Street & Technology*, 1 May 1994.

42 **"Junius Peake . . . been governor and vice chairman"** "Exchanges. Quest for Opportunity: 10th Anniversary Special Report," *Wall Street & Technology*, 1 July 1993.

44 **"Send me your order flow"** Author interview with Alex Jacobson, ISE.

44 **"Dominion Securities 'loved it'"** "Bernie I hardly knew ya; Bay Street insider Doug Steiner was once inspired by Bernie Madoff. How, Steiner wonders, could he have believed in someone who turned out to be crooked to the tune of $50 billion?" *The Globe and Mail*, 27 February 2009.

44 **"paper examining the Madoff scandal"** Greg N. Gregoriou and François-Serge

Lhabitant, "Madoff! A riot of red flags," EDHEC Risk and Asset Management Research Centre, January 2009.

45   "payment for orders . . . was a necessary evil" Author interview with Ed Mathias, Carlyle Group, private equity firm.

45   "By 1990, Madoff was trading 275 NYSE stocks" Ivy Schmerken, "The Bulls and Bears Come Out at Night; Electronic Trading.

45   "his employees went on to work" Author interviews with former Madoff employee, headhunter Ben Ross.

45   "Cincinnati exchange . . . using Preferencing" Craig Torres, "Heard on the Street: How Street Turns Your Stock Trades to Gold," *Wall Street Journal*, 16 February 1993.

45   "don't like what we are doing" Ibid.

45   "By 1989, Bernard L. Madoff" Author interview with Peter Chapman.

Chapter Three

48   "Her father, Abraham Hershson" "Abraham Hershson, Retired Executive, 89," *New York Times*, 17 March 1990.

48   "Hygiene's pink shares traded" *SEC News Digest*, 21 September 1961.

49   "one Madoff investor who had been referred through Engler" Author interview with son of Madoff investor in Bay Area, California.

49   "Madoff was the opposite of risk" Author interview with relative of Madoff investor.

50   "Cohn, who was known as Sonny" "Cohn, Declaire & Kaufman Fined $3,500 by Big Board," Dow Jones News Service, 2 October 1979.

50   "a so-called two-dollar broker" Fed. Sec. L. Rep. P 93,272 in Re the Revenue Properties Litigation Cases. Appeal of Cohn, Delaire & Kaufman, 451 F.2d 310 (1st Cir. 1971).

50   "Cohn partnered with Madoff in forming Cohmad" NYS Department of State, Division of Corporations. Selected Entity Name: Cohmad Securities Corporation. Current Entity Name: Cohmad Securities Corporation. Initial DOS Filing Date: February 19, 1985. http://appsext8.dos.state.ny.us/corp_public/CORPSEARCH.ENTITY_INFORMATION?p_nameid=1075519&p_corpid=975028&p_entity_name=%63%6F%68%6D%61%64&p_name_type=%25&p_search_type=%42%45%47%49%4E%53&p_srch_results_page=0.

51   "Christensen . . . eventually became an elder statesman of the trading floor" Author interview with Frank Christensen.

51   "Hirshon, who had started his Wall Street career in 1927" NYS Department of State, Division of Corporations. Selected Entity Name: Hirshon & Company, Incorporated. Current Entity Name: Hirshon & Company, Incorporated. Initial DOS Filing Date: May 08, 1919. County: New York. http://appsext8.dos.state.ny.us/corp_public/CORPSEARCH.ENTITY_INFORMATION?p_nameid=3369&p_corpid=3005&p_entity_name=%68%69%72%73%68%6F%6E&p_name_type=%25&p_search_type=%42%45%47%49%4E%53&p_srch_results_page=0

52   "Alvin J. Delaire, Jr., and his wife, Carole, went skiing" Team guest list, Interbourse, Zermatt 2004.

53   "Murphy would often stop by and have lunch at Madoff's" Author interview with Michael Murphy.

53   "Peter DaPuzzo and his wife, Mary Jane, also socialized with both Madoff couples" Author interview with Peter DaPuzzo and Mary Jane DaPuzzo.

55   "Madoff was one of the few broker-dealers who stayed open" Ibid.

55   "Chais . . . receiving cumulative returns as high as 900 percent" Madoff Trustee Irving H. Picard complaint *v.* Stanley Chais, www.madofftrustee.com.

56   "former clients of Avellino and Bienes were able to set up new accounts" Mark Seal, *Vanity Fair*, June 2009.

56   "Madoff lowered the returns he was promising" Michael Bienes, PBS *Frontline* (www.pbs.org) interview transcript.

57 "Madoff's Ponzi was unraveling" Markopolos testimony to Congress, 4 February 2009.

57 "upward of $7 billion" Department of Justice complaint, December 2008.

57 "Jacobson. Then the head of investor education" Author interview with Alex Jacobson.

60 "big Madoff clients 'would get executions that seemed impossible'" Author interviews with former clients of Madoff.

60 "Steiner was immediately impressed by the trading room" "Bernie I hardly knew ya," *The Globe and Mail*.

60 "NASDAQ's trading committee . . . 'we always met in his offices'" Author interview with Ed Mathias.

60–61 "For someone . . . making $20 million a year" Author interview with former Madoff employee.

61 "Bernie did have his quirks" Julia Fenwick in Miles Goslett, "I Just Can't Live with That Camera—It's Not Square." *The Mail on Sunday*, 4 January 2009.

62 "Peter Madoff 'started screaming at us'" Author interview with former Madoff employee.

62 "Cohmad executives . . . had worked . . . at Cowen and Company" Robert Jaffe, Marcia Cohn, Jonathan Greenberg, Finra.org BrokerCheck records (www.finra.org).

62 "Spring . . . worked at David J. Green & Co." Richard "Dick" Spring, FINRA broker.

66 "Robert Jaffe was paid roughly $100 million" Secretary of State William Galvin exhibits in February 2009 complaint *v.* Cohmad, www.sec.state.ma.us/sct/sctcohmad/cohmadidx.htm; "involved parties" at Cohmad: Marcia Beth Cohn, Robert Martin Jaffe, Maurice Jay (Sonny) Cohn, Stanley M. Berman, Alvin James Delaire, Jr., Jonathan Barney Greenberg, Cyril David Jalon, Morton David Kurzrok, Linda Schoenheimer McCurdy, Richard George Spring, and Rosalie Buccellato.

63 "Madoff stopped making payments on Cohmad accounts" SEC *v.* Cohmad et al., www.sec.gov/litigation/complaints/2009/comp21095.pdf.

64 "Cohmad also steered Madoff investors to use" Nina Mehta, "It's a Cohmad Mad Mad World," February 24, 2009, MehtaFiscal, http://mehtafiscal.wordpress.com/2009/02/24/cohmad-mad-mad-world/.

64 "Burt Ross, former mayor of Fort Lee, New Jersey" Andrew Tangel, "Ft. Lee accountants had deeper ties to Madoff," *The Record*, Hackensack, N.J., McClatchy-Tribune Regional News, 6 March 2009.

64 "Marder's firm name appears" Robert Chew, "The Bernie Madoff Client List Is Made Public," *Time*, 5 February, 2009.

65 "Louis Boston, whose flagship store" Jean E. Palmieri, "Louis to Emphasize Men's Sportswear," *Daily News Record*, 19 September 1990.

65 "Kiton suits . . .once . . . you've had filet mignon'" Peter Walsh and Jean E. Palmieri, "The Best Customers in the Best Stores," *Daily News Record*, 17 April 1998.

65 "Jaffe initially denied" Casey Ross and Jenn Abelson, "Broker tied to ex-Hub mob leader Jaffe did business with Angiulo in '70s," *Boston Globe*, 23 December 2008.

66 "he golfed and did the charity circuit" Interview, Beth Healy, *Boston Globe*; "Jaffe's Role Studied in Madoff Case," NPR: "All Things Considered," 5 December 2008, www.npr.org.

66 "a common practice" Shannon Donnelly, "Palm Beachers call Bernie Madoff arrest 'knife in the heart,'" *Palm Beach Daily News*, 15 December 2008.

66 "one-third of the Palm Beach Country club" Josh Sens, "Bernie Madoff's golf memberships provided the perfect venue to run the largest Ponzi scheme in history," *Golf* magazine, 1 June 2009.

66 "Shapiros donated $14 million" "Shapiros Commit $14 million for Planned Admissions Center," 22 January 2008, www.brandeis.edu.

67 "Brandeis school newspaper" Ariel Wittenberg, "Who are Carl and Ruth J. Shapiro?" *The Brandeis Hoot*, 3 October 2008, http://thehoot.net/articles/3785.

67   "sons of . . . 'Hank' Greenberg" Leslie Scism, "Splitting Heirs: One Son Leaves Dad, Another Stays Behind" *Wall Street Journal*, 14 June 1995.

68   "Ruth had a penchant for secrecy" Author interview with former investor in Madoff.

68   "Kashar was paired up with . . . A. J. Delaire" Author interview with Mark Kashar.

69   "Cohmad displayed a mixed reaction to its relationship with Madoff's firm" Lars Toomre, Toomre Capital Markets/Insights, www.toomre.com.

69   "In a November 21, 1991, letter" Exhibits, Secretary of State William Galvin complaint *v.* Fairfield Greenwich Group.

71   "market technician Steven Nison" Scott McMurray, "Japan's 'Candlesticks' Light Traders' Path," *Wall Street Journal*, 8 November 1990.

73   "Madoff hired Neil Yelsey" William Power, "Heard on the Street: Salomon's Quiet Mood of High-Tech Trading Will Boost Its Stock Price," *Wall Street Journal*, 2 February 1994.

74   "They did it on a massive scale" Author interviews with former Madoff employees.

75   "alternative trading networks" Greg Ip, "Trading Places: The Stock Exchanges, Long Static, Suddenly Are Roiled by Change," *Wall Street Journal*, 27 July 1999.

75   "the spreads . . . shrank to one cent or even less" "Why has trading volume increased?" Rutgers University, 29 February 2008.

75   "Decimals 'killed everyone' " Author interview with former AMEX executive.

76   "By placing before SEC investigators reams of information" Suit *v.* JPMorgan Chase, 2009 cv 4049 MLSMK Investments Company *v.* JP Morgan Chase & Co. and JP Morgan Chase Bank, U.S. District Court, Southern District New York, April 2009.

76   "Madoff also lied . . . about how much money he was overseeing" "The Madoff affair: Dumb money and dull diligence," *The Economist*, 20 December 2008.

76   "Madoff's explanation for this discrepancy" Hugo Duncan and Nick Goodway, "Two Years of Lies Kept SEC at Bay," *Evening Standard*, 11 March 2009.

77   "by lying about the number of clients" U.S. Attorney Southern District of New York Lev Dassin, Manhattan Federal Court, 10 March 2009, criminal information, 11 counts filed *v.* Bernard L. Madoff.

78   "hedge funds controlled $1.3 trillion" FBI Web site, www.fbi.gov/page2/march07/hedge_fund.htm.

78   "We never got any hedge fund business" Author interviews with former Madoff employees.

79   "market makers would not socialize with the people from the seventeenth floor" Author interview with Doug Kass, Seabreeze Partners, Palm Beach, Florida.

Chapter Four

81   "Frank Christensen dropped in" Author interviews with Frank Christensen.

81   "a scare from the SEC, which had shut down two of Madoff's main fund-raisers, Frank Avellino and Michael Bienes, in 1992" Randall Smith, "SEC Breaks Up Investment Company That Paid Off Big but Didn't Register," by Randall Smith, *Wall Street Journal*, 1 December 1992.

82   "Eleanor Squillari, thought there was only one business" Mark Seal, *Vanity Fair*, June 2009.

83   "Technically, it was nothing of the sort" Author interview with Richard Baker, former Louisiana congressman, head of Managed Funds Association, Washington, D.C., lobby group for hedge fund industry.

83   "Chief among the big money scouts was Fairfield" Helyar, Burton, and Silver, "Madoff Enablers Winked at Suspected Front-Running."

83   "four of his five daughters" Author interview with Sherry Cohen, former Fairfield Greenwich employee.

84   "Busson was luring in new investors" Katharina Bart, Dow Jones International News, 15 December 2008.

84 **"Access International Advisors was another feeder"** "White Paper: Impact of 2008 Events on Hedge Funds, Funds of Funds and Service Providers," 2 March 2009, Infovest21 White Papers.

84 **"He can't be a fraud"** Author interview with associate of de la Villehuchet.

84 **"Santander later admitted"** Thomas Catan, "Switzerland Investigates Santander," *Wall Street Journal*, 19 June 2009.

84 **"Fairfield at least was up front"** Author interview with Michael Toporek.

85 **"Hollywood types, such as screenwriter Eric Roth"** Madoff investor list (www .madofftrustee.com), Roth lawsuit *v.* Stanley Chais , Picard *v.* Chais, 09-01172, and *Picard v. Bernard L. Madoff*, 09-11893, U.S. Bankruptcy Court, Southern District of New York (Manhattan).

85 **"control DreamWorks Animation studio"** Rob Golum and Andy Fixmer, "Katzenberg Says Madoff Did 'Extraordinary Damage,'" 8 January 2009 (Bloomberg).

85 **"Even Elie Wiesel"** Angela Montefinise and Brandon Guarneri, "Insult to Injury at 'BERN'ED SHUL," 17 May 2009, *New York Post*; "Elie Wiesel Donors aid Madoff-hit Elie Wiesel," *The Jewish Chronicle*, 3 April 2009; Tom Hays, "Wiesel recounts meeting Madoff, losing millions," Associated Press, 26 February 2009.

85 **"The senior Mr. Merkin had known Madoff"** Peter Robison, Janet Frankston Lorin, and Joshua Fineman, "Merkin Intimidated Co-Op Board While Building Funds," 9 January 2009 (Bloomberg); Author interview with Michael Steinhardt.

85 **"We thought he was God"** Wiesel speaking at *Portfolio* magazine panel, 26 February 2009.

85 **"There's a whole industry of these third-party marketers"** Author interview with Thomas Lauria.

86 **"They had serious disincentives to vet out"** Author interview with Doug Kass.

86 **"Annette Bongiorno, was recruiting"** David Voreacos and David Glovin, "Madoff Key Aide Bongiorno Recruited Her Neighbors as Investors," 2009 February 14 (Bloomberg).

86 **"introduced to Madoff by a man named Sonny Cohn"** Author interview, Madoff investor via Cohmad.

87 **"superfast electronic community networks"** "Who's Who in ECNs?," *Wall Street & Technology*, 14 June 2000, www.wallstreetandtech.com/story/WST20000614S0003; jsessionid=PL04YINFGMNEEQSNDLPCKH0CJUNN2JVN.

88 **"Englander, a former AMEX trader"** Marcia Vickers, "Inside Wall Street/The House of Izzy," *Fortune*, 14 November 2005.

88 **"the sheer scope of the fees Madoff was leaving on the table"** Erin Arvedlund, "Don't Ask Don't Tell," *Barron's*, May 2001.

88 **"That's how they entice you to become a client"** Thomas Lauria, ibid.

89 **"other industry parties for the legitimate broker-dealer"** Security Traders Association, STA of New York, 9–11 April 2003, *Traders Magazine* website www.tradersmagazine .com/photos/2003_10909/19915-1.html.

89 **"RBC had clients"** Author interview with Robert Picard.

89 **"the Rye Select Broad Market name"** Christine Williamson, "Homework saves crying over Madoff; Institutions heeded the red flags raised by hedge funds of funds," *Pensions & Investments*, 22 December 2008.

90 **"the world's top-earning hedge funds"** Paul G. Barr, "Hedge Funds Fear Redemption Season," *Pensions & Investments*, 6 November 1998.

90 **"Citadel in Chicago"** Hal Lux, "Boy Wonder" (Ken Griffin, founder of Citadel Investment Group L.L.C.), *Institutional Investor*, 1 September 2001.

90 **"explain irrational investor decisions using psychology . . . using . . . Kahneman . . . and Tversky,"** "The Psychology of Investment," *The Economist*, 23 April 1994.

91 **"they go mad in herds,"** *Extraordinary Popular Delusions* . . . Charles Mackay, public domain, www.archive.org/stream/extraordinarypop014178mbp/.

91 **"confidence of key investors"** Neil Behrmann, "Madoff fools Notz Stucki and UBP with steady non-volatile fictitious returns," Infovest21, 2 February 2009.

91   "Notz Stucki admitted that over the years" Pierre-Alexandre Sallier, "Notz Stucki compensates its customers," *Le Temps*, 24 April 2009.

92   "Schulman became one of the biggest advocates" Alistair Barr, "Madoff's rise fueled by leverage, controversial fees; Scandal shows how hedge fund business relied on trust, relationships," MarketWatch, 18 December 2008.

92   "one of Bernie's biggest salesmen" Author interview, former AMEX official.

93   "Social psychologist Robert Cialdini" Len Fisher, "Madoff's Willing Partners," *Washington Post*, 20 December 2008.

93   "all of these can be faked" Ibid.

93   "a different sort of cheat" Ibid.

94   "Cheats can prosper" Ibid.

94   "Joe Geiger, a managing director" Hung Tran, "GAM Reveals How It Dodged the Madoff Bullet," FINAlternatives, 20 March 2009.

94   "I was introduced to a feeder" James Newman, letter to Ermitage clients.

95   "Aksia, which in 2007 penned a letter" Aksia letter, December 2008, signed by Jim Vos.

95   "Madoff paid them to be the front door" Author interview with Lita Epstein.

95   "Con artists know people's mental roadblocks" Author interview with Patrick Huddleston.

96   "spurred some industry changes" Author interview, UBP official.

96   "An independent administrator" Author interview with Reiko Nahum.

96   "Metzger supports mandating independent custodians" "Madoff Ponzi Scheme and Need for Regulatory Changes"—Leon Metzger, Congressional Testimony by CQ Transcriptions, 5 January 2009.

97   "Vos noted the lack of" Aksia letter.

97   "As early as 2002, Ehrenkranz and Lehman struck" Lehman Brothers 425 filing with SEC, 8 September 2003.

98   "peer-to-peer learning group for high-net-worth investors" Tiger 21 Web site www.tiger21.com.

98   "support group for multimillionaires" Gary Rivlin, "Where Everybody Knows Your Portfolio," *The New York Times Magazine*, 14 October 2007.

98   "the man at Lehman Brothers lost" Author interview.

98   "Tremont, which she opened in 1984" Mario Gabelli, Tremont SEC filings.

99   "her real talent" Greg Newton, "A Talented Talent Scout," *Barron's*, 31 July 2006.

99   "a buyout vehicle called Lynch Corp." Anna Robaton, "Mario Gabelli: He's CEO of Little-Known Stock That's Something of a Stinker," *Investment News*, 14 June 1999.

100   "known as the CSBF-Tremont Hedge Fund Index" Greg Newton, "A Talented Talent Scout," *Barron's*, 31 July 2006.

101   "the Madoff–Tremont relationship was so significant" Putnam Lovell opinion, Tremont SEC filings, www.sec.gov/Archives/edgar/data/880320/000095012301505828/x52116dmdefm14a.txt.

102   "Kingate was overseen" Infovest21 Staff, "Movers and Shakers," Infovest21 News Provider Service, 2 February 2009.

102   "three big ones: Fairfield, Kingate, and Tremont" Iain Dey and Kate Walsh, "Posh Europeans drummed up sales," *The Sunday Times*, 21 December 2008.

103   "Kingate initiated . . . in 1994" Kingate Investor Files "Derivative" Lawsuit John Bruhl *v.* Kingate Management Ltd et al., 09601510, filed in New York State Supreme Court, 15 May 2009.

103   "Another Kingate fund was operating as far back as 1992" ALTIN 2002 marketing materials and annual report.

103   "Syz marketed Kingate" Ibid.

104   "By 2005, pension funds . . . love affair" Mary Williams Walsh and Riva D. Atlas, "Pensions Risk Billions in Hedge Funds," *New York Times*, 27 November 2005.

104 "There were many seasoned market professionals" Author interview with Christopher Miller, Allenbridge.

Chapter Five

106 "the septuagenarian had fallen asleep" Author interview.
107 "Overall, 2007 was a fabulous year" Fairfield Greenwich 2007 compensation records and marketing materials.
108 "Walter Noel founded Fairfield Greenwich" Fairfield Sentry Class A Shares Offering Memorandum, July 2003.
108 "Noel had graduated" April 2, 2009, updated biography in the *New York Times*, http://topics.nytimes.com/top/reference/timestopics/people/n/walter_m_noel_jr/index.html.
109 "Corina, the eldest" "Corina Noel Is Engaged," *New York Times*, 12 February 1989.
109 "party hosted by hair stylist Frédéric Fekkai" "Super Bowl champs will be honored in Greenwich," *Stamford Advocate*, 27 April 2008.
109 "Antoine Bernheim's popular industry rag" Stephen Taub, David Carey, and Joseph Epstein, "The Wall Street 100: compensation was way down in 1994 for Wall Street's highest earners," *Financial World*, 4 July 1995.
110 "their main $6 million home on Round Hill Road" John Christoffersen, "Manager's luxe life on the line in Madoff case," Associated Press, 29 January 2009.
111 "a money-losing futures fund called TAPMAN" Vicky Ward, "Greenwich Mean Time," *Vanity Fair*, 1 April 2009.
111 "Piedrahita began to show some of his main characteristics" Caroline Waxler, "The Walter Noel Chronicles: Meet Andrés Piedrahita, Son-In-Law," 26 December 2008, www.businessinsider.com.
111 "Fairfield Greenwich cofounders bought a shared interest" Kaja Whitehouse, "Madoff Sell-Off," *New York Post*, 9 February 2009.
111 "Also in 2006, the Noels paid" LexisNexis, mortgage records, Walter and Monica Noel.
112 "Fred Kolber & Co." Steve Fishman, "Card pro earns his fortune in big game of options," *Success Magazine*, 27 October 1985.
112 "Walter had been surviving" Sherry Shameer Cohen, http://metrojournalist.blogspot.com/.
113 "Noel was never a partner in the options trading business," Author interview .
114 "Tucker had also married well" Deaths: Schneider, Norman, *New York Times*, 16 July 1999.
114 "John Donachie, one-time head of compliance for Fairfield Greenwich Group" Author interview with John Donachie.
115 "Jeffrey Tucker was a 'hardworking guy'" Author interview, former associate of Fred Kolber.
115 "Empire Racing Associates ... elected Tucker" James M. Odato, "Racing bidder gains players; Magna, Churchill Downs, heavy hitters in racetrack industry, and horse owner Marylou Whitney join Empire in bid for state franchise," Capitol Bureau, *Albany Times Union*, 17 August 2006.
115 "Sheikh Mohammed bin Rashid Al Maktoum—the ruler of Dubai" Dennis Yusko, "Dubai ruler adds stable to realm: Saratoga's legendary Stonerside farms is sold for $17.5M to train horses like Travers winner Bernardini," *Albany Times Union*, 18 January 2007.
115 "Equine Advocates, a charity for rescuing slaughter horses" Maria McBride Bucciferro, "Horses benefit at sanctuary," *Albany Times Union*, 23 August 2002.
116 "Tucker bought other farms" Dennis Yusko, "Stone Bridge Farms for sale: $18 million: 426 acres, opulent homes listed by fund manager who lost $7B of clients' money in Madoff fraud," *Albany Times Union*, 11 April 2009.

116   "hedge fund investing . . . in China" Li Xiaowei, "U.S. Expert Predicts Big Future for Hedge Funds," *China Daily*, 14 January 2006.

117   "Chester . . . and Irongate" Author interview with John Donachie.

118   "only dukes not there were the Dukes of Hazzard" Jose de Cordoba and Thomas Catan, "The Charming Mr. Piedrahita Finds Himself Caught in the Madoff Storm— Colombian lived lavishly and sold a fund that fed the scam; He says he was a victim," *Wall Street Journal*, 31 March 2009.

118   "fund of funds sought out . . . low volatility" Author interview.

119   "the daughter of the Haegler family" Keith Dovkants, "The Gilded Family Who Fell to Earth," *Evening Standard*, 19 December 2008.

120   "after Madoff's arrest—UBP issued a detailed letter" UBP document.

120   "head of research, Gideon Nieuwoudt" Cassell Bryan-Low, "Inside bank, alarm rang— Switzerland's UBP stuck with Madoff despite warnings," *Wall Street Journal*, 15 January 2009.

121   "British gossip columnist Taki Theodoracopulos" Taki, "Marked men," *The Spectator*, 7 February 2009.

121   "Werner Wolfer was a Swiss banker" Commentary by Ann Woolner, "Madoff Victims Suspected a Crime, Just Didn't Care," 2009 January 30 (Bloomberg).

122   "Ken Nakayama . . . was doing what he loved" Author interview.

124   "Walter Noel . . . on the big money circuit" Author interview, former associate Fred Kolber.

125   "Noel's sons-in-law got paid much more" Fairfield compensation worksheet.

125   "Charles Murphy . . . snapped up the mansion . . . for $33 million" Josh Barbanel, "Every Man for Himself," *New York Times*, 25 January 2009.

125–126   "Jeffrey Tucker had got a whiff of the big money" Author interview, former associate Fred Kolber.

128   "AIG decided to take a look" Author interview.

128   "warned Walter Noel face-to-face" Author interview with member of the Greenwich Roundtable.

Chapter Six

129   "with her husband Erwin Kohn" Nelson D. Schwartz and Julia Werdigier, "Madoff ties bring down a brash Viennese banker," *New York Times*, 8 January 2009.

129   "brokerage firm called Windsor IBC" FINRA BrokerCheck brokerage records.

130   "he was there every year without fail" Author interview with Doug Engmann.

130   "exchange officials from around the world" "NYSE Hosts Latest Intercourse Challenge, Wins Golf Tourney," *Securities Week*, 23 July 1990.

130   "star money manager Felix Zulauf" Beth Belton, "Program helps high rollers invest in Europe," *USA Today*, 7 June 1990.

130   "unique way . . . to invest in European equities" Michael R. Sesit, "Eurovaleur Offers New Team Approach for Big Investments in European Stocks," *Wall Street Journal*, 5 June 1990.

132   "Kohn wasn't just a banker" Author interview with William Browder.

132   "crestlike seal of twin lions" Matthias Wabl, "Sonja Kohn Wooed Bernard Madoff Billions with Medici 'Fantasy,'" 2009 February 19 (Bloomberg).

134   "Glenn Gramolini, a Geneva-based asset manager" Helyar, Burton, and Silver, "Madoff Enablers Winked at Suspected Front-Running."

135   "Medici controlled the Primeo funds" Matthias Wabl, "Madoff Wasn't Friend, Pain Is 'Unbearable,' Kohn Says," 2009 January 15 (Bloomberg)

135   "commissions of more than 800,000 Euros" Zoe Schneeweiss and Matthias Wabl, "Bank Medici Ensnared by Madoff Losses After Winning Fund Award," 2008 December 24 (Bloomberg).

135   "she funneled as much as $8 billion" *Format Magazine*, Austria, 1 June 2009, www

.format.at/articles/0922/525/243071/das-geheimnis-medici-bankpraesidentin-kohn-madoff-beraterin.

135 **"Paris-based BNP, for instance, issued"** Schneeweiss and Wabl, "Bank Medici Ensnared."

136 **"Horst Leonhardt from Austria, says that Kohn didn't disclose"** Horst, Leonhardt *v.* Madoff, Medici et al., 2009, civ 2032, SDNY, filed March 2009.

137 **"Kohn allegedly made two transfers to . . . Gibraltar"** *Profile* magazine, 29 May 2009, www.profil.at/articles/0921/560/242678/geldwaescheverdacht-sonja-kohn-ermittlungen-medici-bank-gruenderin.

138 **"Leveraged Capital Holdings"** LCH marketing document, 1999, 30th anniversary of asset management.

138 **"with the backing of Edmond de Rothschild"** Mike Foster, "Backers reduce weightings in Soros' Quantum funds," *Financial News*, 13 April 1998.

138 **"Georges Karlweis"** Stanley Reed, "The Rothschilds' Hedge Fund Guru Georges Karlweis is courtly, conservative—and a big winner," *BusinessWeek*, 10 March 1997.

140 **"UBP launched D-Invest Total Return"** "Genève, bastion historique de la gestion de fonds de hedge funds Angélique Mounier-Kuhn," *Le Temps*, 13 September 2006.

140 **"UBP wasn't reckless"** Author interview, former UBP employee.

142 **"the Qatar Investment Authority's executive director"** Camilla Hall, "Madoff 'Killed' Hedge Funds, QIA's Al-Abdullah Says," 2009 March 12 (Bloomberg).

142 **"black boxes"** Kat Slowe, "Ithmar Capital predicts hedge funds 'extinction,' " ArabianBusiness.com, 03 April 2009.

143 **"Irving Picard . . . went after Bank Safra"** lawsuit, www.madofftrustee.com.

144 **"as the school of kings, Le Rosey,"** Sarah Veal, "In Switzerland, Democracy at the Summit," *International Herald Tribune*, 17 February 1993.

144 **"Busson and Thurman would sometimes have dinner with Bernie Madoff,"** Eleanor Squillari and Mark Seal, *Vanity Fair*, June 2009.

145 **"Busson ended up redeeming out of Berger's fund"** Neil Behrmann, "Judge instructs Bear Stearns to repay $160M to Manhattan Receiver," Infovest21 News Provider Service, 15 February 2007.

145 **"Berger was convicted"** Boris Groendahl, "Time Runs Out for Charges Against Michael Berger," Reuters, 8 April 2009.

145 **"ARK (Absolute Return for Kids)"** Cassell Bryan-Low, WSJ BLOG/Deal Journal: "Hedge Fund Charity Gala Much More Low-Key," 4 June 2009, blogs.wsj.com/deals.

145 **"the hedge fund industry is a force for good"** "Diary Arpad Busson," *The Spectator*, 14 June 2008.

146 **"GAM, a hedge fund of funds"** Yael Bizouati, "GAM Expands Fund-of-Funds Team: Alternative manager brings on two former Condor execs," *Investment Management Weekly*, 7 April 2008.

146 **"Catching a fraud is practically impossible"** Stephanie Baker and Tom Cahill, "Uma Thurman No Help to Arpad Busson in Madoff Fraud's Nightmare," 2009 January 8 (Bloomberg).

147 **"Nicola Horlick and her company Bramdean"** Martin Steward, "Madoff scandal asks industry awkward questions," *Financial Times*, 1 February 2009.

148 **"cash out of Madoff accounts with just ten day's notice"** "Bramdean Alternatives Limited," Unaudited Interim Report and Condensed Half-Yearly Financial Statements for the period from 1 April 2008 to 30 September 2008, Regulatory News Service, London Stock Exchange.

149 **"Haussmann also revealed one of the hedge fund industry's dirtiest little secrets"** Haussmann Explanatory Memorandum, February 2007.

149 **"It works like this with rebates"** Author interview, hedge fund manager.

Chapter Seven

153 **"Vinik, who ran Fidelity's well-known Magellan mutual fund"** Steven Syre and Charles Stein, "Hedge Fund Chief to Close Operation—Former Magellan Manger Jeff Vinik says it's time to refocus, spend more time with his growing family," *Boston Globe*, 27 October 2000.

153 **"Then came Eton Park. Eric Mindich"** Gregory Zuckerman and Henny Sender, "Huge Hedge Fund Launched Successfully Under Eric Mindich, *Wall Street Journal*, 3 November 2004.

154 **"known as a 'lockup' in the hedge-fund world"** Riva D. Atlas, "Hedge Funds' Glitter Fades (but Not for Investors)," *New York Times*, 5 November 2004.

155 **"Paredes, then a professor at Washington University School of Law"** Paredes draft paper.

156 **"One German billionaire even took his own life"** Carter Dougherty, "Facing Losses, Billionaire Takes His Own Life," *New York Times*, 6 January 2009.

156 **"volatile short-selling of Volkswagen"** Daniel Schäfer in Frankfurt and James Mackintosh, "Hedge funds may sue Porsche over VW," *Financial Times*, 15 March 2009.

156 **"Ackles, who represents the Hedge Fund Association"** Author interview with Mitch Ackles.

190 **"the perceived edge was Madoff's ability"** UBP letter to clients.

157 **"Pacific West Health Medical Center Employees Retirement Trust, which invested in Madoff"** Pacific West, Repex lawsuits *v.* Fairfield Greenwich et al.

157 **"there were no third parties independently confirming"** Gregoriou and Lhabitant, "Madoff! A riot of red flags."

159 **"the Baer client began taking notes"** Author interview with former Julius Baer banker.

159 **"Bank lending is inherently more expensive"** "Banking Survey—securities displace banking," *The Economist*, 2 May 1992.

160 **"functioning as a "shadow banking system"** Emily Barrett, "Pimco's Gross Sees Banking System Emerging from Shadows," Dow Jones Newswires, 8 January 2008.

161 **"Cerberus Capital Management, a hedge fund"** Dennis K. Berman and Monica Langley, "Driver's Seat—Sign of the Times: A Deal for GMAC," *Wall Street Journal*, 4 April 2006.

161 **"Lampert of ESL hedge fund"** "Store closing costs, lower demand hurt Sears' net; Shares jump as Kmart increased its operating profit the first time in two years," MarketWatch .com, 26 February 2009.

162 **"$7 trillion of their savings in mutual funds"** Managed Funds Association, 2009.

162 **"just sixty-eight hedge fund firms in existence"** Kaja Whitehouse, "Hedgie Horrified—Investor's Letter Strikes Back at Hedge Fund Industry," *New York Post*, 21 November 2008.

163 **"It's outrageous . . . I am appalled and disgusted by the activities"** Letter, Sandra Manzke, 2008.

164 **"Citigroup was so eager to bring Pandit on"** Heidi Moore, WSJ BLOG/Deal Journal: "Citigroup's Troubled Tale of he Tape," Dow Jones News Service, 20 November 2008.

164 **"Pandit's Old Lane fund was sucking wind"** Eric Dash, "All Told, the Price Tag for Citigroup's New Chief Is $216 Million," *New York Times*, 14 March 2008.

165 **"Hedge funds were even starting to inspire class warfare"** David Segal, "Anguished silence fills Bear offices; Employees sad, unsure of future," *Washington Post*, 30 May 2008.

165 **"Bear Stearns hedge funds"** Kate Kelly and Dionne Searcey, "Bear Stearns purchase came with legal woes," *Wall Street Journal*, 16 March 2009.

165 **"They made money at the expense of others"** "Amazon Defense Coalition: Chevron Makes Multinational Monitor Magazine's Top Ten List of World's Worst Corporations," *Multinational Monitor* magazine, Business Wire, 26 November 2008.

167 "CalPERS, which invested $11 billion in hedge funds" "CalPERS to Expand Private-Equity, VC Investments Reuters," *HedgeWorld News*, 8 June 2009.

Chapter Eight

169 "regulars at industry networking events" www.tradersmagazine.com/photos/.
169 "Shana Madoff, Peter's daughter who had been hired out of law school" Gregoriou and Lhabitant, "Madoff! A riot of red flags."
170 "signed by Enrica Cotellessa Pitz, Madoff's controller" Massachusetts Secretary of State William Galvin complaint *v.* Cohmad, exhibits.
171 "Madoff didn't allow broker-dealer employees to keep paper on their desks" Author interviews with former Madoff employee; Julia Fenwick interview, Goslett, "I Just Can't Live with That Camera."
172 "Lazard valuation report of these businesses" Confidential document shopped to Wall Street firms after Madoff's arrest.
173 "Frank was rude all the time" Author interview with son of Madoff investor.
173 "Archbishop Molloy" David Voreacos, David Glovin, and Patricia Hurtado, "Madoff's 'Street-Smart' Aide DiPascali Was Investors' Go-To Guy," 2009 January 16 (Bloomberg).
173 "Bongiorno and DiPascali were kindred spirits" David Voreacos and David Glovin, "Madoff Key Aide Bongiorno Recruited Her Neighbors as Investors," 2009 February 14 (Bloomberg).
174 "Robert McMahon, who worked at Madoff" Author interviews.
175 "Velvel recalled" "Investing with Bernie Madoff: How It Happened, What Happened, and What Might Be Done, Part I," 19 January 2009, http://velvelonnationalaffairs.blogspot.com/2009/01/investing-with-bernie-madoff-how-it.html.
176 "Lautenberg of New Jersey, which invested with Madoff, sued Peter" Lautenberg suit *v.* Peter Madoff.
177 "According to Teri Ryan, the whole Madoff family is to blame" Daniel Ryan, Teri Ryan *v.* Peter, Mark, Andrew, Ruth Madoff et al., 09101616 in N.Y. State Supreme Court, February 2009.
179 "to Teri Ryan, there was no separating Madoff family members" Daniel Ryan, *Teri Ryan v. Peter, Mark, Andrew, Ruth Madoff* et al., 09101616 in N.Y. State Supreme Court, February 2009.
180 "Cohmad . . . not to use e-mail at all" SEC fraud charges *v.* Cohmad, 2009.
181 "Annette Bongiorno had her own office" Tom Lauricella, Amir Efrati, and Aaron Lucchetti, "Painting the Scene of Madoff's Crime," *Wall Street Journal*, 29 January 2009.
181 "phony stock trade confirmations" Amir Efrati, "The Madoff Fraud Case: Probe finds fresh details on Madoff trade tickets," *Wall Street Journal*, 10 March 2009.
182 "and the Vancouver Stock Exchange" Dominic Lau, "Stratus says exchange clients Y2K ready," Reuters.
185 "Paul Konigsberg" Tom Lauricella, Cassell Bryan-Low, and Jeanne Whalen, "The Madoff Fraud Case: London office used in cash ploy, filing says Madoff transferred money from U.S. to U.K. and back," *Wall Street Journal*, 13 March 2009.
186 "Madoff investor Steven Leber" 09-80593 U.S. District Court Southern District of Florida, Leber *v.* Paul Konigsberg, Konigsberg Wolf, 20 April 2009.
186 "account number BONY 621 . . . and JPM 703" SIPC affidavits re Madoff bank accounts, Securities Investor Protection Corp. *v.* Bernard L. Madoff, filed in U.S. Bankruptcy Court, 5 May 2009.
188 "Stephen Raven, chief executive of Madoff Securities International" Marietta Cauchi, "Madoff Securities Intl Ltd: Not Part of NY Bernard L. Madoff," Dow Jones Newswires, 12 December 2008.
189 "'It was like going to a lavish wedding,' Fenwick recalled" Goslett, "I Just Can't Live with That Camera".

189   "Gaffen visited the Madoff operation" Author interview.
191   "NSX . . . had once been known as the Cincinnati Stock Exchange" Ivy Schmerken,
        "The Bulls and Bears Come Out at Night; Electronic Trading," *Wall Street & Technol-
        ogy*, 1 September 1990.
191   "Madoff paid Bear Stearns substantial fees" MLSMK Investments Company *v.* JP
        Morgan Chase & Co. and JP Morgan Chase Bank, 09 cv 4049, U.S. District Court, So.
        District NY, 23 April 2009.
192   "Chase representatives met with Madoff" Ibid.

Chapter Nine

195   "Markopolos came to view Madoff as a domestic enemy" Markopolos testimony to
        Congress, 4 February 2009.
197   "Manion . . . was tough and smart" Author interview with Fran DeAngelis.
198   "QWAFAFEW, where finance nerds could get together" Author interview, Herb Blank,
        Rapid Ratings.
199   "Zoe Van Schyndel, a onetime SEC employee" Markopolos testimony to Congress,
        4 February 2009.
200   "We were losing a tremendous amount of business" Author interview with Ron
        Egalka.
201   "Casey, Markopolos, and their lead research assistant Neil Chelo puzzled over"
        Markopolos testimony, Egalka interview.
203   "Harry's strategy is like Bernie Madoff's" Markopolos testimony to Congress, 4 Febru-
        ary 2009.
205   "Neil Chelo, also a Chartered Financial Analyst" Ibid.
205   "Frank Casey, a former U.S. Army airborne infantry officer" Ibid.
208   "In a 1934 memo, Pecora wrote" Ferdinand Pecora, memo to the Senate Banking
        Committee chairman, 1934, National Archives. Pecora was author of "Wall Street
        Under Oath: The Story of Our Modern Money Changers."
209   "Geffner was SEC 'class of '91'" Author interview with Ron Geffner.
210   "WorldCom securities fraud case" "Preparing for Alternative Asset Management Reg-
        ulation: A Roadmap for Planning Cost-Effective, Asset-Building Infrastructures to
        Meet the Coming Regulatory Requirements," FinServe Consulting, www.finservcon-
        sulting.com, May 2009.
210   "Cox was an enthusiastic supporter of Newt Gingrich's" Adam Zagorin and Michael
        Weisskopf, "Inside the Breakdown at the SEC," *Time*, 9 March 2009.
211   "blocked Aguirre from deposing John Mack" Author interview with Gary Aguirre.
211   "Pequot Capital's Art Samberg shut down" Alistair Barr, "Pequot closing in midst of
        government probe; Investigation cast 'cloud' over hedge fund firm, Samberg says,"
        MarketWatch, 27 May 2009.
212   "BATS, based in Kansas City, hired Swanson" Stephen Labaton, "Unlikely Player
        Pulled Into Madoff Swirl," *New York Times*, 19 December 2008.
213   "Mark McKeefrey, Fairfield general counsel, and Amit Vijayvergiya, Fairfield's chief risk
        officer" Transcripts, Massachusetts Secretary William Galvin complaint *v.* Cohmad,
        exhibits.
215   "Tucker testified, either Madoff or DiPascali turned on a screen" Ibid.
216   "Fairfield employees worked furiously to produce evidence" Ibid.
217   "'allegations of Madoff being a Ponzi scheme were never even investigated,' said
        Thomas Gorman" Author interview with Thomas Gorman.
218   "The SEC comes in and they tick off boxes on a checklist" Author interview with Rick
        Stone.
218   "Bernie is a fraud" Markopolos testimony.

Chapter Ten

221   "**Lord Jacobs of Belgravia was bitten**" Suzy Jagger, Miles Costello, and Christine Seib, "Madoff's client list shows how his web spanned the worlds of Hollywood and UK Establishment," *The Times*, 6 February 2009.

222   "**Greenfield has filed a lawsuit against the NASD**" Author interview with Richard Greenfield.

223   "**Flagler . . . long line of millionaires**" *Florida: A Guide to the Southernmost State*, Oxford University Press (1939).

223   "**cosmetics queen Estée Lauder . . . for lunch**" Bettijane Levine, Los Angeles Times Service, "Cosmetics Pioneer, Mogul Dies at Age 97," *Miami Herald* , 26 April 2004.

224   "**Sullivan, the youngest of the Florida connections**" John Holland, "Madoff Ally in S. Florida Tells What Went Wrong," *South Florida Sun-Sentinel*, 31 January 2009.

224   "**'You son of a bitch—it's over now,' Bienes said**" PBS *Frontline*, www.pbs.org transcript.

226   "**St. Thomas Aquinas High School, where Monsignor Kelly is the principal**" Michael Sallah, Patrick Danner, John Dorschner, and Ina Paiva Cordle, "Floridians fleeced," *Miami Herald*, 6 February 2009.

226   **Bienes claims** Harriet Johnson Brackey, "Charities Still Feeling the Pain in Wake of Madoff's Fall," *South Florida Sun-Sentinel*, 24 May 2009.

227   "**Mrs. Panstreppon . . . researches fraudsters**" Talking Points Memo, //tpmcafe.talking-pointsmemo.com/talk/blogs/mrs_panstreppon/atom.xml.

230   "**Madoff's fund was pitched to Sands as a no-risk investment**" Josh Hafenbrack, "Legislator Needs 2nd Job, Savings Gone in Madoff Fraud, Sands Consults on Side," *South Florida Sun-Sentinel*, 8 June 2009.

231   "**Jose Lambiet, columnist for the *Palm Beach Post***" Author interview.

231   "**Fisher had already lost $200 million—with . . . KL Financial**" Jeff Ostrowski, "Judge Denies Bail to Man Charged in Investor Scam," *Palm Beach Daily News*, 4 April 2009.

232   "**Jaffe . . . made withdrawals from his Madoff accounts**" SEC complaint v. Cohmad, June 2009.

233   "**I believe Ruth had some part in this**" Author interview with Richard Rampell.

235   "**Andrew Schneider is the founder of HedgeCo.net**" Author interview with Andrew Schneider.

235   "**even in the savings plans of law enforcement**" "West Palm Beach Police Pension Sues Collins Capital," Infovest21 Staff, 11 June 2009.

237   "**Picower's attorney, William Zabel**" Jane Musgrave, "Palm Beach residents who claim Madoff bilked them are being targeted over profits they made," *Palm Beach Post*, Cox News Service, 7 June 2009.

238   "**Picower Institute for Medical Research and two for-profit . . . companies**" Mary Jacoby, "Complex web benefits foundation founder," *St. Petersburg Times*, 8 July 2001.

240   "**mini Ponzi scheme in Venezuela**" "Venezuela judge orders arrest of 10 brokers," Reuters News, 5 November 1993.

Chapter Eleven

242   "**Leon Levy's memoir, *The Mind of Wall Street*,**" New York: Perseus [permission pending from the late author's wife Shelby White]

242   "**Upon Heller's recommendation**" "Merkin's Art Adviser Bought Expensive Rothkos, Lost Millions" lindsay Pollock, 2009 January 8 (Bloomberg).

243   "**Merkin didn't particularly like the Rothkos**" Author interview with Victor Teicher.

244   "**Merkin . . . had been asked to pen essays**" "McGraw-Hill Professional to Publish 75th Anniversary Edition of Graham and Dodd's *Security Analysis*; With New Commentary from Today's Most Prominent Value Investors and a New Foreword by Warren E. Buffett," PR Newswire (U.S.), 5 May 2008.

245 "Stevenson . . . gained entry to the building" Michael Gross, *740 Park: The Story of the World's Richest Apartment Building* (New York: Broadway, 2005), www.mgross.com/writing/books/740-park/

245 "It was not easy to gain admittance" Teri Karush Rogers, "Peeking Behind the Gilded Walls of 740 Park Ave.," *New York Times*, 9 October 2005.

246 "Keynes . . . outperformed the market" Asher Meir, "Madoff's 'perfect storm' of misconduct; Private investors are free to risk their money as they see fit, but institutions are obligated to high standards of prudence," *Jerusalem Post*, 19 December 2008.

246 "NYU . . . resisted . . . Merkin stayed silent" Memorandum of law opposing Merkin motion to dismiss, New York University *v.* Ariel Fund, Ezra Merkin et al., N.Y. State Supreme Court, Index No. 08603803/2008.

246 "Founded in 1886, Yeshiva was" Lee Mitgang, "'Torah U'Mada:' Yeshiva University Marks Its Centennial," Associated Press, 14 September 1986.

247 "started in 1948 by Rafael Recanati" Joe Brady Stamford, "Minimal concern as field narrows," *Tradewinds*, 18 April 2008.

247 "Recanatis would be known as" Mirit Gal-Edd, "The Rockefellers of Israel," *Jerusalem Post*, 23 August 1991.

248 "Merkin, his siblings, and their children . . . hold about 37 percent" Overseas Group SEC filings.

249 Ezra parted company with Joel Greenblatt" "The Monster Mensch," *New York* magazine, 22 February 2009.

251 "Merkin reaped . . . $470 million in fees" Zachery Kouwe, "Manager gives up control of funds after Madoff loss," *New York Times*, 21 May 2009.

251 "Goldman, a twenty-year veteran of Wall Street" Peter Robison, Janet Frankston Lorin, and Joshua Fineman, "Merkin Intimidated Co-Op Board While Building Funds Madoff Lost," 2009 January 9 (Bloomberg).

252 "In 1982, Nash and Levy sold Oppenheimer" Abha Bhattarai, "Jack Nash, 79, Pioneer in Hedge Funds," *New York Times*, 2 August 2008.

253 "Nash focused on short-term trading" Tom Cahill, "Jack Nash; Visionary Investor, Mentor in Mutual, Hedge Funds," 1 August 2008 (Bloomberg).

254 "Teicher was convicted in 1992" NYU lawsuit *v.* Merkin, Deposition transcripts N.Y. Attorney General Andrew Cuomo *v.* Merkin and Gabriel.

255 "Merkin farmed out money to Feinberg" Greg B. Smith, with Douglas Feiden and Thomas Zambito, "Madoff's Pal Feels AG Wrath; Cuomo Charges Merkin in Ponzi Ploy," *New York Daily News*, 7 April 2009.

255 "Merkin told *BusinessWeek* magazine" Emily Thornton, with Susan Zegel, Joseph Weber, and Lorraine Woellert, "Q: What's Bigger Than Cisco, Coke, or McDonald's? A: Steve Feinberg's Cerberus, a Vast Hedge Fund That's Snapping Up Companies—Lots of Them," *BusinessWeek*, 3 October 2005,

256 "Olmert . . . told the Associated Press" "Israel Govt Sells 9.99% Bk Leumi Stake to U.S.-Based Funds," Dow Jones International News, 15 November 2005.

257 "Stamos . . . introduced Merkin" Ianthe Jeanne Dugan, "Failed Hedge-Fund Firm Bayou Sues Investors to Return Money," *Wall Street Journal*, 13 September 2006.

258 "Jack Nash pulled his money out of Madoff" N.Y. Attorney General Andrew Cuomo suit *v.* Merkin, Gabriel et al.

261 "Andrew Gordon" Thomas Zambito, "Merkin Warned, Still Lost Millions—Documents," *New York Daily News*, 18 April 2009.

Chapter Twelve

265 "Herb Blank of Risk Ratings" Author interview.

265 "Squillari noticed that Madoff left his appointment book" Mark Seal, *Vanity Fair*, June 2009.

265 "Ruth . . . was withdrawing $10 million from a Cohmad" Massachusetts Secretary of State William Galvin complaint *v.* Fairfield Greenwich Group, exhibits.

266   "Joan and Ruth each inherited just over $1 million" Anthony M. DeStefano, "Papers suggest Ruth didn't know she put mother's assets into her husband's firm; Experts say that raises doubt she knew of fraud," *Newsday*, 18 June 2009.

266   "Little did we know" Joe Lauria, "A Foot Soldier for Madoff Looks Back on His Service," *Wall Street Journal*, 23 March 2009.

273   "Daniel Celeghin . . . Casey Quirk" Christine Williamson, "Institutional funds of funds suffer 9-month drop of 37%," *Pensions & Investments*, 15 June 2009.

Index

Access International Advisors, 84, 203–4, 221
Achenbaum, William, 232
Ackles, Mitch, 156
Advisory business/hedge fund, 54–80
  appeal to investors, reasons for, 90–94, 104–5, 119, 122, 146–47, 157–59
  auditor for, 95, 157, 259
  Avellino and Bienes closing, impact of, 56, 81–82
  beginning of, 47–48
  and Cohmad Securities, 48, 50–51, 62–66
  connection with legal operation, 54–60, 75–76, 79–80, 157–58, 170, 172, 187
  DiPascali, role of, 173–76, 178
  employees, 79, 173–76, 180
  explosive growth of, 81–83, 119
  fake trades, executing, 181–82
  as fraud/Ponzi scheme. See Ponzi scheme
  fundraisers/feeders. See Feeder network
  invisibility of operations, 7, 78, 79, 90, 93, 124, 126–27, 183–84, 201, 235
  JPMorgan Chase knowledge of fraud, 192–93
  Madoff secrecy/lies about, 76–79, 82, 90, 158–59, 178, 180, 215
  Markopolos uncovers, 195–206
  old computer, Madoff use of, 94, 181–84
  performance fees, absence of, 88, 91, 114–15, 148–49, 198
  primer broker, absence of, 88–89
  registration with SEC (2006), 77
  returns paid from. See Returns
  SEC filings, fraudulent, 76–77
  seventeenth floor, appearance of, 170–71
  suspicions/red flags, 7–8, 88–98, 114–15, 118–19, 120–21, 136, 146, 157–59, 192–93, 198–203
  technology used, 181–84
  trade tickets, phony, 76, 181–82, 194

unraveling of, 56–57, 205–6, 263–65
withdrawals in 2008, 263–64
Aguirre, Gary, 210–11, 219
Aksia, 95, 97
Al-Abdullah, Hussain Ali, 142
Allen, Sarah, 96
Allison, Michael, 20–21
Allwin, James, 153
Alpern, Ruth. *See* Madoff, Ruth (wife)
Alpern, Sara (mother of Ruth), 21, 266
Alpern, Sol (father of Ruth)
  background of, 21–23
  as fundraiser, 25–28, 47–48, 177–78, 222
Alpern & Heller, 21, 26–27, 177
ALTIN, 103
Ambrosino, Dominic, 270–71, 275–76
Ambrosino, Ronnie Sue, 4, 270–71, 275, 276, 278
American Depositary Receipts (ADRs), 185
American Jewish Congress, 194
American Stock Exchange (AMEX), 34–37
Anderson, Semone, 181
Angiulo family, 65
Arab investors, losses to, 142
Arenson, Cynthia, 25–26
Arenson, David, 26
Ariel fund, 48, 84, 244, 250–51, 253, 257
Asch, Judi, 19
Ascot fund, 48, 84, 228, 242–43, 244, 251, 257–61, 272
Asness, Cliff, 160
Austria, Kohn, Sonja, 84, 129–37
Avellino, Frank, 26–28, 226–27
Avellino and Bienes
  copycat version of, 228–29
  as fundraiser, 27–29, 48, 177–78, 228
  knowledge of fraud, denial of, 28–29, 224
  as Madoff victims, 224–27
  re-open as Mayfair, 225–26

Avellino and Bienes (*cont.*)
  SEC shut-down of, 56, 81–82, 91, 118, 129, 178–79, 225–27

Bachenheimer, Doria, 217
Bacon, Kevin, 85, 172, 221, 243
Baker, Richard, 83
Banco Santander, 84, 86, 117, 142–43
  victims, payments to, 84, 143
Bank accounts, Madoff's, 186–87
Bank Leumi, 256
Bank Medici, 84, 130–37
  Kohn's funds, 134–37
Bank of New York Mellon, Madoff
  account, 186
Banque Syz & Co., 103
Baroni, Lisa, 277
Bear Stearns, counterparty trading with
  Madoff, 191, 193
Beauchamp, Ed, 51
Belfort, Jordan, 23
Benton, Dan, 153
Berger, Michael, 92, 145
Berger, Paul, 211
Berkman, Jay, 227
Bernard, Christophe, 120
Bernard L. Madoff Investment Securities
  Bear Stearns counterparty trading with,
    191, 193
  clients, policy toward, 72–73
  connection with illegal operation, 54–60,
    75–76, 79–80, 157–58, 170, 172, 187
  and crash of 1987, 80, 92, 129, 240
  and crash of 2008, 57, 63, 165–66
  electronic trading, 23, 37–43
  family employees, 67–70, 72, 91, 169,
    179–80
  founding of, 20, 23
  front-running suspicion, 77–78, 121–22,
    128
  global reach of. See Global business
  growth of, 26–27, 30, 45, 206
  as legitimate business, 12, 24–25
  Lipstick Building location, 53–54, 81
  London office. See Madoff Securities
    International (London)
  as market maker, 36, 45, 54, 70, 79, 134,
    171, 207–8, 225, 240
  options, use of, 56–59, 69, 148, 157
  order flow, payment to clients, 38, 43–46
  peculiar practices, 67–72, 78–79
  revenues/profit, 172
  SEC audits of, 77, 171–72
  SEC investigation of, 212–18
  statistical arbitrage unit, 73–75

Stratus system, use of, 182–83
  and third market, 30, 35–38, 44
  traders, role of, 70–73
  trading room/offices, 59–61, 71, 169–71
Bettencourt, Liliane, 204
Bienes, Michael, 26–28
  charitable contributions of, 226–27
  knowledge of fraud, denial of, 28–29, 224
  as Madoff victim, 226
  See also Avellino and Bienes
Biggs, Barton, 154
Bin Juma Belhoul, Faisal, 142
Biondo, Adriane, 5
Bish, Keith R., 103
Blank, Herb, 265
Bloomberg terminal, 156, 218–19
Boesky, Ivan, 237
Boiler Room, 23
Bonaventuri, Dan, 180
Bongiorno, Annette
  as fundraiser, 86, 173–74
  role in firm, 86, 175, 181–82, 184, 194
Bowman, Larry, 153
Braman, Norm, 172
Bramdean Asset Management, 147–48
Breslauer, Gerard, 85
Broker-dealer, use of term, 24
Browder, William, 132
Brown, Matthew, 117
Bruhl, John, 103
Buccellato, Rosalie, 69
Bucket shops, 23–24, 162
Bull, The (yacht), 187, 266
Busson, Arpad "Arkie," 84, 144–47, 273

Cacioppi, Theodore, 11–13
Candlestick charting, 71
Cap d'Antibes residence, 13, 72, 266
Cardile, Robert, 173, 175
Carlson, Dale, 37–38
Casey, Frank, 56–57, 196, 200–201, 205
Casscells, Anne, 153
Celebrity investors, 85, 172, 221, 272
Celeghin, Daniel, 273
Cerebus fund, 249, 251, 253, 255–56
Ceretti, Federico, 98, 102
Chais, Stanley, 55–56, 85, 228, 269, 271
Chapman, Peter, 33–35, 38–39
Charities and foundations
  due diligence requirement, 239
  as incentive for wealthy, 238
  Madoff victims, 85, 249, 257, 272, 276
Chelo, Neil, 201, 205
Cheung, Meghan, 198, 217
Chew, Robert, 220

Chin, Dennis, 1–2, 4, 275, 277
Christensen, Frank, 37, 54, 81, 87–88
Cialdini, Robert, 93
Cincinnati Stock Exchange, 35–36, 41–42, 45–46, 58, 191
Citigroup, decline (2007), 164
Cohmad Securities
    as feeder network, 48, 50–51, 62–70, 86–87, 170
    fraud, cover-up, 170
    mission statement to clients, 69
    office of, 170
Cohn, Marcia, 68–69, 86, 170
Cohn, Maurice "Sonny," 48, 50–51, 68–69, 86, 170, 223. See also Cohmad Securities
Cohn, Milton, 69
Collar trade, 59
Colomby, Harry, 17
Cooperman, Leon, 153
Cox, Christopher, 210, 219
Crash of 1987, 55, 80, 92, 129, 240
Crash of 2008, 57, 63, 87, 165–68, 192–93, 263
Credit Suisse, 157–58
Crupi, JoAnn "Jodi," 175
Cuomo, Andrew, 260

Dale, Chris, 187–88
Daly, Michael, 268–69
DaPuzzo, Peter, 34, 53–54
Dassin, Lev, 2, 266, 268
Decimalization, 56, 75, 207
Decker, Peter, 98
Delaire, A. J., 68
Delaire, Alvin, Jr., 50–51, 68, 140
Delaire, Alvin, Sr., 50
de la Villehuchet, René-Thierry Magon, 84, 203–4, 221
Denver, John, 272
de Picciotto, Edgar, 5, 91, 117, 120, 137, 139–41, 157, 203
de Picciotto, Michael, 117, 120, 140
Derivatives, 122
Dinvest Total Return, 140
DiPascali, Frank
    plea bargain, 237
    role in firm, 78–79, 173–76, 194, 215
    and unraveling of Ponzi, 263
Donachie, John, 114
Dumb money, 46, 117

Earn-outs, 100–101
Eberle, Fletcher, 17
Egalka, Ron, 196–97, 200–201, 204–5

Ehrenkranz, Joel, 97–98
Ehrenkranz, Sanford, 97–98
EIM, 84, 143–47
Electronic trading, 37–43
    and Cincinnati Stock Exchange, 35–36, 41–42, 45–46, 58, 191
    and hedging, 36
    Intermarket Trading System (ITS), 34–35, 41–42
    London office, 185
    Madoff Integrated Support System (MISS), 42
    and preferencing, 45–46
    profits gained from, 36–38
    statistical arbitrage unit, 73–75
    Straus system, 182–83
    trading procedure prior to, 23, 37–38, 40–41
Elie Wiesel Foundation for Humanity, 85, 249
Elstein, Sanford, 17
E-mail, archiving prohibited, 180
Employees
    of advisory business, 79, 173–76, 180
    DiPascali, role of, 173–76, 178
    e-mail, archiving prohibited, 180
    family employees, 67–70, 72, 91, 169, 179–80
    ignorance about fraud, 78–79, 172–73
    as investors, 172, 174
    treatment by Madoff, 180–81
Englander, Israel "Izzy," 158
Engler, Michael, 5, 49
Engmann, Doug, 234–35
Epstein, Lita, 95
E-Trade, Versus Technologies, 44
Europe, 122–50
    Access International Advisors, 84, 203–4, 221
    EIM, 84, 143–47
    FIM Advisors, 84, 98, 102–3
    Kohn, Sonja, 84, 122–28
    London office. See Madoff Securities International (London)
    Madoff appeal to investors, 139–40, 148–50, 204
    and Markopolos investigation, 203–4
    Notz Stucki, 91, 137–39
    Safra Banking Group, 142–43
    Union Bancaire Privée, 96, 102, 119–21, 140–42
Eurovaleur, 130, 132

Fairfield Greenwich Group, 106–28
    Chester and Irongate funds, 117

Fairfield Greenwich Group (*cont.*)
  due diligence failure by, 123, 126–28,
    215–16
  Emerald funds, 216
  as fund-raiser, 48, 83, 92, 95, 102, 105,
    107–8, 118–21
  Nakayama investigation of, 122–24
  and Noel family, 108–10, 116–17
  partners, 107, 110–11, 113–16, 117–18
  post-arrest, 216, 271–72
  SEC interview with, 212–14
  Sentry Fund, 88–89, 91, 107, 121,
    123–24, 157, 192–93, 205, 228, 272
  suspicions/red flags about, 123–28
  warning about Madoff to, 127–28,
    214–15
Fay, Sharon, 45
Feeder network, 148–49
  Alpern (father of Ruth) in, 25–28, 47–48,
    177–78, 222
  Avellino and Bienes, 26–28, 48, 177–78
  Bongiorno in, 86, 173–74
  Cohmad Securities, 48, 50–51, 62–70,
    86–87, 170
  commissions to, 27, 62–64, 66, 69, 83–
    84, 86–87, 101–2, 114–15, 132
  European, 122–50. See also Europe
  Fairfield Greenwich Group, 48, 83, 92,
    102, 105, 107–8, 118–28
  Florida connections, 222, 224–39
  functions for Madoff, 199
  and Kohn, Sonja, 129–37
  Konigsberg in, 186
  and Manzke, Sandra, 83–84, 89, 92,
    98–104
  M-Invest Ltd, 120
  and Ponzi unraveling, 263–64
  post-1990s fundraisers, 83–87, 92, 95,
    98–104
  post-arrest, 271–72
  Ruth (wife) in, 223
Feinberg, Stephen, 161, 249, 253, 255–56
Felder, Raoul, 166–67
Felsen, Brian, 4–5
Fenwick, Julia, 61, 188–89
FIM Advisors, 84, 98, 102–3
Financial World, 37
Fisher, Jerome, 231–32
Fisher, Len, 93–94
Fitzmaurices, 276
Fix, Charles, 132, 263
Florida-based victims, 222–41
  feeder network connections to, 222,
    224–39
  See also Palm Beach

Foley, Mark, 234
Forbes, 36
Foundations. *See* Charities and foundations
Foxton, Willard, 269
France, Access International Advisors, 84,
  203–4, 221
Freilich, April, 236
Frenville, Rudolph, Jr., 28
Friehling, David, 157
Friehling & Horowitz, 95, 157, 179, 259
Frontline, 28
Front-running, 77–78, 121–22, 128
Fund-raisers for Madoff. *See* Feeder
  network

Gabelli, Mario, 98–100
Gabriel Capital, 48, 84, 228, 243–44,
  249–57, 251, 253, 257, 260, 272
Gaffen, David, 189–90
Galvin, William, 68–69
Game theory, 93–94
Garrity, Michael, 199
Geduld, E. E. "Buzzy," 32, 60
Geffen, David, 85, 221
Gerber, Pati, 48–49
Gibraltar Securities, 23–24
Gieger, Joe, 94
Glantz, Edward, 228
Global business
  Arab investors, 142
  European network. See Europe
  Madoff efforts for, 129–30
Goldenson, Daniel, 260–61
Goldman, Laura, 251–52
Gordon, Andrew, 261
Gorman, Thomas, 217–18
Gramolini, Glenn, 134
Grasso, Richard, disdain for Madoff, 38, 40
Greenberg, Jonathan, 62
Greenblatt, Joel, 253
Greenfield, Richard, 222, 231, 232
Greenspan, Alan, 162
Gregoriou, Greg N., 44
Greisman, Harold, 127
Gross, Bill, 161
Grosso, Carlo, 98, 102
Grübel, Oswald, 31, 157, 158

Hadassah, 272, 276
Hall, George, 45
Harris, Ira, 222
Haussmann Holdings, 138–40, 149
Hedge funds
  avoidance of Madoff, 78
  capital introduction, 88

and crash of 2008, 165–68
CSFB/Tremont index, 100
Europe, access to, 140–41
funds of hedge funds, 138
future reforms, 273
growth of industry, 78, 83, 85, 138–39,
   152–54, 159–62
investor access to funds problem,
   162–64
low volatility, 84, 89, 91, 118–19
Madoff's bogus fund. See Advisory
   business/hedge fund
origin of, 151
pension fund investors, 103–4
primer broker, necessity of, 88–89
rebates, 149–50
SEC enforcement actions, 155
SEC registration (2006), 151
self-clearing, 158
as shadow banking system, 159–61
structure/operation of, 155–56
third-party marketing of, 85–86
top funds, 90
unpredictability of, 118
vetting, importance of, 145–46
Hedging, and electronic trading, 36
Heller, Sherman, 21
Herald funds, 134–37
Hershson, Abraham, 48–49
Hirshon, Walter, 51–52
Hoffman, Roger, 51
Hollander, Stan, 19, 23
Horlick, Nicola, 147–48
Horowitz, Jerome, 157
Horwitz, Daniel, 1
Huddleston, Pat, 95

Ineichen, Alexander, 138
Interbourse, 130, 234–35
Intermarket Trading System (ITS), 34–35
Internet, precursor to, 41–42
Investors
   attracting, main methods, 47–48. See also
      Feeder network
   claims, settlement of, 269–71
   collusion with Madoff, 93–94, 105, 119,
      122, 219–20
   courtroom speakers, 3–4, 275–76
   early clients, 25–27
   European compared to American, 221.
      See also Europe
   Florida residents, 222–41
   Hollywood personalities, 85, 172, 221,
      272
   Jewish. See Jewish community

Madoff appeal, reasons for, 8, 49–50, 83,
   90–94, 104–5, 119, 122, 146–47,
   157–59
Madoff policy toward, 72–73
Madoff promises to, 6, 27, 49–50
secrecy encouraged by Madoff, 7, 96,
   135, 136, 151, 199
suicides of, 204, 269
taxes paid on returns, 270
turning Madoff down, 89–92, 94–95,
   239–40
Israel, Sam, 92
Italy
   FIM Advisors, 84, 98, 102–3
   UniCredit, 131, 135–36, 142, 147

Jackson, Winnie, 181
Jacobson, Alex, 44, 57–59, 93
Jaffe, Robert M.
   as fundraiser, 50–51, 62, 64–66, 69, 86,
      222, 223, 230–33, 264
   as Madoff victim, 241
   as neighbor, 112
   SEC suit against, 232
Jewish community
   Catskills vacationers, 25–26
   charities/foundations, 85, 249, 272, 276
   in Florida. See Florida-based victims;
      Palm Beach
   fraud, impact on, 272–73
   long-time investors, examples of, 48–51
   and Merkin, Hermann, 246–49
   and Merkin, J. Ezra, 249–50, 256
   socialite circles, 26, 66, 84–85
   See also Investors
Jones, Alfred Winslow, 151, 154
JPMorgan Chase
   Madoff account, 186, 190–91
   Madoff relationship with, 191–93
   suits against, 193
   suspicions/red flags of, 192–93

Kahneman, Daniel, 90
Kang, Detective, 11–13
Kantor, Norman, 228–29
Karlweis, Georges, 138
Kashar, Mark, 68, 71–72, 75
Kass, Doug, 79, 79–80
Katzenberg, Jeffrey, 85
Kelly, Vincent T., 226
Kenn Jordan Associates, 227
King, Larry, 272
Kingate funds, 98–99, 102–4, 272
   Global, 84, 99, 102–3
KLM Asset Management, 228–29

Kluiber, Rudy, 153
Kobren, Eric, 153
Koeppel, Nora, 16
Kohn, Sonja, 48, 84, 129–37
  disappearance of, 272
Kolber, Fred, 112–13
Konig, Salomon, 239–40
Konigsberg, Paul, 185–86
  as fundraiser, 186
Konigsberg & Wolf, 186
Kroll, Dick, 196–97

Lampert, Eddie, 161
Lanesborough Hotel, 189
Latin America, Safra Banking Group, 139,
  142–43
Lauer, Matt, 11
Lauria, Tom, 85, 88–89
Lautenberg, Frank, 176
Leber, Steven, 186
Leonhardt, Horst, 136
Levitt, Arthur, 73
Levy, Leon, 252–55
Lhabitant, François-Serge, 44
Lipkin, Eric, 175
Lipstick Building, 53–54, 81
Litt, Marc, 2
London office. See Madoff Securities
  International (London)
Long-Term Capital Management, 79, 254
Loomis, Carol, 154
Lovell, Putnam, 101

Mack, John, 210–11
MacKay, Charles, 90–91
McKeefrey, Mark, 213–14
Macklin, Gordon, 34, 36
McMahon, Robert, 174–75, 180, 182–84,
  194
Madoff, Andrew (son)
  education of, 179
  Madoff confession to, 13, 57, 265
  role in firm, 37, 67, 72
  turns Madoff in, 11–12
Madoff, Bernard L.
  arrest of, 11–13
  background of, 13–21
  bank accounts of, 186–87
  Bull, The (yacht), 187, 266
  confession to family, 13, 57, 265
  courtroom demeanor, 2–3, 268–69, 275,
    277–78
  early life red flags, 20–21
  exchange events, attendance at, 130,
    234–35

family, protection of, 3, 268
financial industry businesses. See
  Advisory business/hedge fund; Bernard
  L. Madoff Investment Securities
fraud, scope of, 2, 6, 30, 266–67
guilty plea, 1–4, 268
guilty plea, rationale for, 13, 269
house arrest, 2, 4, 266
illegal operation/Ponzi scheme. See
  Advisory business/hedge fund
on investment strategy, 7, 49–50
investors/clients of. See Florida-based
  residents; Investors; Jewish community;
  Palm Beach
losses, amount of, 276–77
media coverage during career, 36, 37, 41,
  43, 44, 45
media exposés, before arrest, 7–8
at Metropolitan Correctional Center, 269
as NASDAQ chairman, 44
personality, early red flags, 17–18
personality of, 52–53, 60–61, 81–82, 171
political activities, 5–6
on Ponzi scheme, 6–7, 12, 268
residences of, 11, 13
revolutionizes trading, 28, 30–46, 73–75
right angles, obsession with, 61
seaplane, commute to work, 51–52
and SEC. See Securities and Exchange
  Commission (SEC)
sentencing, 275–78
social circle, 51–53, 112, 144, 231
sons. See Madoff, Andrew (son); Madoff,
  Mark (son)
Versus Technologies, 44
wife. See Madoff, Ruth (wife)
See also Investors
Madoff, Mark (son)
  Madoff confession to, 13, 57, 265
  role in firm, 37, 67, 72, 189–90
  turns Madoff in, 11–12
Madoff, Peter (brother), 61–62
  biographical information, 15, 20, 179
  and electronic trading, 36–37
  financial industry, accomplishments in, 5
  joins firm, 23
  knowledge of fraud, 218
  Madoff confession to, 265
  personality profile, 61–62
  role in firm, 67, 176, 220
  suits against, 176
Madoff, Ralph (father), 13–15
Madoff, Ruth (wife)
  assets transferred to, 266, 277
  background of, 14–15, 21–22

as fund-raiser, 223
at holiday party (2008), 265–66
inheritance claims by, 266
knowledge of fraud, 218, 233
married life, early, 22–23
role in firm, 68, 218
and secrecy, 67
sentencing, absence from, 275
style of, 53
withdrawals before arrest, 265–66
Madoff, Shana (niece)
    education of, 179
    and London office, 188–89
    marries SEC officer, 189, 211–12
    role in firm, 62, 67, 169
Madoff, Solomon David (grandfather),
    14–15
Madoff, Sondra (sister), 15
Madoff, Sylvia Muntner (mother), 13, 15
    SEC litigation against, 23–24
Madoff exception, 207–8
Madoff Integrated Support System (MISS),
    42
"Madoff Investment Process Explained"
    (Markopolos), 197
Madoff Securities International (London),
    61, 184–90
    electronic trading, 185
    as family bank, 184–87
    Madoff London hobbies, 188–89
    money laundering from, 185–88
    ownership of, 185, 186–87
Madoff Victims Coalition, 270, 278
Mainzer, Dave, 41
Malkovich, John, 221, 272
Manion, Ed, 196–98, 219
Manzke, Sandra
    charges/suits against, 272
    as fund-raiser, 83–84, 89, 92, 98–104
    on hedge funds, 163–64
    losses of, 149, 162, 168
Mar-a-Lago
Marder Sosnik, 64–65
Market maker
    defined, 70
    Madoff as, 36, 45, 54, 79, 134, 171,
        207–8, 225, 240
Markopolos, Harry, 8, 55–57, 195–206
    background of, 198
    fraud, method of uncovering, 56–57, 196,
        200–204
    SEC, reporting Madoff to, 196–200
    testimony of, 55, 91, 195–96, 201,
        218–19
Marston, Carol, 15

Mathias, Edward, 44–45, 60
Maxam Capital, 98, 102, 104, 163
Mayfair Bookeeping Services, 225–26
Mendelow, Steven, 228
Meriwether, John, 79, 254
Merkin, Hermann, accomplishments of, 85,
    246–49
Merkin, J. Ezra
    biographical information, 242–46
    charges/suits against, 256, 260, 272
    college endowments managed by,
        245–46
    in financial industry, 244, 249–58
    as fund-raiser, 48, 84–85, 228, 249–52,
        256–58
    warnings about Madoff to, 98, 258–62
    wealth of, 242–45, 248, 251, 258, 260
Metropolitan Correctional Center, 269
Metzger, Leon, 96–97
Midwest Stock Exchange, 41
Miller, Christopher, 104
Mindich, Eric, 153–54
Minkow, Barry, 23
M-Invest Ltd, 120
Money laundering, and London office,
    185–88
Montauk residence, 13, 78–79, 171, 189,
    266
Mora, Jeffrey, 153
Moss, Frederick, 46
Murphy, Charles, 125
Murphy, Michael, 32, 34, 53–54

Nadel, Arthur, 92
Nahum, Reiko, 96, 158
Nakayama, Ken, 93, 122–24
NASDAQ
    Madoff as chairman, 44
    Workstation, 42
Nash, Jack, 252–53, 258–59
Nash, Joshua, 258–59
Nasi, William, 266
National Association of Securities Dealers
    (NASD), 34, 44
National Market System (NMS), and
    Madoff, 33–37
Newman, James, 94–95
Newton, Greg, 104
New York City residence, 11, 266
New York Stock Exchange (NYSE), 34–37,
    40
Nierenberg, George, 3–4
Nieuwoudt, Gideon, 120, 121, 141
1973 Masters Vacation Fund, 229
Nison, Steve, 71

Noel, Walter, 48, 83, 106–15, 124–25. *See also* Fairfield Greenwich Group
Norman F. Levy Foundation, 186
Notz, Beat, 137–38
Notz Stucki, 91, 137–39, 140
   Pendulum and Plaza funds, 91, 138

Options
   functions of, 57–58
   use by Madoff, 56–59, 69, 148, 157
Order flow, payment to clients, 38, 43–46
   controversy related to, 46, 206–7
   SEC approval, 206–7

Pacific West Health Medical Center Inc.
   Employees Retirement Trust, 157
Palm Beach
   fallout from fraud, 234
   feeder network connections, 86, 224–39
   history of, 222–23
   Madoff residence, 13, 266
   Madoff's memberships, 223
   Madoff victims, 222, 231–32
   police pension fund and Madoff, 235
Palm Beach Country Club, 49, 66, 222–24, 231–33
Pandit, Vikram, 164–65
Parcesepe, Aldo, 191, 193
Paredes, Troy A., 155
Paulson, John, 167
Peake, Junius, 42–43
Pendulum fund, 91, 138
Penny stocks, 99
Pension funds
   European, 146–47
   hedge fund investors, 103–4
   Palm Beach police, 235
Peppard, Jamie, 227
Pequot Capital, 98, 103, 153, 210–12, 219
Performance fees, absence of, 88, 91, 114–15, 148–49, 198
Perone, Herb, 184
Picard, Irving, 143, 181, 187, 235–36, 269–71, 276–77
Picard, Rob, 89–92, 132, 147
Picower, Jeffry
   foundation of, 237–39
   as fund-raiser, 222, 236–39
   illegal activities of, 237–38, 269
   phantom returns, 236–37, 270
   special returns to, 235
Piedrahita, Andrés, 83, 107, 110–11, 113, 117–18, 120, 140
Pink sheets, 31, 33

Pioneer Alternative Investments, 102, 135–36, 142
Pitt, Harvey, 209
Pitz, Enrica Cotellessa, 170
Plaza fund, 91, 138
Ponzi, Charles, 5, 6
Ponzi scheme
   beginning, theories of, 54–56, 79–80, 92, 172–73, 204–5, 240, 267
   family knowledge, 179, 218
   Madoff on, 3, 12, 268
   Markopolos uncovers, 195–206
   operation of, 6–7, 54–57, 76, 89, 102, 119, 176–77
   SEC disclosures, phony, 76–77
   unraveling of, 56–57, 205–6
   withdrawals, impact of, 63–64, 205, 263–64
   See also Advisory business/hedge fund
Portnoy, Jay, 15–20
Posner, Brian, 153
Powell, Greg, 226–27
Preferencing, operation of, 45–46
Primeo Executive, 134–35
Primeo Select, 134–35
Prop trading, 70

Qatar Investment Authority, 142
Quick, Leslie, 51

Rampell, Richard, 233
Raven, Stephen, 188
Ravens, 15–16
Raymond, Mark, 228
Reardon, Erin, 175
Rebates
   hedge funds, 149–50
   from Madoff to clients. See Order flow, payment to clients
Referrals to Madoff. *See* Feeder network
Regulatory agencies, failure and Madoff, 7
Reilly, Kevin, 51
Returns
   huge, to special investors, 232, 235
   phantom, 236–37, 270
   promise to investors, 27, 95, 194
   regularity as tip-off, 55–56, 59, 84, 91, 107, 118–19, 134, 136, 201–2
Reverse conversion, 124
Richards, Lori, 189, 211
Robbins, Norman, 229
Robertson, Julian, 7
Rosa Mexicana, 265–66
Ross, Burt, 273, 276
Roth, Eric, 85

Russia, Kohn marketing to, 84, 135–36
Ryan, Theresa and Lawrence, 177–79, 218

S&P Investment Group, 227
Safra, Edmond, 91, 137, 139, 142
Safra, Joseph, 142
Safra Banking Group, 139, 142–43
    victims, payments to, 143
Samberg, Art, 98, 103, 211
Sands, Franklin, 230
Saxl, Richard, 104
Schiava, Yanko Della, 83, 116–17
Schneider, Andrew, 235
Schulman, Bob, as fund-raiser, 83–84, 89, 100–101, 104
Schulman, Dr. Martin, 51
Schumer, Charles, 172
Sebah, Charles D., 103
SEC. See Securities and Exchange Commission (SEC)
Secrecy
    of investors, encouraged by Madoff, 7, 96, 135, 136, 151, 199
    of Madoff, about business, 76–79, 82, 90, 158–59, 178, 180, 215
    and Ruth, 67
Securities Acts Amendments of 1975, 33
Securities and Exchange Commission (SEC)
    admiration of Madoff, 209, 212
    audits Madoff, 77, 171–72
    Avellino and Bienes shut-down, 56, 81–82, 91, 118, 129, 178–79, 225–27
    Bush era decline, 210–11, 219
    competitive markets agenda, Madoff support, 35–36, 39–40
    failure to find fraud, 209–10, 216–19
    investigation of Madoff, resistance to, 199–200, 206–12
    investigates Madoff, 212–18
    and Madoff exception, 207–8
    Madoff filings, fraudulent to, 76–77
    Markopolos disclosure to, 196–200
    operation, changes over time, 208–10, 218
    order flow payments, approval of, 206–7
    regulator, in Madoff family, 189, 211–12
Securities Industry Association (SIA), 40
Securities Investor Protection Corp. (SIPC), 271
Sedgwick, Kyra, 85, 221, 243
Sentry Fund, 192–93
Shapiro, Carl
    amount invested (2008), 264
    as initial large investor, 51, 66, 91

Palm Beach connection, 66, 222, 223
    special returns to, 235
Shapiro, Ellen, 65, 230
Shapiro, Mary, 222
Short-sale rules, 207–8
Siebert, Muriel, 171
Silverstein, Larry, 272
Smart money, 117, 139
Smith, David, 94
Sorkin, Ira
    advice on plea, 13
    in courtroom, 1, 276
    as Madoff victim, 272
Soros, George, 7, 118, 139, 149, 152
Sosnik, Bell & Co., 64–65
Sovereign wealth funds, 142
Spain, Banco Santander, 84, 86, 117, 142–43
Spielberg, Steven, 85, 172, 221
Spitzer, Eliot, 155, 200
Split strike conversion, 8, 59, 104, 124, 134, 175, 196–97, 201–2
Spring, Richard, as fund-raiser, 51, 62, 118
Squillari, Eleanor, 82, 265
Stack, Brian, 153
Stamos, Peter, 257
Statistical arbitrage unit, 73–75
Steiner, Doug, 44, 60
Steinhardt, Michael, 249–52, 255
Stillman, Charles, 186
Stone, Rick, 233
Stratton Oakmont, 23
Stratus Technologies, 182–83
Stucki, Christian, 137–38
Stucki, Notz, 91
Subprime mortgage crisis, 264–65
Suicides, Madoff victims, 204, 269
Sullivan, Michael D., as fundraiser, 224, 226–27
Sunny Oaks Hotel, 25–26
Swanson, Eric, 189, 211–12, 217
Switzerland
    EIM, 84, 143–47
    Notz Stucki, 91, 137–38, 140
    Union Bancaire Privée, 119–21, 140–42
Syz, Eric Charles Max, 103

Teicher, Victor, 253–57, 259, 261–62
Telfran Associates, 228
Thain, John, 87
    Mar-a-Lago, 231
Thema fund, 134
Theodoracopulos, Taki, 121
Third market, 30, 35–38, 44
Thurman, Uma, 144

Tiger 21, 98
Toomre, Lars, 69
Toporek, Michael, 84–85
Toub, Philip, 83, 116–17
Trade tickets, phony, 76, 181–82
Tremont Capital Management, 83–84,
    89–90, 92, 95, 98–104, 272
  Broad Market Fund, 89, 102, 104
  Rye Select, 90, 102, 104, 235, 272
Trump, Donald, 231
Tucker, Jeffrey, 83, 107, 112–16, 126–27,
    215–16
Tudor-Jones, Paul, 144
Tversky, Amos, 90
Two-dollar brokerages, 48, 50

UniCredit, 131, 135–36, 142, 147
Union Bancaire Privée, 96, 102, 119–21,
    140–42

Van Schyndel, Zoe, 199–200
Velvel, Lawrence R., 175

Versus Technologies, 44
Victims of fraud. *See* Investors
Vijayvergiya, Amit, 213–14
Vinik, Jeff, 153
Vos, Jim, 97

Walbert, Richard, 32
Wall Street & Technology, 41, 43
Weiss, Anthony, 131
Weissman, Richard, 165
Wetherhill, Christopher, 99, 100, 103
Wiesel, Elie, 3, 85, 249
Wilpon, Fred, 172, 194, 229, 257–58
Wolfer, Werner, 121–22

Yelsey, Neil, 73–75, 179

Zabel, William, 237
Zeus Partners Limited, 142
Zuckerman, Mort, 256–57, 260
Zulauf, Felix, 130
Zweig, Jason, 95–96